Of Effacement

Inventions Black Philosophy, Politics, Aesthetics

Edited by David Marriott

Of Effacement
Blackness and Non-Being

David Marriott

Stanford University Press
Stanford, California

Stanford University Press
Stanford, California

Printed in the United States of America on acid-free, archival-quality paper

Library of Congress Cataloging-in-Publication Data
Names: Marriott, D. S., author.
Title: Of effacement : blackness and non-being / David Marriott.
Other titles: Inventions (Series)
Description: Stanford, California : Stanford University Press, 2023. | Series: Inventions: black philosophy, politics, aesthetics | Includes bibliographical references and index.
Identifiers: LCCN 2023018087 (print) | LCCN 2023018088 (ebook) | ISBN 9781503628786 (cloth) | ISBN 9781503637252 (paperback) | ISBN 9781503637269 (epub)
Subjects: LCSH: Philosophy, Black. | Black people—Race identity—Philosophy. | Identity (Philosophical concept)
Classification: LCC B808.8 .M37 2023 (print) | LCC B808.8 (ebook) | DDC 126—dc23/eng/20230726
LC record available at https://lccn.loc.gov/2023018087
LC ebook record available at https://lccn.loc.gov/2023018088

Text design: Elliott Beard
Typeset by Motto Publishing Services in 10/14.75 Freight Text Pro

Contents

Le Noir n'est pas (Frantz Fanon).[1] The essays presented here proceed from a long meditation on the meaning of Fanon's troubling idea of the "n'est pas," undertaken in an effort to understand—through a philosophical-genetic approach—how this notion exceeds the categories (as well as principles) of blackness as meaning or concept.[2]

First, the book claims that the n'est pas cannot be determined as experience or representation—more precisely, its excess can neither be subsumed nor reproduced as *Dasein*, for it frees blackness from any obedience to ontology, and so detaches it from any servitude to philosophy. This book thus avoids any ontological—or more exactly, *eidetic*—attempt to reveal the n'est pas. The n'est pas cannot be measured in terms of being, since its subtracting intuition surpasses limitlessly the sum of those intuitions that saturate it; the n'est pas should rather be called an incommensurable, or immeasurable, abyss. This lack of saturation, however, does not always or even first of all suggest limitlessness; it is often marked by unforeseen crystallizations, permitting different aggregations to be foreseen on the basis of different arrangements and effects. As the crystallized phenomenon passes beyond all finite summations—which often cannot be seen—all syntheses must be abandoned in favor of what Fanon calls the abyssal whose infinitesimal end precedes and surpasses compositions of being.

The n'est pas must also account for how those saturated depths occur in their exorbitant splendor and wretchedness.

When Fanon introduces the n'est pas it is to question how blackness is what is given to be seen, each time, according to a perspective that is total as well as partial, conceivable, and always comprehensible. The n'est pas is not limited to these registers; nor is it a thought of *disclosure* to be affirmed and confirmed as such. The n'est pas shows us how our intentions and intuitions are often cut off from the real; that our perspectives prevent us from knowing and recognizing how our vision is structured by irreal elements, and so, how we are led astray by our own passions and attachments. At each stage of our descent, we see something emerge as chaotic, monstrous, and react to it in pain and distress; but we are unable to attain it, being equally incapable of telling apart knowledge from something lost or desired. In this way, the saturated depths cannot be foreseen, for the delusion that saturates reality, forbids black particularity from being distinguished as particularity, thereby annulling its possibility as invention. Consequently, because these depths could not be intuited, all possible paths leading down to them could also not be foreseen. Similarly, the n'est pas challenges the *conatus essendi*[3] of being, from being considered apart from race war and a black will to power. Black power is, in fact, a power that is beyond power. *It is not an object to be had—* it is a power that begins by withholding itself and thus remains inconceivable to any object as its effect. The n'est pas must thus account for the ways in which conatus goes to war against blackness as a power which is neither true nor the good. It must teach us the cure for our powerlessness, and precisely because blackness can never be the means of obtaining a cure. In this sense, blackness is strictly an auto-immune relation in which every struggle to discover and appropriate it ends in suspense and incomprehensibility.

Let me note, however, two points to avoid misunderstandings. The status of the analyses offered here remains to be determined. Moreover, there is no terminology that can convert or translate the n'est pas. Neither judgement nor freedom are up to the task, nor spirit or revelation. Unlike certain themes of philosophy or psychoanalysis, the n'est pas does not coincide with either mastery or knowledge; nor is it a presence grasped in representation and its concept; nor is its meaning hidden in the semantics of the verbal form to be. I say absolutely that the n'est pas does not constitute a concept—it is the dark *invisable* of reason—for it is not *determinable* or *meaningful*.[4] Nonetheless, the relation between blackness and the n'est pas presupposes certain relations. To make sense of those relations this book has recourse to the notion of *effacement*. This word is not a metaphor. But it does manifest a structure, as Lacan might say.

A privileged example of effacement is found in the existent. In the modern era it has been the fate of black life to be valued according to its nullity and its fungibility. If to live means to fulfill the freedom of one's essence, to reach it without hindrance—immanently; and only what is free can be judged as living, black being enters history as the definition of unfree life that also undoes the relation between being and existence. The sign of this unfreedom, whether in law or politics, is manifested by the *corpus exanime*, which is the relic of a life that is above all not living, and whose existence causes a ripple or shudder in those living on. According to Fanon, this *corpus exanime* affects us even before we know what it is, or rather precisely because we know it only delusorily: as *méconnaissance*. Misrecognition offers us only a semblant life (we could also say an image that effaces), and yet is, at the same time, imposed on us with a power such that we are submerged by what shows—and thereby hides—itself, to the point of fascination.

Another privileged example comes from art. To love only the art that plunges one into total darkness is to make an idol out of darkness.[5] It is not to grasp how black art is the sign and worship of its own darkness. The n'est pas crystallizes this semidarkness, but not as revelation or enlightenment. For it foresees what art cannot foresee, i.e., that darkness cannot be aimed at, meant, or intended. Consequently, the n'est pas precedes any apprehension that wrongly applies "knowledge (of the object)" to the *non* that unfolds as the black excess (of form, materialism, or structure). The n'est pas is not merely a fact of structure.[6] Such a thought is too pious. But the n'est pas is not pious—or more precisely, it is because it is not limited to a black imagining of form that it passes beyond any piety of form (it has no connection to form as affect). In that sense, it is as opposed to aesthetics as it is to religion or any other form of consolation. It is the dark *invisable* of reason. As for us, the art that opposes itself to the judgement of form is not thereby opposed to violence, the saving violence of form, the lawful violence of the tabula rasa. Only the art that wages the cruelest war on black pain and suffering makes the n'est pas appear. This art that crystallizes the n'est pas destroys us. It destroys the law that makes blackness complicit with the suffering pain of its existence. As such, this art is directly experienced as the unbearable.

Accordingly, the n'est pas cannot be borne. This consideration derives solely from realizing that when the black gaze cannot bear what it sees, it suffers effacement, and, because what cannot be borne, concerns what cannot be seen—*the thought that is nègre to thought*—then to think the n'est pas is to think what we are incapable of knowing and incapable of reaching. It concerns an effacement that our being cannot sustain. This effacement informs what is recognized as our necessary weakness, because it keeps within the limits suggested by our idealizations and fantasies. We have so little knowledge of the n'est pas that we do not know it (how it invades our thoughts, and all the forms of consciousness and unconsciousness). Disturbed as he is by the contemplation of the n'est pas in his own being, Fanon dares to say that blackness is not capable of recognizing it—as a thought, or *cogitatum*. Indeed, he says that we suffer from a bedazzlement that tries to universalize our wretchedness instead of trying to think it—or think it better. But I would suggest that this is because we are weighed down by it, that is to say that our wretchedness weighs too much, and precisely because blackness is so weightless a thought. There is no doubt that this weightlessness is heavier than the world. Beyond the in-itself and the for-itself of the disclosed, this weightlessness burdens me; it burdens me in my solitude and in my exile from the world; it burdens me because it causes me to fall, without end, without protection and without defense, in oblivion. But it also burdens me with a strange dishonor which harasses me from the first moment each day. It is easier to bear this weightlessness than to see my dishonor exposed: what else can I do, given the insecurities, fears, and miseries of black existence? For the author of *Black Skin, White Masks*, black being has become something empty, weightless, yet quickly evaporating, lost to itself, expelled from itself in so far as it is a desire without ex-sistence.

This is why blackness cannot be too much occupied and distracted, that is to say, when we imagine that judgment and justice in the world will unburden us of our cares, we are advised to avert our gaze from the n'est pas, and to keep ourselves fully occupied with the promise of the mountain or tabernacle.[7] Therefore, if you can see something in the darkness around you, and if you can find something to hold onto in this limitless, unfathomably deep loss of experience, why, if the n'est pas is so removed from knowledge or object, does it reveal to you this absence in your essence, why should you not be able to know, with an even greater certainty of reflection, what the n'est pas reveals to you as the *invisable*? In this dereliction—which I am imagining was also Fanon's—we experience the n'est pas as a nearness that is also impossibly far. The n'est pas, according to Fanon, identifies here an *informe*—not of being—but an *informe* that is without form, for it subsists as the dark tain of every mirror. These mirrors show us that there is another world, but only the abyss leads us there. It follows from all this, first, that these mirrors conceal nothing but our own disappearance, so that we only become visible in our disappearance, or that disappearance from life is what defines black life. Secondly, wrapped in such cloaks of disappearance we cannot even see whether we are enrobed or denuded. There is thus an intolerable presumption in such arguments, although they seem to be based on an illuminating wisdom, which is neither sincere nor reasonable, unless it makes us admit that, since we do not know of ourselves as we are, we can learn it only in the incommensurability of the seldom seen or found.

Of Effacement

Part I
Ontology and Language

How does blackness take place in language? Is language subjected to blackness instead of only representing or enunciating it? And if so, when Fanon writes of blackness, that it is n'est pas (is not), where should one look to make sense of this n'est pas? One could look to philology (see Chapters 2 and 3), not in the sense advanced by Edward Said or Paul de Man, but in the sense advanced by Werner Hamacher, who writes, in *Minima Philologica*: "Philology emancipates the interval from its border phenomena."[1] This definition makes evident that philology is more than a rhetoric of topoi and tropes, for what it discloses are *the spaces in between* history and phenomenology, or grammar and rhetoric. Thus appears those "black" swarms or magnitudes that surpass the spacing of time (topos) and the time of spacing (trope) that are so evident in what Lacan calls *lalangue* (Chapter 4).[2] Those black intensive magnitudes do not, however, prioritize philology. For even when Said defines philology as the "detailed, patient scrutiny [of words in their 'worldliness']"; and de Man defines it as "mere reading . . . prior to any theory," neither definition can make sense of the n'est pas.[3] Both end up with philology as the effect of something prior: language and/or reading. Said, for example, writes: "reading is the indispensable act, the initial gesture without which any philology is simply impossible."[4] The act of reading is thus said to form part of the moral-political obligation that makes philology possible; namely, to subvert *and* affirm *humanitas* as the essence and priority of world literature [*Weltliteratur*]. What is never put into question is philology as the topos where reading makes legible its own genealogy as a history of interpretation.

De Man also shows himself to be more interested in topos than that of the n'est pas, and to that end cannot teach us how to read black texts.[5] Does his idea of philology, as a philosophy of rhetoric, offer us nothing else but an encounter with language, an encounter with its baffling apriority? Is this why he repeatedly returns to the word "prior" in his return to philology? Hence his evident interest in the structure of language *prior* to the meaning it produces, and the teaching of literature as a rhetoric and poetics *prior* to it being taught as a hermeneutics and a history. To return to philology is therefore to return to the priority of language over history or hermeneutics, or to return to what we cannot conceive, or barely receive, without confronting this prior question of apriority. Language is therefore always *prior*—and subsequent—to the return that illuminates it. That illumination arises from philology's blindness. Like Oedipus, its blindness is both prior to, and what establishes the priority of, its transgression. Whoever finds himself smitten by the love of words owes this love, most often, to the return that overlooks the priority of language to philology. There is no cure for such blindness, for the only means of obtaining clear sight obliges us to put out our eyes in our returning to it.

Philology is thus doubled: it is always the trope of a return that language and/ or its reading makes intolerable, not to say miserable, because philology is always the effect of the "return" it produces. The question then arises as to what this return is symptomatic of—or coincident with? As if the dispute over *which* return was warding off the greater anxiety, their shared recognition that what is prior must come from somewhere else, from outside philology? An apriority that cannot ever be reconciled with, or decided as, philology? In following these arguments, I should make it clear that there is no basis for making one concept of priority take priority over the other. For to argue in these terms is inevitably to maintain the apriority that marks the limits of philology's return. But what is revealed by the n'est pas is contrary to this pathos or dialectic; and thus explodes the idea that black philology can ever begin in the sublimated return to itself. Whence the insistence that in these two rivalrous returns, *nigra philologica* is never, in fact, returned to, but precisely forgotten *in the return to it*. Of course, de Man's emphasis on structure rather than on historicity, on rhetoric rather than on hermeneutics, is explicitly reversed in Said's own return to philology. Here priority is not so much a sight blinded, but the means, the mediating point, where history meets wisdom in imaginative understanding. (Mediation is also the great principle of black philology and the great principle of its worldliness. See Chapter 2.) The idea that philology can be equal to the historicity of language via a dialectic of imagination, is to know "the constraint they [literary texts] impose on us [and presumably also the constraint we impose on them?]."[6] To read is to acknowledge the mutual constraint of duty and obligation; fidelity to the text—in its worldliness—is the means of obtaining historical wisdom and understanding. Once again, philology is what allows us to see the priority of topos without falling into blinding presumption. "[P]hilosophy deals with the true, philology with the certain . . . both the true and the certain lay claim to belief, both to urgency, both to conviction." And: "Eloquence is what makes possible an understanding of the true and the certain . . . Eloquence involves not only the best use of words, but also their most *copious* articulation."[7]

Philology, in its eloquence, confirms and delimits truth in its certainty. But if, qua urgency, philology remains in exile from the world of conviction, it reintroduces warring incertitude into the belief on which it stands, and which is the true homeland of the mind. At once the best, most copious articulation can no longer be solidly established as the inviolable sign of the true and the certain; and the most eloquent philosopher finds himself in the world of uncertainty. He speaks in enigmas, aporias, ironies, and equivocations, as though he moved in a barren desert, as though he lacked the conviction to choose truth, as though he could not choose without wavering, as though, unsure and awkward, he was incommensurably poorer in these raids on the inarticulate. The most copious comparatist, the most eloquent philosopher none the less lacks all philological conviction. Philology speaks of its exile from the true and the certain, frankly, and has no conviction in its philosophical concept, which is like the unhappy incertitude of the mind.

In this first part I will suggest that such incertitude is necessary to black philology, otherwise it cannot grasp, and so defend, what drives its eternal return to, and exile from, our original nature in the homeland of our being. Thus, black philology is not the congenial pursuit of *philía* and *alētheia* as tropes of return, for it constantly needs to be diverted from the dread, misery, and dejectedness of its own apriority. These two contrary drives give rise to a confusion of trope and topoi, which leads black philology to seek satisfaction in the consolation of an imaginary originality—of world, race, and language—which can be returned to once it has overcome the obvious difficulties of knowledge and interpretation, and only then can it open the door to understanding and wisdom. *Nigra philologica* is the result of a constant wretchedness which is its own secret idealization. For how can it know—legitimate—itself without conflict over what, paradoxically, both founds and escapes it? But that dispute also conceals a more wretched outcome in the reading of philology itself; namely, the perpetual struggle of renewed ide-alization that also craves the threatened miseries that root it. Hence the excite-ment of knowing, of conceiving the properties of ancient languages that are in-deed boosted by the endless, insoluble problem that they exist for us only as what could never return.

That is why philological knowledge [*Wissen*] is said to emerge from a principle of "perpetually renewed understanding [*perpetuierte Erkenntnis*]" without end.[8] For this is how philology establishes the "unique, unexampled" truth that is the foundation of its reading.[9] Unique and unexampled: for philology is not just a di-alectic of knowledge and judgment, but an ideal (of critique and historical judg-ment) that must delude itself into imagining that each text is indubitably itself but also the unexampled ideal of its own unity. Moreover, *this unexampled uniqueness is never arbitrary nor unambiguously final.* For the understanding which consti-tutes this uniqueness, and which gives it historical life, is the outcome of an inter-dependence—a mediation—of philological cognition and understanding [*Erkennt-nis*].[10] Why this dynamic mediation? Because philology attends to the unique as a "deciphering operation." As such, every ciphering operation is dissolved again into the "cognitions from which they arose."[11] Dissolution occurs essentially as a dis-closure of language itself. According to this unique unexampled singularity, philol-ogy is not only a deciphering that reveals or discloses. Rather, philology does not resist resistance (as operation), but guards it (in its singularity). The point is not to unclose apriority, in the sense of a return. Rather, one can only decipher philolo-gy's own enciphering priority. Thus, what is posited or asserted entails a process of deciphering that must be "understood *as* written in cipher."[12] The foundations and principles of such hermeneutics is therefore compared to a "lock that snaps shut again and again, and explanation should not try to break it open," for to seek a key to such hermeneutics only works to close what is already closed off.[13] And this is true for the reading of all texts. We must thus decipher not what is revealed, but the *unique* relation of language to its own *black* particularity: that particular-ity is always already posited by language, and so prior to the limits of judgement, but what is hermetically written is also precedent to predication or knowledge, for what it signifies is both prior to the lock and its closure. Or, if you prefer, what black philology is concerned with is the ever-singular emergence of the n'est pas that escapes both dialectical sublation and the conventions of sense. If it is her-esy to reduce the singular to exemplarity, black philology is heretical in interpret-ing the "is not" as the task of *all* textual understanding.[14] Because it consists of singular occurrences, the n'est pas speaks everywhere where black life is (not), in its most enciphered modalities. The n'est pas speaks in every black interlocution but is also incapable of ever being said. Rather, the n'est pas is where black language denies, unknows, and doubts itself. When confronted with the n'est pas, blackness is the beingness that consists, but cannot be thought, in terms of apriority. But then, it is what remains to be said which becomes the problem of its philological understanding [*Erkenntnis*], since the unconcealing of black uniqueness never takes into account what is unconcealed by the n'est pas—its *refusal to be* "mediated subjectively in cognition."[15]

But is there another way of thinking about blackness and the language of black texts? My focus on Lacan's neologism *lalangue* and on the African trope of Esu is not by chance (Chapters 2 and 4). Indeed, when Lacan writes of lalangue in *La Troisième*, he also says "ce n'est pas par hazard" (it is not mere chance) that it occurs in language.[16] Lalangue is not subject to chance, for, like Esu, lalangue shows us the wondrous splendors made possible by language. The collisions of signs, signifiers, or tropes made possible by lalangue also make manifest letters whose singularity is not mere chance (n'est pas). Lalangue is an attempt to account for these amazing manifestations that trouble and oppress *any certitude of language* in analysis. Lalangue is the manifestation of homophony, but homophony is not the congruence of meaning and chance. Lalangue renders possible what happens before language happens, whether as alterity, form, sign, or event. Perhaps this is why Lacan says that "the '*non*' of denial and the '*nom*' that names is no coincidence" either. If the homophonous structures of language (*la langue*) show coincidence they should not therefore be dismissed as merely coincidental. What can we infer from his analysis? It is interesting to note in this regard that it is due to Lacan's focus on lalangue that he rejects the *la langue* of the linguists, but not entirely: to accept the echo between *voeu* (wish) and *veut* (want), for example, is also to accept the precedence that arrives as a prepossibility of predication (wish) or judgement (want) as such. The reason for doing so, and the only one to be found in Lacan's writings after Seminar XX, is merely that the unconscious is also made up of various homophonies: the unconscious is that which *lacks* the ability to situate the coincidences (of lalangue) as topological or lingual possibilities. Even homophonies in speech situate a nonlinear relationship between sign and representation, language and contingency.

In this sense, I agree with Jean-Claude Milner when he writes: homophony "transforms radically everything that can be theorized about the Unconscious and its relationship to the fact of *lalangue*."[17] He also says, "*lalangue* is homophony, but homophony does not belong to *la langue*."[18] Why not? He offers us some intriguing answers. Firstly, linguistics resists lalangue. Or it does not see what coincidence—the symptomatic logic of its signification—offers to the ideal time and space of the sign in its enjoyment or possibility. In brief, homophony is immediately read as homonymy. Is that all they have to say? They also confuse the precedence of prepossibility, the n'est pas that precedes the positing of language, with the negative motif of arbitrariness (Saussure) or with the positive motif of homonymy (Chomsky). Linguists do not want to recognize the homophonous pre-essence of language in what they envisage as the coincidences of homonymy. Sounds and spellings may coincide, but that coincidence has no relation to meaning. It is clear then that it is only the doxa of *langage* that prevents them from accepting lalangue, and by their rejection they have become resistant witnesses; and, what is more, in doing so they remain opposed to the unanticipated, nonhomogeneous opening of a homophonous n'est pas within all language.

As a result of this n'est pas, just to be clear, I am referring to a lalangue that precedes its "own" possibility as lalangue as well as the concept and essence of an essential, noncoincident chance in language. It is not just that there exist homophonous phonemes, letters, word plays, parapraxes, and so on, that are not accidental, but that the n'est pas interrupts any philosophical logic of representation, namely, those examples by which the n'est pas of *la langue* occurs as lalangue—and only in this sense—becomes lalangue's performance of itself. Indeed, it precedes language itself to such an extent that it remains ungraspable as language. Let us say that lalangue, being neither object nor law, is the unrepeatable and unfathomable trace in any time or sequence, network or code. In a word, lalangue has two essential characteristics. It is "the [presignified] deposit, the alluvion" that precedes the positing of language: it is the archi-lettering, in whose archi-communion or archi-sympathy "a group handles its unconscious experience." (The word "group" brings together lalangue with that of community, and philology with that of an emotional bond or tie in a community of ends—we shall interrogate that proximity in what follows.) Consequently, lalangue echoes the *not* of the n'est pas in the marks or traces it leaves on speaking being. Once again, it is hard not to read these deposits as traces—a means of diversion and inescapable danger—that allow us to procure, without mastering, meanings that we would rather not know. What seems clear is that the question of lalangue and of mastery are intimately related to each other. The speech act that inadvertently confuses *wish* with *want* is not, at the deepest level, mere confusion, but the means through which the subject ardently, disturbingly, sets out in pursuit of their insatiable liaison.

Lacan uses the word "swarm" to describe lalangue's manifestation.[19] Swarm suggests something more than matheme, mathematization, or geometry. It suggests something more than law or code, knot or topology. And in order to make sense of this word we need to grasp lalangue as a kind of imminence, or pre-presence that is unmediated in the singular infinitude of this imminence, for these swarms can never be correlated to the ordering of syntagm or paradigm, nor that of semantics or concept. We shall be exploring these textures, independent of the signifier and notions of its mastery, in the pursuit of a black philology. We shall also try to account for the ways in which Esu, in his fecundity and mediation, echoes *phileîn* or *lógos*. But we must also acknowledge that the swarming magnitudes of lalangue cannot ever constitute a science, not least a philology.

Unless we bear these cautions in mind, we risk reading lalangue as mere play, performance; or as simply meaningless contingency. And if these are all pseudo-representations that is because they risk essentializing lalangue as simply horror or disturbance to a world of ordor. Perhaps this is why Milner evokes lalangue as an alternative to racism, the racism of representation, which he accuses of reducing the lettering of "life" to that of essence.[20] But is lalangue entirely separable from the lettering of a certain whiteness? And what does it show us, if not that there is a n'est pas that unsettles, disturbs, the white ordering of lalangue in Lacanian psychoanalysis?

One

N'est Pas

Fanon: "le Noir n'est pas un homme."[1] And this other text, by Pierre Macherey, from an essay on Althusser and Fanon: Is not the racially interpellated subject "the spokesperson or the echo of a remark of which *he is not*, himself, the author, and which does not come out of his mouth in a spontaneous fashion, but which has been dictated by another voice, a voice that remains silent?"[2]

We have yet to understand the being that is not, whereby it is the echo of a silence that cannot be communicated except through gaps—ruptures— in language. How do we recover the moment of its silence, before it can be established in the realm of being, before it is bleached white by ontology or representation? We must try to hear, within this silence, the yet to be understood experience of blackness. We must pose the question of its being anew, before its reading can crystallize around the question of what it is, or, as Fanon conceives of it, is not, and the question of whether blackness should ever be considered a conventional form of *humanitas*. To describe this experience of non-being, this echoing that turns ontology on its head, as a voice speaking without authorship, without origin, and as though a voice overheard, is to know that blackness cannot be uttered without at once being echoed by a voice that is not: n'est pas.

This is doubtless more than a question of reading. To explore it we must renounce the usual methods of psychoanalysis or philosophy. We must never allow ourselves to be guided by what we may know of being (whether as an unasked question or as an alterity somehow unaccounted for or disavowed). None of the concepts of phenomenology, even and especially in the implicit sense of intentionality, consciousness, or affect, must be allowed to exert an organizing role. What is imperative is the gesture that attends to the undecidability of what blackness is, and not the "science" that reads it as invariably a question of force, power, ideology and violence (and I would add to that: identity, desire, and faith). What is originary—in Fanon's phrasing of the n'est pas—is the caesura that establishes the distance between humanism and black personhood in general. This is why Fanon prefers other terms such as "persona" or "mask." As for the hold exerted by ontology upon blackness as criminality, pathology, excess, one might say that undecidability characterizes these debates insofar as the n'est pas derives from this caesura from the start. We must therefore speak of the n'est pas without judgement, right, or obligation. We must speak of the n'est pas as *something else entirely*; and we must leave in abeyance everything that could figure it as a literal truth. To speak of the n'est pas is to speak of a void instituted between humanism and the limits of the human. For the n'est pas is absolutely other to what blackness is or claims to be.

Only then will we be able to understand why blackness poses a question that has yet to be formulated, and for which similarly there is still no answer. Indeed, the one thing that will keep us from understanding the n'est pas is inherent to blackness itself. To explain why let me briefly turn to the ambiguous ways in which blackness has been read by philosophy, or a certain philosophy; a reading that is, in a very originary and very violent way, unable to pose, let alone answer, what it is that makes blackness both black *and* undecidable. Here silence and speech, being and non-being are inextricably involved: inseparable since they are not yet distinguished, but are nevertheless misrecognized each as the other, the one in relation to the other, in the undecidable exchange that separates them and that allows neither knowledge nor testimony to prevail.

I

Let us see then how being echoes this n'est pas, and whether its echoing is ever given to experience.

It has become commonplace to say that a subject is subjected by what it assays. The classical analysis of ideology has shown how each subject is marked, assailed, by authority.[3] Each subject is interpellated as if in response to the voice of someone speaking. And what is implanted is a whole causality in which the subject comes to know itself as substance, body, historical life; hence the subject is always the effect—the echo—of the voice whose authority it answers.

But *whose* voice? It is precisely this question that motivates Pierre Macherey's critique of Althusserean interpellation. Where, Macherey claims, in the classical scene of interpellation, the question posed by the enigmatic call [*appel*] of ideology is understood by all because *each is forced to answer from his or her place in language*, and each is hailed (by a *hey you!*), why assume that we all turn around [*retourné*] in exactly the same way? Could it not be the case that there are some who are so very differently *determined* by the situations they find themselves in? Situations where the relation to the sovereignty of the state is at once the mark, the provocation, the insistence of *something* else; the result of an additional (not to say aberrant) separation? On the contrary, perhaps there are subjects who experience the effects of power not in terms of being seized, or that of a subjection revealed, as happens in the classical schema, but more in terms of being neither heard nor spoken to, but reduced precisely to the effect of an obliteration? If respect follows on from recognition, it is quite clear that there are those whose marked distinction is inscribed, and irreparably so, by nonrecognition. It happens every day. In persons of color, for example. Whence Macherey's three challenges to the Althusserian formula:

(i)   for the subject who is *made to be* black there is "the feeling of not being a subject like the others, but a subject with something added, or perhaps we should say something missing"; accordingly this subject "is not [*n'est pas*], like the one of whom Althusser speaks, a turned subject [*un subject retourné*], but a doubled subject, who is divided between an I and this *more (or less) which cannot be recognized or connoted as such*;[4]

(ii) whereas the Althusserian formula of subjection "draws its efficacy from its purely verbal character: it is projected from behind, from a source systematically concealed from sight," the subject of color "is constituted as such in the order of the visible, in plain sight, so to speak, and this changes everything"; it is an actual encounter "between two intersecting gazes";[5]

(iii) as such, one does not become a subject of color "except by entering into a relation [*rapport*] with others"; a situation which, because it unfolds in plain sight, "brings consciousness into the foreground and presupposes no reference to an unconscious [in contrast to Althusser who famously compares ideology to the unconscious]."[6]

In all three instances, the only universal rule is: the positioning of the subject by ideology is not delusory or imposed, and each *turn* is, in a certain sense, to give oneself up even more. But this does not justify the further belief that interpellation "isolates the one who receives it, suspending the relations that he or she might entertain with other people," and merely because we are all considered to be subjected in exactly the same way.[7] In other words, the privilege given to the *retourné* barely suffices as an account of social differences. In cases 1 and 2, Macherey thinks that the iconic *"tiens, un nègre!"* [look, a nigger!] from Frantz Fanon's 1952 text, *Black Skin, White Masks* offers a differing account of subjectivation. Indeed, Fanon's extrapolation of the effects of the *tiens* brings it much closer "to the data of lived experience." Because Fanon's (*hey you!*) is a phenomenology rather than a transcendental function, it does not issue in the specification of the subject (as simply seen)? How is that? In case 2, Macherey's notion of an encounter "in plain sight" implies that there is no turning around for the black subject, just a "gaze that fixes him"[8]; but in case 3, which Macherey thinks comes closest to Fanon's supposed phenomenology, sight becomes marked by a sense of "objectivity" that is more troublesome and is described as follows:

> What first strikes us in this exposition is how it underscores the cumulative nature of the process by which is installed—in the mind of someone who, here, says "I"—the feeling of not being a subject like the others, but a subject with something added, or perhaps we should say something missing, since the addition in question is color, a characteristic with negative connotations, the absence of colorlessness: we begin with an observation, tied to the intervention of an external stimulus, an onlooker's gaze on his body and his skin, an observation that exhibits an objective status from the outset; there then develops, in the mind of the one undergoing this test, a growing psychic tension leading from amusement, which is a form of acceptance, to the feeling that something unacceptable is happening, something strictly unbearable, at least under normal conditions.[9]

Whatever the virtues of Macherey's general construal of Althusser's theory (we will return to that question in a moment), it seems fairly clear that he has not at all grasped Fanon's main argument in *Black Skin, White Masks* concerning *le vécue du Noir*. This may be because, just as Althusser's account of ideology has to be understood, I am suggesting, on the basis of the universality of the "linguistic or symbolic order," so Fanon's own thinking of the subject who is made *nègre*, which we shall soon see is also indebted to a radical rereading of Sartre, also has to be understood on the basis of his earlier treatment of an apparently quite different account of *subjectivation* to which Macherey rather surprisingly never refers in these contexts. In that account, in which the ear and the eye are not simply solicited but held, so to speak, Fanon describes the moment when ideology speaks through the black subject as the *feeling* of being *handed over to a gaze*, a gaze *that makes the visible inseparable from an absolute dereliction*. This interpretation is not one of cause and effect—from external stimulus to psychic tension—for it is not certain that the gaze is reducible to any realist schema of apprehension. Its objectivity is not one of vision, but that of a quasi-transcendental structure that upsets the *moi*, the ego, because, strange to say, it makes the "nothing" appear that the subject already echoes. Inasmuch as the black is always *on guard* before any actual racist encounter, and inasmuch as this guardedness, moreover, is startlingly focused on the unconscious ideology of negrophobia, what is manifested here is not an encounter with an alienating *vision*, but a "nothingness" now out in the open.

This nothingness is not something *seen*, in the form of an experience; but nor is it to be confused with an actual turning around. Hence, Fanon gives the example of a black philosopher on his way to study in France: "How can we explain, for example, that a black man who has passed his baccalaureate and arrives at the Sorbonne to study for his degree in philosophy is already on his guard before there is the sign of any conflict?"[10] What Fanon puts forward here is in fact very different to Althusser and Macherey. In general terms: to be traversed by the gaze is not equivalent to a transcending subjection. The transcending here is of another order. Blackness is not the result of authority or subjection; it is the enigma of its own disquieting in-plenitude. The invasion of the *tiens* does not correspond to any object or representation. Yet it does make palpable a vertigo that is the result of a truly enigmatic interpellation. Or as Fanon puts it: the *moi* is on guard because it is surrounded by its own fantasy of intrusion, which it sends back, wards off, so as to eagerly await its certain appointment. What you walk towards is already within you, and what you so strenuously strive to avoid is already there facing you, fierce and inexorable. We are close here to an overwhelming sense of anxiety. It is indeed an anxiety, but strange, shifting, changeable. The *moi* is forced to say: there is something that returns, paralyzing reason, and is more intimate, more disturbing than any thought or call could be. If we refer back to this struggle as disquieting, what seems to be at issue here is a resistance that takes the form of a submission; and an enticement in whose ardent pursuit one comes abruptly to an end: as *nègre*. Here, body and sense remain indeterminate or can no longer be determined. I mean: the *nègre* has no meaning as essence and bears no relation to an object. What it does is to *return* (and not simply *turn*) the "I" to a nothingness that is absolutely exterior to being. The connection between vision and gaze, between word and identification, remains the effect, then, not of power, but of an endlessly traversable distance between subject and its hallucinated seeing of what cannot be seen. The imago is the best way of describing how vision gets clothed by a significance that empties it of sense, reference, world. The former acts as a confirmation, so to speak, that one was already subjected by the latter; the *noir*'s enigmatic relation to the *nègre* is already *there*, in me. Think of a machine that despises the *moi*, and precisely because the *moi* is the machine that despises the black form of interiority, at once wanting recognition and despising the need for it. To be hailed as *nègre* is hence always to be lacerated by the imago (the imago launches being beyond what it permits us to see: not only toward the nothing in its nudity, not only toward fantasy or discourse, but toward the coldness of a preexistence that extracts blackness from language, where it remains undeciphered, unknown). Thus, the feeling of a violation that is both absolutely other and radically intimate. Hence the effect of the gaze that is all the more intensely received because it is doubly impenetrable. The n'est pas does not encounter being but discloses a non-being beyond being—a nothing that is neither *in* language nor *outside* it.

Phenomenology cannot think the n'est pas because it can only think it as a negation, a finite encounter. But Fanon suggests something altogether different. There is a nothing that transcends being itself: an "is not" that obliterates being as *selbst*, subject, ipse. The black light of such a sun annihilates being as *alētheia*. Why! Because there is no light that can reveal the elemental and obscure ground of blackness as *medium*? Or because such a wish is conceited, pointless, uncertain? And there is always a risk of absurdity in such illumination. However traumatic the n'est pas may be, it persists as a *monstration* where all the threads are hidden.[11] Such threads reveal scars. But the hand that guides them, back and forth, is not strictly intentional, nor malicious. Anti-blackness is the façade, but what braids, or threads letters into words, words into voices, is a recurring hostility that is never simply ideology or apparatus. This is why the *tiens* is not a game of hide-and-seek (which belongs to the whole Althusserian-Hegelian ontology of recognition). For Fanon, in brief, recognition is subjection; but the gaze offers us a different dialectic, and it does so quite openly. The gaze does not reveal to us some petrified architecture. On the contrary, what it *holds* and grasps and *darkens* is not a call to subjection; but an impersonal *non-moi* invaded by an unlocatable sign. For what it reveals it also keeps secret, with the result that its revelation (in speech) introduces a kind of involuntary enigma, and one that leads us to imagine a flaw that is immanent to experience.

Consider, for example, the famously obscure opening of "The Lived Experience of the Black Man" (which comes just after the iconic *tiens* episode):

> There is in fact a "being for other," as described by Hegel, but any ontology is made impossible in a colonized and acculturated society. Apparently, those who have written on the subject have not taken this sufficiently into consideration. In the weltanschauung of a colonized people, there is an impurity or a flaw that prohibits any ontological explanation.[12]

Inasmuch as recognition gives us access to being, it dominates being, exercises a power over it. But when Fanon says black being is given to be seen, because it is obliged by being for others [*für andere, l'être-pour-autrui*], he presents a refusal, a denigration. Consequently, since the only thing that makes us human concerns vision, we are taken aback to discover an alterity that makes being impossible, prohibited, excluded from the genus as thoroughly wrong, flawed, prohibited.

What is this impurity that places me outside of myself, but that also nullifies self-knowing? And how is one to account for this flaw that speaks from the side of the real (that is, the place where what is seen is negated, prohibited)? This account of ontology as centered on prohibition is, according to Macherey, complicated by Fanon's own treatment of "the limit that speculation on the subject of being qua being encounters," that is to say, a being that is also "being qua not-being [*être en tant qu'on n'est pas*], which is not the same thing at all," but even that more complex account, in Macherey's view, presupposes a being that "teems with the unthought and the unsaid" (and of which Sartre's notion of a *néant de son propre être*, mentioned in *Black Skin, White Masks* and of course in many other places by Fanon, and explicitly linked by him to a desire not to be), is a telling example.[13] Macherey uses this account to underscore the point that racial difference has no experiential equivalent. But Fanon's critique of ontology—of which the *tiens* scenario is a key illustration—suggests that there is a difference *within* the very category of difference that cannot be represented by or reproduced *as* difference even if we thenceforth read it as what results directly from the discovery of difference. Fanon's extremely subtle point is that blackness does not have a language of its own, or: what it reproduces, what it utters, is a ventriloquy (in the proper sense of the term) that *speaks by itself.* In other words, contrary to the notion of interpellation, blackness has no articulation, for even its difference is borrowed; the result is a language whose idiom is that of the n'est pas. The relation between the Other and the black does not consist in vision but in an absolute difference. There is never such a thing as a relation or encounter; what the flaw reveals is a transcendence without presence, a certainty without security. This is why one cannot *not* feel its violation. Nor can one turn toward it, like Orpheus. For to turn toward it is to have it all the more inscribed as an epiphany that *nègres* (with each *pas* a surrendering to an infinity of the *least*). Consequently, the experience of the *nègre* removes any other that might delimit it. The black has no *retourné*—and its subjugation has nothing to do with reason or judgement. We recognize in it a flaw that overwhelms the entirety of its being.

The shock of such scrutiny, the disordering of being by disorder, must therefore serve as an example of why the n'est pas is not an *experience*, but a judgement in *opposition* to sociality.

The n'est pas, certainly, is a very paradoxical object: without figure, without oppositional term, without remainder. In short, it is what has always been said, but also what interrupts being-said: it is essentially what remains in place, by being out of place: a corpse that *corpses*.[14] In *Black Skin, White Masks*, the problem of this n'est pas—the problem of situating the non-being of the black—is ontological rather than ideological, then, not because it starts from the problem of how people are subjectivated by their interpellation, but how certain subjects have to assume a being that is *not* in order to be recognized as subjects. For Fanon, as we know, this contrary situation takes on the unmanageable weight of a *that within*[15] that can be neither introjected nor expelled (the *moi* is seized by it though it resists it; it opens the door to it even though the *moi* comes after its founding). In brief, non-being is not the same for everyone and, in fact, the being that is made not to be (n'est pas) is not entirely a question of ontology (and so is different from Sartre's *néant* or *rien*). The placement of this n'est pas within a theory of ideology is therefore designed to solve a theoretical problem. That problem is not simply that of an unsaid (in Macherey's language), but refers to the effects of a prohibition that is maintained in being and is reproduced as a non-being that blackens. It is a problem that Fanon, in his early work, primarily engages via Sartre—not to say Freud and Hegel—and which has to be understood on the basis of his treatment of the moment at which the black understands that it is also *nègre*, or perhaps was always already *nègre*, a moment that Fanon puts foreword as belated, namely *nachträglich*. Or, the discovery of one's racial difference is always a belated discovery.

In *Black Skin, White Masks*, Fanon suggests that the drift of Sartre's demonstration—in *Being and Nothingness, Black Orpheus*, and a host of other texts—in fact underscores why ontology is unable to think this black deficiency of being, its impurity, and precisely at the point where its prohibition introduces a more menacing untimeliness (and of which it could be said that blackness is *nachträglich* to even Freud's notion of *Nachträglichkeit*) and in a way that complicates how Sartre understands the relation between consciousness and being:

> For once this friend, this born Hegelian, had forgotten that consciousness needs to get lost in the night of the absolute, the only condition for attaining self-consciousness. To counter rationalism he recalled the negative side, but he forgot that this negativity draws its value from a virtually substantial absoluity [*absoluité*]. Consciousness committed to experience knows nothing, has to know nothing, of the essence and determination of its being.[16]

When is a negativity truly negated? When it is unbeknownst to rationalism. For we can never be sure of its manifestation or consequences. To *impose* an idea of black lived experience (faith and benevolence apart) is not to engage with it, but precisely to drown it in abstraction. This is the situation that Sartre has forgotten. It is not surprising, therefore, that negation can be revealed only virtually; the absolute has a positive value, an ethical structure, *because* it does not consist in being grasped as mere negative essence, or as a loss circumvented by reason. That is why blackness is compared to a virtually substantial absoluity. Its endurance is not like the hardness of a rock, but the experience of a destitution that *petrifies* (moreover the imago that freezes all laughter, also ineluctably sunders all space, shape, movement; here petrification expresses a *corpus exanime*). This means concretely: blackness is not a knowledge acquired by reasoning, nor a thought to be *worked* (but never absolutely) by a dialectic of disclosure and manifestation, but a nothing whose splendor remains hard to grasp. What makes blackness both absolute and virtual is also what makes it incomprehensible to both reason and ontology as traditionally understood (by which Fanon means: the languages of essence and determination).

Let us briefly consider why. In *Being and Nothingness* (1943), Sartre argues: for being to appear there has to be a corresponding state of consciousness, for being in-itself (*an-sich*) or rather within-itself (*in-sich*) does not appear on its own; being presupposes something that is nonpresent and nonevident and that is its actual ontic foundation.[17] Being only appears *for* somebody, which is to say for a subject: its appearance must therefore be ontically grounded in something that is outside itself before it can be determined for a subject. The priority of being over appearance is thus deduced not from the side of the object—which is transcendent to our experiences of it—but from a subject (or self) consciousness that is entirely apparent to itself, and which is nothing more than its intentionality. Whatever the phenomenological precision of this argument, for Sartre self-consciousness has no content in or through itself, all content is given it from the outside. More, it is a "non-substantial absolute" because "it exists only to the degree to which it appears"; this is why the place from which it speaks is a "total emptiness (since the entire world is outside it)."[18] Since self-consciousness is empty, insubstantial, a non-being, a *néant*, that is ontically, transitively dependent on being, it is always in an intentional relation to what carries it, namely, an *en-soi* that is identical to and completely filled by itself, and that has no emptiness or internal division. Rhetorically, there is no attempt here to go from the language of ontology to that of racial difference. And yet, in those texts in which the question of racial difference is explicit, Sartre presents racial self-awareness as either an escape from self-consciousness (that he describes as irreal) or as the embrace of race as a quasi-objective essence (that he describes as a deluded self-objectification). In both instances, the subject intentionally denies (or inauthentically refuses) its own being. However, as the citation from Fanon suggests, what these two examples fail to grasp, and what Sartre forgets (in his turn to phenomenology), is the extent to which the subject who refuses to be black is never able to escape the negrophobic effect of that refusal on his or her psyche, so that the response to the imago is not the feigned escaping or embracing of difference, but the sudden disclosedness (what Heidegger calls *Erschlossenheit*) of an *en-soi* that is paradoxically full of its own non-being, and is overwhelmed by all the *négatités* that come with it: shame, despair, and guilt—that is to say, all those feelings that leave a residue and that cannot simply be negated at the level of consciousness. This is what Fanon means when he says that the black subject remains haunted by a virtually substantial absoluity, for every experience of it empties itself of everything absolute, or transcendental. In a word, blackness cannot know itself eidetically as spirit. In going on to say, after reaffirming that consciousness is dependent on being, that the black has no actuality of being but also no possibility as being, Fanon makes the appearance of this n'est pas into a fundamental challenge to ontology. Blackness becomes an absoluity that can only affirm itself as a n'est pas (and consequently as a forbidden possibility), because its "*être été*" (being made-to-be) only appears insofar as it is not, and as something less than a *rien* but never quite a *néant*. But this non-being is not the subject's own. "[T]his reconsideration of myself, this thematization, was not my idea," Fanon writes.[19] As a matter of fact, the black is the subject who allows non-being to appear—he assumes it as his essence, and his way of being is being-made-to-be-the-*en-soi*-that-is-not (n'est pas); blackness is the *être été* that reproduces itself as a n'est pas: where then is its contradiction, where is its impurity?

To answer, we must, despite the epistemological paradox of the object, say: blackness is the expression of a perpetual effacement. Silence, or *retournement*, is denied us, not because our speech has no status, or we don't speak clearly or well, but because *all speech is on the side of an anti-black law*; or rather, between sign, phonē, and articulation, language appears to occupy a place that is *daubed* by a negative instance that forces it to speak. To speak black or white is still to have a role imposed: either that of a shimmer or blemish added on, or that of an obligatory delusion that is also a failure to speak at all. Or else the speaker is hampered by what is said without being said, what is absent: the idiom of a law that simply communicates the *ban* (the affective politics) of negrophobia. In this case what is unconsciously said can only be expressed, so to speak, by its effect: the effect of a being that is excruciated. This is why any lapsus in speech is irreversible. A white idiom can only show black delivery as impure, bad, comedic; as a failure to speak "properly," and will either try to correct or perfect it by a judgement that is akin to a condemnation. Anyone preparing to speak "Parisian" (among other blacks) will, then, be conscious that each pronounced word articulates a n'est pas that is always on the side of a racial law. But not being is not being nothing, and deficiency is not a negation, but rather contains an affirmation of another sort in itself. A deficiency of being may be indistinguishable from the fault that empties it, but this deficiency does not exclude the power, the affect, of absoluty that is the fault line of its very structure (a point that is as hard to express as it is to grasp). In other words, what has been or can be produced as *nègre* also raises, in a very profound way, what counts as subjection.

Yet, what is it then that gives the *nègre* such power? It has power for it escapes power. It is a word that crosses distance and yet establishes distance. And what it expresses murders every black existent. For the *nègre* has no face (and what it shows, what it gives, commands with unconditional authority, and consequently passes all understanding as sincerity or deceit). It negates sense but does not do violence to truth or language: the *nègre* is an epiphany that opens language to the rich density of *non-sens*. What is perhaps most chilling is the fact that we think we are hearing a word, a question, a praxis, however, what inscribes itself in the relationship between orality and word is a kind of obscene uttering—identified with the perversity and violence of the word, *nègre*—that is equally persecutory and condemnatory. Fanon immediately lays out the significance of this conflict for the psyche, whose brutal spontaneity introduces into the *moi* what is not-me (a hallucinogenic *non-moi* that transports and abandons, inhibits and resists). Whence its interest, for Fanon, as an image that paralyzes the power of *black* power. Yet the *nègre* has a power that at first glance power does not have: it distresses us (as Fanon has remarked) not because it possesses truth; but because it corresponds to a *real* that is neither emancipatory nor transcendent. Since it opens up being in caricature, openness is in a sense suspended, and independently of any intent or desire we may have. The black is stuck, paralyzed before a prohibition not because it is emptied of *être en-soi*, but because, contrary to Sartre, it cannot *emerge* into the world as *nègre*. The *nègre*, in other words, is not encountered on the way to being, like an obstacle, but rather in what lies beyond it: the deficiency by which the *noir* finds itself lacerated, severed, scattered (which is what passes for the black experience of the world). And this allows Fanon further to play on the fact that in French, the word *être* is not just a transitive verb in the present tense but also can be used in the passive voice, which Macherey has perhaps not succeeded in grasping in his more simple account of ideology.

Everything that could be taken as evidence of this apparently negative virtually substantial absoluity, then, would be in fact the positive condition of the impurity or flaw by which the black knows nothing (n'est pas) of the essences and determinations of its being. For our purposes here, the essential part of the analysis is that it implies that ontology has itself forgotten how black being-for-others is structured by this n'est pas. We are constrained by that absoluity (it is not simply an escape as Sartre has it) *and* that constraint is not simply the power of an unsaid—that is, the anonymous voice of ideology speaking through the subject—but an enigmatic prohibition. As a result, *since the black is made not to be, rather than an inauthentic failure to be*, the *être en tant qu'on n'est pas* is not just the expression of deficiency but manifests a n'est pas and consequently involves something more like a warning sign, an interdiction, an essential ban or exclusion, however evanescent or fleeting. And this being-made-not-to-be, which explicitly alludes to Sartre's "être été" in *Being and Nothingness*, appears to have a characteristic that could be described as the ideological response, in culture, to the very possibility of black desire.[20] (This could be linked to other figures in Fanon of a disallowed or forbidden path, such as the "prohibitions and barriers" in *Wretched of the Earth* and the more general figure of zones and blockades).[21]

These are the main elements that provoke Fanon and Sartre's divergent views: it is because Sartre emphases a Marxist dialectic that Fanon insists on the *unforeseeableness* of what imposes itself as the irremissible weight of the n'est pas. This hypothesis would then bespeak an essential limit for how Fanon understands Sartre's phenomenology in its efforts to go beyond négritude. There is a relation here with a *beyond* that has to be thought of as more originary than either consciousness or ideology. And who can doubt that, if we dream of an absoluity and our dreams happen to be where absoluity is ineluctably invoked, which is a common enough fantasy, and if such absoluity gives rise to our freedom, we should think things had been turned upside down? Such flawless phantasy is only possible when we are awake. For while the dream lasts, we are unable to be in the possession of this phantasy-identity, which allows us to enjoy a being that is no longer black. For what we cannot know is whether we are awake when we dream of being white, or are more than ever asleep, that is to say, in a deeper, blacker sleep that has to be repressed. Not just because blackness is an unbearable condition, but because the condition itself, regardless of how it affects us, necessarily hovers between a state of knowing and not knowing, caught as it is between a delirious disavowal of the *nègre* whose dream this is, *and* an anti-black phantasy in which blackness is negated. It is impossible to say in either instance, that to dream oneself white is to be as if one were asleep (i.e., no longer *nègre*), or that to dream oneself as black means that we can no longer be asleep (i.e., *nègre*), as if being non-black could only be dreamed in this way, like that of a veil drawn over a whitening surface.

Because it cannot be decided whether it reveals or hides, or because such absoluity can only forget (must forget) the virtuality that determines it, blackness is like a trance to the very extent that it remains entranced by whiteness. As a result, since what induces us to seek what we are (not) is a benevolence offered only in phantasy, it cannot be authorized as a principle of symbolic consistency. There is no certainty, even when we awake, as to whether blackness is really now dreaming itself, or whether such doubt presupposes the "white" enjoyment of such constraint, and so puts to an end any "black" freedom from such desire, and, in this sense also, *receives* the belief as an excess that derives *from* constraint. The cure for this may be liberation, but how does one take possession of one's imaginary? And is that ever really a good thing to do? Moreover, no one can be sure, apart from deliria, whether he is dreaming as black when awake or black when dreaming, because when we dream, we are just as firmly convinced that the stereotype is true, and that fetishism is just a dream on which racist discourse is grafted, and from which we shall awake when our desires converge with reality.[22] Although Fanon never to my knowledge makes the connection explicit, this complication of the Hegelian notion of the *pour-soi* is of a piece with his own ambivalent fascination with Sartre's notion of nausea, as we shall see. And the sense that even if, for Sartre, it is through the subject that nothing (the *néant*) comes into the world, the black subject cannot "be its own nothing," for the thing that makes it into non-being does not belong to it, and is not its own doing, for it does not seek to determine itself as non-being (and thus as a *néant de son proper être*) but discovers that its non-being is outside of itself, and so beyond authenticity or intentionality. In other words, the struggle (what else can one call it?) to be black does not *presuppose* negation or resistance. Nor does it presuppose a relation to an other. If it is not enough to be ontically black to be consciously so, nor is it enough to identify as black to be black in one's drives and desire.

II

Returning to *Black Skin, White Masks*, and leaving aside for now Fanon's initially enigmatic alignment in that text of blackness and ontology, of blackness and impossibility, let us try, the better to grasp what Macherey has wrong here, to understand the overall argumentative structure of Fanon's text (its reading of negrophobia as ideology). Fanon claims that negrophobia is endemic to the system and institutions of the colony and is itself grounded in a moment of inaugural violence that it cannot ever simply integrate or absorb. This claim is not simply an empirical or historical claim about existing systems or institutions (although the question of how the de facto violence of the colony becomes de jure, legitimated by a logic of racial sovereignty, is also at stake). This founding violence does indeed seem to have something of the character of the Althusserian version of interpellation, in that it is radically constitutive of the subject and thus marks a complete subjectivation within whose interruptive, decisive character we have been associating with the temporality of the "tiens" episode. But to capture this violent structure—the performative power of negrophobia—it is telling that Fanon's discourse comes up against its limit: it has to move away from both the language of phenomenology and that of psychoanalysis, to grasp the meaning of what he calls the n'est pas. To give just one example, which occurs after the introduction of the "*schema épidermique racial*": "I approached the other [*l'autre*] . . . and the other evanescent, hostile but not opaque, transparent, absent, disappeared. Nausea . . ."[23]

On the basis of this claim, Fanon will argue that this founding violence does not simply disappear along with the (white) Other who institutes it, but that the trace of it remains as a kind of nausea. To the extent that which is thus instituted as *nègre* is not just a system of domination with its predictable outcomes (and Macherey concedes in all three of his cases that negrophobia is not repressive in this sense), then the decision not to be *nègre*, in as much as this is ever a decision, always takes place in the nauseating recollection, as it were, of that ungrounded foundational moment. Insofar as we are dealing with a prohibition that is itself absent, evanescent, decisions made in the name of freedom are then always in principle, however unknown in fact, imprisoned within the formal instituted framework of a racial law (what Fanon calls "imposition") within which anti-blackness is judged and pronounced. Fanon gives this imprisoning a very strong characterization in terms of aporia, in that on this view *any* decision to not be black to some extent attests to an interdiction at the level of being. The White Man [*le Blanc*], he writes, "had no scruples about imprisoning me," which is the reason why the "I" here is not only outside of itself [*être-la*], but experiences itself as *the effect of a call that is nihilating.*[24] Every time that the subject hears the word *nègre*, every time that it tries to affect a correctly subsumed white example, according to a determinant judgement of what it ought (not) to be, it experiences this nausea by which the ego hemorrhages into an experience of aporia. This emptying out, this lessening: the terms converge on the concept of effacement in ways that remain to be understood, and that will force us to revise our understanding of Fanon's relation to Sartre, Marx, and Lacan.

Freedom, then (as opposed to resistance or complicity), always entails, however minimally, this moment of nausea in which negrophobia uncovers the vicissitudes of this *être-la*. Macherey would not deny this; indeed, this is just where he thinks that Fanon (as opposed to Althusser) is right, but he thinks that nothing in the structure as laid out so far justifies what he presents as Fanon's refusal of the unconscious. After a further argument that attempts to show that negrophobia in general gives rise to a nausea that is certainly related to that described by Sartre in the context we are exploring, Fanon lists and discusses three aporias in the sense we have just given, and it is here that we will be able to understand the general logic of the *être-la* that Macherey is overlooking. Although all three of these aporias (which overlap to some extent, or perhaps can be thought of as redescribing one and the same impossibility from three slightly different angles, in terms of what Fanon calls the interdicted accomplishment of an infinite desuturation) are germane to the questions here, and the nearest Fanon comes actually to saying what the *être-la* is in the context of the third, it is actually in the first that the logic in question is most readily understood.

The first aporia, "an object among other objects," reveals how blackness is possessed by a voice that is not its own. We can thus say that the appearance of the *nègre* is consequent to the disappearance of the subject (its evanescence), and for there to have been a subject, there must have been something other than the subject for its being to just disappear from the world—what, in a different context, Fanon calls the *existentiale* situation of vertigo and nausea. This much we have seen Macherey concede. On the other hand (this is what Macherey seems not to have grasped when he claims that for Fanon "one is never a subject pure and simple, or a subject in an absolute sense, but only ever a subject in a situation"[25]), the action or decision to not be a subject (or to be a subject condemned and judged as deficient) must nonetheless still have a relation to absoluty and thereby to a certain loss. Fanon describes the situation as follows:

> Locked in this suffocating reification, I appealed to the Other so that his liberating gaze, gliding over my body suddenly smoothed of rough edges, would give me back the lightness of being I thought I had lost, and taking me out of the world put me back in the world. But just as I get to the other slope I stumble, and the Other fixes me with his gaze, his gestures and attitude, the same way you fix a preparation with a dye. I lose my temper, demand an explanation. . . . Nothing doing. I explode. Here are the fragments put together by another me.[26]

Let us pause at the image of the two slopes. On one slope we discover the imago that confines us, and in whose suffocating movement we discover the *eidos* that obliges us to leave the world because blackness has no essence as world.[27] On this slope gravity means: a lightness that is now heavy, an absence that is now lived, in whose intoxicating humiliation blackness is neither light nor sensible. The point is that if lightness could be regained, the black would, in his idealism, confidently enjoy blackness as an immanence, and, if he has never been anything but lightness, he would have no idea of what he lacks. But he finds himself burst apart, fragmented. And there is no image (no essence or signification) to reabsorb his recantation. Instead, he finds himself at a distance from world, and is equally incapable of becoming world. Where then is one to go in this state of affairs? The world is foreign, uncertain; and every appeal to the Other is not granted. Indeed, those appeals—rather than referring to the infinity of an Other—disincarnate the ego in the ordeal of its suffering, including the very language of doubt, cogito, ipseity. Is there, on the other hand, another way down? There is no certainty on the other slope. The attempt to descend deeper ever deeper within being, to find the essence of being as rhythm, eroticism, nonviolent logos, élan vital, possesses nothing but falsehood; so false that even the desire to counter destiny with myth, to proclaim a dark Dionysus, only proves how far blackness is from things in themselves, from the categorial law of understanding. To seek its truth as a thing only fixes being as a thing, to be known only in so far as it presents certain attitudes and gestures. It is the contrary that must be affirmed: the n'est pas that confounds consciousness and reified forms of being and obligation. And yet the n'est pas is unobtainable.

This is why blackness is a paradox to itself. The gaze that reifies me must at one and the same time be the gaze that frees me from reification, and thus gives me back my world, yet without my being able to present a world. The gaze thus contests or suspends my access to the world. This means that the "I" that aspires to the world can never simply or confidently be known as world. On the one hand because of the desire that defines the decision as such (in its contentment and wretchedness); and on the other because the "I's" belonging to the world will again be subject to the same aporia as that of the object. This means, says Fanon, that blackness has to invent, or more properly, reinvent the world in its discovery of it as lost (and each case is, *ex hypothesi*, a loss that is *already known*). This moment (however fraught) then repeats, in however minimal a way, the founding violence of the exclusion itself, as already described. In short, for blackness to be in the world, it must, in its self-presentation, be both liberated and excluded. It must preserve itself as fixed or suspended in order to reinvent itself as free or transcendent in each case. For without reinvention, it will not be able to avoid the servility that "freely" affirms the essence of its negrophobic principle. Each time it is fixed, each time it finds itself excluded by a white interpretation (narratives, values, reasoning), it knows that the gaze that reveals infinity is not a true Other, but a phantom, a monstrosity, the repository of white absolutity. At least, if the gaze that guarantees it in no uncertain terms is also what censors, or nihilates, then to be repeatedly seen by it, which always happens in part and according to the necessary iterability of negrophobia, is to be returned to being not as tragedy, but as farce. It is, however, a disturbing either-or that says that the black can only enjoy a semblance of freedom if he overwhelms or supersedes what he is; or if, because he doesn't know yet what he is, that he must suspend the decision, or stop at the undecidable, but always violently resolved, that is to say, buried, dissimulated, repressed blackness of his being. Here, the *être-la* is what founds (and so exceeds) the n'est pas by which being appears. Or, more tellingly, here blackness learns to become one with its disappearance rather than the appearance of its being.

Macherey would perhaps say that this is just the kind of situation he is describing in his first case (i.e., the gaze as a logic of domination).[28] If that were so, then at the very least his criticism of Althusser would be unjustified because to that extent they would in fact be agreeing. But it seems as though they are not exactly saying the same thing. Macherey's description of "a specified subject, a normed subject, a subject for and under norms," which is supposed to capture the "(apparent) legitimacy" and the "(real) efficacy" of racist interpellation, and despite its claim to be essentially a correction of Althusser, in fact systematically minimizes the elements of complicity (the desire to be put back into the world), of violence and undecidability, in Fanon's account.[29]

Indeed, it seems that the question of decision, what it establishes or makes happen (in the sense of being the enigmatic point of a pathological inability to decide), is the object of Fanon's second aporia. The point here (Fanon also formulates this argument in the wake of his polemical exchange with Sartre) is that for the black "to make myself known" (in the sense of being recognized, that is, as a consciousness that is aware of its freedom), there must be a recognition by others that "all I want is to be anonymous."[30] In this sense, "anonymity" means a little more than not being noticed; it refers rather to a desire to be recognized as not *nègre* even though what is recognized as *nègre must* be a misrecognition, a situation in which the desire to go unrecognized by a misrecognition is always an *impossible* recognition. On the one hand, this involves a tension between being a subject pure and simple in the sense of being-for-others and the singularity of the situation that we have already laid out and that Fanon redescribes as an undecidable "descent" between two contradictory but equally imperative injunctions (so a kind of double bind): to become white insofar as one is condemned as black but always in the awareness that one's whiteness is impossible, heterogeneous, and irreducible, and, on the other hand, something that seems just as pernicious, and that the least one can say about it is that it is not immediately perspicuous. In a related but distinct movement, there is a point, prior to the misrecognition of recognition, which, in the imaginary identification with a white object, the black subject is compelled to effect a complete dissolution of itself. Let us briefly examine this dissolution; it involves a *devouring* [*dévorant*] which aligns with and reinforces this white superego, which has all the inexorability of a law, and an internal persecution that is the consequence of a guilt that is already hateful. As Fanon puts it in his chapter on "L'expérience vécue du Noir": if the black child is guilty, it is because it must sacrifice itself to a superego that never fails to condemn it precisely so as to dissipate the child's black inner world.

Thus, to be black means: embrace one's deficiency, impurity, and necessary disappearance as one's most singular possession. Fanon says that blackness is the experience of that which, though heterogeneous to what it means to be human, and what ought, and yet cannot be human, is not yet in being. In a certain sense, it is not yet this "not yet," but nor can it concede to humanism what it so often proclaims: that what lies beyond the "not yet" is never a question of being, but of time and waiting. "And in one sense, if I had to define myself I would say I am the one who waits."[31] How does one test out this waiting, if blackness is not the thing for which one waits? How does one wait when what is awaited always escapes you (which shows you that what is already awaited is simply too far away, or reveals a "not yet" already engulfed by the infinity of what one is not)? Without this vicious circle, Fanon says, apparently repeating an earlier point, the decision not to be black would not be a decision and would amount to a negrophobic imposition. Throughout all of this fraught characterization Fanon comes back to the assertion that "the proof was there, implacable. My blackness was there, dense and undeniable. And it tormented me, pursued me, made me uneasy, and exasperated me."[32] The point is that if blackness is undeniable, to have the density of being to which we shall be increasingly attentive in what follows, then it must exceed or suspend not merely the generality of what it means to be a subject, to which it nonetheless retains the relationship laid out in the first aporia, but also the idea that the decision to be is something that is never simply done or made by a subject; in the sense that there would first be a subject in its self-identity and relative self-sufficiency, and that would subsequently come to make (or suffer) a loss of being on the basis of that subjecthood. Consequently, the relation of being to the "not yet" would then follow a different trajectory—from imago to drive, rather than from image to ego. In a way that is certainly still Sartrean in its inspiration if not its details, Fanon will argue that a thinking based on the subject will be unable to account for blackness. Even if one wanted to say that the subject was made black or that blackness happened to it, in Fanon's view, the word and concept "subject" would severely block and limit that thought (just as earlier we were able to criticize Sartre's subjectivist account of self-certainty). As often around these matters, Fanon is quite vehement: "I was not mistaken. It was hatred; I was hated, detested, and despised, not by my next-door neighbor or a close cousin, but by an entire race.[33] And: "Victory was playing cat and mouse; it was thumbing its nose at me. As the saying goes: now you see me, now you don't. . . . And in one sense, if I had to define myself I would say I am the one who waits."[34]

Undecidability, then, seems at the very least to involve an appearance that also involves one's disappearance ("now you see me, now you don't"); an awareness (belated) of ontological hatred; and a "not yet" that makes every *kairos* impossible to witness or attain. To that extent, and contrary to the Sartrean account we were reading earlier, if the white subject is entirely characterized by its transparent emptiness (since the entire world is outside it), and to some extent is the consequence of what happens or befalls it as a simple event or contingency, for the black subject, as Fanon puts it, the world is already *there (être-là)*, aversive, hostile, even hateful, and what befalls it is expected. This aspect too, which Fanon is again suggesting must be present, however minimally, in any decision (not) to be black (the decision not to be *nègre*), suggests an opacity that, in a word, blackens ego, cogito, and bodily schema. Further (and this aspect of Fanon's discussion seems entirely absent from Macherey, though not from Sartre), this trial or ordeal of undecidability is not simply a transient moment (thought of as an impasse in a Hegelian sense). The undecidability that I am (or perhaps, given what we have just said, the "it" that is hated, or that is added, *the it that is me*) that is at once seen and unseen, (and, once witnessed, produces nausea)—this *it* remains marked by undecidability, and according to a pervasive logic of alterity its *être-là* is never simply *there*, or, more precisely, it is *not* an *il y a*.[35] And it remains marked by undecidability in the mode of spectrality, which will, as we shall shortly see, be a crucial aspect of Fanon's thinking and one that will make his theory of subjectivation slightly different again from Althusser (and a fortiori Macherey's). The specter that wakens me to being remains with me in the question of incertitude for the one who is black (for in questioning its appearing, as black, I too recognize my own uncreated presence; to look at the specter is also to consider what constitutes it, and what is excluded from it; but doubting what something is is not the same thing as saying that it is an "is"). Certainly, the real must lend itself to a figuration, to a concept, but for Sartre the actuality of the *en-soi* is not affected by this appearing *before* appearing. For Fanon, on the other hand, the figure and concept of blackness introduces a schism that alters being; it is not present in itself, but refers to something that has been cut open and amputated. Moreover, this hemorrhaging challenges not only the subject's consistency but its ontic presupposition as an existent. It is not so much dependent on how being appears, but a realization that blackness reveals the being of an appearing dependence. "I am a slave not to the 'idea' others have of me, but to my appearance," Fanon tells us.[36] This is why it cannot be surmounted or sublated, but remains caught, lodged like a ghost in an undecidable decision, which it either blindly follows or affirms as the law of its existence.

After some remarks about how this situation reached in the first two aporias (something in you more than you, undecidability of the decision [not] to be as coming from somewhere other than the subject, whose arrival or refusal I do not master or control) might lead to madness or neurosis (which will again bring us back to Freud) and other remarks about a reluctance (if not an outright refusal) to align the sense of being "too late" said to be at work in these descriptions with the idea of racial difference, Fanon moves to his third aporia. This final turn will explicitly bring us back to Freud but also suggest a way in which the Sartrean and Freudian versions of ontology cannot be separated as rapidly and cleanly as Macherey seems to think, and needs to think, in order to sustain his reading of Fanon's own interpellation.

The third aporia: "I wade in black irrationality, I am up to my neck in it, as a rational response to white irrationality," at first seems little more than an inversion of the adage that we must meet unreason with reason. The reason that is unreason is thus the reason why I have turned to irrationality. And here another essential question appears: Why is the logic of inversion *already* slavish? In positing separation is it not already implicated in that which it denies, and so incapable of going beyond it? What could be more contrary to the rules of dialectic than the unhappy consciousness that encloses division within itself but always fugitively, without regard to transformation or resurrection? For Fanon, this inversion ruptures the kind of ecstatic irrationality at play in Senghor's négritude and, most importantly, affects the relationship between jouissance and knowledge. Just as he comes up against something unreasoned in being-for-others, Fanon realizes that the turn to black irrationality is also a symptom of the desire to make himself known. For the knowledge of what it means to be black in a certain sense comes before knowledge and blocks it. And even if it were possible to counter racist scientific knowledge with black poetic knowledge, that decision would still take the form of the *être-nègre* whose inversion belies the bourgeois notion of subjectivity that defines the irrationalism he is trying better to understand. Hence Fanon's irritated, frustrated response to Sartre's "*Black Orpheus.*" Again, what Sartre forgets, or pays insufficient attention to, is how inversion is a falsehood, a contrariety, and one that makes it harder to conceive of blackness without *mythos*. Moreover, in positing blackness as a transitive-transitory relation to historical knowledge *as such*, rather than the consequence or effect of historical knowledge, Sartre never recognizes the "not yet." This shows that Sartre, in his desire to make négritude the outcome of a dialectic that precedes the distinction between reason and unreason, that *must* precede it, or more precisely, put it out of its reach, makes blackness into an unhappy unconsciousness that can only find itself outside of itself. Consequently, we can really only know ourselves when we perish in a "white" dialectics of inversion. Having written on this elsewhere, I won't go into any detail here.[37] But Fanon's response, "so they were countering my irrationality with rationality, my rationality with the 'true rationality,'"[38] recalls the discussion of *Being and Nothingness* that we described earlier. There we saw how a simple submission to the call of ideology puts an end to any doubt, for the moment one is summoned, speculation ceases and one's destiny is about to be decided. The difference here, however, has precisely to do with the quality of the urgency that Fanon ascribes to racial thinking: eschatological as it may be in a certain sense, here the belief that race is a destiny does not seem to occur *at the end* of discussion or deliberation, nor even exactly *as an outcome* of such discussion and deliberation, but, through its intrinsic irrationality, cuts short deliberation and discussion, which are in principle irrelevant and which, however necessary they may be to the prospects of a reasoned response to blackness (and blackness is never simply a question of reason, says Fanon) are necessarily displaced by a phantasm whose existence is sui generis.

And so, it is not surprising that Fanon immediately invokes here not consciousness but indeed an "impulsiveness." Négritude is the acting out of an "impulsive position" that is driven to see in blackness an *en-soi* that is complete or "immanent in itself," and precisely because it refuses to see or know how it is itself unreasoned, driven by the desire not to be.[39] But this desire to make blackness into an immanent moment of decision (in the sense of invention), to make it into an *is* rather than an *is not*, is always preceded (structurally and epistemologically, says Fanon) by the moment of negrophobic interpellation. This is why, as Fanon points out, the decision to present blackness as an *en-soi* is never a question of rationality (*verständlichkeit*) or negation; but is the result of a subjectivation that is always and everywhere the imperfect, incomplete imbrication of one's being. Or, as Fanon puts it, "Où me situer? Ou, si vous préférez: où me fourrer?" Where do I fit in? Or, if you prefer: where should I put myself?[40]

III

Irony as the negative is the way; it is not the truth but the way.
Kierkegaard, *The Concept of Irony*

This questioning is in fact a constant one in Fanon, first appearing in his published work as the famous final sentence of *Black Skin, White Masks*: "O my body, always make me a man who questions!"[41] The emphatic, exclamatory distinctions of Fanon's texts are often in tension with the precarious, even agonistic nature of what is being expressed, in as much as they concern the *irony* of a certain metaphysics, and that is more or less explicitly alluded to many times in Fanon's work, functioning as a kind of watchword or slogan but never once given a precise definition or a detailed reading. In *Towards the African Revolution* (published in 1964 but based on articles from 1952–1961), for example, he writes: "It thus seems that the West Indian, after the great white error, is now living in the great black mirage."[42] In the essay "West Indians and Africans," first published in *Esprit* in 1955, Fanon suggests a possible connection between irony and what he refers to as a "defense against neurosis," provoking him to state that, in the West Indies, irony (and incidentally the reference to the great black mirage returns us to the context of the third aporia and the racial-cultural politics of négritude—irony is in fact used to question the somewhat impassioned invocation of négritude), is paradigmatic. In the essay, Fanon's reading of négritude, which does not mention explicitly his own earlier reading in *Black Skin, White Masks*, though he does invoke irony as a kind of dissimulation, helps us see how the three aporias presented separately in *Black Skin, White Masks* are related in the general thought of an irony that is both psychoanalytic and historical (the resonance with Macherey's analysis of the *unsaid* in *Pour une théorie de la production littéraire* [translated as *A Theory of Literary Production*] is something to which we shall return):

> Jankélévitch has shown that irony is one of the forms that good conscience assumes. It is true that in the West Indies irony is a mechanism of a defense against neurosis. A West Indian, in particular an intellectual who is no longer on the level of irony, discovers his Negritude. Thus, while in Europe irony protects against the existential anguish, in Martinique it protects against negritude.[43]

The explicit invocation of irony as a defense against anguish and neurosis is clear here, but the idea that irony also names a dialectic of black history (in the Antilles, in Africa) may not be so obvious. So in the essay we find: "Until 1939 the West Indian lived, thought, dreamed (we have shown this in *Black Skin, White Masks*) composed poems, wrote novels exactly as a white man would have done"; but "in 1945 he [the West Indian] discovered himself to be not only black but a Negro [*Nègre*]," a discovery that came from the reading of Césaire's *Cahier d'un retour au pays natal*.[44] And again, in 1939, the West Indian "was continually recalling that he was not a Negro"; but "from 1945 on, the West Indian in France was continually to recall that he *was* a Negro."[45] What happens between 1939 and 1945? Fanon cites two linked events: the publication, in 1939, of Césaire's *Cahier d'un retour au pays natal*; and the forced deployment in 1943 of ten thousand racist Vichy sailors in Martinique after the fall of France. According to Fanon, the confrontation with white racism forced Martinicans to analyze their metaphysical fabulations apropos of French imperialism, but it was Césaire's poetics, defined specifically as a *négritude*, which permitted them to ask the question: am I a *nègre*? A question that acted rather like a parabasis in that it interrupted and intruded upon the illusion of West Indian society and rhetoric. Martinicans were forced to rethink the strictly ideological relation between "being neither white nor Negro" (a class definition), and the function of such rhetoric when faced with negrophobia. The result was an acute crisis of thought and experience, memory and desire. In the first, history is not so much a defense against irony as the most ironic of discourses; and in the second, négritude is the means by which anti-black black racism can be expressed and denoted. Which is as much to say that the desire to be, or not to be *un nègre*, forestalls what one is and is a defense against what one appears to be but is not. The irony here has a very specific meaning, which the reference to Vladimir Jankélévitch's *L'Ironie* (1936) makes more complicated than it might at first appear. What is it that makes négritude an ironic poetics? *Négritude* is essentially the convergence of different signifieds in a single signifier, according to which blackness is both excessive and subtractive, both concept and unreason, both truth and pseudology. It is this specific element that, for my part, I call a *parabasis*: "parabasis is the interruption of a discourse by a shift in the rhetorical register," writes Paul de Man, which is also linked to an interruptive "intrusion" (as such, the word not only gives us a different way of thinking about the "tiens" passages, but also about Fanon's reading of them).[46] The oscillation between error and mirage would suggest that the parabasis is permanent in the sense given to it by de Man in his reading of Schlegel: that the interruption—the interdiction—takes place successively, infinitely, so that we could say that *blackness is the permanent parabasis of an anti-black allegory.* Irony refers to its necessary undoing and what, historically, links it to an economy of aberration. This is the logic of an excess that is infinitely subtractive, and a dialectic that is structured by enmity. "I mean, for example, that the enemy of the Negro is often not the white man but a man of his own color."[47] What disrupts desire is, then, the disillusion that permanently blackens all irony. But there is no recuperation in terms of an historical dialectic, as we saw in Fanon's response to Sartre, for the great black hole is a mirage, and even irony cannot expose what it really is, for what it reveals is an enmity launched against one's own impossible reflection. And just as, when considered historically, blackness is a mirage, in the same way, when considered as irony, it reveals a negrophobia or—the same thing—a négritude that henceforth makes comprehensible an enmity of which irony, formed as a defense, is the most precarious, suspended, and interrupted of signs.

Simplifying greatly, it seems to me that there are two very different ironies, or allegories of irony, at work in Fanon's writing. Irony as history, as a black neurotic defense against blackness; but then irony, or its parabasis, as the point where blackness vanishes infinitely, to a point where no form of knowing could ever reach. Accordingly, where Macherey's sense of interpellation seems to come primarily from an unequivocal, supposedly unironic account of being spoken, Fanon's reference to irony, or, if you prefer, black irony, which by its interruption and utter ambiguity gives one the impression that defense and enmity have changed names and even content, spells the end of the fantasy that black subjects could ever know each other, or be known as black, which is enough to cause existential anguish and metaphysical crisis. For if it is the case that blackness or, more precisely, its allegory, presents both a challenge and a defense, the one thing that Fanon insists on is that this allegory also points to the perpetual irony of the same (illusory, condemned, murderous) encounter with what is considered to be *nègre*. Let us consider these two oppositions.

Firstly, in the West Indies, the decision to *be* is always troubled by a desire that, we know, both idealizes and repels blackness, and so is unwilling and unable to decide between them, and so chooses neither. Irony offers an illusory escape from such indecision; whether this derives from a good conscience (Jankélévitch) or a bad conscience (Sartre), the refusal of apodictic certainty (the assertiveness of ideology), is not simply evasive, but nor is it resistant. Fanon accuses the black ironist of being *defensive*, that is to say, the failure to decide between content (truth) and form (appearance), or between white (message) and black (medium), gives rise, historically, to an aporia that cannot decide between illusion and error. I do not believe, in fact, that blackness can proceed without a certain undecidability as to its object (as we know, nothing is more resolutely elusive and paradoxical than the language of racial authenticity). Nor do I believe that *le vécu noir*, heir of a thousand anecdotes and fables, at once mythic, ideological, and stereotypic, can be divested of irony without the risk of further illusion. If black irony invites complicity with negrophobia, it also diverts us from the meaning of that clandestinity. Hence Fanon's criticism of the metaphors by which West Indians express their superiority to Africans, and the vision that subsists through them, that of a feeling of racial inferiority hidden behind the *nègre* as signifier. It is this argument, itself ironical, that explains why blackness is inevitably experienced as a permanent parabasis. (I am referring here to the word *intrusion* rather than, say, imposition, or interpellation, and the trope by which it is communicated: the metaphor that makes blackness appear as a black hole, and the various invocations of a paradoxically repelling attraction, as an asymptote that famously touches on its own negation, but in a way that is always liminal, indecisive, because it refuses to know what it already knows, and will not verbalize the words, or the concepts, that would free it from such equivocation.)

Contrary to Jankélévitch, then, for whom irony reveals the truth behind illusion, perhaps it would be better to say that blackness is disclosed by a distance incapable of being traversed or negated. Here, speech misses being because it is diverted from it, indeed the more diverted language is, the more it can be enjoyed as a negrophobic distraction. To ask "am I *nègre?*" is thus to be confronted by an illusion that attests to something displaced, something unsettling that diverts the mind from all ethics and politics. As such, any wish to reascend the two slopes (of existence and nonexistence), or to climb back down from them (from abjection, say, to liberation), is already diverted by a parabasis whose only thought is to stop blackness from being thought. Black irony would thus be the equivalent of a distraction. Existence is not *first*—before existence blackness consists of a n'est pas that orients it, that places it *in front of* the nothing that it echoes. This is why Fanon says the black is always a stranger to himself: unable to relate to the Other, he not only puts into question his freedom, he cannot recognize his destitution, nor can he stop himself thinking about it (this is the definition of Fanonian denegation). The n'est pas refers to a being who enjoys such separation, and whose jouissance is separated from its nonexistence. If, then, one were to try to answer the question (how is blackness possible?), one would need to deconstruct this very opposition between irony and history, irony and truth.

The second, much more recent opposition, of a more Marxist aspect and largely tributary to the Althusserian paradigm of science/ideology, is that of the *unsaid* of literature. Or: literature makes us aware of what it cannot say or is prevented from saying. The unsaid is the limit of ideology, but it is through it that ideology speaks. Hence it both structures and fissures the semantic codes of the text (a limit that literature mouths silently). At the very end of his introduction to *A Theory of Literary Production*, first published in 1966, Macherey gives a brief summing up of this unsaid structure, which establishes: "that absence around which a real complexity is knit."[48] This absence is determinate but not determined. The unsaid is then seen as the absent (though coded) residue of what the work *cannot say* or necessarily leaves unsaid; it is (the real, historical) elision that "founds the speech of the work" (if we define that speech as a kind of "vanishing" without which it could not be heard) that precedes its meaning *as* history (if we set meaning in opposition to its denegation—a word that Macherey borrows from Lacan but doesn't really define as such).[49] Just as the opposition surface/depth implies a hermeneutic vision, so the unsaid/meaning opposition implies an ultimately dialectical vision (under cover of a logic of confrontation): there is a reduction of the unsaid to that of a symptom (the idea that each work is "haunted by the absence of repressed words which make their return"), and of the symptom to history, where the unspoken "receives the means" of its "realization." Literature, the trace of the unsaid, and because it is specifically this trace, then makes negatively explicit its historic function, which Macherey here describes as its production. Accordingly, it is the task of any Marxist reading to show how the work establishes, symptomatically performs, and ideologically assumes its history, in the same way that the "*unconscious of the work*" establishes repression (the way an abscess reveals an underlying disease), in order to lance the process of its suppuration.[50] Hence, we arrive at the paradox of an unsaid that governs any reading as such, the entire pertinence of an indetermination (in relation to form, ideology, discourse, or history) that has no signified, yet through which everything happens or is produced as the "real" of the work.

I should like to suggest that the unsaid is what haunts every literary production. How, then, can we read or interpret it, and how does it relate to the *situation* of blackness? To answer this question, we will need to inquire more closely into the relation between language and ideology. To do so, I will use as my example Macherey's later reading of Fanon's *Black Skin, White Masks*. Accordingly (as I concluded at the beginning), we will see how blackness is produced—sutured—by a theory of reading that concedes that the essence of ideology is the production of a universal structure but in ways that make blackness itself invisible, which is absurd.

Let us take first the opposition of the unsaid and meaning, of subjection (*l'assujettissement*) and interpellation. No doubt how we read includes a certain relation to how we, in turn, are irreducibly read. The Marxist structural analysis of ideology is wholly based on the conviction (and the dialectical proof) that we subsist by how we reproduce ideology. In brief, to occupy the grammar by which we are recognized as subjects we "*must answer*" the call of ideology, for there is "no possibility of dodging it" or its logic of reproducibility—the effects of ideology can be varied without altering this underlying structure.[51] That Macherey should then say of the black that the "operation of selection" also takes "the form of a relegation," as implacable and as it is overdetermined, has exactly the same narrative (or, more precisely, structural) function as *l'assujettissement* does in Althusser; for example, the way in which the subject "is called upon" is functionally necessary to how it expresses ideology.[52]

The error, however—and it is here that we must modify Macherey's reading of blackness—would be to forget the irony by which the black realizes its untruth. What this (forgetting, as we have just said) forgets is not what brings about the content or the signified of selection, the racist forms of understanding that are assumed to be already *there* (*être-la*), but the form, the signifier, or if we prefer, the permanent parabasis by which the subject is desutured and *as such is never symbolizable*. For blackness is articulated around a position that has no here-there (*juste là*); its signified is a never-having-been-there (or is more akin to a kind of hallucination), as we have shown in Fanon and even more clearly in his reading of psychoanalysis. Further, Fanon attempts to bring to light—without reference to verisimilitude or allegory—an interplay between voice and signifier in which the black (or more exactly the black who is ideologically whitened) *does not need the "tiens" to be heard for it to have an effect*, for the place it is communicated *from* is already echoed by a drive *toward* it, a n'est pas that is located at the *other* end, as it were, of desire and reality, of subject and ideology. Moreover, this drive is *absent*, it necessarily slips away from any image or history of meaning. Thus its relation to a certain neurosis: even though it is full of malice and a certain defensiveness, this is an irony that has no symbolic code, genre, or disposition, whatever the material uses of ideology.

Hence we can no longer *see* blackness as the overdetermined effect of a structural situation. Blackness is not relegated, but effaced; in the black, there is only whiteness, or, more precisely, the black in its blackness is only a denegation of form—consequently, *there is no subject of blackness*. We can say metaphorically that the black is subjected not by what he is, but by what he is *not*: neither host nor parasite, the *nègre* resolutely intrudes as an obscene intrusion; it confuses distance and limit, not because of nausea, and not even because of autoimmunity, but because it is an abolition that is freely chosen (that is, a self-effacement that is always a forced choice). Doubtless, this is why its voicing is not primarily phenomenological (Macherey) nor *automatic*

(Althusser), *but that which recedes*, as it were, from discourse, truth, and ideology. What is more ironic, more undecidable, more interruptive, than this structure by which blackness experiences itself as fixed in its effacement, and that declares itself free in its chosen unfreedom?

IV

Now let us turn to the second opposition, that of irony and history, which is in effect the opposition of Fanonism and Marxist phenomenology. There is a kind of intermediate step here that will lead us to the parabasis that we are trying to understand in the irony Fanon is invoking. Here too, we must refine our vision of what blackness is (or is not).

What enables Macherey to question Althusser is, as we have seen, the belief that the theory of ideology is blind to the functioning of difference. It is a blindness that is symptomatic, unsaid. And therefore, says Macherey, has to be decrypted. The features of the unsaid are, of course, undeniably drawn from Althusser, or at least from his idea of a symptomatic reading (the belief that what is unsaid is both absent and what grounds the text in a *real historical rationality*). To read symptomatically is thus to expose the unsaid of discourse, but also to let theory bring its own diversion to an end. So, like any discourse that claims to expose what is absent, how does one finally know that one has grasped the truth of ideology? How does one distinguish the unsaid from ideology if the former surreptitiously persists, constantly repeated by the work, without its meaning or signified being anything but what is *meant* by ideology? These propositions seem to be both excessive and insufficient: excessive because meaning is always returned to its referent, and the text thereby becomes the incarnation of an absolute reference; insufficient because the operation of *conversion* or *decryption* is never explained in all its depth. A word on this last point.

We know that the unsaid of the work, what determines at once its task and its limits, is the ideology that takes place by never taking place *as such*. There is no text without repression, and here is why: All literature begins as the sign or allegory of a displacement; and each reader who would know this must also come to know what is unsaid. But, to think this, critique must be able to make repression representable, for why otherwise would we read it. A Marxist theory of reading must thus expressly become the structure, the code, by which the unsaid emerges as the resolution of its ideologically re-pressed reference. Now, the irony of blackness (the black irony of thought) has essentially nothing to do with reference or repression. Of course, it can include symptoms, but it does not need to be repressed for it to be uncon-scious. Fanon constantly talks about how blackness is the depositary of a cultural hatred that directly opens a black hole *within* the psyche, and in ways that are necessarily unknown or ambiguous, but no less real or trau-matic for all that. Blackness is the trace of an unsaid that intrudes, but what intrudes has no determinable meaning beyond the intrusion itself to the point where blackness is the experience of a paradox: *an unconscious affect that is itself not unconscious.* It is better to speak, more neutrally, of a form that lacks repression, or for whom repression is lacking. Let us even add, per-haps: without arrival—or at least without the appearance of arrival—intru-sion does not function as a meaning (a signified that is unsaid), but is the ef-fect of an entire culture. But even here we are not really going far enough, for what remains to be described is a vanishing that is neither an event nor an occasion, and so cannot be dialectically overdetermined as something un-said, or simply interpellated.

Whence Fanon's view of a black n'est pas: a figure that does not lend it-self to figuration—or even that of production—a figure that subsequently is not a *verneinung*; a figure that is not tropological, but that reveals a dra-matic antithetical turning point that Fanon characterizes as a *contrecoup* or ricochet, that is, an adversative signifier that throws one off balance, out of kilter, off guard. In the "tiens, un nègre!" example: such a moment is fore-grounded not by the various metaphors, but by the exclamation mark that suggests that the gaze cannot be grasped as readily or straightforwardly as Macherey suggests—that is, not as an intruding sense or intention, but as a punctuation without content. By carrying this distinction to its conclusions, we shall be working toward why blackness requires a different language than ontology. For the moment let us recall that the n'est pas is, as Fanon says, the paradoxical figure of what cannot be figured, and that it is indeed with-out phrase or sentence, even though it can be echoed, or relayed, and in re-spect to which the word *black* is little more than an antilogy, whose signified opens onto a perpetual parabasis in which Fanon suggests we experience the impossible: "I made up my mind to laugh myself to tears, but that had be-come impossible."[53]

Such sentences make it obvious why the n'est pas is not the work of a repression. But they also make it quite clear why the n'est pas cannot, consequently, be conceived as an existential situation. To explain why, consider
the following passage from *Black Skin, White Masks*, which I cite at some
length:

> One of the traits of the Antillean is his desire to dominate the other. He steers
> his course through the other. It is always a question of subject, and the object is
> totally ignored. I try to read admiration in the eyes of the other, and if, as luck
> would have it, the other sends back an unpleasant reflection, I run the mirror
> down: the other is a real idiot [*un imbécile*]. . . . Each of them wants *to be*, wants to
> *flaunt himself*. Every act of an Antillean is dependent on the Other—not because
> the Other remains his final goal for the purpose of communing with him as de-
> scribed by Adler, but simply because it is the Other who asserts him in his need
> to enhance his status.[54]

So what is the Antillean's relation to the other? It is marked by one generic
feature that attaches it to an idiocy that is indeed foolish and that, not surprisingly perhaps, does not distinguish it from a complex rhetorical irony:
the obligatory desire to be "full of myself," and to declare to the other that
this "wish for fulness" is already, in itself, the sign of an insufficiency that is
both litotic and rhetorical. If these sentences of Fanon's are deeply ironic, it
is because they show how the black desire to *be* is already foolish because it
cannot fulfill itself (and presumably because it is mediated, dependent), and
for whom the other is of the same order as a reflection that renders not plenitude but its opposite, a self-image that is inclined to be suspicious (of itself)
because the other is inattentive to my (fictitious) exemplary status.[55] These
sentences, in their complex rhetorical inversions, seem to me, then, to present black identity as a kind of pseudonymous delusion, and one marked by
a rivalrous relation to another that, on this view, is in fact an ironical self-
relation. What we must grasp here is not that such irony might *seem* foolish,
but what it bespeaks is a claim to being that is radically displaced from being
and that Fanon habitually describes as an antagonym.

This is not all. The black is a *comparaison* that itself has no status, in the
sense given it through the pages of *Black Skin, White Masks*, with its image
of a distrust that is *itself* negrophobic when viewed from a black perspective, and that bespeaks an envy of the white *néant* that it lacks, such that it
masks what is missing and cannot ironize away. This insight has considerable

consequences for Fanon's understanding of interpellation since it corresponds to a confusion—not so much of appearing with phenomena—but of the *néant* with cogito, as if the other that besets me (and who plunges me into a black hole) could be simply annulled, or again, dispensed with, along the lines of a chiasmic reversal. So when Fanon writes: "The question is always whether he [the other] is less intelligent than I, blacker than I, or less good than I," what is being thematized ironically is also an example of foolish undecidability (and, indeed, of mirage and error).[56] Amidst such uncertainty and gnomic inversion it is hard to tell apart desire from a kind of pathological narcissism that, in a further paradoxical twist, also communicates a form of mastery and satisfaction, but one that can only perform itself as a kind of ontological stupidity, as is further evidenced by the fact that it is so obviously haunted by what it is not, a n'est pas that Fanon draws attention to as an obligation that makes the decision to *be* both constrained and aporetic. Put another way, it is clear that, if blackness is n'est pas, a *non-étant* otherwise repressed by phenomenology, clinically it signifies not so much *"a being by which nothingness comes to things"* (the words are Sartre's), but a nothingness whose being is a thing, and that reproduces itself as the imprint or turning point of a destitution that is also its most luxurious possession.[57] It follows that, for Fanon, blackness is not a dialectical struggle between an *en-soi* and cogito, but an aporetic struggle over the status of what is lacking, and one that is linked not to how one is seen, or how one imagines oneself being seen, but to *a disgrace of being* stupefied by irony.

Condemned, unconscious, prohibited—and yet performed: let us say that blackness cannot affirm, or choose, itself, for it is already chosen—by which I mean that it cannot pass from indecision to a transformation of what subordinates it; the paradoxical gravity, and fate, by which it is at once undecidably mad, foolish, and deluded; and, as is so often the case, bespeaks an almost religious love for what would destroy it, and that luxuriates in both the choice and the experience; an inheritance based on culture and not on pathology (and consequently is never *just* a question of unconscious desire). The n'est pas certainly has some affinity with a symptomatic morphology, but it differs from it on one fundamental point (the predicates associated with these aporias imply a self-blinding irony that, once again, is never simply ideological). The n'est pas (whose form is derived from a logic of corpsing) cannot be resolved (*aufheben*), nor negated; for as Macherey shows perhaps in spite of himself, it speaks to the ways in which blackness is the depositary of culture, how it is excluded, not just selected; out of kilter, not just turned around; nihilated, not just subjected.

To return, in conclusion, to the concept of interpellation that I discussed at the beginning: in my opinion, it must consist today not in trying to see history within the unsaid of the text. In *Black Skin, White Masks*, the unsaid is not the form of the text but that which can never be said and which I would prefer to call, at least in this chapter, the permanent parabasis of a black allegory. The problem of what it means to be a subject can only be treated in relation to what I call an undecidable question; and which, to continue the metaphor, can be summed up by saying that, if hitherto we have read black texts as stupidly referential (as identical to their situation), it would be better to read them as the place where blackness is suspended or interrupted (as a question of authenticity), whose irony, as Fanon describes it reading Césaire, is nothing but an abyssal infinity—which envelops and absorbs nothing other than the black hole of its relation to both ontology and destruction.

Two

Nigra Philologica

To Signify, then, is to master the figures of Black Signification.
Henry Louis Gates, *The Signifying Monkey*[1]

The previous chapter ended with the question of the n'est pas in black speaking being: how does one know who is speaking it when it has neither sign nor presence? How does one speak—let alone represent—the anguish of a non-presence? Or think a thought without a thinker (a thinking that has yet to be thought *as* blackness)?[2]

Everything turns on this paradox. The n'est pas—in the obscurities of its writing, and not in its sense—neither uncovers nor reveals blackness; but conceals and withdraws it from being. The task of making it speak, even in philology, is thus beyond logic or semantics; nor can it be sought in grammar or rhetoric (the forms, figures, schemes, and tropes of understanding). The n'est pas must precede judgement and figuration, for it is always already given to us as the pathos of a being that cannot posit itself as sense or meaning, essence or ontology. So how does one read it? In what follows we shall explore two answers: those who think blackness is a kind of figural philological mastery and those who think it is a singular n'est pas that literary philology cannot understand.

I

I will begin with *topos*. To venture into it is to be placed as place; to be rhetorically commonplace. But any rhetoric of place (topos) can only take place beyond place (*atopos*). In other words, the black propriety of place has no place,

it can never be in place, for there is no place for what it is *not*. (For all definitions and principles of a black propriety of being are placeless and so cannot
be looked to express *topoi*. The placeless ones, on the contrary, have become
accustomed to being taken, stolen, in exile, and are taken aback when presented with propositions, which understand nothing of atopos. We therefore
need to proceed with other definitions and principles of topos or atopos.)

I will speak, therefore, of Esu, this mediator between *vernaculus* (native)
and *verna* (a slave born in his master's house).[3]

As the figure of mediation, and also of a writing of mediation, Esu is the
mediator who allows us to know our own rootlessness.

Knowing topoi without knowing our own rootlessness makes for bad
philology.

Knowing our rootlessness without knowing our origin makes for black
despair.

Knowing Esu strikes the balance because he shows us both rootlessness
and origin. He is the pure means in which the very mediacy of language manifests itself as prophecy and as witness.

As a result of this irreducible mediacy he gives us the spoils, the riches;
the crowning glories of a *black* semiosis.

As the "ultimate copula," he rejoins language and being, thought and history, grammar and rhetoric, blackness and philology.[4] As the ultimate "figure [and reader] of indeterminacy," he assumes that being is *pólemos*, that
one is multiple; for no idea comes near him without critique, for his power
is one of infinite multiplicity.[5] In short, Esu *"is* the dialectical principle" of
disillusionment and unveiling, of critique and self-critique.[6] And his greatest
mark is the prodigious figurative power that, via mediation, rejoins-sublates
(*Aufgehoben*) that which is *not* (n'est pas) to that which is.

Yet because we are incapable of attaining this goal by our own efforts,
philology is the means that we employ in our striving toward it. That striving can be interpreted in two different ways. It is because we are alienated
from the modern world that we value classical blackness as origin. This is
the philological motive of every act of reading black texts, including those
of philosophy.

Yet we know that those origins represent an ideal at which black philology is striving, regardless of our steadfast conviction in its decisive impossibility. What else does this striving, and this impossibility, proclaim but that

there was once a unity of trope and topos, of which all that now remains is the empty print and trace of a black *hermeneutica sacra*? Thus the black philologist tries in vain to combine *gens* with logos, seeking in language a general knowledge of community, which is not there so as to overcome the racial essences that are, since this infinite abyss can only be filled with the infinite, signifying fecundity of interpretation; in other words by black philology itself.

Now it is not possible to have one without the other, for what is rejoined can be destitute and barren, as well as having nothing to say or express. This is why Esu is not only a god or sovereign power; he is also the power of mockery. That power masks and distances rule (propriety) and everything we call our own (ipseity). There are places (topoi) where even Esu's dialectics must be called n'est pas, and non-places (*atopoi*) where Esu's speech must be no longer sayable or translatable. ("Nothing" here denotes what cannot be said or pledged, that which is too absurd for any predication or assertion of mastery. An excess that has no content and cannot be communicated as anything, not even the philosophical promise of "*to have said it*" before denying, believing, or doubting what is said. Here blackness happens *before* we know how it comes about as the excess of language.)

In Esu and through Esu, therefore, we find our place. Through him, being returns to itself as the pathos of return, its realms, its cities, its homeland. But only through and in philology can return take place and teach us both meaning and knowledge. Knowing Esu is to find ourselves in a strange place, but it is also to go toward a certain trajectory of place: the historicizing philology of blackness. Here, we draw closer to the origin, not further away.

To grasp this copula is to know and have *ase* (power). Ase is both de facto and de jure black power, that is, "the force of coherence of process itself," which is itself an ingenious hypothesis of logos *as* mediation.[7] Without Esu as mediator, the logos cannot communicate to us, and without philology as the mediator of mediation, the words, signs, and signifying power of logos cannot be known. Without mediation, the hermetic rules of ase would no longer be decodable or meaningful. Without Esu as mediator, the logos (as origin) cannot attain concrete form. Through Esu, therefore, we know logos. But to know logos, we need to know the philological rules of its decipherment. For Esu "connects the grammar of divination [the validity and value of true ase] with its rhetorical structures [figures of interpretation]."[8] This is why Esu is the necessary mediator, and why without him blackness cannot grasp its origin. Hence, Esu is both the figure of mediation and the constitution of mediation itself.

But at the same time, we need to know mediation because of our rootlessness, because we lack nothing less than knowledge of our origin. We can know Esu only by knowing our own self-relation, and what determines this self-relation is blackness as rootless mediation. It is at this limit point that the literary critic, Henry Louis Gates, considers philology to be a dialectical principle of blackness. His formulations of black literary scholarship with regards to philology will be our main concern in this chapter.

To know black philology without knowing this rootlessness is thus to not know the true relation between topos and verna. It is not to know how slavery had an impact on logos (as an event without mediation), nor why blackness is without place (without sacred topoi or figures). So what is gained through the understanding and knowledge of *nigra philologica*? What does the return to philology *as method* add to the *certainty* that such a thing as a black logos had existed not as a question of hermeneutics, but of reality? And if we study Esu the trickster, will we be able to see why history is no longer the mediator, and slavery is no longer without mediation, but parts of a whole?

The result is a new mastery of mediation and a new myth of place. For to know blackness without origin is never enough. All those who have claimed to know black existence as rootless only have futile proofs to offer. But to prove that blackness is rooted we need the solid and palpable proofs of philology. By showing how blackness has a sacred meaning in the world and through this a logos we are, therefore, no longer rootless. And the recognition that blackness has always articulated itself through *African* topoi thus proves that it has a legitimate foundation in philology. What is Esu but the name and promise of an initiation into philology? Moreover, an initiation that says incomparably more about acts of reading and decryption than about *bildung* or *Wissenschaft*.[9] In "Africa" we thus discover a signifying that is as natural as *vernaculus* and a *philologica* that is just as venerable as that of Europe. At least this seems to be the promise of Gate's seminal *The Signifying Monkey* (1988), from which the above principles are taken.

The philological principles that Gates concerns himself with are all to do with roots (*etymon*) and debt (*schuld*). With admitted entrepreneurial spirit,

Gates wants to make blackness reveal itself as figurative wealth. It is deplorable to see blacks without any trust in their African past. Everyone thinks about the present and the future, but when it comes to thinking about the African past, people lack the requisite speculative faith. But without trust in the past, how can we amortize the future? This is what makes philology so important. It provides us with the criterion by which the limits of historical knowledge can be overcome. Philology sets the limits by which rootlessness is no longer an unsecured debt and gives us a promissory note for the future (like selling ancestry because we can now be sure of its future value). For what mediation embodies is a philological promise (to us the creditor) that the absent black logos will no longer be indebted to the debt form of who we are; but will bring us together in shared obligation and trust. The more impoverished one is symbolically, the more one sees the promise of capital wealth in the realm of *symbola*. The past underwritten as a stable referent or use value, thus becomes the ultimate guarantor of the value (of blackness as) value, whose "ancestryness" will allow us to maintain a proper sense of justice and history. For the past *must* be read (valued) if the possibility of debt redemption is to be meaningful. Black philology thereby becomes both the ends and the means by which all values of exchange-mediation become measurable against reparation, in the same way that rootlessness is measured against the unpayable debt of origin. After all, without mediation, neither credit nor debt can be wagered as speculative returns. Black philology thus aims to create wealth out of the perpetually renewed debt of mediation, and it does this without recourse to a fundamental reserve or guarantor of value. Why? Signifyin(g) has no faith in the measurability of value and no interest in the final redemption of debt. What matters is that the past as a debt *without limit* becomes the pledge of a fungible debt that can be "read" without limit—as the undecidable figure of black mediation. This is what makes Esu into the figure of speculative mediation. He is the principle that does not force us to choose between meaning and sign, or thing and symbol, for he is the metaphor for how trope and meaning are always mediated by something else, namely, the unsecurability of black fungible debt. The black world knows this, for it is a good judge of signifyin(g). And what signifyin(g) signifies, according to Gates, is an unavoidable trickery, or mockery, devoted to the ambiguities of language. Tricksters are always mediators, and mediations always tricks. (But language is the mockery of a mediation that can never be sublated as either trickery or mediation.) And what they produce as logos is pólemos (or strife):[10] the subversion of nothing less than language, and, perhaps, the suspension of blackness itself as an allegory of subversion. In this sense, mediation cannot be guaranteed as truth, but nor can it be verified as logos or meaning.

So how does one master or secure it? Why believe that blackness—or its logos—categorically announces itself in this capacity for surplus enjoyment? And why assume that to encounter trickery is to encounter the indubitable signifying power of black discourse?

Signifyin(g) is neither a language of representation nor one of devotion, and yet in *The Signifying Monkey* it carries a lot of interpretive weight. What is its role? Do we indulge it because it is somehow natural? No, rather we enjoy it because it opens up a rift between white grammar and black speaking being, and because it sets an *a priori* limit on the reliability of all linguistic knowledge. I mean what signifyin(g) offers us is not reference, but the polemical embrace of genealogy through which the intensional aspect of meaning and trope can be discerned. As such, it depicts a "parallel, discursive" onto-political universe that only becomes visible in black semantic modes of figuration, for example, the dozens, toasts, the lie, riddles, boasts, and so on.[11] To be sure, all of these ritualized exchanges of language share a common form, one marked by the exchanging of symbola (the mark and tests of language), that in turn secure an obligation to respond in order to repay the "debt" (the principal owed to language itself).[12] Signifyin(g) is thus the exchange of what cannot be exchanged, or rather it establishes the place of exchange (topos) as one of unpredictability (trope). Without unpredictability or indeterminacy, the laying down of a mark (*horos*) cannot circulate as a debt owing, nor can it become an internal pledge of signifyin(g) value. For unable to circulate without unsecured symbola, signifyin(g) cannot repay the obligation that acts as its security in both the witnessing (the performance of it) and as an object of exchange.

In his reading of signifyin(g) as philology, Gates thus focusses on its consequence for the interpretation of black usages of language. Taking part in it is, crucially, less a matter of representation, than the *writing* and expression of a series of obligations in which blackness moves from identification to exchange. While Gates suggests ancestryness is what emerges from these exchanges, he is unable to avoid reading blackness as anything more than a formal principle wherein symbola constitutes the referential function of ownership and possession. Accordingly, the very idea of mediation, which is supposed to rejoin being and logos, only takes on reality for the philological understanding of language itself. For if signifyin(g) is a "pledge" (horos) that one receives from the other, it only has value as an indeterminacy that does not itself mean anything outside of the locus of language, with the result that it cannot secure the value or validity of "black" pledging. (Moreover, if there is no marketplace for the pledge of ancestry, then it cannot secure any future option on earnings.) There is thus no foundation of, and no philology for, signifyin(g) that is not undermined by the obligation to posit it as object or property. Hence where its meaning fails, reading becomes a counterfactual allegory. Signifyin(g) thus presents an infinity of discursive universes that expose another way of reading, and one that depicts an allegory of reading without end or respite, and one that astounds in the way it engenders figural supposition and opposition, but always as narrative metaphors of their own unreadability.

When blackness signifies itself, it thus forces philology to become the means through which mediation *speaks through* the mediating figures that language brings forth. Some would read signifyin(g) as conventions or mores (and Gates does this repeatedly). But one can also read it as a subversive praxis that puts representation, inspection, and figuration to work at the precise point where all attempts to grasp *topoi* as *trope* (conceptually or figuratively) can no longer be determined and so break down. And, since figurative trickery cannot exist without debt, doubt, or speculative conflict, there is no truth in it, or, if it is true, its truth must be a mockery of its reading. In either case black philology is obliged to humble itself before the failed mediation that mocks all figure, structure, or form, which seems to be the only thing that black rhetoric is.

However, Gates does not present breakdown as the work of black philology. And simply because signifyin(g) rejoins figure and trope in a higher onto-political form. Gates's analyses remain largely determined by semantic distinctions between paradigmatic and syntagmatic levels of linguistic utterances, and by a literary hermeneutics that privileges metaphor over immediacy of meaning. Reading becomes for him the event of decryption-mediation. Even in terms of reading Esu, reading itself is governed by a higher law. That law is logos that is given form, not as faith, but as a kind of transcendental figuration that makes mediation into a kind of philological event in the black world of figures. Insofar as it shows us our rootlessness and our ase as a dialectics of indeterminacy and unreadability. In black reading, the world of ase is no longer lost to the world, but becomes something lasting and immediate; it informs me of the language of African gods, on the one hand, and helps me understand their esoteric forms, the traces they leave of themselves in the mediated presences of black texts. This necessary bond that links trace—and thus ase—with figure is supposed to comprise the means through which the esoteric signifier is secured. But if reading stops there, allegory allows us to proceed further: Esu *has* himself *to be* read as a metaphor of indeterminacy, and blackness is the figure that infinitely produces itself as the metaphor of that metaphor. The whole premise of black philology thus comes down to a name-calling (pólemos) that is an allegory of its own unreadability, and yet one which clings to that outcome as the greatest philological superposition of a black reading of texts. In short it is as indeterminacy that blackness reads itself and that is why it *has to* read unreadability as the blackest trope of its language.

Thus, if one is to practice a black philology of texts, that philology has to situate itself as, literally, *Esu-'tufunaalo*, that is, as the "one who unravels the knots of Esu."[13] But how does one unravel a knot, when no tying is equal to it? How does one untie a knot that is infinitely indeterminate? Although Gates rather confusingly describes these topoi as hermeneutic *metaphors*, I must confess here that I prefer to advance the principle as a *topology of mediation*. Why? Because these knots are not so easily severed by interpretation. (Or is it because these knots already assume place, shape, and temporization? And by that very token, words cannot untie the very relations by which mediation is being thought as enciphered?) And I must state here if mediation involves a reading of *itumo* (to untie or unknow) and *iyipada* (literally to turn around or translate), it kind of matters whether the predicative copula is that which joins or is that which severs. Indeed, does it make any difference to topos if it is repeatedly (i.e., philologically) confused for a trope? "If Esu is a repeated topos, for my purposes he is also a trope," Gates tells us.[14] A black philological reading of Esu thus seems to depend on whether we consider him indeterminate when he speaks as trope, or meaningful when he is no longer readable as topos? But insofar as the unensurability of Esu is neither a topos of trope, nor a trope of topos, then perhaps we should look to decipher him in *another* sphere, and one, preferably, beyond the reach of either? Anyone who considers the place of Esu in *The Signifying Monkey* has to confront the language of place, and, in its monarchical-racial discourse of gods and people, decide whether philology takes the place of pólemos in the production and creation of customs of naming, dissing, interpreting, and worship.

On the other hand, if topos is always trope, at least implicitly, then what could it possibly mean to say that philology is also a monkey, that is, an interpretive emblem of signification?[15] In every philology—and all are, according to Gates's presentation, allegories of self as animal—topos humanizes animality, but trope does not animalize humanity. Hence the figure of the monkey, which is itself an anthropomorphic metaphor, suggests that there is something aberrant about blackness; that is, it cannot be epistemologically grounded as animal or human, but nor can it be grounded as an emblem in the strict sense, say, of vice or virtue, of weakness or strength. To be sure, as fable, it can never grasp itself simply as animal nor, as logos, know itself as human, precisely because it makes both undecidable as language and/or thought. To repeat: if place is already figure, what would it mean to consider blackness as a being placed by allegory, and attribute to that placement a movement that is always *masked* by figure, which means that the figurative function of language precedes not only being and topos, but also any certainty of reading? The relation between the two, which Gates provisionally calls "a mask-in-motion," is what interests me here as a concept or metaphor of decryption-translation, although as we shall see, a metaphor that also calls attention to itself as a *metaphysics* of a *trace*—the monkey as the "trace" of Esu—a trace that always involves philological *transferences* (Gate's word).[16] If I insist upon the significance of this word *transferences*, I do so for two reasons. On the one hand, because Gates is concerned with black texts as "enigmas, or riddles, which must be read or interpreted, but which, nevertheless, have no single determinate meaning"; rather, reading here presents itself as a kind of fatefulness, or divination.[17] On the other hand, the word *transference* seems to mark out that what is being proposed here is a *general system of divination* that cannot even recognize itself in these signifying patterns and their complex interweaving of different threads, histories, traditions—the copula by which blackness is always at a distance from itself, or is always diasporic, displaced, without rootedness, or homeland.

(And if the copula can only be thought as transference, as a philology of transference, then is predication not already bound to go astray as atopos? Further, what would it mean to assent to it as the measure—and so the figure—of black signification and communication?)

Therefore, peremptorily, is black philology working here as a kind of discreet wish-fulfillment, without the means to secure itself as either past or future? Yet this would suggest that the debt to be repaid has no secure meaning or cannot be secured as meaning; philology is thus unable to mediate itself as the praxis of mediation, for it cannot conceive of a *black* demand, instruction, critique, or promise, and least of all can it rejoin *Erkenntnis* to its praxis of reading. If there is a black praxis of tropes, then the one thing it cannot depend on because of its supreme indeterminacy is blackness, and yet this is its very reason for being. However much philology searches for black topoi or tropes what it cannot find is the figure that is the figure of all tropes, for its meaning cannot be given. Thus there can be no rhetoric of black tropes or grammar without assuming a large number of philological principles connecting race and language. But we must not forget that the n'est pas cannot be grasped, or mediated, by such principles. Indeed, it is a rootlessness that can never be *written*, read, decoded. Now, we know that the opening chapter of *The Signifying Monkey* describes a "myth" of origins; and that one could say, in effect, this myth is marked by a topos of placelessness, which remains, as a process, infinite, "never-ending"; and if this anti-topos must be read, it can only be read as a trope, for its locus is missing, and so it cannot be located in any topos, for blackness is a-topic.[18]

That is to say, if there is transference (during the course of any return to philology), what could it mean, then, to think it as situated in a dissemination that turns back upon itself so as to subvert itself, a return that is only truly black in so far as it subverts itself? But this return, which relies no less on rejoining being and ontology, leaves a major part of the implications of its reading unexplored. In Gates's theorization of black figuration, blackness is both the power of figuration and the figuration of an identifying power that cannot be known outside of its charismatic authority. We can only deduce it, as supplicants and martyrs, through the traces it leaves in our transferences—that is, our philology. In this context, blackness reproduces itself, at least philologically, as a sacred topos and value whose traces—as parody and authority—can be seen in the words and figures by which black sociality

inscribes itself in charismatic black speech. But by the strangest or most logical of paradoxes, the black logos can only present itself through the riddles
and symbols by which it retreats from language. What seems clear is that
these figures can only take place (topos) without taking place (atopos). In
other words, the logos is the necessary, imperious effect of tropes in which
blackness *cannot be posited* as topos or trope. A paradox, then: as the figure
of an imperious de-position, blackness cannot be apprehended as time or
space, or even as the time of spacing, and we shall say why this atopos also
bypasses any pattern or rhetorical order of signification or of trope. If the
signifying monkey is the "great trope of Afro-American discourse, and the
trope of tropes," this is tacitly because what it signifies is itself the tacit mon-
ument to that which allows for neither trope nor topos.[19] I would even say
that the myth not only takes the form of that which cannot be heard, located,
or read as anything but myth, but also as the failed narrative of both origin
and dislocation. The topoi of these various tropes—of mediation, of logos, of
origin—are thus mere tricks, riddles, of a transferential origin. And thereby
do not so much delineate a site, advent, or inter-locution as a desire to decipher the philological encryptions of desire—only in this way is signifyin(g)
double-voiced (as black and rootless; as bound and in exile).

And if all origin myths are shadowy, "buried or encoded," "ambiguous,"
"enigmatic," scattered through "several concealed fragments," then how can
they even resonate as topoi? In effect, Gates cannot claim to know these
myths as a "guiding force," for he addresses them as primal loci of a language that is always figurative, and so displaced, suspended.[20] He speaks of
roads, pathways, courses through a "maze of figuration" that takes him on
a necessary indirect course from cryptogram to code, grammar to rhetoric,
enigma to mastery, and yet each time interpretation is put on display as a sacred work that allows the reader to understand the book of fate, what we get
are further riddles. Beyond that, there is nothing but the promise of a mediating commonality linking blackness to its logos, and nothing but the allegory of mediation. But the language of the sacred does not correspond to any
object that is not already encrypted by tropes. These roads and pathways,
mazes and crypts thus refer to something that cannot be known because
they lack the ability to locate blackness beyond the figurability of any referential claim. In any event, the analogy between philology and priesthood
that Gates provides refers to black philology as that which *sacrifices* itself to

discourse, and necessarily keeps watch over truth on one hand and understanding on the other. But this decoding is itself the referential illusion of a
meaning that never arrives at its destination in logos. We will not be able to
read without this initiation into mastery that *governs* (Gates's word) the indeterminacy of black texts, nor can we avoid reading the power produced
within it as logos—and this, first of all, is what it means to read black texts.[21]
To this extent, to read is no longer a figure of knowledge but the masking
of unreadability itself; "figure" is the maze through which every referent of
blackness, including the very language of ludic pathways, can only appear
through the very language of amazement, but it is not merely the referent
and figure of amazement that waylays; it is also the remainder of the referential and figurative loss of amazement itself.

The open-endedness of these interpretive principles can function, of
course, only within the system of their propagation, and within the history and grammar that links them to various ritualistic oral practices. But I
would say that this in itself—the function of mediation and linkage—quite
openly conveys a sense that (contrary to the notion of open-endedness)
there is no black philology beyond this desire for a "perpetually copulating
copula."[22] There is no purely and rigorously mythic writing. The so-called
origin myths of black writing are, by right and by principle, not only due to
an empirical or archaeological deficiency, for they function not only as a system of signs, of spoken or written writing, but also offer us a syntax, a spacing, between the raw and the cooked, the different and the same, the pro-
fane and the sacred. And an examination of the structure and the necessity
of these hierarchies quickly reveals that they signify precedence before they
signify "signifyin(g)" itself. Better put, if the African gods speak in language,
as Gates reminds us, and only initiates can interpret what they say, then the
sign is always inscribed in mastery—its idolatry, institution, and transmission. What is odd about *The Signifying Monkey* is the silence on the question
of black philological mastery—the politics that it makes manifest, and the
relation of that mastery to that of language. If the sovereign is always *two in
one*, not binonymous, or dual, but *two in one*, then, like the king's two bodies,
sound and concept, and what permits either of them to function, to present
themselves as such, is the *process by which mastery is rendered and renders itself.* If there is no pure sign, nor absolute sovereignty, then there can be no
purely open-ended philology either, for the power that establishes philology

is always bound to the sovereign; it is what lets the meaning of sovereignty be heard; and is what teaches us how to listen so that mastery can always remain audible in both the written and the spoken sign, but also in every *sens* of the word. Philology is the mask of sovereignty, and what discloses it as word in its worldliness.[23]

What else can the black philologist do, then, but verify the imperious demands of ase, and so grant its principles true historical legitimacy? If all philology is an allegory of power, however, it does not follow that all allegories are *necessarily* philological.

We've said that Gates returns to philology in order to form a speculative response to the crisis of black rootlessness. And because that crisis is implicitly understood as a debt relation, knowledge of one's roots becomes a kind of speculative surplus value, insofar as the acquisition of its "occult ability [beyond any referential restraint] adds value to itself" (the words are Marx's).[24] When we know what it means to dwell, we understand better how the world is indissolubly bound up with logos, and how understanding depends on language. But the price we pay for understanding must depend on a racial debt, not on life and labor, which can never be paid off. We see therefore why, having no value, blackness becomes the sign of value itself. It may be because of its infinite productivity, but it is enough to say that such prodigality explains why blackness may well be the privileged sign of a knot that adds to itself in unraveling itself.

Strangely enough, it is this transmutation of *Dasein* into surplus value that gives blackness an allegorical value for the language of philology; it becomes the middle point between meaning and nothing, infinitely remote from historical understanding and promissory life. And in this, it exposes the value-creating powers of language itself, that is, those productive labors that are always hidden by the hermetic secrets of philology. Equally incapable of mediating the nothingness from which philology emerges and the allegory by which it is engulfed, blackness is, then, language. And it can never be founded on anything other than an allegorical indebtedness to language. It is the transcendental rootlessness of a language that is always deceived by its own transferences onto certainty and stability, and by virtue of being nothing but a n'est pas.

Others could draw conclusions from this involving numerous claims about exile, loss, and the *political* languages of home and community.

Others could draw conclusions about the errancy that is first of all indissociable from the experience of mineness [*Jemeinigkeit*].[25]

For example, the rhetoric of *ipse* is often at its most transferential when it is compelled to defend the language of what one calls one's own. Perhaps this is why Gates, who says that black tropes are ruled by atopoi, constantly uses tropes of sacred topoi to postulate being as logos, speech as meaning; but in a way that cannot know how blackness comes about, or becomes an event, for despite itself and despite what he says, its signifyin(g) value is always in excess of (or surplus to) what is indicated or enunciated *as* black.

In the perspective of these n'est pas, blackness can speak of nothing but the limits of its own impossibility. It is not certain that philology or comparative linguistics, for example, can turn that nothing into a law, since there is no reliable criterion by which the n'est pas can be grounded as mediate or immediate, as referentiality or figurality, for it is impossible to know it as a principle of part or whole. Since the figurative power of ase is also the power of figurality, every hermeneutic demand to know it, to be subject to its law, must also know that every reading of it must also fall under the "law" of the n'est pas. The n'est pas renders intelligible what all figure revokes. For it cannot be strictly figured as logos or as law, for the n'est pas offers no possibility of deciding between them. Gates has not grasped the consequence of the n'est pas for his reading of black tropes—his philological hermeneutics is, understandably enough, *a demand for even nothing to have meaning*, to have a communicative structure as address or trope. *But the n'est pas is beyond this imperative, and yet this imperative is what subjects philology to the n'est pas.*

It will be objected that such a reading misses the significance of openendedness, that it can never be reduced to a negative unity, but rather extends a semiosis, which is irremissible. But why assume that the *open* is the mark of a benevolent rather than a destructive opening? Is that not also idolatry? More, from what point of view can it be said that blackness marks the difference between mythic and sacred violence—when it ceases to be rooted, and so loses any sacred character it might have had, or when it becomes the site and discovery of a lawmaking transformation? What arises from these crises is the image of an indebtedness that belongs to neither the written nor the oral traditions of Africa, but permits us to refer to the signifyin(g) mastery of all the steps [*pas*] black languages have taken; but these are *pas* that no longer belong to mastery. I want to say that the n'est pas is the abyss of such speculation. For it has no meaning as past or future. But neither can the n'est pas belong to philology, to the idea of a *slavery* that is also historically the mythic beginning and filiation of black *theōrein* in *The Signifying Monkey*, but also a host of other Afro-American texts. Here, therefore, we must refer to a n'est pas that resists all the oppositions, including those of rhetoric and grammar, myth and philology. The n'est pas that resists these oppositions, and resists them because it exceeds them, is neither a mask nor a revelation, a meaning nor a method of interpretation; for it belongs neither to sign nor phonē in their usual sense; and is located, as the strange atopic place of being and language, speech and writing, *between* the apprehension of blackness as *pólemos* and what links it to divination, and the reassuring illusion of a black logos.

How then does one read the n'est pas? It goes without saying that it cannot be *disclosed* as law or myth. But what of power? In *The Signifying Monkey*, we are told Esu is a power to be summoned by sacrifice, will; only by giving something up can his sign be made manifest, present, and his lordship be shown in all its multiplicity as something *born(e)*: and his being-present is always a synthesis, a mediation, the means by which 2 becomes 3.[26] Now if signifyin(g) is a 3, the third element by which being joins itself to difference, a jointure that makes possible representation as such qua sign, that is because his ase can never be represented as presence, it can never be offered precisely because it is the result of an offering. So rather than a dialectical element, as Gates suggests, we could say Esu is the being that reserves itself in the movement of difference and at a very precise point—at the point where blackness mysteriously occults and disappears itself from the determinable, from knowledge, from the system of signification. For its ase is also the disappearing of disappearance as mediation, synthesis, logos, or meaning. Its fatefulness, then, is the endless detour of figures of relation, of topoi, of writing, of trope. In such appearances, propitiation is indistinguishable from radical indeterminacy.

If Esu is always absent, as Gates also insists, I would argue that is because he cannot be "render[ed] present in the open-ended signification process of which it consists."[27] If Esu is indistinguishable from aporia, then that which *he is not* (n'est pas) cannot be rendered as aporia; and consequently, he cannot be read as either present or absent, as either concept (*begriff*) or substance (logos). And yet while I agree that there is no direct access, or contact, with truth or meaning, why delineate this indeterminacy as due to the fact that Esu "governs" understanding as exchange? That is, why hasten to recall that the indeterminate is the predicate of power, and only in order to acknowledge the superior, and ineffable, working *of* sovereignty? Such demarcation is never put in question but is confirmed as the "predetermined meaning" of black being and truth, or, less anthropologically, as the black power of language itself. Esu would be a language or trope that is, then, irreducible to ontology or representation—or metaphysical reappropriation; he would be that which inscribes fate and that which exceeds any onto-theological system (which is how Gates is still seemingly thinking a language of divine writing). For Esu is the writing of a copula that *penetrates*, displaces, defers, any *arché*, system, or logos. And that copulation is literally *nègre* for the philology which produces it as sign, reference, or history.

For the same reason, Esu is not the "trope of tropes" but the atopic trace of a différance within every topos that defines the quest for blackness as origin, and precisely because it has no rightful beginning as mastery or lordship, and no principle that is not already—metaphysically, metaphorically—enslaved by the thought of origin. This is why the word *writing* in *The Signifying Monkey* fails to question its own transference onto aporia as the true secret of a black hermeneutic tradition; the postulates, axioms, or definitions of a critical discourse that still wants blackness to *mean*, and so enslave itself once more to the tasks and rituals of a philological formulation. It's a formulation that is just as mythic as the strategies and topoi employed by philological racism. Philological racism because this strategy of reading is not a simple strategy in the sense that strategy orients a tactics toward blackness as figure, or as the figure of figure, but because the schema is still one of *racial* mastery, of a racial *system* of interpretation, that also proposes an entire reading of a field, a tradition, an archaeology. Moreover, that system clearly assumes that *race* has a single principle of referentiality and address, a single end—an essence that is being's presence to itself—which philology then teaches us how to worship and love via certain words (*negro, negra, nègre, nigra*, etc.) that make present that presence and prescribe it's meaning. (But if such tropes demand to be read as black, the philology that teaches us their value must also teach us about their power and tell us why that power escapes power as "demand," "law," "rule," or "mastery.") If there is a certain ambiguity in this tracing of blackness, it no more follows the diacritical contours of a homonym—signifyin(g) as racial essence and content—than that of its symmetrical and semantic inverse—the homophone that conjoins difference and différance (i.e., *blackness* as ideology, *blackness* as the bond between God and man). While Gates admits that he encountered great difficulty in arriving at a black version of Derrida's neologism, that is because his calculations remain at the level of the word, both semantically and politically. The concept of *signifyin(g)* is a case in point—the decision to drop the "g," or render it silent, referring to how the word is spoken by black people, rather than how it is thought. But what goes missing here is the racial law that traverses such silences; and that deems the transmission of black speech as insignificant, as missing being, logos, reason. The parenthetical marks around that gap do not, to be sure, elide that genealogy, but nor do they have the power (the ase) to distance the analysis of black speaking being from such constraints.

By means of such strategies, Gates underlines both the strength and limits of his project, insofar as blackness still seems to supersede the very opposition between signification and convention, lending itself not only to a rhetorical versus semantic orientation, but to a new *form of enslavement*, namely, of the signifier by rhetoric. And a method whereby value is once again contracted to semantics.

I would say, first off, that différance is not a figure of *doubling*, even though it does seem to me to reside in a question of mastery, for, as Derrida insists, différance "is maintained in a certain necessary relationship with the structural limits of mastery." On the one hand, the words *certain* and *structure*, also indicate a limit in how mastery is being thought, or how différance constitutes a *racial* limit to the mastery of thought; but what is certain is that the *a* (in its silence) refers to a *we*, a community, for which mastery remains the most irreducible historical question.[28] As a result, the structural effects of racial mastery on language are not taken into account, or if they are, they are not yet perceived as a racial question of différance. By contrast, even though Gates also refers to *we*, or *our*, when discussing the *value* of signifyin(g), he does so rhetorically, and not structurally. Rhetoric becomes the locus of a black convergence with mastery and reading becomes the exchange place that allows black subjects to come to an understanding of their mastery as différance. This difference in the différance of mastery will become central in what follows.

———

We know that the verb *signify* has two meanings here that are quite distinct. For example, in *The Signifying Monkey*, to signify is to trope, and to trope is to signify. In this sense, the black word *signify* is a signifier that "wrecks havoc upon the signified."[29] "One is signified upon by the signifier."[30] The consequences of this are as follows: to signify as black is to disclose "the free play of language itself," and to wreck havoc on "white" referential meaning.[31] Nowhere is this characterization of blackness more striking—and nowhere more ironic—than that of a skew that defers and is indirection; and that maintains a refusal, a resistance, that announces itself as a reversal in which words become symbola. *Signify* in this sense is to reverse, and to take turns, consciously and unconsciously, showing the *limit of value*, or, and equally, to suspend or annul signifiers of mastery. In this sense, every act of divination that seeks to speak the truth must use the language of truth to critique and displace truth and the discourse of mastery.

The other sense of *signify* is less common and more indefinable: to revive something dead, absent, mortified, petrified, murdered. When dealing with the unfigurable, signifyin(g) is an inventory of blackness itself as a kind of death in, or as, language, but this is a death from which each act of speaking emerges, presents itself, and precisely as a prosopopoeia of a différance that cannot be determined, enjoyed, or derisively performed *as a self*. Rather than triumph, or mastery, in brief, here what is most noticeable is the interruption of figuration by the nonfigurable.

Now, although Gates completely overlooks this aspect, it is central to the question of a mediation between blackness and logos. We can illustrate this aspect with a key distinction. At one point, Gates tells us that "signification is the nigger's occupation."[32] How does "nigger" signify signification? The word signifies a certain property or a conjunction of properties in which we glimpse both the senseless power of language and the mockery of the authority of sense or of meaning. "Nigger" does not, in the scheme of things, signify authenticity as an event of meaning, for what it poses—and thereby deposes—is the falsity, the duplicity, of any positing of a black language. *Nigger* deposes what black language posits. Thus "signification is the nigger's occupation" because it cannot compensate—either rhetorically or ontologically—for the loss of blackness to that which has no origin, sign, or style, and which signifies nothing more than a n'est pas within the order of meaning.

However great the signifying power of "nigger" may be, it is never able to be anything but an occupation, a labor, a task. Furthermore, if reading is unable to present that power as anything but slavish, then it is unable to avoid either the racial imperatives of philology or its positing of black language. To announce niggerdom as occupation persists as philology for the precise reason it fails to grasp how "nigger" cannot be the expression of an already constituted black subject, nor can it ever be the constitution of black signification. For "nigger" denotes a language without language, or a language that is opposed to language as destiny, logos, fate. This clearly means that, being neither a name of place nor ancestryness, "nigger" is exempt from the enjoyment of surplus value; it is the only referent entitled to validate the topology of the n'est pas. More deserving of illegitimacy than genealogy, "nigger" necessarily has no guarantee than its difference from black difference. It is the errant force (pólemos) of a language that remains irremediable as the means for attaining the end of self-constitution; it is the enemy that makes blackness recognize the infirmity of its own nature, its indignity, its vanity, its despair. This is why "nigger" is immediately and irreducibly indifferent to signifyin(g) as play, form, or aesthetic meaning. "Nigger" is not interested in rhetoric, grammar or trope; for it is the *différance* of black signifyin(g) to language, and thereby brings signifyin(g) closer to the limits of a mastery that neither Gates (nor Derrida) can think. "Nigger" is the différance that cannot be constituted as a spacing or infinite temporalization of time, sign, or life, for "nigger" is precisely the scission of trace and figure; it is the difference that wrecks the jouissance of tropes. But, because "nigger" brings us close to the infinite and multiple ways in which blackness continues to be mythically thought, it is also necessary to the value that signification denotes. And we will see why that which lets itself be designated *nègre* is neither simply signified nor signifier, for what it announces is something other than mastery, or its enslaving passion in the context of interpretation, and thereby the figure that is always obscured by means of this repression (or transference). (We will return to this point in the second part of this chapter.)

———

Summary of the argument so far. Signifyin(g) as topos, signifyin(g) as trope. How are they joined, mediated?

We began with the problem of their meaning, since this is how Gates begins. Signifyin(g) is said to be a form of irony, of protest, "protest" standing equally for dissimulation and mockery. Signifyin(g) *represents* the vernacular as parody. It takes the *place* of difference in racist discourse. When that discourse speaks of whiteness, makes fun of it, condemns, or judges it, signifyin(g) exemplifies a semantic and logical riposte or inversion. What Gates is describing here in order to define it as a semantics or logic is a classically determined notion of the sign as representation—what he cannot do is think the signifier (Esu) in its *différance*. And this determination presupposes that the sign, which defers presence, is conceivable on the basis of a *black* presence that it differentiates, and mediates, and/or reappropriates. According to this classical semiology, the substitution of the sign—via irony, pastiche, parody, and so on—for its ostensible meaning is both *rhetorical* and *locutionary*: rhetorical due to an intensional play of substitutions; locutionary due to a written or verbal representation of ritualistic speech, with the structure itself being one of mediation between the two.

In attempting to put into question the ideas of mediation, or indirection, one would need to see blackness as something like an originary *dissemblance*; but one would not call it originary in the extent to which it represents the values of parody, or resistance, which are all assumed to be signifiers of an authentic black praxis—that is, what people do, and say, and have always said. To put into question the rhetorical and performative characteristics of black signing, to oppose them to an originary dissemblance, therefore would have two consequences.

(i) One would no longer consider différance as a trope, which here means its rhetorical use of signs, and which constitutes a culture of ritual naming (in thought or language), *governed* by and mediated by self and presence.

(ii) And therefore one puts into question the authority of black presence, or of its symmetrical inversion as irony or parody. Thus, one questions the limit that has always constrained us, which still constrains us—as a problem or system of philological thought—the drive to formulate the meaning of blackness in general as "the unity of presence and representation," and in a way that can only think that opposition as simple absence, or parody.[33] Already it appears that the type of question that remains unasked throughout, which cannot be asked, is the extent to which black beingness remains irreducible to this notion of the sign, and that already signifies a parody of the signifyin(g) formulation of what blackness is, or means, or makes present. I note here that this is more than a reversal, but indicates a dissemblance that can no longer be conceived as semantic mediation, and what Gates says in *The Signifying Monkey* about black parody, about what must be liberated from traditional, literary notions, must also apply to his own severe, decidedly non-parodic reading of parody, of the black tradition, black experience, and so on. Hence when Gates writes: "The blackness of black literature is not an absolute or metaphysical condition," rather, blackness can be discerned only through "specific uses" or constraints; this implies that blackness can only be realized through the experience of its constrained reading, including that of philology.[34]

But every question concerning these "specific uses" is soon reduced to "an act of rhetorical *self*-definition."[35] Most of the semiological patterns outlined as signifying relations are hence reduced to an image, a psychological sign, or imprint—that is, presence. Now insofar as Gates (correctly or incorrectly) divides Afro-American literary history into those who give this sign presence (good) and those who render it absent (bad), it should be clear that parody, mediation, inversion, and representation, are constituted solely by their ability to give the blackness of the literary sign presence, and so nothing distinguishes them, or relates them to one another, other than this metaphysically absolute opposition. (And that opposition is itself the aesthetic effect of mediation as ideology.) If blackness can only be discerned through close readings, as Gates claims, what is seemingly never read is this determination (the referential constraint of a non-referential positing, which is nothing more than the positing of the philology it contests, and yet affirms).

Again, this principle of presence, as the condition for black signification, affects the totality of blackness: presence remains the concept, the ideal meaning of blackness; and its mediation, by tradition, custom, and philology, is what Gates calls the blackness of blackness. We do not have to go into all the problems posed by these definitions here. But even when Gates is discussing cesuras, breaks, ellipses, and the like, what matters to him is whether the utterer is, or is not, "a *master* of this compelling mode of evoking presence by absence through indirection."[36] What philology subsequently bequeaths to us is this indirect mode of evoking—signifyin(g)—a presence that incarnates itself as something more and less than mastery.

The first consequence to be drawn from this is that blackness can never be present in or as itself, can never arrive without mastery. Essentially and repeatedly, every concept of signifyin(g) is inscribed in a system within which signifyin(g) is the art—the presencing—of mastery. Rather than the différance of mastery and slavery, blackness then is no longer simply a praxis, but rather the trope that makes mastery present in general. For the same reason, blackness, which is not a concept, nor simply a word, becomes the self-referential unity of form and mastery—that is, it is the act that always *names* itself as rhetorical mastery, and what blackness names is no more than the topos ("the desired space") that "create[s] a space for the revising text" of black philology and tradition.[37]

The blackness of which Gates speaks is itself, therefore, neither simply a rhetoric nor an ontology. It refers to an experience in the singular. *The black experience.* And all that black philology is meant to do, or should do, is implicate the relation by which black texts mediate (and are mediated by) such experience.

II

Still, it is the mask that attracts us to blackness, and rightly so.
For therein is contained, as well as reflected, a coded, secret,
hermetic world, a world discovered only by the initiate.
Henry Louis Gates, *Figures in Black*[38]

The phrase [the changing same] captures strategies that I designate
as *the mastery of form* and the deformation of mastery.
Houston A. Baker, Jr., *Modernism and the Harlem Renaissance*[39]

What is the relation between reading and mastery? According to Gates and Baker, my two primary examples here, the question of mastery is always a dialectic between *form* (understood here as trope) and *tradition* (understood here as a coded, secret, hermetic world—a "valued repository of spirit").[40] But, on the other hand, form is already *masked*, is the effect of a mask: in language, in speech, in writing, blackness is the ludic form that conceals, and thereby reveals, a signifying that is equivalent to a mask. But, if blackness is the masking that reveals itself, what can never be fully seen is that which *does not conceal, does not reveal* this masking; and this is the meaning of *alētheia* in the black reading of texts. For not only is blackness masked, but its masking conveys the motif of a "spiritual consolidation of the race" from the outset.[41]

What is performed as mask (from the Latin *masca*), and by means of the *mas* or *maris* (meaning "doll" or "puppet")—is an encoded difference whose principle is that of revelation and dissimulation, which nonetheless produces, in a veiled and modified way—signs of difference that are also signs of authenticity. Blackness, therefore, if it is originally masked, can *only perform itself as mask*, can only mask itself to reveal itself, act like a clown or buffoon in order *not* to become a clownish referential relation, to the extent that the mask comes by way of loanwords from Latin and Arabic. The *dictio* and *persona* of the mask are thus forged from the same hermetic gesture; and what is said here of the mask can also be said of its mastery. The unmasking of the mask is fundamental to its black rhetorical function, yet Gates is careful to caution against simply equating the mask with mastery given the role it plays in the very possibility of *black* speech. And if that speech cannot be heard without being masked, one should not try to master it because it *willingly* plays the role of a mediating, irreducible complicity. Since the mask is coded but has to be so, and since blackness is the mask of its own utterance, so philology reveals itself to be the true discourse of mastery. For Gates, the mask that both allows and resists sublation (meaning) is, therefore, simply philology. Or language. The manifestation of the mask is, to be sure, produced by a thinking of transference—of *philía* and debt, of the continuous debt of *philía*—in the way meaning is masked, disguised by predication. It may be that what it illumines is how blackness is misappropriated by all forms of hermeneutics and exegeses. It is the reading of what takes place as the loss of place (atopos), but always in the mode of trope, of *symbola*, that rejoins it to what it always was in the realm of speculative dialectics. For blackness to be *articulated* (monstrated), it must therefore simultaneously announce and withdraw itself from the truth of its speculative concept. To be "loaned" a word without reappropriating it, if one did so, would be not to oppose it, but to be enslaved by it, by its referential authority and meaning. Such is the signifyingness of the mask that blackens being, and that shows the blackness of the signifier insofar as it darkens every manifestation. Thus, the mask is both origin and that which hides itself as origin. It is the *prosópeion* that conceals itself as figure and is the figure of concealment. All readers of black texts are thus indebted—to the meaning of the mask—because reading risks being improperly vigilant regarding the mask of meaning; the disclosure of the one can never be an argument for the rectitude of the other.

The signifyingness of the mask is so intricate a principle that it is easy to confuse it with referentiality or figurality, so we should be careful not to draw false conclusions about blackness as language, revelation, or power. However, Gates and Baker do not always avoid this problem. What is being denied from the outset is the principle that allows them to see what the rest of us cannot see even when it is in front of us: that coded, secret, hermetic world whose true representation remains indexed to its philological deciphering. What is it about signifyingness that is so clearcut, so clearly seen as a principle by them, and yet can hardly be seen by anyone else? Perhaps they are just better readers-philologists, but is the reading of black texts solely a question of making something appear? By their own account, only philology can disclose black speaking being—I say *disclose* since we are talking about concealment—and it has to do so philologically, that is, it must act as, or coincide with, a mastery that has race as its own essential or reigning principle. Which means that masking is the metaphor (the hermeneutic string) that *shows* blackness speaking itself, *in principio*, as sovereign? But how can a mask found itself as both form and (the power of) foundation? What does it mean to speak black but to be part of a community of interpretation in which every lexis and diction is a bond, a pledge, and every thought or word spoken both the wealth and servant of an imagined or ideal community? And if, consequently, what we see does not belong to either being or phenomenality, is it necessarily better to posit this encoding as dissimulation or disclosure? Might there not, at least at the level of logic, be another way of looking at blackness than that of a revealed concealing? Equally, should we not abandon this vision of language as a kingdom of ends? This will be our question, and consequently what will be disclosed by it is an endless suspicion of disclosure.

And a suspicion of this suspicion: because critique often seems to rely on the revelatory promise of its own end.

Since language, which Gates says is also a kind of masking, is what allows us to mask, how are we meant to read black texts as "a form of masking"?[42] For both Gates and Baker, the key to black rhetoric lies in the vernacular, for it is here where blackness becomes present and attains presence. Dialect is where black forms no longer pander, or are subservient to, or are imitative of, mastery; dialect is where blackness *masters*, and so eludes both slavery and stereotype. In such mastery, black language is no longer "a mere relic of a slave past," but bespeaks a new dialectical relation to the past and the present.[43] In a slight parody of Hegel, we could say that in masking, the black subject says [*spricht*] more than it means [*meint*], for it does not say [*sagt*] what it means [*meint*]; but then how could we possibly know it if it always remains in the dark, obscured by various maskings?[44] The idea of a mask is always an allegory of that which remains ungraspable, while guaranteeing its status as irony, as the undoing of trope by the desire for understanding. To read blackness sovereignly would, it seems, be akin to no more than, paradoxically, exposing what is masked, which in and of itself, is always the limit *to* mastery. To be exposed is, literally, to have no hiding place, and consequently to feel vulnerable and surveilled, or idealized and appropriated. One of the founding insights of black philology is thus to point out that the most weighted *symbolon*, oddly, is often the least readable because its proper meaning is a conjecture of figures, and allegories, passions, and errors. It is a matter of judgement without meaning. These figures remain readable only because it is impossible to read their unreadability as a sense *in* being, or as an *ab-sens* of sense.[45] To understand blackness is, then, a hermetic act that "*translates* experience into meaning and meaning into belief."[46] We must therefore follow the paths of these obscurities, since there is a danger of deception on every side.

But what are the rules for such translation? It seems to involve a dialectic between being a *hare* ("did you attempt to follow the movements of an autumn hare through sedge-brown, October woods?") and a gorilla (or a monkey and a lion in the case of Gates).[47] Note here how the animal metaphor of a lure that induces interpretation to seek out *causa* also suggests a wandering, a movement, an inadequacy between trope and meaning that is inherent to philology. If the hare (or sign) is always too near, or too far away, from what it refers or signifies, or is always displaced, withdrawn, from the promise of its capture, then why chase it if it can only show itself in disguise? And if the trace—the signifier—that blackens both language and sense disguises itself in this way, as masquerade, why assume that the trace reveals reference rather than an a-topos we can never be sure of reaching? (After all, it is not only gorillas who are duped by impossibilities seen in mirrors.) Since there is no trickery without display, and no interpretation without capture, what Baker is suggesting in these hermeneutic metaphors could be extended to sign and understanding in general: that what matters is what is traceable structurally as "black," or what may be rendered as such; but first it is necessary in order for black eloquence to be established, or be read as such, that historically what comes first is the mask and its value, which is inextricable from myth, fable, ritual, community. As the hare metaphor implies, blackness is *the trace of an absence that withdraws itself from disclosure and dissimulation*. And what it leaves behind are the masked traces of that concealment. All the more so when we realize that the lure hides nothing except the deceitful promise of capture; a deception by which reason is tricked in turn. A deception that derives its strength, not from power, but from nothing; and this, in fact, is how it strikes the imagination—as a trace whose original nature is *ex nihilo*. We are precisely in the situation where the hunt transforms cognition into parody and at the same time disallows any pursuit other than via an ambiguity that always seems obscure to both judgement and interpretation. Both the production and erasure of the trace are not acts of capture by philology, but the philologist being acted upon by their own desire for capture. The pursuit is endless, since the capture of black performative power (*ase*) is itself a figure that masks itself in the pursuit of a hare through sedge-brown October woods, and, as such, is bound to overlook the elusory concealments in what appears to be the mastery of every lure. By the same token, the pursuit of any *nigra philologica* is bound to fail, for, in all rigor, those who seek it can be said to mask all the fables that go a-hunting for black cognition or hermeneutics.

Our previous analysis of beast fables perhaps responds to this fundamental conundrum, which neither Baker nor Gates resolve in their simple recourse to hermeneutic metaphors. Is not the blackness of these animals at bottom the space between—between, for example, irony and pedagogy, and the metaphor that animates it, the philological mastery in whose inventory blackness is always *elsewhere* to human being? By naming hare, rabbit, gorilla, lion, monkey, as figures of enigmatic revelation, black philology's task is to put into words something that is hard to put into words. To render the trace of something that hides itself as trace, and not because it conceals itself, but because there is no means of revealing it without further concealing it. An ontological paradox that makes judgement necessary—and impossible.

This, then, is the paradox that both Gates and Baker explicitly envision as a kind of black vernacularity: black uses of words, patterns, tropes, are read as allegorical objects. They also function as unlocatable symbola—as loaned objects indifferent to linguistic values. But again, these allegories are not something that can be understood in terms of mastery, for there is no philological agreement on how they should be read. To write in the vernacular, at least formally, if not necessarily in content, in the formulations put forward by Baker and Gates, is to designate blackness as hermetic difference, as the movement by which language both puts itself on display, and codes any display, or any exterior referral in general, and by which a black idiom is thereby evoked as the historical trace, of differences. And that also goes—or rather especially goes—for the vernacular as the law of *genuine* deception. We ought to demonstrate why concepts such as form, mastery, the rhythmic, metaphysical principle of tradition, and mask, remain in complicity with what is at issue here, namely, a metaphysics of race as trace, as the excess of deformed presence. But what I want to focus on here is the sign itself—enclosed within a logic of representation—that is used to underline this belief that there is a "distinctively black meaning" that can only be understood, philologically, as a secret style, or code, that is somehow beyond ministrelsy (that is, bad mimesis) because its self-formation is understood to echo that of the tribe, or ancestor (i.e., good mimesis). In any event, what is understood by means of mimesis, as the will to this collective understanding, is never questioned as such, but is instead naturalized as the meaning and value of what it means to genuinely speak as black.[48] What cannot be put into question, then, is the mask as the black will *to* representation; and to object to this as a kind of metaphysical racialism would be, above all, not only to dispute whether blackness *can ever* be understood (as code or mastery), but what would it mean to be *mastered* by it, and precisely insofar as it does not correspond to self, history, philological understanding, or any thought of tribe, or of value.

Now if we consider the chain of signifiers by which masking lends itself to certain notions of value, according to the necessity of context, what interests me is why either author has recourse to good and bad forms of mimesis. How is it that a black copy of white form is deemed "second-rate," "mediocre," "pale by comparison," a mispronunciation; while a black imitation of black dialect is seen to be a coded deformation, the willed reclamation of an achieved eloquence?[49] It may be that there is such a thing as a good politics of mimesis, and simply because it has no image, value, or referential property that can be unequivocally read as politics. But can mimesis ever *be* black? I am not speaking of imitation, but of its writing; the fact that blackness must speak in dialect is, in a sense, not the same as saying that every dialectal mark signifies nothing but the name or promise of an authentic blackness, and therefore cannot, in any sense, signify either a "slavery" to meaning nor a "meaning" of mastery.

Let us take just one example. "'Gwine,' for instance, is still commonly found in black speech . . . in which speech actually occurs."[50] Who uses the word *gwine* (present participle of go)? Who but black people, who consequently make the word into a kind of promise for black speech itself? To say *gwine* is thus to be reconciled to the actuality of what is being described as a genuine example of blackness accomplished as speech act in a community of ends. Yet it is far from evident why this locution simultaneously announces what it so self-evidently asserts. If *gwine* is only meaningful to those who say it, and who know its code and convention, that is because the meaning posited exceeds all the acts and positions from which its *Dasein* can be uttered. Or: *gwine* cannot be established as an example without its figurative truth falling into a kind of slavery. The figure thus makes visible the historicity that enslaves it as a meaning-affect. Nothing is more erroneous here than confusing speech acts with the ways in which people perform the ardors of their exemplary narcissistic enslavement by language. It is not because of history, people, or place that *gwine* has resonance, and nor is it valued because it makes present, or brings into presence, a sacred topoi (Esu), thereby allowing us to understand and grasp the immediacy of value, and thereby re-forming the present in terms of what it is not, the past. *Gwine*, instead, could just as easily be read as the différance—the transference—that severs past and present, resonance from meaning, and, by the same token, *gwine* would denote everything that is no longer resonant, that is no longer, in our terms, metaphysically recognizable as severance, as the singularity of black speech or sound. In constituting itself, in dividing itself from concept, or a certain way of looking at the world, *gwine* is what might be called an impossible philology, or the becoming-present of a dislocation that has no

meaning other than temporization. Or what it points to is not the constitution of an originary figure—or primal topoi—but the quasi-transcendental
trace of an unfulfilled communion, a communion that cannot ever be understood in any other way but an aporia of time, sense, and world; and regardless of the phenomenological or transcendental language of mythic revelation, or sacred relation. For if the black word is a mask, what it speaks is not
presence, meaning, or relation, but the *aporon*, the impasse, that fissures the
movement of all signification. For what can never be posited is language itself, for what *gwine* reveals as language is a relation that is relationless; a going that can't be translated into representation.

Could not blackness then be the aporia—the differentiating movement—
that masks itself as representation? Such a signification would not be a positing of form or mastery, nor would it seek to divide itself between a rhetoric
(of tropes) and a formal imitativeness (of mastery) to be judged historically.
And above all, since it is formed from the verb "to blacken," it could give rise
to a new historical semantics. Here, we need to remember, that as always, for
Gates, signifyin(g) is also a ritual of decoding, and that what is decoded is
the blackness of blackness. I believe that Gates is sincere when he says blackness both presents and is the work of negation. For what it does is rhetorically reverse those tropes that, to be sure, seek to imprison it. However, if
blackness is the work of negation, it must also negate, or turn away from, all
representatives and concepts that seek to produce it as the *other* of time, history, or spirit. In Baker and Gates, if blackness negates, what it negates is always immediately referred back to the semantic and ontological purities of
that which can never be negated—the trickeries, the mediations, by which
blackness grasps itself as dialectical mediation. The aporia is thus limited to
the display of a negative simplicity: blackness is, and blackness ain't,[51] but
what precedes the ain't is always retrievable as a meaning, a topoi, that precedes signification, and whose originary act is conceived of as an original act
of signifyin(g) by which it becomes and so affects itself as black. And this is
why blackness *is* mastery. Or: it is the meaning and sense of a meaning and
a sense, that invariably grasps itself sovereignly in the act of signiyin(g). It
does not say what it means, for what it means—as predication—is first and
foremost *a force that governs* that is in neither speech nor ipse, and that cannot even be said to take place as actuality or ego, but is more like a nothing
that is not and is not *not*, and is therefore irretrievable as thing or signifier.

But why presume that this act makes it possible to translate the blackness of blackness—which in either text is the decisive point? And why must translation be the process by which the power of deformation can be displayed as mastery? It could be argued, of course, that mastery cannot be translated without being made servile to representation or understanding; for it must first be read but is never simply identical to how it is read (for it is said to be nothing other than an incongruent indirection), and this is why mastery cannot be pronounced and cannot be performed as mastery.

Mastery, thus, cannot master itself—it is deferred, traduced, by the signifyin(g) incongruities of blackness. In other words, blackness cannot give form to the *is* or the *ain't*, for its "form" is aporia. Therefore, blackness neither is nor ain't. Let us say: it is neither the *is* as the withheld—suspended, subsumed—form of the *ain't*. Nor the *ain't* as the no less unoccupiable negative form of the *is*. Neither the *is* nor the *ain't* of ontology. Thus, the *is* that is the abyssal—perpetually impoverished, unsaturable—form of the *ain't*; and the *ain't* that is the infinitely finite form of the *is not* (n'est pas).

Arguably it is this philological irony that is to be understood as the logical effect of blackness, including what thereby can never be understood as an irony of logic. In effect, if we accept Gates's language of irony, in its meaning and its syntax, we would have to conclude that irony is language itself, or that there is no language that is not always already mastered by irony. And in this case, notably, one would also have to conclude that, as the "consciousness [or 'superconsciousness'] of the language," blackness cannot be thought as figure, meaning, or mediation, but as the non-mediated affiguration of a sign that is always the *nigra* that makes language both possible and impossible.[52] In all these cases blackness is the aporia whose irony is neither that of a lion, rabbit, monkey, or gorilla, but that of a n'est pas that remains incomprehensible to all forms of speaking—and species—being.

Now if we refer, once again, to the n'est pas, that is because blackness is a deformation that is always distanced from itself. The language of blackness (which consists only of its difference from itself) can only signify blackness in meanings that deny, asperse, or ironize it as other than language, and thereby as a speech without language, and whose signifyin(g) exposes the irreparable abyss of language itself. This implies that there can never be a black language identical to itself, for it can never be inscribed in language; and regardless of whether language is understood figuratively, hermeneutically, philologically, or historically. Blackness is no more *black* than it is *masked*: it is only readable, figurable, in its unreadability, and this is also of course what makes it absolutely black.

If, hypothetically, we maintain the notion that blackness has no language, then it also has no relation to community, history, logos, or race, but it is more like the hare, or the monkey, that can never be reached as either a metaphor of presence, or as a signifier of absence; and this is equally valid for trope, speech, revolution, or mastery. (Elsewhere I suggest that blackness is the différance of capacity and incapacity, and, in the relation of speech and language, forbids the essential delegations that Gates, throughout his discourse, traditionally wishes to delineate as a tradition of representation.[53]) The practice of a hermeneutics or a code supposing "a hidden, or internal polemic" between texts, and also supposing in the practice of this polemic a play of revision and inversion, a spacing and temporization, a double-voiced articulation of difference—all this is no more than the outcome of a hermeneutic principle mistakenly read as a ground, in whose promise of totality there is nothing more than the promise of its fulfillment.[54] The hermeticism, which grounds the entire project, is also a logic (of revision) grafted onto a metaphysics of totality, with blackness treated as the anticipation itself of totality, but it is always both behind and ahead of itself, as a kind of *arché* that is also precisely the result of a certain telos. Whence the repetition of its central concept of the sign, which always returns the black phonē to the metaphysical presuppositions of *the* race.

One might be tempted by an objection: given that the black text is a *speaking* text, only in its written form, it only becomes a signifyin(g) sign by means of inscribing itself in a system of differences. Certainly in this sense, the speaking or signifying monkey could not be present to itself, as speaking or signifying, without différance. But why then conceive of a presence, and of a presence to itself of the subject in the hermetic traditions in which it is fated to signify, and to grasp itself, according to Gates, as the sign that signifies black mastery, authenticity, beingness?

Such a question thereby suggests that, prior to the signifier *blackness*, and excluding any trace or différance, a tradition is presumed that returns us to philology and that founds this expansive vision of blackness. In *The Signifying Monkey*, Gates calls for the opening of that tradition, and for philology to be its horizon and its determination. The problem with his conception is its reliance on a transference that is both pre-positional (prior to any to-poi) and pre-propositional (prior to any trope). And that this horizon, before blackness becomes a sign in the world, is what gathers it into a circular relation, into a presence, and one that is "before" slavery, that is before *its* enslavement by racist discourses of (philological) mastery. And what holds for blackness also holds here for signifyin(g) in general. Just as the category of black signifyin(g) mastery cannot be, and never has been, thought without reference to racial presence as *arché*, or logos, so too the subject as signifying consciousness has never manifested itself except as a mastered self-presence. When certain words are repeated in a signifying duel, and one finds oneself trying to pay off the black debt owed to them, words that are so apposite that it would be nigger to change them, then every speech act must become "nigger": this is the sure sign of black dialect. That is, the envy and rage, the irony and perversity that is constitutive of all ipseity, is what ex-poses the nigger, in the very moment in which speech appears to be most black, for nigger is the passage and repetition of all self-relating black speech acts in their deformation and their mastery. The privilege granted to a dialectics of mastery therefore signifies the privilege granted to anti-blackness; and even if one describes blackness as a transcendental understanding of absence, and this is implicit in both Gates and Baker, this is because they grant precedence to an anti-black semiology of language, which they both unwittingly resemble, and incessantly reproduce as the figure of all possible figures in black, as the primordial *sound* of black existence, as the historicity of what it means to be *too* black.

This "ontological circle-structure," to borrow a phrase from Heidegger, remains caught in a racial metaphysics of the sign.[55] But what makes these texts—and so much of black critical theory—circular is the way black presence is invoked as a phenomenality, whose status must be presupposed as the exception and the possibility of blackness in general, whose meaning is a self-presence that is always the "effect," the "revision," the "parody," or "irony" of anti-blackness; an *après-coup* that thereby always understands itself, grasps itself, via an anti-black presupposition.

Thus, one comes to posit blackness—and specifically the consciousness, the being-performative of presence—no longer as the determination and effect of a tabula rasa, but as the black irony of understanding and interpretation. A determination and effect within a system that is no longer resistant to presence, and which avoids the entire question of resistance (except as a *formal* question of signification). This is a system, then, that no longer toler-ates the opposition of high and low culture, nor that of resistance and com-plicity, and precisely because it is complicity itself—the cynical and aesthetic dissimulation of blackness as form and experience. Having formulated form as the ontological circle-structure of mastery or enslavement, these texts of-fer no further commentary on the différance of blackness itself to both sign and language (or rather: power and authority).

Is there an alternative to the circle? The issue is not one of deficient un-derstanding, but of a different understanding of what blackness is and is not. Here everything is at stake, and yet perhaps nothing really is. A point al-ready made by Fanon in a series of explosive analyses that, arguably, have yet to be read. Let's recall that for Fanon, blackness is the locus of an uncon-scious that puts into question its very possibility as a *Dasein*. Blackness itself is never present; it is only the différance of drives and desires, or, paradox-ically, there can be no blackness without the n'est pas that *belongs* to it, for it is not separable from the nothing that binds and blinds it, which is some-thing more and less than anything, and which is the belated effect of what I call the "not yet" that is always awaited and always deferred in its waiting (and is as far removed from mimesis or mastery as possible). Moreover, this n'est pas is not veiled, hidden, or encoded, nor is it the disguised possibil-ity of *Dasein* as such, and so the result, as it were, of the incessant decipher-ing or unveiling of texts qua understanding. The n'est pas cannot be under-stood, circumscribed, or reproduced as a value of truth, a black truth. Nor is it present, visible, hidden or given as a coded secret that puts this (mimetic) ambivalence on display. Its only advent is the tabula rasa; that is to say, the inscription of a discord without measure, that signifies a measureless differ-ence of blackness to philological understanding, as such it is infinitely finite to the categories of being, politics, and culture.

It is historically significant therefore that when Fanon speaks of irony, he speaks of its metaphysical value, for in this theory of irony (which is also that of Gates, Baker, et al.,) race is always linked to a question of self-understanding, or to what disturbs it. But in his formula—blackness as un-happy consciousness—the n'est pas is described as a movement that is not exterior to black being but rather determines it from the outset, and af-fects every possibility of *Dasein*, including ontology, phenomenology, and hermeneutics. Again, irony here is qualified by a permanent parabasis or suspension, insofar as it cannot be communicated, or comprehended, nor appropriated as form, ground, or principle. Wherever the n'est pas is located, it is not as a topoi, or trope, but as a not-yet that nevertheless marks the subject as a moment of incomprehensibility, and one which disallows any simple narrative of ontology, ipseity, or mastery.

Here we are touching on another decidedly more obscure meaning of "gwine," whose enigma turns on an anticipation that is the making-impossible of language as what disappropriates and de-authenticates understanding. In the opening chapter of *Black Skin, White Masks*, Fanon pursues what it means to go from dialectic to a language in which one never belongs, nor possesses; but one that nevertheless enables a conscious-unconscious calculation that one will be *less black* in so going; and, on the other hand, how this going makes evident an impossible presence, and an irreversible expenditure of libidinal energy, and one that opens *onto a greater loss*. A classically "white" black locution is accused of being just as alienated as its black dialectal refutation; both are signs of a nothing, a lack or defect exposing language's false racial promise. There is something unpromisable   non-sublatable—in these black speech acts. The majority attack anyone who deviates from its rule, its illocutionary law. One thereby consents to it because it shows something other than a promise, and not because it promises mastery. For one can no more refuse it than one can refuse speech. And this other law can no longer be understood as the measure of ego or self, nor as an economy of signifiers, or lexemes, but as the absence of measure, or, as it were, an impropriety that interrupts the hyperbolic demand, request, or hope, that blackness *signifies*; or that it could ever be a making-present, a performative, or *free* understanding of itself without magically turning white. What Fanon's reading thus discloses—and perhaps immediately forecloses—is a *nigra philologica* that is measureless because it cannot be brought together with meaning, and thus cannot be taken as evidence of an intentionality, of an ipse. Elsewhere, in a reading of this chapter, I have attempted to indicate what might become of this going from dialect to *another* way of speaking, that takes into account this possibility and impossibility as a singular altercation with blackness itself.[56] Rather than the signifiers of a tradition, of inauthenticity, Fanon's reading calls attention to something that is decidedly more complex and enigmatic. Namely, an understanding that is displaced, and that reinscribes that displacement, not at the level of semantics, or even that of the signifier, but at the level of a *lalangue*, a black *lalangue*, that exposes itself insofar as it returns to itself, for what belongs to it does not belong to it, but to others, to whom nothing belongs but a failure to represent, and so to name, and without which there can be no being-with [*mitsein*] with either self, community, or other.

Or perhaps what we see here is what happens to language when its non-mastery frees us to access the aporia of our own otherness?

For the question of what makes belonging understandable in no way implies that it is possible, only that such a belief is the absent *causa* that becomes ek-sistent in all black signifying. Contrary to the metaphysical, dialectical, racial perspective of a system of black meaning, we must conceive of a signifying in which the subject always "dies" to meaning, and in which each act of communication and understanding is disclosed as something that is infinitely finite in both its loss and its possibility, for it is no longer even possible to utter a word without this exposure, and abandonment to, everything that one is not, and never was before. If every positing of a white interlocution comes from a place where it is impossible to posit, a place where every black-white positing is implacably opposed and postponed, it is not because the inability to roll one's rrrs in the correct place is the fault of ontology alone, or of what is hidden, made absent, by ontology. That is just the fantasy of mastery. Rather, what interrupts the desire to speak, to posit, to show oneself as white, what exposes it as a fantasy, is that which exceeds mastery, for it has no meaning as absence or presence. Here a certain alterity—to which Fanon gives the name "contrecoup"—emerges as the figure of an impasse that is decidedly more aporetic than the Hegelian trope of mastery. In this echoing, and between it, what flashes out is the longing of language itself; which doubtless means the longing of an unconscious to discharge itself in representatives, proxies, delegates, but without any possibility of arrival *in* language. In this sense, the contrecoup concerns how *lalangue* marks the unconscious, and how the unconscious is irreducibly the after-effect, the contrecoup, the delay, of a *lalangue* for whom even the notion of trace, or of différance is inadequate. The language that turns toward itself, that no longer conforms to any communicative code of mastery, is a language that tries, but always fails, to speak its own incomprehensibility. Let us call this the *lalangue* of *lalangue*. And it is this language that blackness, in its impossible, incomprehensible whiteness, speaks.

Which is to say that what I am here calling a *nigra philologica* cannot be circumscribed by a psychoanalysis, an aesthetics, or a philosophy. When Fanon uses the word *sociogeny*, he shows us how the *nègre* can only be determined as the thought of différance in the understanding, language, and society of anti-blackness. More exactly: the *nègre* is the anti-project of a white-black *Dasein*. He is not. Accordingly, he is the other that I turn away from; he is the path that, in turning away from, I find myself in my desire for self-certainty. This alone is certain: the *nègre* cannot be thought other than a point of departure. But what makes him so threatening, and so infallibly subversive, that language always leads back to him? In the colony, it is impossible to secure a semblance of self, to return to oneself, without his presupposed repression. As far as the choices go, those who seek to whiten/ darken black elocution; those who seek to repress or convert black speech acts, want to see *nègre* die as a performative, and precisely because *nègre* weighs down everything that proves the humanness of black existence. This point is fundamental to Fanon's critique of ontology, of any idea of a black presence. In brief, language speaks from a place that is anti-*nègre*; but once again this prohibition is impossible to secure, and so can only half-speak [*mi-dire*] its presupposed truth.

Can the *nigra philologica*, for these reasons, ever avoid this *mi-dire*?

There is no simple answer to this question.

In a certain sense, to read "the vast and terrible text of blackness," is not so much to set out in search of absence or presence, but to set out *from* it.[57] And that figuration is "the nigger's occupation." As its occupation implies, *nigger* is a praxis. It is a saying that is without being—without, for example, productivity or value. And yet, Gates offers this task as the thought of its black meaning, or as the truth of black meaning. What remains forgotten is that there is no such thing as "nigger", and in this respect what it discloses is merely its difference from being, and non-being. Philology chooses to reveal the "nigger" to us via loanwords that, in each case, show how skillful we are at reading masks. But these alētheic signs have no value as presence. Rather, to speak "nigger" is to find oneself essentially misunderstood, or rather disfigured-disguised by what it makes manifest. Insofar as "nigger" masks the difference of blackness from Being, and thus of the difference of Being from every manifestation of blackness, "nigger" is thus a cryptonym for that which occurs as neither being nor entity, neither essence nor logos. And its verbally understood essence confirms the figuration of what remains incomprehensible to blackness as being or object. *It is precisely because the nigger cannot appear in its being that it cannot be mastered nor captured.* Thus, he makes present a difference that is no longer readable as lure, mask, or ancestryness. The nigger figures incomprehensibility for the black signifier, as Fanon reminds us. In his prohibition, what speaks is what can never be secured in place as a signifier, for the nigger is, in a certain and very strange (overdetermined) way, that which never belongs to language at all, and therefore can never be troped, figured, or employed as a figure. The nigger or *nigra* can only be written as the trace, or the différance of what it is not, the n'est pas—for the *negra*, *nègre*, does not belong. He is the hare who is always caught or, more exactly, he is the scent of what we believe we are chasing but who always escapes, effaced as such. In this sense, it is better to say that the nigger brings to light the *un*-sayable effects of a perpetual hunt or transference through which blackness learns how to commodify, to ruin, its own luxurious noncommunication.

Perhaps this is why he is the trace—the thread [*montrer*]—of that which can never be presented, that can never manifest itself as figure or *figura*, fate or destiny, disclosure or mask.

In section 56 of *Minima Philologica*, Werner Hamacher refers to how predication has become "the (ideological) central *topos*" of our epoch, but in a way that cannot be contained by any topos, yet holds open an a-topy or u-topy.[58] The path—the movement—that leads from one to the other does not bring this opening into being but is what holds it open. Not only that, the opening is also a withdrawal, or a concealment that opens language to itself, but also suspends it. In the hold, I suggest, language was open-ended, and remains not yet open. This is what I want to call the a-topos of *nigra philologica*, and its reading begins with this: with the advent that is not (n'est pas), but that points to its own dissimulation as an opening. Far outside of any outside, and yet from the outset the most intimate, the most predicated opening to interiority, the n'est pas is the most marked and the most erased, effaced a-topos, or non-site of blackness. As such its opening makes legible that which is always already read, and that which is incomprehensible, yet to be read; the n'est pas is that which therefore disorders language, for it is already on the path of an *es schwärtzt* that is, consequently, beyond articulation. A path that is unsecurable, beyond otherness or understanding, and is therefore, once again, nothing more than a violence of opening.

What remains to be thought is why this opening exposes itself and unfolds as *nigra*?

And here the question of reading returns, but so, too, does that of a path beyond-toward language.

Perhaps this is why the notion of signifyin(g)—in the stricter sense employed by Gates—has to be written via a series of opposites: function-event, history-repetition, code-structure, symbol-essence?

The failure to think the *différance* of these pairs thus suggests the following paradox: at the very moment when the signifyin(g) figure, the fundamental object of black rhetoric, is discovered, it is in danger of seeing its figuration obscured by the emphasis on an endogenous reality, race, which is itself supposed to be in conflict with a normative, prohibitory external reality that imposes itself on various disguises. We have indeed the figure, in the sense of a product of the imagination, but we have lost the structure. Inversely, with the theory of transmission we had, if not the theory, at least an *intuition* of the structure (signifyin⌈g⌉) appearing as an almost mythical datum, which in any case transcended both the event (of slavery) and, so to speak, its rhetorical afterlife in the discourse of black philosophy-literature. The ability to elaborate the figure was, however, if not unknown, at least underestimated.

However, it is not entirely evident that trope or topos are the best means to reach the *nigra*. Firstly, they presuppose that philology understands blackness as a praxis of mediation; for they insist that black philology can only reach mastery via an *Erkenntnis* that we showed to be wholly deluded. Then the position assumes that the sense of blackness cannot be established from blackness itself, but by means of interpretative traditions and hermeticism. According to Gates, therefore, the praxis of mediation lies in knowing how to keep to the course of the philological hare, even though the hunt is perpetual and capture indeterminate. But it is evident from this chapter that this too is ambiguous; to be rooted in blackness does not mean going after philology, but rather being able to necessarily follow the scent left behind by it. Interpretation is always a cipher of what is negated and preserved as philology, and hence the only way to discover what black saying and meaning is, for Gates, is to perceive the mask that falls between what blackness says and what it truly means. And, although these masks can only be seen as ciphers, these masks allow us to see what blackness always was in its rootless indeterminacy. Finally, his view assumes that philology can rejoin the evidential to interpretation according to preconceived laws of mediation, and to reject mimetic errancy, even when it is perfectly lucid and explicit, in favor of a higher form of knowledge (*Wissen*). Apart from the fact that such knowledge remains one of fable (Esu), nobody can fail to see that its etymological investigations are excessively indebted to race myth. But the decision to follow a fable does not necessarily lead to greater certainty, rather it leads to nothing but further deciphering. Such is the aporia implicit in *nigra philologica*.

As far as this aporia is concerned, we have already noted above that it is inconsistent with the language of the n'est pas, and for this reason alone I reject it. For if philology has to rely on the proof of mediation, and on the self-certainty of that relation, my argument throughout has been that the n'est pas cannot be so depicted. Indeed, we have tried to connect the arguments about mediation to certain figures of rootlessness. If blackness is to find itself, or what it was, it must acquire a new self-relation or self-certainty. We accordingly spent some time asking why topos became the endless realization of a black structure of language (logos)? We saw that for Gates, Esu expressed the endless capacity to both figure and present both the concealment and unconcealment of logos that, for Gates, constitutes the signifyin(g) essence of blackness as such. Esu announces possibilities, or rather possibility *tout court*, in his rendering of blackness as both figure and deformation. Yet if Esu is also language he must also disfigure the figures of existence that black philology grants the very being it forms. Thus rather than presence, what Esu renders is the *depossibilization* [*Entmöglichung*] of blackness.[59] But neither Gates nor Baker, I believe, were able to pursue the political consequences of such a thought.

And for two contrary reasons. It would be taking a very limited view to describe as follows the evolution of Gates's ideas during the period around 1988: from an historical semiosis of figures, to the establishment of an ultimately racialized *genealogy of origins*, to the historical-philological constitution of ancestry based on genetic codes, or the hermetic codes of racial genetic science.[60] If we intended, which we do not, to present a step-by-step account of the development of his thought, we should have to distinguish at least two other currents in this period.

The schema underlying the rhetorical theory of *The Signifying Monkey* is itself based on a constantly invoked fantasy of ancestryness. That fantasy permits certain figures to appear, or disappear, but what can never be presented are the original fantasies (*Urphantasien*)—of roots and debts—which themselves can never be presented: that is, the trace that appears to manifest itself as slavery qua event, or figure. In fact, the trace that profoundly links ontology and phenomenology is the slavish origin of a fantasy that is integrated in every structure of the original fantasy of slavery. Which is why blackness is rootless only in fantasy, not in the fact of its historical enslavement. Always repeated, always the origin, always the enigma of time, memory, and black being, the original fantasy of slavery justifies its status as being always already there. Slavery, then, as the figure *before* figure. Or as the trope, as Gates once famously put it, of tropes.

There is a tautology here, a fractured circle: slavery erases itself in presenting itself, enslaves itself in mastering itself; like the silent g of signifyin(g), it displays, with redoubled significance, the original fantasies that are the origin of black tradition, structures, and speech.

The annunciating and reserved trace of this movement is disclosed as a metaphysics, and especially in the attempt to present it as a theoretical model of representation. And especially in the Gates and Baker texts, which take the absence of a real object (slavery) to reproduce the experience of something missing but always in the hallucinated form of its loss. It is this fundamental lack that the signifier fills—signifyin(g) recovers the hallucinated object and links it with the earliest experiences of the black speaking subject as a subject of desire.

Thereby a myth of origin can be comprehended as what is presupposed, made legible, by its figurative expression. Philology is both its promise and its legislation. Gates claims to have recovered a fundamental structure of black desire. But *The Signifying Monkey* is the theoretical construction of its loss, yet one always preserved as loss, as fantasy, which tries to cover the moment of separation between *before* and *after* (slavery), while still containing both (as the trace, the revoicing of sign as absence and presence). In case anyone is misled by the *between*, philology here represents a mythical moment of disjunction between trace and erasure, between the two stages represented by enslavement and its hallucinatory revival (as a preserved, inscribed sign), between the object that satisfies (the race) and the sign that describes both the object and its absence: a mythical moment at which slavery and desire meet in the common origin of an original loss whose very loss is sheltered, retained, endlessly displayed.

The origin of signifyin(g) would therefore be the moment when blackness, disengaged from any reality, moves into the field of fantasy and by that very fact becomes the racial origin of language. The moment is more mythic than genealogical in time, since it is always renewed, and must have been preceded by desire, otherwise it would be impossible for such desire to be conceived as rediscovered ancestry. But this is because the black logos can never appear itself, as such. It is always fragmented, fissured in its appearance. It is neither object nor its sign: it is not the representation of a signifier, but is itself represented as if signifyin(g) an enslaved scene, in the earliest forms of fantasy, that cannot be assigned any place in reality, but which seem to be a primal staging of slavery itself in the political landscapes of blackness. There is no blackness without this politics, this staging in which logos and sign are always mythically enmeshed.

If blackness concerns an irreducibly mediate, figurative relation to itself (to its concept, or interpretation), then it can only reproduce itself by reference to an analogical "apprepresentation"; it can only be understood as written in cipher, for only then, paradoxically, can it be seen for what it really is. Consequently, it is only as cipher that it can be the object of philological knowledge. In the *nigra* what is revealed, in principle and a priori, is the history of a question that perpetually repeats itself as a question *of* history, rhetoric, mimesis, mockery, and politics. In its philology, however, one necessarily begins not with rhetoric, but with its veiled meaning, and in a similar fashion, with its deciphering. It is wholly different with the n'est pas. Since it does not consist in figuration or in predication, it does not belong to any *theos* or *logos*. For the n'est pas cannot rejoin proof to understanding; and it refuses to be compelled by the distinction between meaning and judgement. It requires neither history nor historicity, neither ancestryness nor signifyingness, to have an effect. Since therefore it cannot belong to either philological nor philosophical judgement, it cannot be interpreted or possessed as a criterion of possession. The reason why the n'est pas remains the unsaid of philology is simply because it puts into question language as philologically understood. For the same reason it cannot be interpreted as *nigra* or *nigger*, insofar as these terms are used to make judgements about black literature and philosophy.

It is therefore far from being the case that the desire to make blackness *mean* can signify what can be inferred from signifyin(g); on the contrary, one may more readily conclude from this that it is principally because the n'est pas resists such ascription that it is blacker than black. And as the blackest figuration is also the most emblematic, the rule for reading the n'est pas must be nothing other than a path that does not lead us to any *there*; not to form, structure, or concept, and not to sign, reference, or language. The n'est pas, in this sense, marks a place that never takes place as place, which thus reveals an origin not in the nature of a beginning or an end, but in that of an opening that holds itself open to what it is not, to the extent that it is the continuous knot of this not. That is why it is untranslatable by blackness, and why instead of mastery, masquerade is the mockery that masks its philological servitude.

Three
Nègre, Figura

From what has already been written, it is clear that philology is not the same thing as the n'est pas. But what about the n'est pas? Where does this "is not" come from—this nothing that does not signify knowledge any more than it represents reason or logic? What philology could interpret it? And what exactly does it show us? But first, can blackness even be a philology? If there is a hermeneutics of blackness, how does it attain an understanding [*Verstehen*] of its object? Singularities rather than monstrations? Judgements rather than allegories (for example, the "evidentness" of black predications and figurations alike)? Every desire to interpret black texts must constantly confront these questions anew.

In the previous chapter we asked: Can black philology posit this unique reality, in other words, without reducing it once again to a subjectively mediated ontology? In a radical sense, the n'est pas is the speech of the nonmediatable that is at once both the production and non-production of a *nonsens* that puts itself outside of itself, that splits and divides itself. *This division is the condition of the possibility of its philology and its radical critique of philology.* Philology thus offers us nothing more than a key to a lock that language snaps shut. On that point, let us see whether the n'est pas is what opens the lock or what closes it even further. Our example here will be the work of Edward Said.

———

Thesis: the following discussion centers on the question of style, but my subject shall also be that of the *nègre*, whose style always reveals to philosophy a force that is *thrusting*, and that *cleaves* and shatters the very thing from which it withdraws, leaving an indelible, irreducible impression. What, then, does the *nègre* force philosophy to say: the perverse pleasure of a violence that is inhuman? Or an outrage and humiliation that reason presents to itself as its foundation and law? The *nègre* not only undoes being, meaning, subject, and logos; it also undoes, or does away with, the pleasures of expiration and/or recuperation.

In *Black Skin, White Masks*, Fanon explains how this figure consists as a kind of paradigmatic metaphor.[1] But to provide a fuller explanation of this, I will give an example from Michel Cournot: "The black man's prick is a sword. When he has thrust it into your wife, she really feels something. It comes as a revelation. In the chasm it has left, your little bauble is lost."[2] This fear that one's little prick will be lost corresponds to the worry that there are ecstasies, pleasures, that only the other can feel, a combination of fear and self-pity that is carried to the point of a real melancholy. If you ask Cournot whether he sees a chasm, he might reply: no, but look how my wife has been altered, changed, left bucking and flushed by the assault! Cournot immediately relates this impression to that of the *nègre*'s penis (on the condition, however, that one consider this "sword" the revelation of a dark jouissance because of the hole it leaves in being). This is the ontological metaphor that is then used to determine, consequently, the *nègre* as both sign and idea, and that involves the feeling of something primordially inexpressible in the one affected by it. It follows from this that there are certain ideas or notions that are common to whiteness and that it is habitually affected by, and which can be conceived as a "blackness" of style.

Nègre

When I search for Man in the techniques and styles of Europe, I see
only a succession of negations of man, and an avalanche of murders.
Frantz Fanon, *The Wretched of the Earth*

We realize, given the ubiquity of anti-blackness, that the debate we seek to initiate between style (as determined by European idioms and genres) and blackness is complex and difficult. It is based, in fact, on a reading of Fanon's own style, and of his reading of Europeanism, a reading that I believe is in need of some redefinition. What is Fanonism? What is its style? Is it enough to describe the Fanonian text as a refiguring of European texts? What, then, of Fanon's blackness? Does blackness have a style, a late style, whose essence is that of Europe? These are questions that recent readings of Fanon have generally not considered.

Though our initial hypothesis—that we distinguish the techniques and styles of Europe, defined by an ambivalent relation to the *nègre*, from decolonial revolutionary writing, for which we are seeking a *black* definition—has so far not been explicitly discussed, it is hard to avoid the conclusion that such opposition is central to Fanon.[3] For example, Fanon, the champion of Caribbean and African literature, when he is defining the qualities of decolonial style (which is, in his view, manifested by the work of Fodeba, Césaire, Depestre, that is, with writers whom he also regards as pivotal to the nation to come), what would it mean to extend this insight to his own work, not so much because it is Martinican, or African, but insofar as it is in dialogue with European humanism?[4]

This question, that of humanism in particular, concerns the *impression* left by Fanon's famous concluding remarks to *The Wretched of the Earth*. Where he asks us to "waste no time in sterile litanies and nauseating mimicries," and where he exhorts us to "leave this Europe where they are never done talking of Man, yet murder men everywhere they find them."[5] And this leads to the thought that preoccupies him throughout his last work, that postcolonial culture, in its wish to surmount these nauseating mimicries, must avoid reproducing the "obscene narcissism" of Europe, for "it is no good sending them [Europe] back a reflection, even an ideal reflection, of their society and their thought with which from time to time they feel immeasurably sickened."[6] This sick narcissism seems to represent, and to see in the *nègre*, an imitation that is also an "obscene caricature"; and is therefore akin to a perverse mirror whose image is woven out of nothing but itself (which makes the *nègre*, if you will, into a zero symbol, or a purely differential one, a metonymy that manifests a servitude inherent to the society and thought of Europe.) What is the *nègre* enslaved by? By European humanism, Fanon tells us. But the enunciation of humanism—on the basis of which an entire argument about mimesis is being made and with it an entire theory of invention, including a theory of mimesis itself as a perverse narcissism—redraws the entire question of blackness as a politics of style, with the effect that it is borne *between* mimetic rivalry (or the racial envy of models) and what suspends (via new concepts) any fascination or seduction by European traditions and imaginaries.

What these concluding words open up is thus the entire question of blackness as non-identity, as simulacrum, and as a new non-dialectical articulation of discourse. But does this emphasis on separation, on refusal, not represent a paradoxical affirmation of Europe? Here, we must return to the usage of the word *Europe* and what defines it—namely, the desire to take one's leave from a certain philosophical propriety, or property of being, by which Europeanism intervenes in Fanon's text, and his theoretical exposition of its style. To do so, let us consider how his account has been read, and for the purposes of clarifying what is meant here by style. My example will be that of Edward Said, who gives an important account of Fanon's doctrine.[7] In Said's reading of Fanonian style, it is perhaps the figure of Europe, especially as discussed in *Wretched of the Earth*, that personifies the most obvious contrast between the two thinkers. It's a reading which relies on four codes or suppositions, four types of statement, then, or four fundamental propositions—each of which defines the value of Fanon's style for Said:

(i) "When I search for Man in the techniques and styles of Europe," Fanon writes, "I see only a succession of negations of man, and an avalanche of murders." Citing this passage in his 2003 book, *Freud and the Non-European*, a title which already presumes too much, and in which Europe remains a foundation, an *arché*, Said comments: "Fanon rejects the European model entirely, and demands instead that all human beings collaborate together in the invention of new ways to create what he calls 'the new man, whom Europe has been incapable of bringing to triumphant birth.'"[8] Why is humanism the figure here of both *telos* and limit? And given Said's own obsession with style, with orientalism as a "style of thought," why this proximity of invention to humanism, which makes the murderous techniques and styles of Europe the condition—the foundation—of Fanon's radical refusal? Can we speak here in terms of a hermeneutic *figura* that can only see the postcolonial as the *fulfillment* of Europe? (We shall come back to this word *figura*.)

(ii) There is a squaring of the circle here, the *summum* of an historical sense that European humanism—its philology, its universalism, its structures, but also, I would add, its *tekhnē* and style—must come to an end precisely because it has no end, or telos, that is not already figured by the idea of Europe as a limit that has to be crossed, sublated. And yet, if Fanon's response to the "whole edifice" of European humanism, and his grasp of "its own invidious limitations of vision," is also a matter of anti-blackness, of racism, Said has very little to say regarding Fanon's key insight: that the techniques of Euro-imperialist domination, described by him as a global system of predation and murder, is always already a question of style—which he describes as one of "ardor, cynicism, and violence," and a "succession of negations."[9] Said does not comment on Fanonism itself as a *black* style, a style that takes as its subject the question and phenomenon of blackness in all of its aspects (by which I mean, broadly, the figure of the *nègre* which cannot by definition be thought figuratively, or historically, because it has no figural dimension in the human or universal, and so can only be *repeated* as that which is hidden by, and conceals, the human, a repetition that, as we will soon see, has to be repeated whenever the figure of a racial humanity comes to define the human as such). So, my question: given how interested Said is in Fanon, and in style, why is his analysis of the former shaped so little by the latter?

We may ask, again by way of a counter-argument, whether Said's work as a whole is too taken up with what he elsewhere calls the European gaze at the other, and for whom the black other is merely a means (an alibi, an ideological vehicle) for a certain activity and presentation of the European as both expression and the affect? Doesn't this just amount to an ontology of Europeanism as style, and one so wedded to its pathos that it is unable to grasp the politics of a *black* refusal?

(iii) "I see them ['these extraordinary writers and thinkers'] contrapuntally, that is, as figures whose writing travels across temporal, cultural and ideological boundaries in unforeseen ways to emerge as part of a new ensemble *along with* later history and subsequent art."[10]

A contrapuntal reading of the unforeseen: here, then, we have a repetition that is also a form of *echoing*, and that modifies what it moves across, or more exactly, that is the figural fulfillment of its own coursing. According to Said, decolonial art is driven to expose the viciousness, the gross distortions of Europeanism, and to tirelessly bear witness to the fact. "The interesting result," he avers, is not only dependence or resistance, but a Europeanism modified by new articulations, "by emphases and inflections that he [the European writer or thinker] was obviously unaware of, but that his writing permits."[11] This *permission*—a word that seems to paradoxically re-fuse Fanon's own emphases on refusal—is indeed why decolonial art fulfills, by repeating, "the latencies in a prior figure or form that suddenly illumine the present."[12]

Once again, we may ask whether this *refiguring* is a confirmation through repudiation of Eurocentrism, and one that singularly fails to go beyond the elegiac *ressentiment* of the postcolonial intellectual as evidenced by Said, but also by Bhabha, Gilroy, Spivak, and others? Does it thereby go beyond a pol-itics of *ressentiment*, of *ressentiment* as a style of interpretation? Perhaps it does, and in that sense, Said is perhaps right to say, to bring out, a *figura* that is inevitably marked by what is repressed, the disavowed obliquity out of which it arises, and the political demand that it implies, and via a style that is always late, too late, belated. But when we come to designate what Fanon means by lateness, by what prevents the fulfillment of his being *qua* being, the issue is precisely what cannot be established as style *or* being, and that occurs as something like a telos that is always experienced as a movement that complicates movement, or blocks any passage, and which shows a *fi-gura* which cannot be witnessed nor fulfilled. Following Fanon, we can say that the *nègre* is always late for it has no beginning, no *arché*, no strategy that could begin it, and is thereby nothing more than the vicious duplicity that, strictly speaking, defines its removal or separation from being as a hole, an absence, a sheer chasm of being. And in whose thrusting, constitutive de-structiveness, whiteness is both undone and radically penetrated by its prox-imation. That is, if blackness is the sword wielded by a certain strategy of reading; whiteness is punctuated by a kind of mythical fetishism.

(iv) In his late work, *Freud and the Non-European*, based on a lecture given at the Freud Museum in London, Said speaks of the strength of de-colonial thought as a kind of cosmopolitanism, which is itself defined as a kind of "disabling, destabilizing secular wound," "from which there can be no recovery, no state of resolved or Stoic calm, and no utopian reconciliation even within itself," as it were.[13] This besieged cosmopolitanism designates a movement, a style of reading, if you will, that is diasporic, wandering, unre-solved. What is at issue here is a style that "refus[es] to resolve identity into some of the nationalist or religious herds in which so many people want so desperately to run."[14] In this lecture, elegiac cosmopolitanism—in the leg-acy of its uncertainties and hesitations—traces a concern not with the *herd* as a figure of difference but with the inevitable ending of Europe (where the politics of its ending also govern a new cosmopolitan beginning or reinvention that, I argue, amounts to nothing more than what Said asks, at the conclusion of his lecture, is the "politics of diaspora life").[15]

I believe that Fanon's arguments about black life and experience also amount to more than a contrapuntal reading of diaspora—but those arguments do not concern that of the herd versus that of the diasporic cosmopolitan, which seems to bespeak a kind of cultural elitism in the styles of exile so invoked. Blackness, in brief, is never simply a question of diaspora. And the *nègre* is discontinuous with respect to the cosmopolitan, for it has no place to be banished from, and is transcendentally disarticulated.

These four codes—telos, limit, repetition, diaspora—do not form a systematic unity insofar as they fail to address the heterogeneity of Fanon's style, or styles, and reduce them to a concept of a thesis. On the other hand, it would be necessary (and these two conditions are indissociable) for each value implied in these four schemas to be decidable within a set of Manichean oppositions, as if for each term there were a contrary: for example, for blackness, for truth, for power, and so on. In fact Said wants to refuse this alternative—he refers to Fanon's "agonized rethinking of the philosophical antinomies" in the name of a subject-object dialectic, no less, but a dialectic that resonates *"outside* Europe."[16] A dialectic that cannot be put "in the service of a higher unity" (the words are Fanon's), but a dialectic in which violence "appears to play a reconciling, transfiguring role."[17] Which leads Said to ask: Does Fanon "suggest that the subject-object dialectic can be consummated, transcended, synthesized, and that *violence in and of itself is that fulfillment*"?[18] This image of violence as a dialectical, synthesizing force is then rejected as itself a caricature of Fanon's thought, which in turn leads Said to present the subject-object antinomy as a Europeanism "imported from Europe," a "foreign intrusion" that is, as it were, incapable of grasping the racial logic of colonial domination (even if, as we have seen, the question of blackness is always subordinated, in Said's writing on Fanon, to a *figurative logic of fulfillment* whether in the form of criticism, politics, or aesthetics).[19] We need (Fanon can help us) to understand why the reading of colonialism as a dialectic (no matter how unresolved and unresolvable the dialectic) is still part of the discursive work of *figura*. Whence the belief that "the point of theory . . . [is] to remain in a sense in exile," but a theory that is still too wedded to the consolations of exile *as* theory.[20] And this leads to the thought that I've been approaching, and that I want to say occupies all of Said's work, in which the notion of exilic worldliness is exactly the result of a complex affiliation to Europe, that is, this theory of the unresolved and unresolvable remains at the level of a *figura*, which he is destined to neither escape nor transcend.

Consequently, where Said argues for a writing haunted by its own elegiac *figurae*, Fanon argues for a radical departure. Where Said seeks a definition of the postcolonial as a contrapuntal relation to European literature and culture, Fanon attacks what he sees here as the "mimicry" of Europe, for the "European game" (by which he means con, strategy, calculus) has ended, or at least must be brought to an end.[21] Where Said champions the skeptical nonconformity of cosmopolitan style, which is, in his view, manifested by certain European works and their colonial forbears, Fanon decries this confusion of invention with the "obscene narcissism" of European thought and society.[22] Where Fanonism is by definition concerned with a restlessness of dialectical movement between reality and thought, Said is concerned with defending cosmopolitan values against dogma and orthodoxy. Something of this impasse (or such is my hypothesis) can be found in all of Said's writings on Fanon, from early to late.

Said does not focus explicitly on Fanon's own rhetoric, but he uses Fanon to address—to represent—the effects of a certain philosophical displacement and reinvention. A good example of this reading can be seen in Said's *Reflections of Exile* (2000), which contains one of his most sustained readings of Fanon, and one that serves to express some of these differences as set out above. Doubtless with regard to what can be defined as Fanon's decolonial *figura*, Said uses the example of nationalist violence to argue how, in Fanon's late work, nationalism continues to *reflect*—Said's word—the violence that lurks within European colonialism, but in the form of a disavowal that *is always translatable* as a denial that rehabilitates what is being negated, and so remains subsumed within colonialism's "unpromising script"—and hence, never truly different from the colonialism that it is the fulfillment of.[23] We have already traced the main outline of this reading. And so, it is possible to say that violence, for Fanon, is literally irresolvable, or incomprehensible, from the point of view of dialectics insofar as it opens up a *décalage* (a flaw, or gap) that can only be read violently, figuratively, as the essence of the nation to come. In dealing with the valencies of Fanon's argument, Said suggests that Fanon positively refuses to translate this *décalage* into a figure of identity, and precisely because such desire remains an imitation of European sovereignty in both its reified and subsumptive character. In short, (European) antinomy must now be reinterpreted as (decolonial) antagonism, an antagonism that arrests European history, and that prevents its figurative fulfillment as the negated term. This is why Fanon separates decolonial revolution from nationalism—which remains a European concept, or figure. It is not nationalism per se which is being rejected but the metaphysical-racial idea of it. To read as Fanon does is thus essentially to be in exile from one's desire to know, to make sense of, and so elide the space for doubt, irony, or what Said, in the conclusion to his essay, describes as an interminable restlessness that, for his part, derives its gravitational strength from a weightlessness that is uncomplicit with any ground or value.

But this theory of reading as *décalage*, as I mentioned at the outset, is still a figural theory of decolonial reading, where, it will be remembered, the end of colonialism is still presented as the *infantia*, or new birth of humanism. Despite Said's emphasis on the secular, clearly the story he wants to tell is not one of dialectical humanism as defined, say, by Hegel or Lukacs, but a story of otherness itself, as a new kind of exilic figure or figurality. I shall first attempt to define this reading before addressing its effective limit and the problems it entails for any subsequent reading of Fanon. To do so, let us now turn to Said's usage of the word *figura* so as to address what follows from it, and what is instituted by it as a theory of reading and of history.[24]

Figura

Now, *figura* refers to a strategy of reading that identifies meaning as a kind of dialectical circuit: that is, a kind of calculation in which the signifier acts as a locus or pivot that comes full circle, as it were, in which the signified returns to itself as a signifier (of history and of interpretation). Just as the meaning of historical events can be reinterpreted retrospectively, so *figura* is the figural fulfillment of a sense of meaning and of history via an act of retrospective realization (rather than a judgment that is teleologically immanent). We may even say that this prospective retrospection changes the meaning of the past itself—that is to say, changes the meaning of how it has been lived to a question of how the past continues to be lived in the present. It is in this sense that *figura* is necessarily, specifically, anachronistic *and* a mirroring fulfillment. Accordingly, in the Saidian text, the relationship of Europe to the post-colony (at the level of theory) is not one of opposites reflecting each other but one of *affiliation*—affiliations that are oblique, unresolvable, which is precisely what enables them to go beyond the mimetic schemas, the reifying grammars (of otherness) by which the postcolonial repeats and exiles colonial genealogies. Hence, the relation between exile and history is one of *figura*. The *figura* that links them is itself a theory of exile, or written in exile, a writing of exile: a history of literature that is written from the standpoint of exile, and at which point style becomes exiled, but commences. In Erich Auerbach's *Mimesis*, history is presented, or presents itself, as an exilic, stylistic movement that includes itself within that history, and precisely in the form of a critical style that is itself grounded in repetition and recognition.[25]

Figura, first, is introduced by Auerbach to address the relation between the Old and New Testaments—and thus the meaning of (spiritual, historical) events as figures *in praesentia*, by which *historia* and *litteria* (or more precisely, their figurative fulfillment) become supposedly signifiable in the *Aufhebung* of their interpretation. An entire theory of interpretation and an entire reading of literary style indeed subtend Auerbach's text which, here and elsewhere, in its literary references, defines the stylistic effects of *figura* as both the practice and resolution of exile, which sees the intervention of the theoretical into the historical, and of history *as* theory:

> Figural interpretation establishes a connection between two events or persons, the first of which signifies not only itself but also the second, while the second encompasses or fulfills the first. . . . Both, being real events or figures, are within time, within the stream of historical life. Only the understanding of the two persons or events is a spiritual act, but this spiritual act deals with concrete events whether past, present, or future . . . since promise and fulfillment are real historical events, which either have happened . . . or will happen.[26]

Figural interpretation is thus itself a figure of fulfillment, for what is signified is the figure of its own truth insofar as its *veritas* encloses-fulfills the figure whose meaning is preserved along with its historical reality. In fact, what we are being shown here is the discovery not so much of a truth that has sloughed off its figurative skin, but a dialectics of understanding that both produces the fulfillment and captures the figural meaning of it as an event. And presumably because "concrete historical reality" only acquires literality by paradoxically being interpreted as a figurative sign of fulfillment, whose literal truth must be grasped as a figure within the stream of historical life.

This is where Said's own response to Auerbach, as can be seen in several works, hones in on his style of interpretation as no less than a grammar of fulfillment. Even though he criticizes Auerbach for his Eurocentrism, he also says that "Auerbach had the capacity to sense that a new historical era was being born" in the former colonies—his works then are, coincidentally, a combination of elegy and foresight.[27] Of course, insofar as Said sees this predicament in himself as well, Auerbach becomes the model, so to speak, for a way of thinking about literary history, which is no less than a postcolonial style that supposedly overcomes that Eurocentric history. Auerbach's style is, as Said says in his introduction to *Mimesis*, strikingly similar to that of the Italian historian, Giambattista Vico, in that it allows us to reexamine the history of the texts "from the point of view of the maker."[28] "That is the main methodological point for Vico as well as for Auerbach."[29]

> In order to be able to understand a humanistic text, one must try to do so as if one is the author of that text, living the author's reality, undergoing the kind of life experiences intrinsic to his or her life, and so forth, all by that combination of erudition and sympathy that is the hallmark of philological hermeneutics.[30]

The consequences of this philological hermeneutics might be formulated as follows (which could also be read as the four ways in which Said addresses *figura* in his work):

(i) The hermeneutical philological treatment of different styles, genres, cultures and textual traditions is not bellicose but friendly, respectful, indeed almost altruistic (all Said's words), and is based on the conviction that national literatures have been superseded by what Goethe calls *Weltlitteratur*, or world literature, in whose universalist conception the literature of the world forms "a majestic symphonic whole."[31] This universalism is exactly what Said attempts to formalize as a theory of humanistic reading and interpretation that I mentioned at the outset; that is, a theory that weaves together traditions of learning and sympathy via a discourse that is itself woven through and through from a worldly stylistics or philology.

(ii) Hermeneutical philology then, by definition, goes beyond national borders and languages in its pursuit of this worldly cosmopolitan ideal of a European universalism, as well as supporting the notion that a cosmopolitanism is thus a certain kind of *verstehen*, or understanding, that is not inimical or hostile to difference, but is heretical and nonconformist towards "the bellicosity of modern cultures and nationalisms."[32] It criticizes provincial values, even as it pursues the parochial order of a Europeanism which it argues covertly and overtly is the meaning of each epoch, style, and genre. Europe, or such is my hypothesis in this chapter, is the *figura* that produces-authorizes the production of its own figurative authority as the world's meaning. Said says of this aspiration that it is "noble" and therefore radically at odds with "jingoistic mass culture."[33] The elite erudition of the philologist is then deemed to be "a calm affirmation of the unity and dignity of European literature in all of its multiplicity and dynamism."[34]

(iii) Such philology gives a new meaning to the word *humanism*—in whose name violence, bellicosity, and bigotry have also been perpetuated—by making it synonymous with a liberation of particular differences from various orthodoxies and certainties. As such, humanism is articulated dialectically as necessarily disjunct and liberating—that is to say, it is a discourse written in, and out of, exile, or diaspora. This is why *Mimesis*, which was written in Istanbul by a German Jew, belongs to an important series of *figurae* in Said's work: texts, eras, tropes, which are read as antitheses that signify the other of European signification, but whose expression itself remains unresolved in their particular (post-colonial) history.

(iv) In the final instance, hermeneutic philology is always a description of the possibilities of its own displacement in history, and as history, even if its search for the particular meaning of that exile corresponds to a kind of paratactical style that can only indicate the milieu, the forms of social belonging, the thought of belonging, at a distance, in suspense. These particular acts of interpretation are singled out, their method grasped, as paradigmatic *figurae*, or figural interpretation, which are marked out for their real, worldly realization or interpretation of historical events. "At last we begin to see, like interpretation itself, how history does not only move forward but backward, in each oscillation between eras managing to accomplish a greater realism . . . a higher degree of truth."[35]

But it strikes me as both odd and apt to find this notion of prophetic fulfillment, singled out as a kind of shadowy exilic figure in itself, and one that is, like postcolonial cosmopolitanism, both tragic—as the sign of a literal-historical separation—and hopeful—when such separation is reinterpreted if not ever finally resolved as truth, as *veritas*. If, as I am suggesting, the practice of this style of figural realism is itself the work of philology-as-exile, one possible reason it is so freighted with poignancy in Said's work is that, as a strategy, it is the stylistic means by which the historical reality of one's otherness can be represented and most importantly signified as both word and event—both a liminal, conflicted sign of exile and of social worldly life. It might be more accurate to say that, in *figura*, the present not only prefigures the past, it allows us to envisage thought as a distinctive kind of pathway that navigates obscurity in its own paradoxical unfolding as worldly will, seen here as "an attempt to rescue sense and meanings from the fragments of modernity"—even if this rescue is bound to perpetuate itself without ever arriving at the telos of a *veritas* now read as the measure of what it means to be in the world.[36]

   We may ask, by way of a counterargument, whether Auerbach's notion of figural realism is as benign as Said seems to think. When Auerbach discusses the term in his famous chapter on Dante, for example, he uses the *imperial* example of "the universal Roman empire [and its function] as an earthly figure of heavenly fulfillment in the Kingdom of God."[37] If *imperium* is also *figura* in its literary references, its peculiar stylistic effects, and finally in its theoretical articulation, then is empire not also one specific event of *humanitas* and its worldly significance? Said's discourse does not evade the question (indeed it is central to his work), but his conception of humanism, at least in his writings on Fanon, must be reconstructed with another question in mind; namely, Fanon's notorious and difficult figure of blackness as an *antihumanism* (as indicated in the concluding pages of the *Wretched of the Earth*), which is generated by a kind of radical refusal of the oppositional form of dialectical reconciliation of *figura*, and that is written in a style that is not analogous to that occupied by "Europe" in Said's work. The *nègre*, as I mentioned at the outset, takes that place in his writings. More philosophically, perhaps,

Fanon asks us to consider a being that is not so much lost to exile, or written as exile, but that is universally looked upon as *the part that plays no part* in life, history, or concept, that has no case that can be represented or fulfilled, and that enters the lists without right or entitlement. The *nègre's* unrepresentability as both sign and historical event is something that presents a limit (to the human) but cannot present that limit in the humanism presented: the *nègre* is thus the event of the unrepresentable, and is always exiled as the material work of representation. Put another way, it is the bearer without *sens* or metaphor, the bar that remains barred between *materia* and *littera* and is therefore, in a strict classical sense, a *res* who, from the very beginning, cannot discover itself as a subject in history, and for whom there is no redemptive end as *figura*, whether as veritas or history, law or critical judgement—which is to say (as Fanon does throughout his work, from early to late): the *nègre* is excluded from the general tropism of *figura* from the point of view of theory or knowledge, and so cannot be brought to presence, as it were, eccentrically, inventively, artistically, in writing, or as a lived aspect of elegiac style.

Significantly, moreover, whereas Fanon insists that he does "not want to catch up with any one," especially Europe, Said stays closer to the sources of postcolonial literature, and what that literature is compelled to express as circumscribed by the imperial contexts that they both inhabit.[38] Sometimes, when describing this agonistic collaboration, Said refers to Vico (his master), or to Auerbach's notion of the *Ansatzpunkt* (the new starting point). There is always a starting point, a discursive plot, that functions as a kind of semantic anchor. In Fanon's reading, such starting points are always arbitrary and violent by definition; they are not merely repeated, or negated; nor do they symbolize a totalizing vision of memory, reflection, or expression. The invention of European humanism was nothing more than the expression of force, a force that upheld a certain idea of the human that doesn't include blacks or Africans. While Said of course knows this, the question of blackness never gets a mention in his discussions of decolonial literature and history. It is not because Said is unaware of this fact and that he denies it, but more because he cannot think blackness within his contrapuntal schema of difference-in-identity.

It makes sense, I think, to see these differences as a sign of their respective efforts to think—reinvent—postcolonial history and culture, and their differing responses to the entire question of violence among other things, and whether there can be a convergence based on humanism, or whether decolonialism demands a new plot and structure. "If we wish to live up to the people's expectations," writes Fanon, "we must seek the response elsewhere than in Europe."[39] This "elsewhere" is perhaps described not as a *Ansatzpunkt*, but as a *pas*, a step, for the response sought for must, in its own way, be impossible to place, and precisely because its destination—the *jus in bello* that cannot be separated from the people's expectations—is not merely a place to be fulfilled but a demand to be lived up to. If the question of justice is the path to be followed, then each *pas* must become more and more a reckoning rather than the illustration of a new unequivocal expression or revelation of truth. We may even say that in Fanon's notion of a step (a *pas* that develops into a more speculative *leap*), there is, from the start, an opening that is emphatically political. Most obviously, in the many references to this *pas*, Fanon seems to be calling for a movement of persistent, relentless struggle. Only that literature that gives genuine support to that struggle is valid. At the same time, though, that validity is not a question of decision or judgement, or of value, but one of force. In contrast to Fanon, Said does not lend his support to this notion that literature can ever be a program of absolute disorder (what Fanon calls the tabula rasa introduced into the world by these *pas*), and violence is replaced in his work by a philology of "worldliness" and by (at least skeptical) historical self-knowledge. Finally, one can see that what is so seductive about Fanon's work for Said is its concern for real historical justice; this also might explain why Fanon denies philological hermeneutics any priority in the revolutionary decolonial struggle, and why *jus ad bellum*, and one that is not simply dialectical, by definition, is preferred as the means to think through the meaning and negation of these *pas* in a world no longer defined by anti-blackness.

We should, in fact, point out that this opposition between philology and force is not my viewpoint. The question of force, in other words, for Said, is where he parts company with Fanon. He makes a point of declaring that he doesn't, in any way, think that violence (here, he follows Fanon closely in not confusing it with retaliation or revenge) can avoid injustice. He also says that Fanon's "great analytical scrutiny" is the product of his encounter, in Algeria, with the products of colonialism—that is, "damaged institutions and damaged spirits."[40] That said, it is precisely on the question of force that Said draws a dividing line between Fanon's analysis of colonial style, and his own.

Nègre as Style

It is worth, accordingly, trying to pinpoint how the problem of style recurs in Said's disagreement with Fanon. To point to the future of decolonialism (as I argue that Said himself points, and as we have so far pointed): indeed, it is precisely on the question of fulfillment—its politics—that Said's reading sometimes gets Fanon wrong, and by wrong I mean confuses his idea of humanism with that of Fanon's. But even here, what first needs to be discriminated is their differing accounts of revolutionary violence as style. The important essay, "Yeats and Decolonization," which takes as its subject Yeats's decolonial style, can be referred to here.

> Yeats's prophetic perception that at some point violence cannot be enough and that the strategies of politics and reason must come into play is, to my knowledge, the first important announcement in the context of decolonization of the need to balance violent force with an exigent political and organizational process. Fanon's assertion that liberation cannot be accomplished simply by seizing power (though "Even the wisest man grows tense/ With some sort of violence") comes almost half a century later.[41]

There are at least two things being said here: politics and reason are the *summum* of revolutionary violence, and it is the difference between the two that redefines force as power and that renders it as *more than* violence (which is accordingly deemed as never enough). Lastly, Said presents this as a point of view that Fanon shares with Yeats. Now, regardless of Said's taste for the heterogeneous, the nondogmatic, and so on, by describing this view as Fanon's (contrary to those readings of Fanon that present violence as simply terror), he misses Fanon's more obvious point: that the opposition between reason and power is nothing more than a camouflage, an illusion, used to disguise the social and institutional fact that violence is always the inner secret, the future promise, of imperial power; and that (racial) violence is not only reified, and totalized, as the truth of power in the colony—violence is also presented as the form through which native recognition and knowledge necessarily has to take place (e.g., as the only thing they understand, which says, of course, why war and justice become, effectively, equal in the struggle for just means as against justified ends). Said's readiness to oppose this violence to reason (rather than the excessive organizational and political form of jouissance in the colony), is symptomatic of his more humanistic faith that sees genocide and annihilation as the aberration of reason rather than its (racist) foundation.

This is why his comparison of Fanon and Yeats (with the latter seen as primary), is not so much prophetic, but performs the figural accomplishment of an opposition that is not so much analyzed as presupposed. Let me, then, boldly spell out why this account differs from that of Fanon's. In *Culture and Imperialism*, for example, Said repeatedly invokes Fanon's theory of violence in terms of a subject-object dialectic: "For Fanon violence, as I said earlier, is the synthesis that overcomes the reification of white man as subject, Black man as object."[42] Moreover, this reified, fragmentary relation can only be overcome "by an act of will."[43] "Thus the subject-object reification in its prison-like immobility is destroyed."[44] Quoting passages from *The Wretched of the Earth* that, in his view, shows how Fanon reconceives imperial social relations by which "he forcibly *deforms* imperialist culture" and its nationalist antagonist in the process of looking beyond both toward liberation, Said fails to extend his insight to the oppositions—of reason and violence, imperialism and nationalism—that he also acknowledges Fanon is trying to exceed. Yet it is unmistakable that Fanon's idea of change, which for Said is presented as a decisionism, a voluntarism, is also calling for "an epistemological revolution."[45] Ultimately, my concern is not with the accuracy of Said's argument, but in how Fanon's style—in its "conscious," "deliberate," and "ironic" repetition of the "tactics of the culture he believes has oppressed him"—is taken to fulfill a dialectical epistemology rather than radically deform it.[46] For Said, such deformation has only one end point—a non-imperialist reimagining of the nation as concept, with violence interpreted as the teleological reversal of antagonism into liberation.

This is how "the true prophetic genius of *The Wretched of the Earth*" is understood: which is how "we are still the inheritors of that style by which one is defined by the nation."[47] More acutely, perhaps, what we inherit are not only affiliations but also signs that we mistake for revelations, and that unconsciously still define us. Whence Said's lifelong interest in, and commentary on, the "styles of being an exile," which obtrude as part of those self-definitions and which are associated with "willfulness, exaggeration, overstatement."[48] Why? Because exile has no limit and no end and consists of uncertainty, obscurity, and obliquity? Or is it because exile, as a real historical event, is what deprives the subject of its place and propriety? Even when, as a word, "exile" allows us to explicitly present what defines it (that is, its figurative meaning and its truth)? Being bound to one's exile is thus like being bound to one's discontinuity, and thereby its affect: a kind of self-separation that is inevitably marked by feelings of falsity or treachery that are formulated as fidelity (where the promise of fulfillment can longer be sought at a figural level). Consequently, the figure of exile—the style or form it "permits"—is that of a joining through separation, the hyphen, as it were, and thereby the thread woven around a gap or hole in being (and what characterizes this *décalage*, as we saw, is the lack of any *adaequatio* or *homoiosis* to which a bearing-witness might attest). What distinguishes exile (including Said's own writings on exile) is thus a kind of melancholic *discontinuity* that is always at the edge or limit of knowability, and that is because it remains either too attached to the idea of crossing a boundary or border (or having already exceeded it, but precisely in ways that reveal a hidden dependency), or that persists in representing the boundary or border as the non-signifiable limit of both being and truth. However, there is also a third writing or style of exile which Said identifies positively with the work of Auerbach, Fanon, and others, that sees in exile a kind of *figura*, whose meaning or *signifiance* is understood to be humanistic in a strict sense, in that it reveals what it means to be in the world, and that Said refers to as the ethics and ontology of being worldly. This seems to be why, by the end of his Freud lecture, Said asks whether postcolonial theory can ever "aspire to the condition of a politics of diaspora life," without suppressing or excluding this hole or gap which always appears in the midst of its articulation and logos, and that unravels its authority.[49] The question of authority brings us back to the question of rule, or how a critic's idea of style—the propriety and property of critical judgment—itself relies on codes of order, coherence, and intelligibility that are institutional, cultural, and ideological (even if, as readers, we often confuse the significance of what is said for the form of its critical discernment).

But what does any of this have to do with the *nègre*? Whose affect—to which we alluded in the beginning—institutes itself as a chasm that is also the sign of an irreducible mark or absence that only seems to emerge, through the other, as the alethic truth of one's castration? I want to say, forcing Fanon a bit no doubt: the *nègre* is the form through which the subject, and consequently, its truth becomes what it also annuls—the alteration that is, *mutatis mutandis*, the loss of whiteness as style. But this is a loss that is also sublated as a figure of truth. The metaphor of the *nègre* sends us right back again to the concept of castration—but from the perspective of an obscene narcissism that can no longer reflect itself; in other words, a writing whose style is deprived of itself (and, I want to say, performs its abolition). Only in this figurative context does the *nègre* become signifiable—namely, as the figure *that has no order of being*, and which in turn is nothing but what impregnates *arché*, system, foundation. In all these respects—that is, in only one respect, that of castration—we are dealing with the essential inarticulation, the obscure impression, that paradoxically endows what delimits it as being. This is also why blackness has no style and no proper name: and first of all, because its systemic effect is also nothing but *nègre*.

Four

Ontology and *Lalangue* (or, Blackness and Language)

> That language be constituted as a real. . . . This is what is called the arbitrariness of the sign, by which is only meant that the sign cannot have any master other than itself, and is master only of itself.
>
> Jean-Claude Milner, *For the Love of Language*[1]

> Philology does not serve. It is a praxis without a master.
>
> Werner Hamacher, What Remains to Be Said[2]

In these two assertions of mastery, the relation of language and mastery is so close that the sign is also a question of mastery and every philology entails a mastery without masters. In neither instance does the sign *serve* (that is to say, *represent*) this mastery, which would in fact be an eloquent and slavish idea of what it lacks, for the idea of the sign—and its praxis—can only be masterful if it is conceived of as independent from the notion of representation that enslaves, poisons, misrecognizes it.

There is thus a connection here between language, or its interpretation, and mastery, but by no means a direct one. The mastery being so evoked is present in every sign, in every representation, but it is also haunted by the slavery that limits or perverts it, in whose every contrary wish to distinguish the sign from its slavery brings out an altogether more slavish interpretation. In fact, if the mastery of the sign ultimately depends on slavish recognition, how does philology ever escape this impasse, this limitation that inaugurates it? What is the nature of a praxis, in other words, that begins from mastery, but *knows itself* to be slavishly constrained?

I think that what we are seeing here, in the image of the sign, is a kind of oddly racial genealogy of mastery, and one that is disavowed from the start.[3] Going one step further, let us suppose that, if mastery is a question of the sign's "whiteness," then representation is the image of its "black" enslavement.

In *Lacan Noir*, I set out to address the theoretical and political issues involved in such reading, and in the name of a black psychoanalysis.[4] On the one hand, to the extent that the phrase "a psychoanalysis of blackness" can be understood as a praxis of "white" investigation, I wanted to ask explicitly whether a black psychoanalysis could speak for and of itself without accepting this image of the sign in which truth, knowledge, and speaking being are all conceived of with reference to a quasi-racial ontology of mastery. But on the other hand, I wanted to ask whether such questioning could even remain a psychoanalysis without also rejecting the latter's interpretation of language—its praxis, discipline, pedagogy, and training. In short, I wanted to ask what a black psychoanalysis *should* be, if it no longer accepted the values associated with *white* therapy? Would that psychoanalysis still be assignable as an analysis if it no longer practiced or recognized itself as a form of mastery? I needed to find a way of being able to ask the question, therefore, in terms of the image of the sign operating at the level of psychoanalytical praxis.

To accomplish this, I decided to take another look at Lacan's theory of the signifier and, ipso facto, his theory of signification, which he explicitly presents as the *summum* of his teaching, but, before I could do that, I needed to explain, with reference to his theories of interpretation, pedagogy, and method, why the patient's unconscious has everything to do with the quest for mastery, power, and authority.[5] Lacan had followed this path after founding—and then dissolving—his own École or institute. But the intervention of his method took early inspiration from a specific theory of the signifier, which gives rise to one of the greatest analyses of language that contemporary psychoanalysis has as its disposal. Whether psychoanalysis acknowledges this or not, Lacan produced a variety of insights into how psychoanalysis presupposes mastery as the image of the sign. Hence, the question of analysis is: not who is master, and who is mastered, but how therapy repeats the fears, dangers, and pleasures of mastery? Lacan's reading of the place of the signifier in the unconscious, however, offers examples of a counter-reading that also forces us to become radically self-conscious of the racial limits of the signifier itself in Lacanian analysis. The racial presuppositions on which the signifier is based (and which Lacan symptomatically reproduces) progressively comes to light during the Seminar. Today, we can recognize them in the famous but somewhat obscure concept of *lalangue*, and can formulate them as follows:

(i) Psychoanalysis is a practice defined not by its method, but by means of its object. This object, the unconscious, does not designate a closed set (of meaning, logic, or representation), but rather is what makes each subject what it is—that is, its subjection to the signifier is considered to be a determining moment: it follows that this subjection, which supposedly has nothing to do with power, also extends to the *segregating* structures of language. And since *segregare* is described as having a determining power, Lacan places segregation at the heart of what he describes as our subjugation by the signifier, to the extent that the *ça* and the *moi* are placed by it alone, and which every utterance either narrates or anticipates, since every sign acts as either a metonym or metaphor of that *which segregates*, and so can do nothing but represent signification as the outcome of a prior segregation. Although this *spaltung* is not so easy to ascertain in that its origin is *lacking*, the real task, or arduous work, of analysis begins from these signifying subjugations, which are to be understood in an originary sense.[6]

(ii) Psychoanalysis is therefore paradoxical; the question of technique is not primary; and the question of analysis is said to consist of an interminable lack of finality that changes, in turn, the place and value of signification: its *sens*, ratio, ex-sistence, homophony.[7] The *real* object of psychoanalysis is thus the unconscious because the unconscious constitutes the *"limit* idea" of the subject in language; in its very manifestation, the unconscious opens the path that leads to the signifier as subject; it allows us to apprehend the subject (in language) and to know, or more accurately, represent, it's subjection and/or enslavement by the signifier.[8]

Moreover, we see that the terms in which the subject as signifier is known—its expression as principle and value—relies on a consistently unaddressed rhetoric of slavery. The alternatives that some attempt to discover for the signifier—namely, the difference between sense and structure, or *jouis-sens* and the real (as Lacan himself puts it)—are only diverse formulations of the originary event-structure of our enslavement by language that constitutes the originary event of Lacanian analysis. With Lacan, of course, any mastery of the sign remains at the center of the problematic, but we will see that psychoanalytic practice consistently confronts the prior question of slavery to, and as, language; in fact, psychoanalysis remains so dependent on the signifier of mastery that its analytical possibility, as well as its many difficulties, are based on it.

(iii) At the same time as it is taking the place of the subject, the signifier changes its character in the Seminar and its evaluation also changes. Insofar as it founds the possibility of analysis, the signifier also constitutes the limit of psychoanalytical mastery. It changes what it means to *pass* through, to complete, analysis; but it also changes the place of transference, negation, and affirmation, when what we think we know of analysis passes into aporia. The signifier remains at the center of this problematic of mastery in analysis and in the unconscious; in fact, analysis remains so dependent on the signifier that its possibility is measured by the possibility of the signifier to *enslave* or *segregate* the question of the sign's arbitrariness from that of *representation*. Indeed, it is solely because we remain enslaved by—obligated, dependent on—the image of representation by which things and phenomena seemingly encounter us, that we believe they *unveil* themselves to us so that we can speak of them, name them, refer to ourselves (our egos, desires, hatreds) by way of this imaginary-nomination-sublation, describe things without equivocation, and produce a subject whose self-representation is formed by the idea of the mastery that we imagine knowledge and the discourse (of the psyche, of the other) to be composed.

Could it be then that the greatest fear for analysis is not the fear that the signifier summons us to a time before our enslavement, before the I (*moi*) loses its omnipotence, but another, more extreme, more intangible fear, the fear that nothing binds me more than this ontological fear of enslavement? *Before* the signifier, before the order of the object, before being, subjectivity, and freedom, we are summoned into presence by an inescapable enslavement that precedes—with a black, hallucinogenic intensity—representation. In this chapter, we wish to ask whether the signifier, understood as slavery, is what frees us from this ontology, and whether, beyond representation and its hold on being, a more urgent question does not emerge—namely that of a white freedom, which appears here less as a metaphor of analysis, than its pathway into thought and judgement?

If, therefore, the signifier constitutes the impossible limit of every conceivable mastery (which it does by discovering that, first of all, everything that can be said in language cannot at the same time be said in every language, and that every form of mastery is a mask for this impossible lalangue, which remains the origin of both subject and signifier), then the sense of a "psychoanalysis of blackness" can only be conceived of as a total reversal of this ontology of mastery, and its white imaginary ideal. If the truth cannot all be said, and truth is nothing other than "that for which words are wanting," then why this obsession with a master-signifier which, presumably, can only ever act out a *loss* of mastery?[9] And if this obsession with mastery is sustained by speaking being and, in Lacan's reading, by lalangue, insofar as the latter is inherently opposed to representation, then what precisely are we meant to take from the racial figure of mastery and/or its subjection?

Far from being proposed as a work of transvaluation (a psychoanalysis of blackness, or the psychic life of black objects, etc.), Lacan's discourse belongs, on the contrary, to a white dialectics of mastery, via a dialectical sleight of hand, analytical discourse is not simply the reverse of mastery, but that which realizes that the truth of the master (the signifier) is in the slave (representation), and if analysis is the practice that allows us to see this false image of the master (as meaning, as knowledge), that is because analysis bears within itself the truth of the slave either in the whiteness of its objects and representations, or in the logic or topology of scientific or mathematical discourse. But, not only must language be able to show such meaning-effects to us (the symptoms to which the signifier refers; namely, the paralysis, the fear, and within these images, *being* itself understood as either *sovereignty or enslavement*), but also those signifiers must be able to show themselves as the limit of our imaginary mastery, and they can do this only in a monstration [*montrer*] proper to language, a monstration that changes the sense of mastery, from originary power to loss and servitude.

What is lalangue? It is paradoxical that the late seminars, which constantly exhort us to look at knots, holes, surfaces, and so on, should also return us to the signifier. In these works, Lacan does not do away with the signifier as concept. He does, however, propose a new conception of its being.

The signifier is not the object of representation, anymore than it is it a sign that could present itself, which would give itself over to language. On the contrary, language is no longer a saying of being; language itself is being, but being is solely the wearing down (*montrer*) of the "thread" by which it consists. An example of this thread is thus the image of a *montrer*, a wearing away that also allows gaps in being to appear; these gaps show plainly enough that something is missing from being, and how, despite this, a fabric can be formed around them and in which they are securely preserved, that is, veiled over. Thus, it is not surprising that Lacan neither analyzes being for itself, nor nothingness for itself. "Language testifies," he writes, it "wear[s] down the thread [*montrer la corde*], by which the wearing of the weave is designated. When the cord is *monstrated*, it is because the weave is no longer camouflaged in what one calls the *fabric* [*l'étoffe*]. Fabric is of a permanent metaphoric usage [indeed, the metaphor of the weave recurs throughout Lacan's work]—it is what . . . would give the *image* of a substance. The formula 'to *monstrate* the cord' tells us that there is no fabric that is not a weave."[10]

In the realm of truth, being, as an *image* becomes the fabric—rather than the point—of what cannot be known; just as, in language, a privilege is granted to the signifier, which slips back and forth through the modalities, or modifications, of representations. The central question of the signifier as *montrer*, then, is: are weaves our means of grasping the gaps (between being and knowledge); or are they what make them *present*, as something that cannot be *appropriated* or *grasped* as language? Are they thresholds, in brief, or limits? If the former, in this connection, suggests danger, the latter suggests security, as it is governed not by caprice but by fantasy, the fantasy that we know everything, and want everything to be kept safe from the vicissitudes of fear and treachery. And yet, it is the passage from the strength and strain of the fabric (*the limits of representation*) to its being worn (or *woven into language*) that appears to define the task of analysis.

What happens, we might ask, when *corde* and *l'étoffe* become entangled? Or when being no longer refers, even unconsciously, to what it knows but suspends thought at what it unknows, at the threshold, so to speak, of what can no longer be camouflaged by re-representation? The metaphor of the weave should be taken literally: it is a matter of producing in the psyche a thread in which understanding can be rejoined to the act of designation. Each thread, then, allows a second one to be foreseen and sustained until it can express, or reawaken, *becoming*. At the same time, as each thread takes hold it is not *equivalent* to that which *succeeds* it. What each *montrer* shows is a weave which suspends all thought and being other than that of the spacing itself (as the effect of a *segregare*), which brings what is not (n'est pas) into being. Analysis illuminates the images by which language wears down (*montrer*) immanence along with internal objects. As such, it leads the ego—or ought to lead it—through the eye of a needle; identified here with the thoughts that dispossess it, that enslave it. Mastery is, by the same token, the image by which the signifer illuminates the darkest recesses of representation.

Monstration does not, then, subsist as a metalanguage. To be more precise, language is articulated (woven) insofar as it is woven out of lalangue. Monstration is the transmutation of a *montrer*—an ahorizonal stitching that has no other quality, no other element than this fabrication (*l'étoffe*) by which language comes to link speaking being and substance, and that remains even in what is thereby designated. In itself and as primary monstration, lalangue is a being-woven. But it is woven insofar as it is the line, boundary, shape, or gap of another *montrer*, which wears away the cord (of the signifier) to a matter (the ring or knot of signification) that is never simply camouflaged but that reweaves itself and fabricates the being of its monstration. Elsewhere, Lacan writes: lalangue is "the deposit, the alluvium, the petrification" in how a group grasps its unconscious experience.[11] A group cannot be taught how to handle this taut cord (the order of being, finite freedom), nor can it find it in reality or the sign, for its true place is the impenetrable weaves of language and not the fabric of knowledge or philosophical mastery. This is why lalangue is the originary *semblance*[12] of being: monstration refers to a wearing away (of imaginary and symbolic structure) on a limit that is nonetheless real; it is the semblant that gives being its beingness, but itself is nothing more than the weave, the weft, that allows the fabric of being to be seen (as the *jouissance* from which both the signifier and lalangue are woven). That is to say: as a fabric (read figuratively as a primal metaphor) it is opposed to (i.e., resists) the wearer (sense), but it is nonetheless the semblant by which language, when clothed as image, differs from the being it weaves (or represents). We cannot think of language as a coat draped over being: this would be to confuse image for substance, mastery for servitude. Monstration is not only the relation of being to signification but the originary essence of the signifier as such. Each *montrer* is the enjoyment and play of the signifier in its difference, just as the fabric (the being of language) is the primal metaphor for how the drive, say, or object, is worn down by the opposition (between jouissance and sense) that belongs to it at the origin—before it speaks in and as language, and thus before it can be dressed or addressed as logos, trope, grammar. Let us say, then, there can be no being without monstration; those exposed holes or gaps that succeed more or less completely in giving being its consistency as presence and absence, negation and affirmation, appearing and vanishing, mastery and servitude.

Lalangue is never therefore on the side of what is said, which is on the side of what is shown (represented); it is what shows the (b)*lack* impossibility of language: there can be no mastery of language, and analysis is the slave that allows this truth to be written (as lalangue, as poetry, as topology or logic), and this is how we also come to recognize the triumph of psychoanalysis's own mastery.

(iv) The discovery of an original connection between the unconscious and language—the second finding its impossibility in the first—brings us to an altogether more difficult question. Insofar as all systems of language (beyond the diversity of their structures and rules) refer to a prior impossibility of speaking and hearing that is no longer a representation but precisely representation's impossibility, how does analysis recognize this impossibility as an advent? (An advent which, regardless of what it signifies, summons this pure impossibility that defines conjointly the object of psychoanalysis and the ultimate foundation of every possible language?)

Now, if one questions the way psychoanalysis historically developed from Freud, one has to see that psychoanalysis has left this crucial question somewhat obscure—namely, the question of whether, if lalangue enslaves us as speaking beings, the signifier can ever free us? Or whether signs should be racially *known*, or analyzed as such, as if all one had to do was merely to utter a racial predicate for it to have an unequivocal, representable meaning? Let us consider as a sort of example the principles that psychoanalysis has explicitly recognized as its own. The first, the "anti-thetical meaning of primal words," does not specify what is here understood as "meaning"—it would be better to say the "function" (or the "writing") of lalangue—on which, however, the unconscious itself depends. Freud's realization that meaning is simultaneously inscribed in two systems, the Ucs. and Pcs. systems, as well as representing different functions (for example, condensation [*Verdichtung*] [selection]; displacement [*Verschiebung*] [combination]), also conveys the image of speaking beings "consistently occupied," as Laplanche and Leclaire put it, "in mastering the primordial unconscious without ever really succeeding—or if so, at what price . . ."[13] In other words, what defines the *I* is a primordial form of mastery; or how the *moi* uses signifiers to try and master *Repräsentanzen* that are present and already there and have always been there: which means, mastery is implicated in the primal incarnation of the unconscious. Our conclusion from this has to be that while that process does not ensue from the effects of mastery, it nevertheless does follow on from the attempt to master, that is, mastery is precipitate in everything—love, hatred, power, violence, envy, and rule. As such, the drive is the unconscious's way of enslaving itself. And this enslavement is perceived only in those *traces, gaps, lacunae* by which mastery works to mark and mask this impossible desire for a totalized, integrated unity. In all these instances (at least in the way psychoanalysis reads its own difference from philosophy), it is the *m'être* signifier—and particularly the *Da* of *Dasein* that emerges from it—that is crucial to the *recognition* of the limits of speaking being in analysis.[14] (Just to add: the white stones that put us on the trail of this *Dasein* will also allow us to take up the pursuit of what, later on, will be termed a black lalangue.) On the basis of a few key metaphors in psychoanalysis's own founding texts—that is to say, those black zones, triangles, navels, pyramids, continents, about which psychoanalysis says there may be nothing to say, but about whose obscurity everything can be speculated, inferred, interpreted concerning dreams, symbols, desire, knowledge, and resistance— we could perhaps conclude that while psychoanalysis involves a study of difference, the theory itself has always conveyed blackness as *the unanalyzable difference or limit*, not only for analysis, but for the language of interior life.[15] For it is the unknown against whose dreaded identification being must protect itself (the *non* or *sans soi*) whose enslavement it also most uncannily resembles. The subordination of ontology to a repeatedly disavowed racial representation thus leaves the principle of this subordination totally undetermined. Likewise, another principle, no less decisive since it founds the pedagogical postulation of the signifier, so much so that it serves as its slogan, "the signifier is what discloses/reveals the subject (of the unconscious) to itself," also leaves undetermined what defines this mediated access of the signifier *to* the unconscious, an access that is nothing other than its own *appearing-sublation* as mastery.

Nevertheless, if we look closely here, we see that behind the unconscious principle of lalangue, and due to this principle, a certain conception of psychoanalysis enters in unwittingly. This is the very conception that presents the signifier first as what "represents a subject to another signifier," and also how this principle constitutes the difference of psychoanalysis to a traditional philosophy of language.[16] It is the conception of the signifier that is borrowed from that of representation from the start. It is borrowed from the *value* of its meaning-recognition-definition in linguistics. This confusion of the signifier—its topology, its logic—with the *reverse side* of mastery, with what makes the subject conceivable as a subject in, and for, analysis, and notably its theory of language, since the latter is based on a linguistic-mathematical (i.e., pseudo-scientific) nomenclature. Arguably, it is this reversal that is displaced, rather than overcome, by the topological symbolism of the Seminar.

We must still ask: How does the notion of lalangue repeat or differ from that of mastery? It is always as the result of a master, or sovereign, whatever form this takes—whether as truth or fantasy, meaning or knowledge—that lalangue reveals-represents the *moi*'s slavish struggle for mastery. One cannot overemphasize the extent to which the notions of mastery, caprice, rivalry, remain pivotal to Lacan and his conception of lalangue. It is not that lalangue condemns us to slavery: but it does seem to produce the *work* (and *knowledge*) of analysis as the singular enjoyment (*jouissance*) of the slave. In the late seminars, for example, the turn to mathemes, knots, tori, and so on, to illustrate the distinction between what is countable, repetitive, consistent, and *castration*—namely holes or gaps in meaning—offers important illustrations of this distinction between mastery and signification. Indeed, in every instance, it is what cannot be named, or what every word lacks, that speaking being utters but supposedly never answers. But Lacan's texts, in trying to convey, via topology, what language "knows" but cannot say— that is, the "cut" that reduces all meaning to slavery, and in attempting to avoid the delusory language of mastery, merely repeats (or fails to master) the problem of signifying mastery, which the concept of lalangue cannot solve. At least, the only subject that a psychoanalysis of the signifier relates is a white-identified subject who passes for, and remains the cover for, the truth of a mastery that is itself "passing" as a racial logic.

In Lacan's Seminar, it is the claim that the unconscious is *like* a language that exposes the full scope of this confusion. This principle posits an analogy: *"the unconscious is structured like a language."*[17] What gives the unconscious to language, and what makes it like a language, is the analogical structure of signifier and discourse, such as Lacan understands it, insofar as the unconscious has a signifying structure. Certainly, a signifier qualifies *stricto sensu* the Freudian topographical concept of the unconscious, but the unconscious owes its formative power (the power to institute, defer, suspend the condition by which psychoanalysis may emerge) to the signifier. This emergence consists in the movement by which the subject is thrown outside of itself by overcoming itself toward its signifying postulate, insofar as its unconscious transcends its speaking being. This distancing into the "swarm" of lalangue is where the unconscious unfolds itself in the struggle that institutes psychoanalysis in its (naive, ontological) purity.

When signification is accomplished as the making-sense of unconscious meaning, the subordination of ontology to language (the unconscious understood as representing the subject) opens the way to the signifying conception of language that will always be Lacan's great discovery. Although it is the master-signifier that can be seen to be never-said, or only half-said (*mi-dire*), the signifier is still subordinated to the task of signifying the failure of mastery in language.[18] This ability to make the *mi-dire* appear is what distinguishes the servility of lalangue at the same time as it constitutes the principal foundation of humanity's immense power of self-deception. Dissociated from truth, composed of meaning-effects, the language of the unconscious is still however subordinated to, entirely dependent on, the representative function of the master-signifier.

But this master-signifier is nothing other than a *philosophical* representation of mastery. As such, it accompanies all the activities by which the unconscious, unknowingly, masters the implicit messages it bears. And yet it is not always clear whether Lacan means an image *disguised* as mastery or a representation that is made to appear as such, and which still remains ambiguous or enigmatic enough to not be recognized as mastery. For this reason, we will need to ask whether mastery is ordained, on whose account the authority of analysis itself depends, or whether it is contingent, and so can be expeditiously dealt with?

If we return to the early paper on logical time, from *Écrits*, we can see the analogical situation we are describing here take on the form of a logic of color symbolism.

> A prison warden summons three choice prisoners and announces to them the following:
>
> For reasons I need not make known to you now, gentlemen, I must free one of you. In order to decide which, I will entrust the outcome to a test that you will, I hope, agree to undergo.
>
> There are three of you present. I have here five disks differing only in color: three white and two black. Without letting you know which I will have chosen, I will fasten one of them to each of you between the shoulders, outside, that is, your direct visual field—indirect ways of getting a look at the disk also being excluded by the absence here of any means by which to see your own reflection.
>
> You will then be left at your leisure to consider your companions and their respective disks, without being allowed, of course, to communicate among yourselves the results of your inspection. Your own interest would, in any case, proscribe such communication, for the first to be able to deduce his own color will be the one to benefit from the discharging measure at my disposal.
>
> But his conclusion must be founded upon logical and not simply probabilistic grounds. Keeping this in mind, it is agreed that as soon as one of you is ready to formulate such a conclusion, he will pass through this door so that he may be judged individually on the basis of his response.
>
> This having been agreed to, each of our three subjects is adorned with a white disk, no use being made of the black ones, of which there were, let us recall, but two.[19]

It is perhaps as a logic that Lacan's rhetorical use of race metaphor—as trope, as image—becomes most explicit in its concealment.

"Logical Time and the Assertion of Anticipated Certainty: A New Sophism," tells, then, the story of three prisoners, who are faced with a "logical problem": based on what he sees in, or on, the other two, each subject must determine the color of the sign he carries on his back, which he does not see. Lacan separates the moment of the gaze, where the subject considers the colors he has before his eyes, and the moment of conclusion, where the subject defines his own color. In a sense, it could be said that in this little Hegelian drama of recognition whiteness becomes the object of all judgement as such.

But in what does the unequivocal assertion of its logic consist? What are the codes or values that allow whiteness to both reconcile itself and to pass through, and so exit, the door of mere appearance to self-certainty?

What is interesting about this drama is the way in which deduction and knowledge is assumed to be the same for all the prisoners; that is, for the subject who wants to know the "secret" of what he represents, the *signified* of his whiteness, he must, as Lacan points out, become part of a bartering, an act of exchange, and an act of knowing that has nothing subjective about it. The point is not to wait for one's whiteness to be revealed, but to grasp what one already is in one's individual difference from others. The time that it takes to *speak* this difference does not concern one's uniqueness as a subject, but, on the contrary, how one's whiteness is already inscribed in a network of signifiers. In fact, the first thing Lacan says is: those who look, but do not conclude, will never *know* themselves to be white, for the moment of conclusion is based not on individual knowledge but on being able to account for the other's ignorance *as if it were one's own*: the difference that can only be deduced from the way the signifier distinguishes difference as a logic of utterances. In other words, to know one's white identity is to be able to logically sum up and tell apart those signs and meanings that defer and differ from the very idea of representation that it is the function of the black disc to symbolize.

Here, then, is the first answer to the question as to why Lacan might have chosen this problem: to demystify the signifier in its difference, which underlies this opposition between whiteness and blackness, is explicitly thematized here as the ability to account for the signifier, not in its whiteness, but in its spoken difference from representation. Remember, too, that perceptual identity is subsequent to recognition and the mastery by which it is fulfilled.

Knowledge and ignorance, signifier and difference—what is it that unites them? Nothing but a desire for a recognition that sees whiteness—as predicate, as object—triumphantly return to itself. One comes not into the world as white but into the question of its recognition. By way of its emphatic recognition, the *I* is able to know itself, to postulate its sovereignty and freedom. But the logic of this discovery is also, as it were, the manifestation of a symbolization in the form of a negation to which the black disc bears compelling witness. So, the sophism that forces each prisoner to conclude "I know I am white or, more tellingly, I know I am not-black" is not, as Lacan says, a temporal logic, but the value by which blackness, far from being part of the opposition between the moment of conclusion and the instance of the gaze, becomes the screen and mirror, the trait and metaphor, for both the problem and its dialectical solution. Put more simply, it is the difference that allows whiteness to reflect on its own genesis as a differential relation. Like the "instant" of castration in Freud, whose meaning is immediately revealed *as* absence, the whole drama of what is and is not decidable comes down to the active and violent indetermination of blackness as a limit to self-knowledge. (Actually, this absence, which does not correlate to any *moi, conatus,* or freedom, is not so much something that is deduced as something that is prescribed *qua* being, mastery, revelation.) Deprived of its claim to speaking being, memory, or ego, blackness is precisely the means that allows whiteness to ex-sist as speaking being: its logic is one of *in-difference,* or rather, the difference that is *pas-de-sens,* or without sense, a *pas* that is always slave, never master, a means, a *non-savoir* for the manufacture of whiteness as predicate and subject of being.[20]

Let me illustrate this idea further by taking another brief look at Lacan's logic. The connection established between logic and language (which everywhere presupposes a quasi-racial connection) entails the *decisive consequence* of the subject being able to account, in a timely and necessary manner, for both his speaking being and his ontology. In his reading of this moment, John Forrester makes the key statement: "The certainty of being white is engendered in the act itself, rather than prior to the act."[21] This can be seen clearly in the syllogism with which Lacan ends his paper: "A human being knows what a human being is not"; "Human beings recognize each other as human beings"; and, "I affirm myself to be human, for fear of being convinced by them that I am not human."[22] What is one to make of the asymmetry between pronoun and number, being and recognition, self-certainty and fear? In the same way what is one to make of the relationship of the *I* that affirms itself and the affirmation of human being *in general* in the name of a will to recognition? The certainty with which the *I* recognizes its humanness—which the whole dialectic of the three prisoners presents as a "white" choice—now turns into a moment of anxiety about the limits of interpretation. Thus, the affirmation that links these propositions about the self's difference from others inevitably becomes the story of its own unbridgeable difference from itself. Lacan's work is directed to analyzing this certainty and this fear, but what he does not do is interpret how the identity of whiteness logically proceeds from the misrecognition that is blackness, and this for three reasons: he misinterprets how white self-certainty makes blackness impossible because it cannot know it; he misinterprets the logic of mastery as a desire for recognition rather than arising from the fearful uncertainty regarding others, from which it derives; he misinterprets decision and desire because he is content to say what is certain or decidable is equivalent to a desire to be white. One has to speak, to say *I*, to be white, precisely to be me (*moi*). But, from what point, or when, can we possibly be sure that the form of our existence matches a *white* psychical reality? Whiteness, Lacan suggests, represents a mastery that is more real than knowledge (the suspense, the fear, that what we know is always less than, or preceded by, a *black* reality).

Now, the nature of monstration does not remain more indeterminate than in the case of blackness; it is explicitly understood that on the basis of its dis-appearing or non-manifestation that the subject be able to tell itself apart from this *not-all* that defines the rules of the game, and, as such, is the wearing away—the repulsing, excluding, stripping, marking?—by which the subject can gradually see itself in its shared fascination with whiteness as mirror. *To show (represent) itself insofar as it is not*, to advent on the condition of its non-being, or non-appearing, means then to discover one's blackness, to enter into the dark night of the signifier, the dark continent of not-knowing, or to step out of the light of the world. More profoundly, blackness foretells the appearing of the *is not* (or *n'est pas*): it designates the advent of a world lost to itself, the emergence of the outside-the-signifier, in such a way that this advent of the outside-the-signifier constitutes the phenomenalization of blackness as the *limit* to being, world, and meaning. When blackness is analyzed for itself and understood as outside-the-signifier in *Écrits* (the ontically white consideration of the signifier having been proposed), the definition of blackness as pure exteriority appears decisive. "[I]t is the fact that neither of them *left first* which allows each to believe he is white."[23] And the dialectical "logic" of hesitation-concluding that is clarified in this way, in the time of logical decision, is precisely what it means to be white and be in the world. "Indeed, a single hesitation suffices for them to demonstrate to each other that certainly neither of them is black . . . which is to say that this time the three subjects are confirmed in a certainty permitting of no further doubt or objection."[24] It is with this certainty beyond doubt of what is out-side of itself that whiteness attains being in the world. Likewise, it with this *Da* of *Dasein* that we see what is never seen: the impossibility of blackness as a color in the phenomenal order of appearances.

The reference to whiteness is, then, a relation of time and language to the conclusive truth of an ontological mastery constituting the explicit content of the Seminar; but I would also add the early writings in *Écrits*. The saying of the *not-all* is essentially revealed to be nothing other than the racial logic of whiteness, this advent of what is outside itself in which the half-said (la-langue) can be seen (or decided upon) and about which the truth (of speech) is given to a subject: the sophism of a logic by which *Dasein* is made to as-sert, to give, to be, to deduce, to make appear, to set free (a person impris-oned, enslaved) by what it *doesn't know but what it has already whitely decided*. This illumination of saying to the appearing world, "this is me, and this is not me," makes logic into a form of racial decision. In *Lacan Noir*, I argue that this "logic" is what grounds Lacan's attempt to rewrite Aristotle's dialectical syllogism in the form of an aporia. My example there is the logic of the *pas-tout* that ceaselessly reaffirms whiteness as both structure and exception.[25]

Is it inevitable that white consciousness can only see the world from its own point of view and understand it in its own way—that is to say, reactively, as a shared fantasy of mastery? What then of psychoanalysis, which seems to rely entirely on a *white* definition of itself, and which seems unable to inter-pret *Dasein* in any other way?

This reciprocity of decision and sophism is the object of a precise analy-sis in Lacan (later on we shall ask what happens to the sophism in a black analysis of its logic). What this sophism (or logic) gives to see, and of which it speaks, is that it is not enough to believe one is white—one must also *know* it. To know being in its whiteness is nevertheless to make something else and something darker to be seen, namely, the advent into non-presence by which blackness comes into the world (via logic and being). "I am white, and here is how I know it . . . I must be white like them."[26] But this also, it seems to me, says something else. It says: one has to know whiteness imme-diately, decidedly, which also conveys how little fear or uncertainty can be tolerated. Beyond the visibility of whatever is unveiled, white *self*-expression leads forward into something else—an anxiety that is prior to judgement and knowledge. Why, then, does this certainty have to be beyond doubt? And why is it not only an event, but an affirmation of a collective truth? We have to ask why, if there is a specific way for saying this "conclusion," the subject must *first* renounce blackness as a possibility in order to say: "I am a white, and . . . therefore I am not a black."[27]

I think this "therefore" has to do with two affirmations: if whiteness is the advent of being into presence (of lalangue into the real), which consists in concluding whiteness equals being, whence the belief, too, that language is obviously structured (enslaved?) by the nature of this advent. Such a dependence is rigorous and must be analyzed in its own right for what it says is: "the *Da* of *Dasein* can only *know* itself as white." That *Da* summons me, calls for me, awakens me into being in my unimpeachable rectitude. And it does so by ignoring, or being indifferent to, or turning away from, the black disc. Or more exactly: by treating the black disc as if it were an answer to a nothing that precedes being, the symbolization of whiteness becomes possible.

For the white subject to enter into the possibilities of language and judgement, blackness thus has to be discarded, thrown away.

If lalangue is the result of a struggle between language and representation, and whiteness a struggle between logic and sophism, then what appears to link them is the advent into a decisionism that consists in the conclusion of a white community. First, the unconcealing-appearing of whiteness *must* be different from what is concealed as black to the point that the concealment consists in this difference and is a direct consequence of it. In section 3 of the logical time essay, "Discussion of the sophism," Lacan distinguishes the imaginary mastery of knowledge from what the subject is led to deduce therefrom: that which is outside of the logical order of hesitation and revelation. Nevertheless, it seems to me that such a difference is posited only when the originary truth of analysis—not as a technique of decipherment but as an art of interpreting—is understood to no longer doubt itself in the world of signifiers.

Second, because the very exclusion of blackness is what passes into the service of whiteness, what is unveiled as *the judgement of exception* is the discovery of a generalized logic of distrust that has race as its condition. Monstration reappears here but always in the form of a knowing in its relation to a non-me, and a black "is not" (n'est pas) that is the inseparable consequence of an in-difference to blackness in the freedom not to choose it. Sovereign mastery is thus inseparable from the ability of dispensing the value of judgement indifferently upon every blackened being—it is only the subject that is black "that gives their hesitation its definite import."[28]

Third, the definiteness of the appearance of the subject to the others who see him as white refers to a still more decisive situation: to the incapacity of blackness to posit the subjection uncovered in, or by, it. From the instructions given by the prison warden, we readily deduce a choice based on equivalence. But in the subsequent narration no one has the option to choose the black disc, because the choice of the black disc consequently gives no one the authority or right to judgement. All authority belongs to the one who rightly chooses the white disc, for now he has the right to interpret, to exercise judgement; on the other hand, those who possess the black disc by right have no power of judgement. The equivalence of thought and negation in relation to blackness is here formulated by Lacan in a direct manner. This incapacity, according to Lacan's explicit assertion, does not create this definiteness; it is limited to unconcealing it (the hesitation—which is more than a hesitation—by which being unconceals itself *qua* whiteness). It is impossible not to see here a paradox that strikes at the heart of psychoanalysis's very principle: that it is psychoanalysis which provides definiteness to black non-being in its contingency, by which I mean the psychic import of not being black. By analyzing, and only in as much as the unconscious is shown to appear, is that import susceptible to being. And yet, here it has been conceded that what appears owes its existence not to the power of witnessing, since the power of witnessing is limited to recovering a phenomenality that preexists its seeing and that would not be able, therefore, to go beyond perception in a genuine ontological sense. No, here (and throughout Lacan's corpus) it is the destiny of the signifier to both open and foreclose the very possibility of destination as judgement and/or meaning.

Now, these three characteristics of the destining of the signifier—here briefly sketched but obviously decisive—are precisely those of the language that is founded upon the white concluding of the signifier and that, for this reason, we will call from now on the *white logic of the unconscious*.

First, each word constitutive of this logic is different from the negative reality—different from the being (*l'étoffe*)—of the signifier each time it is invoked. Therefore, just as the defining conclusion-appearance reveals itself as indifferent to all that hesitates precisely because it differs from representation, this difference that separates itself from all that it designates (or sees itself as) black is the reason why each word of the language of the white world turns out to be hurrying on from this hesitant black referent. In an astonishing conclusion (to this essay on the necessity of a white conclusion), Lacan denounces classical syllogistic logic when he says that "it posits itself as assimilative of a barbarism" even in its universality.[29]

In fact, by means of its hesitation to the sophism so designated, the logic of the signifier could just as well name something else, the word "white" being applied in this way to a confusing logic of difference that nothing (besides a racial convention, a racial nominalism) is able to dispel. Conversely, and always by virtue of the hesitation that is established between logic (signifier) and being (white), two different hesitations-conclusions are able to qualify such negativity. This is the situation that Lacan denounces as the universal barbarism of the syllogism by which man is assumed to know who he is and who he is not (i.e., not man, not white). But why, we must ask, does this knowledge and the image conserving it have to take on the form of an assurance to defend itself against the anguish and precariousness of not knowing—which Lacan refers to as the danger of being exposed as black?

Solely because language cannot decide that which is not me—the black and he who is not human—solely because the signifier cannot itself penetrate into what each subject claims to say and about which—decisively or indecisively—it can only slander, imprison, delude, judge; accordingly language does not contain within itself the reality of which it speaks. Difference and conclusion are here only the consequence of this primary ontological insufficiency. But then, does not this third characteristic of the language of the unconscious obviously carry within itself the characteristic of the logic of the world—that is, the original and definitive incapacity of blackness to posit the reality that the unconscious unconceals but never creates? The most decisive characteristic of the language of the unconscious that humans speak, and that defines the not-all that cannot be said and is contained in this impotence, is also seemingly the sign of the impotence of lalangue (on which language depends).

Let us turn to Lacan's Seminar XI and the section, "The rat in the maze": "If I have said that language is what the unconscious is structured like, that is because language, first of all, doesn't exist. Language is what we try to know concerning the function of lalangue."[30]

We are following Jean-Claude Milner's commentary by observing that the things that lalangue *exceeds*—*de savoir* (knowledge) and *enunciation* (speaking being)—that is because the unconscious comes into presence by way of lalangue. Lalangue, whether I speak it or not, "speaks" me. They—truth and knowledge—show themselves to us as the *limits* of beings who speak. And yet, they do not take their place among the part objects (the a's) that surround-define us, those gaps threaded through the place from which we speak. They are present (as gaps, as minuses), but as a sort of woven absence. Present in this way, evoked by the analyst's word, they appear, absent in the same way a hole opens in fabric: *although appearing they are not there* but only as the effects of a monstrated image.[31] This is the enigma of the analyst's speech: to make these effects appear and thus seem to give being to them in such a way, however, although said or spoken, language does not exist. Lalangue gives being by withdrawing being from speaking being; it provides language, but as not-being (*non-savoir*). Lalangue awakens thought to thinking by exposing thought to the limits of language.

This is why lalangue is black—that is to say, it reveals a form that is illegible as law, rule, subject or object, and one that cannot be found in the operations of speaking being or its logic. For, as Frantz Fanon points out in his seminal reading of Lacan, the necessity to speak well for the black *colonisé* effectively eclipses and disarticulates black speech as form and meaning (*sens*). More importantly, the need to speak French—in its purity—restricts and constrains black speech further still. This is why, at the outset, black speaking being is intrinsically unreadable as mastery or enslavement. In a sense, it cannot express itself without betraying itself; or rather, it says too much but never enough, and is all chance or confusion. It can only be heard, therefore, as *la langue*'s counter-image; as a sound that has no sign or witness. In black lalangue, reason itself is at its least secure and is rendered as anguish. When Fanon refers to an *x* that *evanesces*, he has in mind a back-and-forth motion that is supposedly the expression of a *contrecoup*[32]; but equally these black accents are spoken as if by ventriloquy, and one that he describes as a fantasy of articulation that makes every word the vanishing-point or the differentiating element of difference itself. The expiation and excess of such expression establishes a connection between prejudice and perversion (one speaks so as to forget one's difference: and pure speech, as Fanon describes it here, echoes a demand that blackness should either split itself off from, *urverdrängt*, or turn against its own signification, so that nothing remains of it but this *purity-as-sign* that remains before and beyond community).

This is why a *contrecoup* is the basis of Fanon's theory of the signifier rather than that of a *montrer*; owing to the force of *segregare*, articulations of difference need to be thought of not so much as (the fabrication of) gaps in being but as warring confederacies. This war resembles a state of siege, with each lexis acting as a kind of militia, attacking every pronunciation as if it were a city, or enemy territory, and generally in handling each signifier as if it expressly delegated submission or allegiance. What Fanon seems to have demonstrated is how blackness is distinguished from signification, and in ways that are irreversible, undecidable, discontinuous, non-totalizable, and, insofar as it is split off from being, transgressive of any existential or representative consideration . . .[33]

Now, analytical speech is not the only kind of language that gives in such a way as to withdraw being as it gives it. Every speaking being does the same; it offers what it names only as a past-presence so that the thing named, as long as it exists only in this nomination and by means of it, does not really exist. The one who says "I did not mean that," does not possess self-certainty by saying that. However, this incapacity of speaking being to produce the totality of what it is, that about which it speaks is not exactly based on speech as such but on the sophism—the knowledge—to which it asks for its ultimate communicative possibility. The impotence that speech (the master-signifier) manifests everywhere flows from the mode of this lalangue and from it alone.

Thus we come back to our introductory remarks: (i) to the original connection of racialized speech and the lalangue on which it rests; (ii) to the disavowed relation, in Lacan's as well as Milner's Hegelian logic, of this lalangue to a primordial *ab-sens* outside the world; (iii) to the importance of knowledge and language that renders this limit—of the known in a purity that can never be known, which also strips it of its mastery, reducing it to these sorts of "lucubrations" (Lacan's word) that the logical sophism provides.[34] In "Logical Time," Lacan describes the will to whiteness as a desire for freedom that is also an act of brutal exclusion. Faith in reason is thereby consequent to the power of an obliterating exhortation. Or, rather, the will to be white has to pose the power of symbolization as the way out of violent affectivity. And, paradoxically, it is logic, as the basis of white political identity, that gives force and legitimacy to the real of its violence. In other words, the basis of the game is the pleasure taken in the risk—the risk that calls for whiteness to be witnessed and blackness to be abolished—that makes the predicament of racial identity the very place where the sign underpins the world's foundation, not in freedom and duty, but in treaty and war. The world, this vast world where everything comes to presence only in a primary absence, an absence Hegel called recollection (*Erinnerung*)—the memory in which everything is there, but in which not anything can be present. Similarly, when Kant spoke of the *a priori* conditions of "all possible experience," and which was in fact only the thread tying understanding to mastery, he too could not—on the basis of what he called representations—posit the not-all (*pas-tout*) of existence; he had to believe in knowledge—that is, the truth of speaking being.

We have many examples of these a priori principles and the anti-blackness that they bear witness to and consist of—and if racial violence is a logical consequence of the a priori, since blackness is attacked with the joint forces of logic and ontology; we need to understand how the analysand's experience of the unconscious is shifted as a consequence of their relationship to it, and why the commandment to become white does not spare any black object, but seeks to exterminate them all. From now on we are going to designate this original *spaltung* of speaking being: "anti-blackness." In this way, the logical sophism, in which classical psychoanalysis-philosophy engages, of conceiving blackness as the non-being of the world, will be dispelled. In the same way, we must dissociate the racial predicates that define speaking being from those that define the revelation of psychic life as an "I" that speaks, and which therefore means "I speak, therefore I *know* what is *said*." These qualifiers are exactly opposed to one another.

The first feature of anti-black signification is that it is a form of *non-savoir*. Blackness revealing itself means that it necessarily experiences itself as imaginary. But this experience cannot be assimilated to knowledge. In lalangue, blackness cannot, so to speak, be named twice, the first time as what reveals or affects, the second time as what is revealed, with the result that the affecting and affected would be presented as two different realities, each finding itself defined by its *knowledge*. Only in blackness, being outside of itself, does its revelation divide itself by destroying itself. The dialectical process that illustrates this situation is the advanced expression of a mastery that can only place blackness in opposition to that of the signifier: in the signifier (as mastery), the *black* world is always already outside of itself. It is already slavish, sublated. In the extent to which blackness is despised, hated, and contrary to reason, it is indeed seen as illegitimate and illicit. These images situate a sign without a signifier. They also situate a transgression that is indiscriminately guilty and innocent alike, and equally irredeemable. An analytic of servitude that no logic can either totally comprehend or exclude.

It is therefore necessary to try and imagine a psychoanalysis of blackness that goes beyond the fidelities and constraints so mentioned.

Irreducible to subjective knowledge, black lalangue marks the place of an original absolute disquietude. Experiencing itself as *nègre*, black life divides itself; it distances itself, impoverishing itself with its own substance by hemorrhaging being. Experiencing oneself as black has therefore nothing to do with the formal and empty syllogism "I think, therefore I am (not)," a sophism that can be seen only in the formal sameness of these terms. In contrast, black lalangue is an immanent process, the fraught process in which life divides from itself; life pulls against itself and departs from itself, thus producing its own winnowing insofar as this winnowing consists in and is complete in an imaginary (white) self-enjoyment. Thus, the process in which blackness reveals itself to itself is identical with the process of its nonbeing insofar as this is understood as self-misrecognition. Black lalangue is a non-self that experiences itself and never stops experiencing itself in nonrelation, and this happens in such a way that nothing ever attaches itself to this self-effacing movement, in such a way that nothing escapes this negative self-abolition.

But in this self-abolishing movement, something else can be spied that is of an entirely opposite character. In the endless advent of black lalangue in its abolition, a n'est pas is born without which an experience of black analysis is impossible. Inasmuch as this experience is an experience of which blackness is imaginary and thus symbolic, the n'est pas in which this experience is accomplished is also singular: it is a life revealed to itself as an unreflexive verb *sans* will, being, predicate, or object; a real whose meaning is impossible.

What we seek to sketch here is the space in which this n'est pas, which ex-sists precisely as the outside-the-signifier, is always misread as the disguise (the *pseudein*) of (white) signifying mastery. The phrase—*outside-the-signifier*—here means a knot where we can no longer pick up the threads linking language to order, and which thereby threatens logic as a form of reason.

The n'est pas that exceeds, by putting into question, the values of logic, reason, and signifier, cannot be contained in Lacan's formula of the cord, and its monstration. Nor can the n'est pas be framed in terms of a clash between *contrecoup* and *segregare* (this is why, as we will see, making the right judgement an obligation only makes the n'est pas more answerable to the most intense forms of hatred, as the experience of a racist unconscious tends to be).

Here, the guiding thread of our investigation again demands our attention at the same time as what we have called blackness as language needs to be further deduced. On the basis of Seminar XI in an implicit way and in *Écrits* in an explicit way, the essential connection between blackness and language could be uncovered as a decisive theme if it is true that the nature of lalangue depends on that of a black *non-savoir* that it always presupposes. If this is true, then another incontestable fact asserts itself: if, as we have just established, blackness disappears, or vanishes from itself originally according to a mode of lalangue radically different from that of the world (namely, whiteness itself grasped in its pure, psychoanalytical essence, as unconscious revelation), then there must be another language than the language of whiteness (a language different from the language constructed out of the noematic meanings foreign to the reality of master-signifiers; in other words, different from the language to which we generally limit the concept of language); this other language would be dependent on the mode by which lalangue proper to the unconscious emerges inasmuch as the appearing of the unconscious is necessarily opposed, signifier for signifier, to the appearing of the unconscious *in* language. This, then, would be a lalangue of lalangue—a secret, or black encrypted cipher.

What does this paradoxical statement imply? First, it implies that there is a lalangue that is not opposed to black speaking being, on account of its making blackness thinkable, sayable, as a non-being beyond all the ontotheologies of the world, for if blackness is a being without a predicate, it cannot be illumined, or unveiled as reflection or shadow; and to that extent, is never only readable as the real essence of philosophy, or the beautiful fantasy of a post-racial ideology. Secondly, if blackness is the *nothing* (n'est pas) between the infinite and finite, as Fanon reminds us, that is because it involves a reversal of the usual properties of visibility and revelation, universal and particular, and precisely because its difference is what engenders being and signification.

On the basis of the black properties of lalangue, we can grasp *a priori* the essence of this other lalangue (which is based on lalangue's unconscious materiality, and which is usually obscured) in the very way through which blackness reveals itself in the world. For the way in which lalangue reveals itself is the way in which it half-speaks (*mi-dire*). And, inasmuch as it reveals its yet-to-be-said-articulation, without communicating itself as this outside of the signifier, then as opposed to every other language, which is always related to a referent exterior to itself, the speech that blackness speaks presents the extraordinary effect that it never speaks because it can never be spoken but is itself intrinsically the absent, non-existent, banned lining of all speech.

(This would be a *montrer*, then, that exposes being in its rectitude: not as the ontology of disclosure or concealment, but as the ethics of its impossibility.)

It does not speak like a *mi-dire* who, throughout the weave of significations, never has any intention but to affect being itself. Blackness's speech intends precisely nothing—and is itself less than everything. This non-speech, or this inarticulacy, swarms within the language used to denounce it. Black lalangue means: absolute disorder and mayhem, and one which declines to articulate itself as syntax or grammar. In principle, if not in fact, these black swarms make the link to what Fanon calls *violence* explicit. As such, they resist both paraphrase and translation. To this should be added that violence in this sense is not solely an experience of war, and therefore engaged in battle with an enemy: we are speaking of the structure on which guilt, fear, passion, and vengeance depends (which is revealed by the oppressed, and by them alone). Someone might object that blackness, in its unconscious function, must be related to itself if it constitutes the content of this lalangue. Does not this self-nonrelation also make the essence of the ego (*moi*) it generates by generating itself (as fugitive, say, or wayward)? What would blackness say, what would remain for it to say if, while having no external referent at all, it were deprived at any rate of saying itself? Would this not be a hesitation that is thereby denied the ability to grasp itself as a hesitation? Or a wild murmuring which, instead of founding violence, could only repeat and tame it?

But what is important to a radical black materialism or poesis is not the ontological essence of this non-articulation, nor its historicity as a fantasy object.[35] Black lalangue is not opposed to discourse; on the contrary, it is the point where the language of whiteness is confronted, however minimally, with an *archia* that is deadly and irreducible. Every signifier that does not stand out against this black horizon, and which does not render this abyssal manifest in this way, draws its possibility from a pathos. *But this is a pathos without pathology.*[36] More, it reduces blackness to value, the value of the already-said rather than the always yet to be-said. Pathos designates the mode of imaginary representation according to which black life represents the human in an originary logos; it designates the material out of which this denudation is made, its flesh; a quasi-transcendental affectivity in which everything experiences itself as black finds its enslaved, mercantilist actualization. In this pathos, force and domination becomes being's content; its wish is its deduction (blackness reduced to the minus-one of metaphor).[37] If blackness originally reveals nothing but its reality as flesh, this is solely because its mode of domination-revelation is pathos, which in the slave instance is entirely connected with a *thematics of marking articulated as such*, this plenitude of a flesh immersed in a slavish self-affection of its suffering (but not of its jouissance or destruction as slave). Hence the moralism and pathos of this figure.[38] In the immanence of its own pathos, this enslaved life is then not any life whatsoever. It is everything except what contemporary black humanism will form it into—that is, as its wild inverted logos.

We see then in complete rigor what the logos, what the speech of black being is. To the impotence of the speech of speaking being, which is incapable of positing the reality of which it speaks, obliged therefore to find it as a mysterious essence that precedes it and which owes nothing to it, the speech of black life opposes the *nègre's* hyper-potency as hyperbole, that of generating (not the semiosis but) the lalangue of which it speaks. This does not mean that flesh has signification, since every signifier becomes a metaphor of its exclusion from the world, the means by which it is derealized. The speech of black life signifies reality inasmuch as it reveals what it is not (n'est pas): the *nègre* generates its own reality by experiencing itself as the limit that does not reveal itself in lalangue but as what sustains it. Thus, the speech of black life reveals simultaneously the reality of what it is not and the *nègre* without which the pathos of its domination-as-phantasm cannot be given life. The unthought of our ultimate, wretched condition, that of being black speaking beings in life, consists of this double denudation and this double caricature.

We must now see by what means the n'est pas—but never as representation—is the only source of black invention . . . And why neither analysis nor philosophy can lay claim to understanding this extraordinary verb.

It is nonetheless the case that this verb doubtless cannot be written as flesh *or* grammar. Let us say, on the contrary, that it is the effect of what is unsaid, and what cannot be said within the order or structure of slavery. Which is to say that it is expressed by a logic of radical *inarticulacy* that exceeds, by questioning, any semantics or semiosis. So, what does it not say, then?

Certain responses have taken shape for the constellation of a black poesis of speech to be investigated. How does this non-speech speak? What does it (not) say? It speaks insofar as it has no life. What does it say? What does it not say in saying? It speaks what it is not. But to whom is this n'est pas spoken and/or said? This is an inevitable question, since even lalangue is addressed to someone and makes (non) sense only as being addressed (but not spoken). Lacan's merit lies in having seen in its radicality a state of things that is often overlooked for being obvious. As one can see in *Encore*, a speech everywhere already present—which gives itself and which says itself—addresses the unconscious to us, allowing it (*ça*) to speak in turn. This privileging of the signifier over that of representation determines our relations and defines what it is to have an unconscious: the subject is "necessary to the function of *lalangue*" insofar as the signifier, via the speaking subject, "becomes a sign."[39]

To put this psychoanalytically, if black speaking being speaks, the one who can hear its speech is the one who is not open to the monstration of its appearing, is the one who is defined by this non-openness, being nothing other than its n'est pas. But who is this, the one who cannot hear the speech of black non-appearance? *How and why is this subject blacker than black?*—irreducibly *nègre*, always not-me? By conceiving blackness on the basis of an anonymous, illicit inarticulacy, one can indeed define some sort of speaking being in the language of force and violent disturbance: every witness to the real is such an event. Certainly, such a speech would appear to be opposed to racist common sense. How can one not see that something like a black rationality is found here purely and presupposed like common sense, if it is true that the possibility of such reason, and thus the possibility of every conceivable black "I"—if the essence of blackness, which is immediately annihilated in every form of exteriority—is born nowhere else than in the place where the *grammars of flesh* are experienced by *nègre*-slaves, especially when their enunciation is made *meaningful* in the pathos of their self-revelation? One could perhaps say that there was, however, no *black* language before slavery, hence such sayings as: black lalangue was heard in the hold of the slave ship *before* it was understood and enunciated as black. Only in this way does black *la langue*, which precedes everything, not speak in the hold; only in this way is there in fact someone who doesn't hear it, the one to whom it has given nothing to be, a n'est pas given to itself in its self-abolition to speaking being—a non-self interminably living its social death in a space removed from language. To speak well of blackness would be to forget what cannot be said, but also what could never be said by those born aboard the slave ships, who spoke a lalangue before language. We can call this a world without words, a world dividing itself into two soliloquies—one remembering the kingdoms of nothing, and one attentive to the experience of a caesura beyond doubt, law, belief, testimony, and witness.

Never spoken but always heard, and therefore a rebellious city within the siege of speech: What the original *nègre* of speech says to every instance of black speaking being is therefore its own separation from speech. Thus is it possible to recognize this speech in that of each subject made flesh or in each of the modalities of its death and suffering. Let us consider the suffering that the slave experiences—beyond the *moi*, law, war or justice—in which the limits of language are exposed, and precisely because "language" cannot be heard in the hold. The suffering slave does not say, for example, that "I suffer in my humanness," which lets one think that one ought to add ultimately to some cause or something like that to the suffering that the speaking being feels. In its nudity, in its fleshness, in its total precarity, in its pure self-difference; what enslaved suffering says is *I am non-nègre*, and nothing else. But it does not say that either—it does not say itself—by saying at any rate I suffer, by forming the meaning of "suffering" whose connection with the "I"'s meaning would constitute the substance of its speaking being. It says itself in such a way that it would not be necessary for the saying of enslavement to be composed of these meanings and to be itself something imaginary. But in itself suffering (*jouissance*) abuts onto the real. If suffering says to us what it says to us without recourse to any moment in the language of communication, then we must ask, "how does it say it" in its suffering lalangue and by it? By becoming more and more articulate (slavish), or by developing an extreme hatred for speech (that is, its system and worship, which is inextricable from an anti-black authorization)? We see therefore why slavery is a speech without an "I," why it is suffering who speaks and suffering who says: the revelation of what, in this way, it tells us is done and by and to black flesh, so that what it tells us of black speaking being is this suffering flesh and nothing else. At the same time that the n'est pas is this speech of suffering, which is only an example, we find before us not metaphor but the lalangue that is the modality of black speaking being; we find ourselves before this lalangue of the real (and not the language of real life), without which there would be no language and no blackness—this black lalangue can only signify emptily, *après coup*, the first n'est pas of our enslaved flesh. Without this lalangue of the real, no black speech of any kind would be able to speak.

As soon as we ask, "how does blackness speak?" inevitably it says to us something more, or less, than its own suffering flesh. And what it says implies an *ien*, as opposed to a *rien* or *nèant*; this *lalangue* is what unfolds from its own suffering flesh and, in fact, this is what makes it possible and impossible. For no suffering ever advents as the suffering of the n'est pas. Since it bears within itself the non-being who suffers it, we are obliged to consider the question of how according to whom this black lalangue speaks. It does not speak by itself, for its own signification does not belong to its own understanding. Only insofar as blackness becomes a sign—is brought by and to language—does its lalangue speak itself, but first in its mastery by the sign, which itself accomplishes, does blackness experience itself as subject. In this way, within the very heart of suffering, black lalangue has already spoken otherwise, in an infinitely abyssal suffering, this abyssal suffering in which blackness embraces itself in the process of its *nègre* yet-to-be-said advent, in the jouissance of the non-knowledge of itself—this uncanny *non-savoir* that lies in every modality of black life, suffering or joy, because in either suffering or joy, it is this uncanny *non-savoir* that makes suffering or joy into flesh inasmuch as its this uncanny *non-savoir*, in this original pathos, which belongs to it, that black lalangue is what gives itself to itself as flesh.

We recognize here, perhaps, a black poesis of thought. I am not speaking of imagining, but of the caesura and the violence that constitutes it. Insofar as this poesis impels us outwards, beyond the white clarity of the world (its meaning and its logic), and beyond our selves, insofar as we withdraw from the universe's primal blackness (the *abyssal*), and shy away from its vicious immediacy, its ties and temptations, it is a black lalangue that speaks to us in our speaking being. It is addressed to every subject not as a being that it enslaves, who would have no means of hearing it, but as the being that speaks the n'est pas of the being that engenders it in its own destructive generation. What each black subject hears as *nègre* may be this lalangue experiencing itself as destruction—and no matter what the vicissitudes of this experience may be in black speaking being. Each black subject has heard this lalangue in the shudder of their own life, when they experience themselves as black for the first time, this lalangue whose n'est pas is itself unsaid, whose speech joins being to this n'est pas—that is immanent to black speaking being. The problem, then, is not one of logic—of disclosure or concealment—nor that of fearful incertitude, but the opposite: the hallucinogenic awareness of a *separation* (a *contrecoup*) that remains obdurate and indivisible. Thus, the impossibility of hearing the *nègre* speak for each black subject, on the condition of them becoming subjects. Forever do we hear the silence of this black lalangue, the muteness in which black speaking being constantly struggles to escape the social death that is black life in language; in which my own life— if I understand the lalangue that speaks in life—constantly tells me I am not speech or life. (But this everyday n'est pas is neither knowable nor bearable, even though it is consistently hateful.)

Nevertheless, it is this uncertainty that is—indeed always has been— condemned as the false image, the *pseudein*, of black speaking being. What then of its truth, its invention, its mastery?

Let's conclude. In *Lacan Noir*, the turn to the question of language in psychoanalysis in its relation to the question of blackness presents two symmetrically inverse phrases. In the first, we find that when language is no longer understood as logic or communication, all of its characteristics turn out to be established on the basis of a lalangue in which it must first of all make that of which it cannot wholly speak be heard (partly said), its speech consisting in the impossibility of the not-all (*pas-tout*). As long, nevertheless, as this lalangue remains imprisoned within the limits assigned to the concepts of truth and mastery since Greece, whiteness will remain the *Dasein* that answers the question of being. Within these limits, the return to the question of language can only be a racialized return. We really see this in Lacan's work (and also Heidegger's), which leaves its mark—philosophically, psychoanalytically, ontologically, and politically.[40] From Lacan to Heidegger *Dasein* is the sovereign decision that knows, and that repeats the same presupposition, language as the negation of representation and, as such, the event that frees itself from the servility of representation, a presupposition that extends the reign of an anti-black negativity everywhere.

Returning now to our opening question: if the ultimate possibility of the logos resides in a purely white syllogism, the apprehension of whiteness as a question of originary mastery very much indicates a racial understanding of language. The signifier is so inextricably tied to its *racial* mastery that any doubt or uncertainty about that mastery entails its failure to speak this fundamental truth of the logos in its very whiteness. And that failure becomes a model for the signifier's servitude as such. The mastery of representation elided by the irony, the permanent parabasis of blackness. Another speaking being thus comes into view, a speech which speaks otherwise, which says something else, which says to the signifier that it is *nègre*, that the *nègre* is what generates the real in its very speaking, who voices the mythic-racial thought of its structure, and that this lalangue, in its condition of social death, embodies a n'est pas from which speaking being has never been separated from and yet testifies to a ravishment (a suffering) that cannot ever be spoken. The speech of blackness is thus the monstration of its social death—and the trait is the black thread on which its loss has been founded, the wreath that the signifier cannot signify until it is coded (represented) as loss (object a). Black speaking being is where the real says itself, unaware of the difference, the indifference, the lie and annihilation of ontology.

We must not see this n'est pas as a speech of the other or even of the world. The relationship of blackness and speaking being are deeper. What is at stake in black speaking being are not those *palabres*[41] of which Fanon speaks—empty chatter without *Dasein* or unconscious correlates, which in analysis is what it means to speak neither truly (*vraire parole*) or fully (*parole pleine*): in contrast to this empty or full speech, the n'est pas does not communicate itself, or possess meaning (*sens*). Nothing comes in answer to the n'est pas; but this *is not* may turn out to be neither a word nor a representation, neither an utterance nor a great resounding event.

If the time of the now is (always) necessary for whiteness to return to its true essence, the one who is n'est pas does not ever coincide with itself, nor does it relate to an "itself." It is neither a superseded opposition, nor does it embrace the half-said (*mi-dire*) in the assumption that this too is the reconciliation of truth with difference. The time of the n'est pas that Fanon speaks of, on the contrary, is the unsaid that remains the never-spoken, whose outside-the-signifier cannot itself be concluded and is also, precisely for this reason, not a choice of being or language, nor a hesitation about necessity or appearance. At once black and ever yet beyond *the* black, the n'est pas never goes beyond the realm of lalangue, it remains as little determined in its end as it is in its beginning: the impossible real of being in its black signification and logic. And because of this *ever yet*, it cannot claim to be the truth of mastery or enslavement.[42]

Part II
Writing and Politics

In Part 1, I explained how the n'est pas cannot be conceived or affirmed as desire, duty, or mastery (the heave into a knowingness that becomes real, the real
as a kind of certainty that brings us back from the dark). But to provide a fuller
explanation of this, I also gave an example: namely that any attempt to attest to
it can only conceal, metaphysically, black power as a signifying power. This concealment consists simply in there being no affirmation, or element of identity, that
could posit it. The notion of the n'est pas therefore cannot be reduced to the
cause or becoming of the black subject, whether it be as an autos or ipse. For
the assertion that black power depends on essence or will (which is here identified with a capacity for knowledge) is an intuition with no concept attached.
The autos is not joined to bios in one identity, for blackness is not (n'est pas). Similarly, when we consider the identification of blackness with an x, we imagine it to
consist as giving meaning to an existence otherwise denied being, and our error
does not only consist in this imagining, but in the fact that we imagine the x to be
the true meaning of black existence, or the real as such, but we are ignorant of
the fact that the x no longer refers to an existent, but to the *non* as such, a nothing where we are unable to conceive of the x as situated in an identity. For even
when we learn later that the x is less than a name or signifier, we still imagine it
to name what it does not name. It is not because we do not know it's true meaning, but because we cannot imagine that its true destiny is to remove black existents from having a foundation in being. It follows from this that every time blackness becomes an x, it does not become an *is*, either in itself or in the world, but
sees the emergence of an "is not" that is no longer adequate, for it mutilates (life,

being, and spirit) and all black ideas of existence. Therefore, insofar as the x is also a n'est pas, in this second part we shall examine why it is always intertwined with a nothing beyond the orders of the subject, its power, mastery, and certitude. To understand this notion, we will need to conceive, if we can, a zero that has no center and no body, and yet is a principle that links being and the real, but which cannot be conceived with any certainty as to its existence. Eventually, we will need to ask, must this zero come to know itself as an x, and must this x in turn be attested to as a renunciation that deplores its past aberrations?

The x and the zero: two terms that are present throughout this book, occasionally with an obscure prominence, but in which can be found the resistances, doubts, and infinite suspension of blackness as politics. The relation between them cannot be identified as means-end events, nor with substance-accident oppositions. Both terms, moreover, are to be distinguished from that of sense or the signifier; neither the x nor the zero take place in the realm of existents, for both name an absence. The x may be cast into zero, but we can only know it through the number, and time, of *conversio*[1]; we can only know black resurrected life through this turning around that is the returning mark of a caesura within the subject, a withdrawal that is also a kind of death, and a rebirth that is also the sacrificial revelation of a nothingness (or n'est pas).

It follows from this that a zero added to the x does not convert it at all, any more than a turning around towards oneself can be converted into an infinite measurement. For there is nothing in the x besides that which annihilates it in the presence of an infinite solicitude, as is clear from the x's pure nothingness. So it is with the mind's conversion from what it is, to a true adoration of faith and justice in what it is not. And that at every step (*pas*), whether involving a return or rebirth, the mind finds itself diverted by the disquiet of thoughts seducing it from what it is (in its original essence) to the deceptions that it also conceives. Put this to the test: there can be no attempt to escape, or flee, racist delusion, that is not itself produced by delusory knowledge; hence I ask: who can know that he is truly converted without first doubting his own erroneous judgement? That is, who can know that he is genuinely on the right path without first knowing his corruption? Then, what norm of racial truth can there be that is more certain than idolatry or deception? Hence the need for a withdrawal that is also a form of renunciation, and a return that is also a kind of faithfulness to the reality of one's black perfection. *Every conversion to an x therefore necessarily begins as non-savoir,* for we do not know its essence. It follows that, if it is the nature of our passions to drive us outwards, even without objects to excite them, it is also clear that every act of conversion reveals a mind under siege from itself. The wholly black truth that conversion reveals at the same time also conceals how enticed we are by anti-blackness even when we do not think about it. Thus, it is true that the x is never equal to itself, and that it is not possible to believe in its essential nature, whether as innocence or knowledge.

Could it be then that the x and zero remain ungraspable by the understanding? That might be the case if their truth was one of logic (*the x is not a proposition*). However, we must avoid interpreting these absent signs as modalities of the negative, for these absent signs are the locus of a radical exclusion. If there is a sort of link (or topological knot) between them, this interval is that of a torus where being is emancipated, not from what it is, but from the belief that it can be liberated from immanence by the light of transcendence. And thus the wager of what Fanon calls, "crystallization." Or what Lacan means by the "indefinitely innumerable repetition of [a] demand" by which the subject is decided in its mastery and enslavement ("*L'étourdit*").[2]

(In the torus the outer is not infinitely beyond the inner, nor is the inner divisible by its outer limits. If the inner bears a relation to the outer, that is because the outer is already the sign of an enfolded interiority. That being so, the x and the zero are unable to be distinguished from each other as distances, limits, or differences. Rather, they are to be understood as the indivisible realization of the concept of the one in relation to the other.)

If anyone would like an example in order to better understand this, I would refer them to what was said earlier about *nigra philologica* in Part 1. For there we inferred, solely from various statements, that the n'est pas discloses the limits of discourse, and so frees blackness from its metaphysical determination as a limit, and so allows another signification to be set forth. The n'est pas discloses, therefore, but it cannot be experienced as a production or sublation. It is the endlessly estranged pursuit of an apriority that cannot be posited as such. In this second part, I hope to explain how the x relates to this reasoning and consequently how the axiom of a zero is founded upon its topology.

The interval between the x and the zero cannot therefore be conceived as a kind of Euclidean space existing independently of the two terms that it separates. For the dimension of the interval opens uniquely into a maelstrom of undifferentiated and yet non-identical relationship. Lacan introduced the notion of a torus to define a kind of intersection distinguished from that of a conjuncture. In the torus, for instance, two empty circles intersect, and both participate in the interval, yet the center of gravity falls outside the volumes of either. The interval between the x and the zero offers a similar kind of link: where exteriority is reconstituted as the interiority of the two looping volumes.

If the notion of the torus functions as a fundamental category of black being, however, the x is the locus where being and non-being (almost touching) become converted into nothing. It is impossible to consider black identity without some inquiry into how the x returns being, as it were, to a zero that enslaves it. In black political autobiography: the x emerges like a shot fired *between* being and its racially predicative logic or syntax (see Chapters 5, 7, and 8). The x is the shot being fired; it opens up a radical possibility in the question *of* being. But what conversion also opens up, aside from the apostasy, the cause of the weaknesses that led us astray, and the means of obtaining a cure for them—aside from all these personal adventures, the x becomes the articulation itself of an unnameable event. The shot that rings out is heard *as a separation in manifestation*. In *The Autobiography of Malcolm X*, for example, the x is never simply a name, or a category. It is what is written and in its continuous writing presents the infinite *distance* of black being in its becoming. By this double movement, the x is situated at the center of the subject in so far as he is outside of himself. That situation underlies Malcolm X's thought on language and revolution and already implies that the relation of the x to the real is the action of a tabula rasa.

Why, then, does the x present itself as evidence of a power that is no longer vulnerable to uncertainty; or as if in the naming of it, instead of liberation, one was able to see something more irrevocable? The result of this surety is that the essence of the x is the authority of this irrevocable event; another, its sudden, disorientating effect on the mind, which, as a metaphor for the limits of knowledge, indicates how truth brings freedom to the mind. Conversion, we could say, shows us how *askēsis* is first deceived and then liberated by *metanoia*. That is why the x is presented in this chapter as a question of deceit and as the mystical act that brings it to an end. If the x cannot be willed, crucially we can never know what will happen when we awake, or withdraw from, or turn back to, zero, and precisely because the x shows us how much we lack authority and justice.

The zero, which is construed as a deathliness in the heart of the psyche, in black living being, is far more enigmatic as a figure. In Huey Newton's famous autobiographical reflections on revolutionary suicide or self-murder, suicide is confronted as a duty or moral law. *Homocidium dolorosum* confirms that the *conatus essendi* is not psychological, but ontological; and that it names a black will to power. Black power is not power, in short, until it exceeds power (as a capacity for life). This situation underlies Newton's thought and already implies a complex realization of resistance *as* reaction, and vice versa. The interval in which the act of being suicided becomes will to power, compels us to abandon binary modes of opposition, in favor of a more dialectical thinking of aporia.

What is the structure of that thought as both a suicidal relation and ontological event?

Newton introduces the notion of the spiral and the arrow. Once again, what is observed to be present at the frontiers of being, renders a union with an alterity that is radically intimate. The spiral refers to black being as a curve around a fixed orienting point, that always circles back to the word, sign, event that constitutes it. And, it must be added, without ever reaching the *nothing* (the zero in its absence). At every turn, our participation in the spiral is not due to our futility, or our dereliction, but to the necessity of an abandoning, a letting go, in which I am somehow committed beyond the limits of finitude. There is a transcendence in the very essence of this dispassionate abandoning, for it marks a separation of black being and truth from the conserving forms of social death.

We should not try to decide on what the point of this zero sum is, nor should we be too keen to follow this black sun as it sinks toward the horizon. Such commitment is strictly a moment of responsibility, even if from such darkness no light returns. Truth does not consist in knowing it; but is the commitment itself. We may recognize this as one example of a thought of what we earlier called the *invisable*. The singularity of which is beyond reason or mastery, self or representation. But even for those who choose to walk along the pure white line (as if only the latter offered terra firma), can they ever be certain that lack of certainty is a far less terrible and harmful a yoke than an abandoning from being itself?

Five

Autobiography as Effacement

Secondly, it [the *constitutive* role of representation in social and political life] marks what I can only call "the end of innocence," or the end of the innocent notion of the essential black subject.

Stuart Hall, "New Ethnicities"[1]

These are the thoughts that drove me to speak, in an unguarded moment, of the end of innocence of the black subject or the end of the innocent notion of an essential black subject.

Stuart Hall, "What Is This 'Black' in Black Popular Culture"[2]

What do we understand by blackness? According to the late Stuart Hall, it comprises an *end of innocence*. Hall speaks, in a manner that is somewhat confusing, of a blackness that is no longer innocent, since it can no longer be understood as such, but he also implies that blackness is always *opposed* to innocence. If the former is a matter of belief, the latter is a matter of knowledge, for what is most remarkable about blackness is always contrary to its concept. The question that insists on being asked is therefore this: What has come to an end: blackness "in itself," or belief in its "essence"? These two "innocences" imply two very different things. But they come together in their *politics*: how will it be decided that an essence is less than its knowledge? And the world, which is founded on anti-blackness: Is this a sure foundation, or a belief that is ill-founded? Hence today, the thought that nothing is surer than that of anti-blackness, which everyone knows is neither innocent, nor has come to an end, but is, on the contrary, the foundation of law, ontology, and politics. Anything that imagines itself innocent is just more ideology, therefore, and the same with knowledge. Since, however, blackness is, or was, never innocent, was the belief one of error or falsehood, and all the more deceitful for being so? Or was it the only infallible criterion of a truth for the world in question? In brief, are we speaking of ontology or of judgement, of reason or of fantasy?

But what is a politics of innocence from a political point of view? What knowledge is innocent in its politics, but not in its essence? The problem seems to arise when blackness becomes an object of knowledge—when it becomes recognized as an autos securely grounded in bios (but only as a life that has no political life, insofar as it is seen as lesser). But if blackness becomes an object of knowledge, it can *only* be known for what it is not, and not for what it is. The difference between knowledge and innocence becomes very murky if what appears to be black can only come to be known when it is revealed to be a n'est pas, an *"is not"* that cannot be *known* as subject, or object. To bring blackness to an end, then, is to come to know a n'est pas that never ends. Politically, this means that blackness cannot be defined in terms of its ends. But the task remains one of grasping its constitution without relation to an essence, which can only be (if its notion is to be grasped [*begriff*]) an advent that brings blackness to an end. Ultimately, one can define blackness only in terms of the specific *innocence* peculiar to it, as the politics of an ending *or* its advent. To vainly seek to clasp this ending-advent as innocent is thus to persist in a delusion that confuses autos with the image of black political life. This is what Hall comes to recognize, much to his rue. The politics of blackness is, then, the institution of what always precedes— and so ends—it: the end that it aspires to become, to know, to make innocently certain. We might say that blackness is always founded on the innocence of what negates it, the ending that it must at once repeat, and the advent that presents itself as the never to be repeated basis of its ending, and this, in fact, is what blackness is existentially, politically, or historically.

In what follows, we shall take Hall literally at his word: we shall seek to lead blackness back to its notion (its philosophically unguarded moment), in order to encounter it in its indefatigable expression of an innocence that is always about to end, and to end in its innocence.

Hence the point is not to know blackness. For if no theory of blackness can essentially know what it is, then blackness itself has no referent; or, better still, it must innocent itself, as Hall has it, of such a desire, or it must become like the child who points his finger at something broken and says: *I am innocent*, unaware that in saying so is to reveal a knowledge that self-condemns. On this, Hall and I are in agreement. Blackness would then be the innocent expression of what we can never know, or think of, as black. Indeed, this would suggest that the signifier "black" must remain necessarily innocent of the very notion of its innocence, for such a claim must always be unguarded, free of the desire (the desire for innocence) and thereby of its guilt. Note that the word "unguarded" in my second epigraph already voices a suspicion that such blackness is unavoidable and yet is always avowable in its unavoidability. Specifically, to not know blackness, or to believe that one does not know it, is to grasp the truth of what cannot be known, or thought of, as black, for there is no last word and testimony on what blackness is.

This corresponds essentially to a chiasmus. In what follows we shall attempt to convert it into a dialectics: a dialectics of conversion. That is, we shall ask what it means to say that blackness never coincides with itself; that it denies reason; that it has no face; and that what it gives often unhinges experience, decision, or praxis. We shall not speak of blackness as a *means* (from its referent to what it represents); but as the nullifying *power* of what it means to think, doubt, or reason. Blackness may appear innocent, but it cannot point to itself without deictics *or* mediation. Nor can it grasp itself *immediately* or *dialectically* without notion or essence. One understands nothing of blackness if one fails to listen to this exemplary n'est pas.

Like the notion that innocently precedes it, blackness is a relation of what cannot be known (as is the case for every existent innocent of its notion) as prudential knowledge. Practical reason is never its end. Knowledge and reason are its means, divine violence alone its end.[3] But this violence, in its interminable appeal for justice, reappears all the more forcefully as an example of pure mediacy. Thus it is never actually violent, but violence in its ending [*Ausgang*], and since that violence is always pending, and this is the real concern of its politics, it is inevitable that it should always appear violent to the means and ends of politics: if blackness is to go beyond the violence of politics, it must disobey any authority that would claim to know or represent it as a politics, whether positively, as an essence, or negatively, as a violence. It is as if blackness must always be the scandal and antiphon of any claim by politics to represent—and so know—it: it is thereby condemned to be the least knowing, or the most naïve, politics of politics.[4] (These dualities will all be put to the test in what follows—and precisely because they produce the essence of an innocence that the political institutionalization of blackness always relies on when it wants to produce anti-blackness, or to become the violence it was always reaching for in law and judgement.)

To begin with, in principle, there are three delegitimations of blackness in these justifications, hence three essentialisms. We shall consider each in turn as an example of the autobiography of an un-thought. (Just to be clear: by "autobiography," what I want to draw attention to is how these thoughts are taken from Hall's reflections on autos, and bios; and how blackness is effaced from the ways in which self-knowledge gets sanctified as restoration and authority).

First, the authority of blackness as reference—that is, its *sens*, or habitual recognition as origin or essence. This is a traditional recognition in which blackness adheres to itself, and despite the inevitable "detour" of its theory, reading, or concept.[5] Here blackness is not assumed to be just one figure among others, but the power of figuration per se. By this I mean that blackness has only one referent, one desired object, one beloved essence: the phantasm and dream of a black totality.

There is the authority of the extraordinary and personal essence of a black *es gibt* (blackness *exists*; we can sense it exactly), which shapes revelation, devotion, heroism, and various other qualities of adherence and recognition.[6] This charismatic revelation, as exercised by various "prophets"—or in the field of politics, lords, rulers, demagogues, leaders, potentates, and so on—focusses on the power of blackness as *alētheia*. Here blackness is nothing but the referential power of a drive for presence, and what persists, ever louder, is the reassertion of an essence before history, tradition, culture.

Finally, there is adherence by virtue of causality, by virtue of the belief in a shared destiny or fate in which blackness functions as both cause and effect. In this instance, blackness expresses itself as a categorial law of obligation. A duty whose obligation does not arise out of respect, but out of a being-in-the-world, whose bearers respond, so to speak, to what they see as a calling.[7]

It is understood that, in reality, obedience to this vocation is no more than a metaphor, or no less than an oblique relation to thought, which involves the way in which the cause is conceived, and one's destiny is represented—the fear and hope that blackness will be redeemed or will be no longer fallen.[8] However, in asking for redemption, black onto-theology not only considers there to have been a fall, but history becomes the teleological expression of a perpetual falling that, as such, is never simply fallen, but signifies an end that is always awaited.

It goes without saying, in the case of Hall, that these conceptions and their inner justifications are read as symptoms of a more general impasse of domination and foundation. Hence, his sense that blackness is a highly nuanced complex of diaspora, alienation, and overdetermination (we shall come back to these commentaries in due course). In what follows we shall be interested in all three types as autobiographical projects: reference by virtue of the phantasms that sustain it, adherence as a principle of power and ideology, and causality as a sign of teleology.

Throughout, we shall focus on how innocence constitutes the *trace*, the *means*, of a black autobiographical politics.

The Autobiography of an Un-Thought

The study of autobiography is caught in this double motion, the necessity to escape from the tropology of the subject and the equally inevitable reinscription of this necessity within a specular model of cognition.
Paul de Man, *The Rhetoric of Romanticism*[9]

1. Innocence Regained

In my two opening epigraphs, whose differing implications we have already touched on, Hall reveals the dilemma that drove him to write, and to speak about, a politics of innocence. Most importantly, autobiography emerges here in the form of a dissatisfaction with how blackness has been thought historically, a discomfort that corresponds, in turn, with the two figures of a *prosopon poien*, the conferring of a voice to what is absent, or no longer, on the one hand, and the uneasiness of that figuration—both expressive and theoretical—as a critical and political project.[10] The concern seems to be with whether one can give voice, or bear witness, to an innocence (however naïve it might be), without the resistance or pathos of trope—but also, and perhaps more urgently, how does one move beyond trope (or prosopopoeia) to dialectics, without thereby reducing or reprimanding blackness to that of its "literal" meaning? Furthermore, what Hall seems to want to bring to an end are those thoughts that try to make blackness consistent, or identical to, its present or past meaning, and so making adherence its heuristic principle.

From this dilemma he set out to make a resolution that will prove to be highly decisive: what is most decisive *for me*, he avers, is to maintain blackness as a *différance*, and, by virtue of this, to insist that it is the dialectical *overdetermination* of any concept or structure.[11] Blackness is, then, nothing less than a figuration vertiginously marked by an x that is both nameless, and endlessly written over, in the sense of an inscription—it is this image that I seek to question, or more specifically, *give voice to*: the notion of a prosopopoeia that is *always dialectically awaited* in the sense of a politics, or a Marxist theory of culture, and which is no more innocent of desire than it ever was a political or historical truth.

Simplifying greatly, it seems to me that the politics and concept of blackness begins with this x, the fundamental understanding of which defines the postwar epoch. One can see this analysis in such classic texts as Frantz Fanon's *Wretched of the Earth* (1961), or *The Autobiography of Malcolm X* (1964), or the early theoretical writings of Eldridge Cleaver, and Amiri Baraka.[12] In all these texts, it is the act of conversion—of that which was deceptive, weak, fallen, but is now pious, sound, strengthened, and by virtue of an obedience to a charismatic restoration—that seems to occupy the center stage, with blackness acting as the *conversive* reading of conversion, which in some way disrupts the innocence or knowledge that is thereby lost or gained. Here, the very fact that we are dealing with an "end of an essential innocence" (in the way that Hall used the term in the 1980s and early 1990s[13]) that prevails—or, if you prefer, persists—provides the basis of the present study. When the end of that essential innocence also comes to define a renaissance of black critical thought from the 1950s on, the resulting question of what it means to read blackness must be considered as part of the differantial weave that Hall, in a quasi-Derridean manner, says necessarily constitutes and suspends any idiom of black identity.[14] In the resulting debate over the meaning of blackness, including Hall's own, innocence therefore does not refer to an immanence posed before representation, which is then seen to coincide with a prior historical moment or advent. No, innocence denotes a peculiar *bildung* of modern blackness. Here we see the emergence of a writing and thinking of autobiography that is itself structured by a principle of error and deception.

Autobiography never wholly overcomes error, which is why it pays heed to restoration. Modern black experience, it turns out, must not only signify deception, it must also represent the conversion, in Hall's reading, of conversion to politics: only in this way can restoration avoid the political error of seeking a new origin whether in that of the *volk, geist, ethnos*, or nation. Or as Hall succinctly puts it: to find oneself already read in those terms is to know that the very attempt to restore, to go back to an essence, is to risk a form of "psychic death."[15] Death, because the trope of prosopopoeia, in its restorative innocence, "deprives and disfigures to the precise extent that it restores."[16]

Hall's texts not only present black politics as a problem of conversion, the key example here being that of black British identity; he also presents conversion as the means to a new cultural politics of identity. Indeed, any attempt to think identity must do justice to the question being asked, which is what would it mean, politically, to bring blackness to an end? Ending means: a blackness that no longer founds itself as a new genuine beginning, in the sense of a repressed or unmediated authenticity. Which also amounts to saying: blackness has come to an end because there is no ethos for its ending. Rather, its politics founds no firm truth but is marked by a beginning that withholds itself. On the contrary, its innocence contains nothing more than an ending that is unmediable. So what one knows of its innocence is an origin to which all knowledge is denied, and so is nothing more than what it is (not): an ending that is futureless, without ethos, or foundation.

One consequence of the question is the fear of losing a stable referent: Can blackness be the basis of a new solidarity? And how might one avoid the injurious effects of such fantasy? All of these questions suggest modern blackness is at a crossroads involving two distinct possibilities: one that attempts to make blackness *innocently* black (that is, a *prosopon* free from racial injury); the other that separates it from such desire (and consequently injures it by bringing it to an end in allegory): neither decision is genuine, both are engaged in mutual deception. Which is, as we shall see, just what the x signifies as the deferred action—and restoration—of black autobiography.

These political debates were not just theoretical for Hall. He experienced them directly.[17] Indeed, his early organizing as a Marxist militant in England showed him two things. Black political formation provided a new concept and illustration of *articulation* (a key term); but Marxism had to be slightly corrected to make that articulation wholly or partly, *emergent*.[18] The point was not to begin with what Marx, in *Grundrisse*, derisively calls "abstraction," for one must go beyond the "confusing fabric" that "the real" presents, by adding more and more levels of determination until one can grasp "the concrete in thought." To grasp material changes in the world, however abstract they might at first appear to be, is to grasp how "different tendencies fuse and form [into] a kind of configuration."[19] In the modern state, reason must show how abstraction is now *constitutive* of social being. Everywhere there is an active configuration, thought must be able to grasp its real relation to material conditions. Marxist philosophy paves the way here for its ability to show how appearances are not just illusions, but the effects of wider ideological conflicts. Hall's early work suggests that the role of hegemony is essential; it explains the force of certain representations.[20] Immediately following these distinctions, Hall invokes black identity as an example of such hegemony, which he variously elaborates as provisional, heterogeneous, deferred, and to that extent, always on the border of restoration and dissolution. Blackness is invoked as a figure—in my terms, an x—that has not only changed its name and even its content over time—from, say, colored to negro, negro to black—but these changes in reference, usage, and rhetoric also express a profound shift in the way blackness is now expressed, which, for Hall, connotes a *positive* difference (and presumably because each epochal shift is thereby less innocent).

The end of innocence that Hall, writing in 1988, first identified as evidence of a new black political maturity, and that he then, later on, in 1992, would invoke, directly, as an "unguarded moment"[21] in his own theory—that is, less a moment of error and more a moment of parapraxis—already performs what I consider to be the real crux of the problem: namely, what would it mean to separate blackness from its determinations, recognized as abstract, that appropriate and expropriate it *as* black? If blackness cannot be thought or practiced without recourse to its racist abstraction, then any attempt to capture this shift, as one between identity and difference say (and it is différance that is here equated with a new cultural politics), will find that ideology and knowledge are not at all easy to separate out, in fact. For if the aspiration of blackness is not just to announce or signal itself as a politics but to claim itself as a new knowledge (at the level of being, but also language), nothing is more ideological than the claim to be speaking from a place that is more knowing, and so less innocent, or from a position that is more or less black.

We assume that a theory, or its politics, can only be justified by its consequences, but Hall's reading of blackness seems to suggest the impossibility of any innocent notion coming into being without also being essentially known as such and so, to some degree, being already ruined. There may be something to be gained therefore by asking what kind of notion is this that produces and determines itself as a dialectics of restoration *and* ruination, and regardless of whether it is read theoretically, historically, or autobiographically? To tease out the implications of this situation, let us reconsider the two main terms of this opposition: that of innocence and that of its conversion. Which is where the figure of a new black politics first emerges in 1980s Britain.

2. Innocence Lost

The question of how to present the end of black innocence without doing so too knowingly, or not knowingly enough, is one that constantly recurs (as my opening second epigraph suggests) in Hall's sense of being assailed by thoughts defined solely by their inadequacy; that is, by concepts judged to be no longer adequate. But one can also see this underlying tension in Fanon's wish to determine the difference between mimicry and invention, say, or in Malcolm X's wish to distinguish between a conversion that remains culturally and psychologically servile and an act that gives birth to a new mastery or analysis of both self and representation. The first act of our own narrative, then, will consist of an analysis of these various transformative causes and effects.

Although conversion can occur in many different ways, it always begins with the self's undoing. Conversion (*conversio*) means: a return that leads to rebirth. The turning round, toward oneself, is itself an act of conversion. Here everything is reversed, and in the turning back, the self comes to know itself through its renunciation. Only by resisting appearances, by turning away from the impure or the sensible, and by knowing the true, is one able to free oneself. The self must turn back to itself, and so convert itself, precisely because it is besieged like some fortress, with the implication that to be converted is to be liberated from a state of siege. And by what is the "I" besieged? By its own doubts, judgements, appetites, and passions. And regardless of whether what besieges is conceived as truth or deception. Perhaps this is why *conversio* is said to be made up of a "liberation within the axis of immanence."[22] *Conversio* does not, then, come from somewhere else, from outside; it consists in a disturbing, disorientating discord in being itself, via a turning back to the self, which inevitably causes one to choose and so act. Is this why Hall refers to conversion as an ending that is at once of political and autobiographical significance? As if the notion were itself a metaphor, a slip, and so less an inquiry into existence than the expression of a discordance. At the same time, is not this very image of a restored filiation (that of a self-reborn) also something indefinable, uncertain, since it never coincides with the self, or its image? So what is the knowledge being claimed as the end of falsehood and deception? What does one know by knowing it, or expose by not knowing it—and how does one *read* this narrative: of a self now different from itself, the advent of self as other? It seems to me that what the act shows is not knowledge, but rather how easy it is to see oneself differently, or in any case, to imagine that one's former self is the cause of all errors (the appearance of a literal truth out of substitutive figure) that this new action discloses. (Hall uses the word *slippery* to describe what conversion accomplishes; how it brings illusion to an end, or blinds us agreeably; or how it rounds on the false rather than the true, or how it corrects ideological illegitimacy by science; indeed, he suggests that to know the causes of error does not mean that one is free from deception. And to know why this is so is to know, in turn, why blackness disturbs any category of self-knowledge or of identity.)

Hall's admission thus demystifies why any desire to *be* innocent must at the same time knowingly innocent itself of any complicity with deception. Our own interest in innocence is much simpler. The surest way to know ideology, apart from its production, is through its deceptive innocence, which cannot be eradicated except through conversion. This perhaps explains why Hall had to turn his back on the Marxian conception of the "last instance" as never innocent enough (or as engaged in mutual deception). Articulation does not show us the truth, but it does show us why ideology is inseparable from the libidinal and political economies that seek to constitute-convert it. Indeed, the above remark is revealing in that Hall seems to be feeling guilt (over his early theorizing) not because of false innocence but because of his own *political* need to not be tricked in turn, with respect to which he may have been too naïve—too blind—in his desire to reach a less deceived understanding of ideology. The same holds true for his theory of blackness: it seems that one can only possess it once one dispossesses oneself of any truthful adherence.

This is why black political innocence coincides with the realization that innocence is genuinely disturbing, for it corresponds to a figure for which no literal-ideological term can be substituted. Let us examine the politics of this trope, the structure of its writing and its affective uncertainty. In what follows we will be wholly concerned with why uncertainty is always the ending and beginning of black innocence as such.

To illustrate why, let us turn to the story of Michael De Freitas, otherwise known as Michael Abdul Malik or Michael X. A man whom Hall knew and who was seen during the 1960s as a radical black leader in England, and who was later hung in Trinidad, in 1975, after being found guilty of the murder of one his "followers." This story is not one of innocence and fall, knowledge and conversion, thereby, but also one of diaspora and law, power and coercion. We'll address the latter in the next section, where I will also return to the question of language, but here I want to focus on the question of what it could possibly mean to read Michael X's autobiography innocently. By which I mean, not only his innocence before law, but his attempt to avoid the dangerous partiality of law, in which principles of error are not only deceptive, but deceive reason through the false appearance of a prosopopoeia—a fiction—that takes its revenge against black lies and deception. (Blackness as a power of deception must be where we therefore start.)

In the following scene de Freitas recounts how he became Michael X while accompanying Malcolm X on a visit to the Midlands in February, 1965:

> He [Malcolm X] got on the phone straight away to Birmingham and told the student organization to book two rooms at his hotel. "I'll be coming up with my brother—Brother Michael," he said.
>
> The Islam student body probably interpreted what he said literally. They booked me in at the Grand Hotel as Michael X—and that was how Michael X came into being. I was not a "Black Muslim." The X was a mistake. When I eventually did become a Moslem, I chose a different name, but the mistake went on.[23]

The x denotes symbolism here, not belief, image but not conversion. This is a false conversion that raises the first of many questions as to when conversion actually occurs: in its experiencing or in its narration, in its writing or in its verbatim reporting?

But there are two odd things about the anecdote: the mistake (which indicates a difference within the colonial histories of blackness) consists of a letter that is embarrassingly mistranslated, that then becomes hijacked by a media that feels compelled to develop the picture (of a fearful British Black Nationalism) the better to control its ideological meaning. Here referential mistake not only becomes autobiographical metaphor; the x comes to be read allegorically as a figure of truth that is nonetheless a lie, and even when truthfully asserting that the figure is a lie, or a mistake that goes on, ideologically no one seems able to escape the deception. Accordingly, in the substitution of x for de Freitas, conversion traces a circuit that leads to the exposure of a deception: blackness as the *prosopon* of a fiction, or what amounts to the same thing, an *articulation* that passes from restoration to disfiguration, signification to autobiographical error.

Which is to say: it is as impossible to dissociate metaphorical substitution from autobiographical error, than aberration from political illegitimacy. For, whether the x is a mere signifier, or simply a written sign, without it, no black autobiographical or radical self can come into being, for what it signifies referentially is also what it elides, and what it weights with being has no reference other than the erroneous implication of a linguistic predicament.[24] The displacement of fiction for figure is not expressive of reference, but is expressive of an illicit conversion of politics into literal error that cannot be eradicated except through deceit. For these reasons, it is simply not possible to correct the mistake that led to the confusion in the first place. Nothing shows us the truth here, everything deceives. The confusion of figure (doxa) for truth (episteme) is, strangely, the very thing—the only thing—that allows black power to appear as autobiographical error. This is why we must recall that any naïve belief in the meaning of the x as innocent, however understood politically, is not the issue here; if black autobiography is aberrant, it is precisely because there is no way to dissociate its referential foundation from the politics of its misreading (a point that de Freitas understands and expresses above). In which case, the x represents a missed encounter between image and belief, black British radicalism and US political culture, for it shows how conversion is hard to tell, for example, from effacement, media image from corrupt expropriation. Therefore, this is not a classic conversion narrative entailing a "before" and "after." Rather, what emerges here—in the context of autobiography—is a referent that has no reliable outcome as a referent, and one whose false appearance can be substituted, overturned, suspended, reversed, by a mere mistaken stroke of a pen.

It is perhaps not unsurprising, then, that in the above passage from *From Michael de Freitas to Michael X*, ghostwritten by John Stephenson, a white civil servant and erstwhile pornographer, to read any story of black converted identity literally is to read it naively, for what is being tropologically substituted is *precisely* what cannot be represented, and what comes into being as a possible mistranslation (in the uncertainty of its truth) cannot be kept apart from the disfigurations that frustrate any attempt to correct or educate it. After all, the x is a mistake that went on. And yet in all of the many writings on Michael X, the prevailing motif is that of trickery, or pretense, of an identity that is performed rather than actually believed or felt. In all of these texts, the x is thus the scene of a simulation in which Michael X, who was the first to call attention to the mistake, is repeatedly invoked as a hustler of whom it could be said that, "on a personal level, [he] did not seem to care about race," but just happened to find "himself in a society in which race was much cared about," and who, accordingly, took up black politics as yet another scam or racket.[25]

What kinds of assumptions about race and culture are being given voice to here? From what knowledge is a lack of veracity being read and judged? Do these readings fail to read the politics and meaning of tropes because they fail to recognize that conversion is never simply a trope to be converted, or do these readings succeed precisely because they already know that a failure to adhere to a black x should never be mistaken for a failure to become black, and despite the widely held belief that blackness can never produce itself politically without becoming an x?

But the most absurd thing here is how the x is taken to be both the cause of error and error itself. For it is precisely as an innocent fiction that conversion is deemed false, duplicitous, and therefore part of a calculated technique of evasion and manipulation. This holds for the above scene far more than for a black politics of innocence, considering the ending of this story is that of a murder of a failed adherent. In the main, it is very difficult to separate the "innocence" of the misreading from the controversy of the later life, even temporarily. However, there were some at any rate who read the conversion as something more than falsehood—that is, as something other than deceit; and who saw in it a truthful positing and a negation. People such as Muhammed Ali, Dick Gregory, John Lennon, Kate Millet, etcetera, all petitioned on Michael X's behalf, in the belief that he was innocent of the charges against him, and precisely because he was never an innocent, by which they meant naïvely black, even if they also tended to present this innocence as crucial to their own seduction by him. That is, they saw something substantive, believable in the x, in its efficacity, and something that complicated the opposition between falsehood and truth.

The result of this confusion is that deceit can both be the essence of justice and sincere prudential wisdom. Or, conversely, what makes black political leadership black is a falsehood that is *both* innocent of politics *and* its lawful essence. And merely according to how prosopopoeia is read as reference, that has nothing just in itself, or as radical adherence whose justness is the sole reason it is accepted. In other words, blackness cannot be converted into politics without the perquisites and prebends of phenomenological illegitimacy and corruption. Which also means: conversion corrupts because conversion is assumed to be at the foundation of any innocence that constitutes itself as a politics, which also allows one to say that illegitimacy is the only measure of black political legitimacy, its existential authenticity.

From Michael de Freitas to Michael X would thus be a text that resists politics, as it is often taken to be, but not because it is an exercise in hubris and self-flattery, but because of the racial violence that founds it, that founds it in the illegitimacy of its constitution-conversion—for there is no resistance to anti-blackness that can present itself as true to politics or law.

We almost never think of autobiographical sincerity as naiveté, and if we do think of it, it is to cast doubt on what appears to be heterogeneous. But in the interpretation of de Freitas's autobiography, the accusation is that it is black power itself that produces false impressions. Black power and the x compete in lies and deception. And error arises from the *failure to reach any understanding* of the deceit of prosopopoeia itself. In a conventional, oddly repetitive manner, we are told: any discourse that declares itself to be radically black must itself be both deceiver and unknowing. In which case, black political autobiography equates to a writing in which sincerity masquerades as truth, a deception that makes any reader who assumes its sincerity a dupe of racist culture. It is no wonder, therefore, that various readers who understand this should slam the book shut in violent antipathy, but is this not a violence that can only repeat the mistake of a literally anti-black reading? We shall not continue in this speculation; rather let us clarify some of its implications.

The patterns of error presented here are thus read as if any adherence to referentiality is itself already formed by error. The explicit linkage of conversion with error thus extends to the writing of black autobiography per se: as figure, the x suffers from the same metaphorical illusion as that of the improperly converted self—namely, its falsehood cannot be corrected by greater knowledge since the act of conversion is itself, in its very manifestation, false, not genuine. The pattern of falsification is the same as that of Hall's essential innocence in "New Ethnicities." Blackness effaces itself, disfigures itself, at the precise moment it converts itself into truth, or lays claim to truth the better to conceal the *power* that permits the very deception of truth at the outset. But the essential point in all this is that Michael X does not himself suppress these aberrations, nor does he deny the mistake in his being named x, which means that he never believed that the x was anything more than an historical or intentional symbol. As the accidental object and not the subject of conversion, he thereby puts literal quotation marks around the autos of his autobiography (which, just to remind you, was ghostwritten by someone else). There is no attempt here to make us believe in the reality of conversion beyond that of its mistakenness. Even when he decides to later rename himself—as black, as Moslem—he is unable to successfully separate restoration from the mistaken effect of a letter read as confessional trope.

Thus, it is all the more surprising to find that this mistake is the point where the literal gives way to a whole pseudology of untruth and deception. Why are these substitutive reversals not themselves errors, given that they found the rhetorical deceit that they then denounce? This question is of no small importance, as we shall see. For it will concern not only how black politics is read, but how truth and untruth, or sincerity and deception (that is, the innocence that is always on the way to being corrupted) becomes ipso facto a way of judging black rhetoric, black politics, as a deception and misrepresentation of the political as such. And, whereas it is generally supposed that the function of conversion is to strip off the form of a servile or deceitful identity in order to restore the true positive content of a regained authenticity, here the use of the x does the very opposite: it withholds the truth of a true nomination, giving us only its simulacrum, and therefore is not easy to tell apart from self-deceit. Hence, what is confusing in its representation is nothing less than the ability to know the difference between the performative dimension of tropes and their meaning or sense. The fact that the letter's message is never revealed, or that it can stand for either truth or falsity, and which will serve as the basis for Michael X's own reading of race as a *mistake that goes on*, is thus negatively made explicit by the functioning of that *from* in the very title of the autobiography. Indeed, Michael X's various changes of identity as he seeks to write himself—like Malcolm X did before him—from hustler to leader, Caribbean "red" to diasporic black, will also suggest that the x provides a prosopopoeia that has no rightful designation, as we see it move from what is literally written to that of self-expression; and from what will be literally written off as a pseudology to that of a radical black symbolism. These rhetorical reversals, by the endless repetition of the same tropological figure of deception, will keep the x suspended between truth and revelation in black autobiographical writing. Moreover, as the question of deciding between innocence and deception begins to invade *all black revolutionary politics*, we will see how criticism renders undecidable the difference between radicalization and manipulation.

When Hall decided to speak about his own experience of Michael X, as told to his 2011 interviewer Les Back, it is interesting to note therefore that he does so by means of similar oppositions: "This is why I think Michael X [whom Hall met before and during the 1950s Notting Hill race riots] is a tragedy, because he had exactly the same formation as Malcolm X, who was from the same hustling background; and Malcolm X became something and Michael lost his way."[26] Since many commentators, in their critique of Michael X, also choose to make a comparison between Malcolm X and Michael, we can combine all of them in Hall's pointed recollection of a young man who, despite wanting to be involved, and to change what was going on to black people in Britain, lost his way and made mistakes, as can be seen in the 1968 autobiography. And, of course, what is deeply implicit in all these accounts is the need to separate desire for meaningful change from the phantasmic demand for it. Alternatively, if the desire to be politically black was given to de Freitas from without then what could it possibly mean for him to perform it, or be equal to it, as the innermost core of his being? And, even more oddly, if the letter always might accidentally arrive in this way as error, then is not the letter already a diaspora in a literal sense, in the *leading away or astray* from what can only be expressed, or addressed, as a politics? As if a letter could itself present a politics in the sheer absence of error or deception? Would this not be a politics that thereby disallows any freedom to politics as will, being, or ethics? And one wherein truth becomes inextricably bound up with absolute decidability?

Thus, it is neither as a tragedy, nor as error or dissimulation, that we should decide the position of blackness with respect to the political. Indeed, I'm not even sure that "position" (a word repeatedly used by Hall to think conflict) is the right word here: my hesitation, or to a clearer extent, my suspicion, has to do with whether conversion can ever be conceived as a position—that is, a principle of articulation that connects representation to contradiction in a way that reduces being to a logic (of determination).[27] For reasons that will become clear, such logic limits contingency to a position that is merely ephemeral, or already determined by the "real" meaning it conveys. Because the x does not function as a ground or honorific but as that which produces unavoidable errors or lapses, Hall can only retrospectively read the story as one of lost possibility (and note here the odd use of the present tense: Michael X *is* a tragedy), for he already knows the outcome of the story he wants to tell, of the death by hanging of a wannabe black leader, rather than the iconic, symbolic outcome of Malcolm X's life and death— namely, a life-death whose value remains constitutive of what Michael X might have become, a life defined by its decisive orientation, rather than one distinguished by mere contingency and error. After all, it was only three weeks after the trip to England, that Malcolm X himself was killed. With the deadly figure of the x, impersonally, taking its revenge.

After all, what prosopopoeia gives—bios to the unknown, the absent— it also takes away from the autos (as self, ego, ipse, or face). Moreover, cases occur in radical black autobiography where the writing of conversion is inseparable from the deadly privations of prosopopoeia, and especially when the life so secured becomes more and more the means to the end of a being conceived as innocent, innocent of those figures that constitute human being, or persons, in the signs and images of anti-blackness.

This is why the x acts like an aporia to the extent to which its meaning always might lead astray those who desire its true meaning be revealed, and who thereby remain blind to the ways that the x might always be the double or counterfeit of such desire: on us as readers of the two fates and the two x's, falls the realization that the relation of rhetoric to politics always might result in a radical or fatal mistake, or a murderous degree of violence, and despite or because of what is sincerely meant or enacted. The x written down thus becomes an allegory of a fall that always just might be the true semblance of black politics (which as such always might be already lost or fallen).

The various readings of the autobiography do not dispute the validity of this allegory on its own terms but question its implicit presuppositions as a philosophy of blackness. But in Michael X's own account what cannot be avoided is: (i) that all forms of political involvement are nothing but mistakes, for what is represented begins by being mistranslated, and (ii) this is precisely why the anti-black world and its media must always generate a narrative about untruth, distortion, and concealment, and specifically, paint the experience of black conversion as a pseudo achievement rather than a virtuous truth.

These two points can now be summarized as follows:

(i) *X is the mistake that goes on.* While asserting that x has no meaning, Michael X, according to several commentators, made this lack into the meaning of a perverse association between black politics and law. The true meaning of the x is thus a perverse, murderous illegalism that needs must be uncovered. Black power is, as it were, just another name for a desire to usurp the place of correct white patriarchal power, which then, by definition, gets imagined to be the avowal of a truth that is repressed as such by black aspiration. But the argument does not stop there. They go on to assert that what Michael X means by "mistake" is the performative mistakenness of black power itself: black political desire is thus designated as either pre-political or inauthentically so because it confuses the desire to be recognized with mere rhetoric, rather than the resolute communication of a substantive truth. Michael X, however, never uses the word truth in the text of the autobiography, but the words "technique" and "effective communication." That what defines the political for him is rhetoric is indisputable, but these commentators, by filling in what the text of the x leaves blank, seem unable or unwilling to accept this definition of politics as no more than a doxa whose racist meaning is now being contested. The notion of black political leadership that emerges out of the encounter with Malcolm X, therefore, does not seem to equate being with truth, for truth is potentially always corrupted by its fall into the meaningless materiality of an x, and the subject is simply the one who always might fall prey to the fetishism of the letter's interpretation.

(ii) *The literal can always be mistaken.* If, as I have suggested, the x is the mistaking of language for sense, then reading itself becomes an allegory of an all too ready attempt to see meaning appear when what determines it is not what is falsely known, but the inability to tell apart what falsely appears from what does not or fails to. The objection to Michael X is therefore double: on the one hand, he is chastised for not being what he seems. And on the other hand, according to the likes of V. S. Naipaul and others, at the very moment that the x appears it is we and not him who have to believe in the reality of the conversion, though we ourselves know this lie to be the truth of anti-blackness. (The sinister aspect of these arguments can be discerned in their anti-black "innocence.") The x is thus read as a racist allegory of truth in which, we are told, blackness, as *autos*, is always the masquerade of its own *aufhebung*, and one that remains blind to the disseminating power of its own untruth in the modern doxa of black power, thereby revealing the deepest truth and untruth of its politics. This seems to substitute an ontological for a rhetorical suspicion. To read blackness as though it can only exist as a deception, and to reduce the complex textual representation of autos to a single meaning (of falsehood), only confirms the anti-blackness of most of these critics. Therefore, it is all the more noticeable that their own reading of Michael X repeats the dissimulations of which they are accusing him: on the one hand, they dismiss Michael X's own suspicion of the literal as a disguise, merely veiling, for a time, a lack of a genuine political message. And so, Naipaul writes: "Everything else was borrowed, every attitude, every statement: from the adoption of the x and the conversion to Islam, down to the criticism of white liberals . . . and the black bourgeois . . . He was the total 1960s negro, in a London setting; and his very absence of originality, his plasticity, his ability to give people the kind of negro they wanted, made him acceptable to journalists."[28] The rivalry over who possesses the truth of conversion, or who has the retrospective authority to narrate and write it, thus spirals forward in an indeterminable pattern of desire and duplicity. If it thus becomes impossible to determine the meaning of x (or even whether there was a Michael X, who is described as a man "without a personality"; "only a haphazard succession of roles"),[29] it is also impossible to know why this business of getting even with the false, with the unoriginal, is so murderously taken up with people getting the exact kind of negro *they* wanted, a want that is taken as the very proof of black duplicity. As I said, the attempt to deconstruct the symbolic authority of the x by showing that its conversion is an act, can only act out this deception by failing to convert figure (doxa) into truth (episteme), to which the attempt owes its very status as a referential act. Naipaul's repetition of the very gestures that he is criticizing does not in itself invalidate his criticism of their effects, but it does problematize his statements condemning their implication. Blackness as untruth is always the semblance of truth, bewitching what we see and what we know, even with seemingly good intention. So also is the task of its reading falsified, which loses its way in what it radically comprehends and what it fails to.

3. Innocence Lost and Regained

In this investigation of blackness, I borrowed from my two opening epigraphs to outline three fundamental terms: reference, adherence, and causality. With these three terms I wanted to propose a phenomenology of modern blackness as a political project and as a discourse. The third term, causality, has yet to be touched on in this analysis. Consequently, it remains vague. As such, it will be the focus of the second part of this study. Before turning to causality, let us conclude this first part by summing up the phenomenological principles associated with my first two terms.

Firstly, we have just seen how, in the effort to read blackness innocently, that is to say essentially, critics can only repeat, on a certain level, the notion of a non-innocent innocence. To read the x, or to apprehend it at the point where it reveals something that is so well hidden that reason is unaware or unconscious of it, is thus to see how the x makes meaningful a deceit that then becomes the origin of a new crime. A crime whose limits are marked by the murderous prosopopoeia of a misreading. In fact, the reading of conversion as deception is already prescribed by the unwillingness to see blackness as anything more than the sly means of a deception. If you want to be able to find the truth of blackness, in brief, one must apprehend it at the point where the eye cannot arrest it, for anamorphoses, deceptive appearances, delusions, are the means by which one finds it. However uncertain conversion might be, however irresolute its conviction, what is commonly pursued by these readings is an invariable association of blackness with literal deceit, which curiously resembles the initialed mistranslation of Michael de Freitas as a black Moslem brother to Malcolm X, a resemblance on which we are told he was always knowingly playing. And the various texts in which this prosopopoeia is transcribed describe a reading that can only repeat the literal mistake that led it to being misread in the first place.

As an illustration, consider the following two citations from Naipaul and Malcolm X:

> An autobiography can distort; facts can be realigned. But fiction never lies: it reveals the writer totally. And Malik's primitive novel is like a pattern book, a guide to later events. . . .
>
> Malik had no skills as a novelist, not even an elementary gift of language . . . But when he transferred his fantasy to real life, he went to work like the kind of novelist he would have liked to be.
>
> This was a literary murder, if ever there was one. Writing led both men there: for both of them, uneducated but clever, hustlers with the black cause always to hand, operating always among the converted or half-converted, writing had for too long been a public relations exercise, a form of applauded lie, fantasy.[30]

> I spent two days just riffling uncertainly through the dictionary's pages. I'd never realized so many words existed! I didn't know which words I needed to learn. Finally, just to start some kind of action, I began copying.
>
> In my slow, painstaking, ragged handwriting, I copied into my tablet everything printed on that first page, down to the punctuation marks.
>
> I believe it took me a day. Then, aloud, I read back, to myself, everything I'd written on the tablet. Over and over, aloud, to myself, I read my own handwriting. I woke up the next morning, thinking about those words immensely proud to realize that not only had I written so much at one time, but I'd written words that I never knew were in the world. Moreover, with a little effort, I also could remember what many of these words meant. I reviewed the words whose meanings

I didn't remember. Funny thing, from the dictionary first page right now, that "aardvark" springs to my mind.[31]

Here we see two differing accounts of writing in prison, of being imprisoned by not being able to write, and two accounts of learning and conversion. Naipaul's comments, taken from the 1974 essay, "Michael X and the Black Power Killings in Trinidad," obsessively condemns what he sees as the misalignment between truth and autobiography. The autos does not refer to truth or referential power, but to an identity simulated, and so is more akin to a fiction than any veridical reality. Fiction is also understood, in its own turn, as more referentially truthful than autobiography because it "reveals the writer totally."[32] Why? Because *prosopon* presents the essence of fiction; more, to the extent to which it restores the deathly, political relation between autos and bios, it shows how blackness is essentially (a contradiction in terms) a naïve form of political life. Autobiography itself, then, can be read as crime fiction, and fiction as criminal autobiography, a chiasmus that ends up revealing the impossibility of reading their difference without arbitrary appeal to skills or effective rhetorical strategies. It is this *imposed* distinction that allows Naipaul to say that the writing of *From Michael de Freitas to Michael X*, in its cliched unoriginality, reduces truth to fiction, autobiography to black power rhetoric. Then, like the stern judge he is, he says such writing can only find expression in a falsely populist rhetoric that confuses the appeal of demagoguery with that of politics, just cause for applauded lie. Which takes us back to the necessity of passing sentence on those who fail to see the difference between naïve pretense and reality, or those who haplessly confuse appearance for reality, and so are unable to flee, or escape from, clichéd unoriginality. Black power, like rhetoric, must thus be condemned as a PR exercise that excludes true inventiveness and originality. And it is because Michael X fails as a writer that his fantasy of black political leadership ends in literal murder. Writing—or language—(if we no longer identify it with style or with literature) is itself murderous of literality. Why? Because tropes are not merely indications or affects, confessions or desires, but are powers that can at any moment disturb reason. To substitute trope for the power of affect is to reduce naming to that of a phenomenology.

That is why the *mutatio mei* (radical change in oneself) is read not as a caesura or break within the self, or as a decision to escape a life that is enslaved, dependent, and constrained; but amounts to saying: black political life is marked out as a fallen, deluded life, and there is no way of distinguishing its autos or bios from a self enslaved by its own lies and deception.

That is why blackness is a fiction of *conversio* rather than the *conversio* of a fiction (and so is unable to grasp the proper truth of power, might, force, or revelation). If the former suggests duplicity, an imbecility of thought and mind, the latter implies a sudden, single, irrevocable event in the life of the mind. Moreover, if the former involves a transition from life to death, mortality to execution, then the latter implies a transition in which one imagines a break, not so much with one's enslavement, but with one's false racial pride, or envy, with the result that in conversion renunciation of all that renders blackness unhappy, subservient, reveals another, less inescapable slavery, indeed a slavery in which a new self and new form are incapable of being born again as *truthful* fictions.

In making the writerly fatally manifest, true fiction (unlike the autos) reveals the last instance of a text when it is isolated from rhetoric, for *it hides nothing*: its function is to reveal, rather than to distort. *To reveal the deadly power of language.* However paradoxical it might seem, only in fiction does death acquire a literal, immediate presence, for only fiction can reveal the prosopopoeia that ends the figural delusion that separates true conversion from false simulation, actual death from the illusory autobiographical self that "dies" in conversion. It is, in fact, the veracity of fiction that separates language from law, that reveals the force of fantasy, the weight of justice as an irreversible event. Fiction thus conceived has nothing to do with lying (representation) but is the total revelation of a truth beyond referent or justice. What makes a fiction a fiction may well be, in Paul de Man's words, a metaphor "metonymized beyond the point of catachresis"[33] (that is to say, beyond injury or error), but what makes fiction into a capital sentence— this cannot be repeated too often—is the moment when conversion tips over into the opposite extreme of a justice that cannot be reversed or gainsaid. The surest way to bring deception to an end is to cause fatal harm to its innocent pretense. Only by killing (blackness as essence, as ethos), Naipaul avers, could Michael become the true kind of deceiver he wanted to be—a point that makes crime in fact inseparable from, and fundamental to, a law separating good from bad writing, black power from truth-telling, the good *demos* from the bad colonial *polis*, the well-executed from the fatally hung.

In the case of *From Michael de Freitas to Michael X*, fantasy becomes murderous only because its lies are not understood for what they are, and precisely because the chain of political desires and substitutions is essentially a relation of deformation at once caught up and enmeshed in a series of referential blunders where the literal has no meaning as innocent. If only we had understood that the x was a meaningless linguistic mistake, people would have understood that Michael X was the falsely-black-manipulator that he always was, and black power the falsely sentimental appearance of politics and ontology. Accordingly, fiction is not itself to blame for deception, but its falsely referential reading as truthful autobiography.

This state of affairs, reassuring as it might sound on an aesthetic level, is, however, rather disturbing if one examines what it implies about black autobiographical writing. For it is not possible to believe that Michael X kills—and is killed—because he can't write without also implicitly believing that what prevents *good* black writing from becoming murderous is its capacity to convert referential illusion into a fiction of "real life." By the same token, to show that only fiction has the power to murder pseudo innocence is also, and perhaps more disturbingly, to show that fiction is never innocent, and that black autobiography can never escape the lethal conversion (of desire into act). The task of policing the false and the fallacious in order to disinter the real from the illicit would thus appear to justify every act of epistemological murder, or (what amounts to the same thing), the execution of truth by force of law. (As if actual murder were the displaced blow, not of writing, but of its rhetorical predicament.) Any attempt therefore to excuse Michael X's "crime" for the crime of his literary innocence must thereby be able to judge the worser crime of referential error. And the more uneducated, illiterate the writing, the more violent the crime of its half-converted inauthenticity. Indeed, the half-converted, like the "half-caste," remains *slavish in its immanence* because, slave though it is, it only becomes more slavish as soon as it tries to forget its slavish appearance, and especially in its promise of black liberation and mastery.

To be free in one's black converted state is thus not to break free from one's enslavement, or, in various philosophical-autobiographical texts, be free from the gaze and thought of that which *blackens* (bile, envy, spite, malice, falsehood, fiction, and so on).

Let me be clear: Naipaul's response to black conversion is unsettling, not because of his claims to know (the essences of truth, the good, etc.), but because of the implicit relation posited between black power and the obliterating power of language. If the latter stands opposed to all pathos, all essences, that is because what it corrupts, it threatens fatally, including all autos and bios. This is conversion's telos and its measure, which also procures for the self a false pleasure in what is renounced. Thus, conversion whitens inasmuch as it distracts (liberates) us from the black imbecilities that enslave (distract) us, and as it does so it saves us from thinking about how we remain mastered (enslaved) by thoughts of liberation in our desire to *be* black. This is why, contra the x, conversion also denotes a liberated enslavement, whose only thought is to escape the fearful punishment of being recaptured, reenslaved, insofar as truth is imagined to reside in an anti-black immanence. Where the text betrays a whole discourse of anti-blackness is the ways in which it suggests blackness is singularly incapable of ever assuming this linguistic power in the writing of autos, except as lie, fantasy, distortion, and displacement.

In seeking to regulate the power of radical black autobiography, both *de facto* and *de jure*, Naipaul's reading must thus overcome the moral authority of its politics and, first and foremost, by passing sentence on its referential validity. But this is a judgement that remains caught in the politics of its own anti-blackness, whose charge of racial inauthenticity itself makes fiction into an inevitable act of real racist violence. Either way, what this argument exemplarily distorts is the relation between autobiography and the fact of a man being put to death. What this emphasis on fiction thus obscures is that the desire to render truth as fiction rather than as law or judgement is itself the result of a confusion between avocation and resolution. The mind that judges innocence false should, however, be wary of taking pleasure in the cruelty of its own innocence. It does not take much to convert this cruelty into literal deception, and, in the process, substitute the cruelty that remains for the figural "accident" of a necessary execution. Above all, what cannot be reprieved is the revenge taken by reason against its own fictionality. This is so, even though it strives to grasp its own foundation in racist error. The threat of murder (to those who perform black power) is thus literally the outcome, not of reason, but of its disturbing fantasy of *the crimes committed by black pseudofiction.* Just as reason suffers for its errors, fiction must be held to account for its laws. Moreover, this error is Naipaul's: it is he who seems to equate freedom from reference with an inability to tell apart the act of murder from the writing down of it. If autobiography deceives, why is fiction any the less deceitful because it asserts its own non-deceitful rhetoric? And if "Malik had no skills as a novelist," why is this seen as a writing condemned by its rhetoric rather than one saved by its absence? On the other hand, if writing is conceived as a technē or skill, why is its exercise any the less artificial (or rhetorical) than that of law or politics?[34] Does this not make rhetoric the actual truth of politics, and murderous fantasy just another act in the game of conversion, whereby truth becomes (or has already become) that which allows the execution of any black subject?

"Malik had no skills as a novelist, not even an elementary gift of language . . . But when he transferred his fantasy to real life, he went to work like the kind of novelist he would have liked to be."

The novel in question, left unfinished at the time of Michael X's death, is thus read as key to the events that follow, as if the life as politically lived can only be believed as fiction, or in fiction, in whose referential system bios can only express itself as the repetition of a murder that can neither be avoided nor known for the autos to absent itself from law. This then would be a "before" that always comes "after" and in a way that binds the literary to the failed conversion it narrates: "Writing [literally] led both men there [to murder]," we are told, or rather black political life can only repeat the false ideological tropes at its origin, and by virtue of the crime that only blackness naively performs as innocence. Consequently, Michael X's attempt to tell his story can only repeat the story of its political failure, or how he has been fatally duped by black power rhetoric. The proof of this is in the sentences he writes and the words by which true opinions are murdered by popular tropes, self-knowledge by prosopopoeia. It also follows that any attempt to make autobiography into political belief, or into the innocence of such narration, will also prove to be a reading duped and thereby seduced by antiblackness. But in the case of someone who is ignorant, and who therefore cannot tell a lie from literal truth, or truth from a lie applauded, why is self-expression seen as necessarily imaginary, and especially when there is no way of distinguishing the literal from the referential no matter how fatal the mistake, and no matter that any presumed innocence may inevitably turn out to be truly murderous?

What seems to justify this belief is the implicit analogy between writing and law, trope and the passing of sentences. Naipaul provides no definitions of "good" political writing but the implications cannot be missed: words in black power autobiography are never innocent because they inflict the injury by which language succumbs to a form of blindness or error. Whereas autobiography fails *because* it cannot recognize the rightful priority of trope over innocence, white over black, fiction over fact; so, in turn, black power narratives fatally confuse their resemblance to doxa with a fantasy of difference. It thus becomes impossible to know what is fact from what is fiction, what is sincerely black from racist fantasy, and so on. The failure of Michael X's conversion is not, then, a failure to align truth with politics, but a failure to know how black political truth produces itself as falsely autobiographical rhetoric. And in the wake of such confusion, it is impossible to tell apart rhetorical murder from state execution, black literary death from fictional error. Accordingly, Naipaul not only condemns Michael X as a writer, but all those who "substitute doctrine for knowledge, and irritation for concern . . . all those people who in the end do no more than celebrate their own security."[35]

This type of admonition may be considered moral, but I think that what is on display here is an obligatory series of rhetorical codes that desire us to make a choice between two kinds of judgement.

The first, the referential (which is still with us, at least insofar as race is presumed to be the primary referent of black writing) is that black autobiography corresponds to *lie* and *distortion*: it derives, as we know, from the belief that *blackness is never innocent*,[36] which relies on an opposition between black life and the life of politics. To encounter blackness is thus to encounter the force of a certain *conatus*[37]—that is to say, an untruth that distresses us because we find it defective, and which we are not sorry to see slip away because, in hurting us, it allows us to correct reason and passion as mutual deceptions. The relation of black life and politics is thus para-doxical: from the autos justifying conversion to the seduction of black power fiction, justice is not the essence of blackness but the laws that seek to correct its rhetorical subversiveness.[38] The converted self condemns itself, not simply because it is wrong to crave black pleasure, or excitement, but because these various diversions are never ends in themselves. So, what is wanted from black conversion is not so much a return to a happier, prior state, but a truth that can be less slavishly enjoyed as the *conversio* of a fiction, and so justifies the violent occupation of a mind already under siege by itself; and that is why black conversion often feels like a state of war and an execution, via the long detour of a *pseudein*—the ardent pursuit of a black achievement of subjectivity. Here the historical reality of black subversion, of revolution, becomes, by way of interpretative metaphor, the literal representation of a black pseudology, which then, historically, becomes the figurative truth of black inferiority. The historical irony is that it is the historical truth of anti-black racism that is disavowed, or its interpretive veracity is now hidden by politically correct rhetoric. Naipaul accordingly bewails what he proclaims to be an absurd truth, and which he says is contrary to reason: that it is racist to deny the truth of racism. Only racism, it seems, can speak the actual truth of race by negating the falsities of black rhetoric.

Yet that initial figure—that blackness is always duplicitous—is already at play in the claim that only fiction can represent the truth of black literality! From this, it remains undecidable whether the x is therefore a figure of corruption or is evidence of a corruption that must be grasped the better to realize its art; or again, to tell a racist truth—that blackness is insincerity— is to know truth as the absence of figure, and at the same time to show how blackness is always absent from true judgement and law. The effect of all this is to make innocence and knowledge, undecidably, the experience of an encounter with a non-innocent innocence that, rhetorically, cannot speak or recognize harsh truths because it persists as a figural cover-up. This would suggest that racist discourse can only establish a *proper* relation between fiction (truth) and fantasy (rhetoric), by making anti- anti-blackness the sign of a sincere rhetoric (anti-racism consists, after all, of an aspiration that cannot free itself from racist rhetoric, since it most typically seeks not only to announce or signal itself as pro-black but as anti-white, solely so as to expel or exclude the latter—just listen to Michael X!).[39] Hence to clearly and distinctly perceive blackness, one must make its rhetoric subservient (so that there can no longer be an absence of truth) to the real, historical reality of racist fiction. It is this argument that sets in opposition, down through the centuries, the reality of blackness as an absence in which truth becomes degraded, mimicked, and so dangerous. This vision also persists, unwittingly (or perhaps innocently), in black political discourse wherein racial truth, instead of being recognized as lie and fantasy, is associated with deliverance and redemption. Despite the rhetorical inversion, blackness is still inevitably represented as a deceptive truth that can never know itself as innocent. The asymmetrical relationship suggests to me that the belief in race as the absence of figure is itself a figure for the most racist of tropes.

The second, much more recent idea of anti-black judgement, which comes directly out of the counterculture wars, is that of *false revelation*. The new cultural politics of blackness (code: black nationalism) is thus seen by Naipaul (and others) as an abstract claim to identity. But for a clearer understanding of this claim, we must note here that its politics, for better or worse, also represents a refusal of the various ways in which blackness has been thought, and consequently read, as revolutionary. And although Naipaul does not focus on the rhetorical forms of this refusal, I want to suggest that this refusal has everything to do with the still unresolved relation between truth and rhetoric in his account. If we define ideology as an enunciative position, and race as its meaning, what emerges in Naipaul's reading is a certain tension that relates to how blackness must be read ideologically, that is to say, rhetorically, as a falsely "imposed" (a dismissive word for how ideas interpose themselves and so necessarily distort and falsify the clear and distinct outlines of phenomena) doxa. Let's pause for a moment on this question of reading. At issue is the fundamental undecidability of blackness as both *parousia* and *eschaton*, or advent and telos. In Naipaul's reading of conversion, what is stressed is its point of completion rather than its movement. He does this because what interests him in conversion is *testimony*: as event, attitude, and condition (*or* mastery, possession, rightful ownership). He is interested in its power rather than in its sincerity. The passage from return to rebirth can be read in this way: we seek conversion by mastering the racial obstacles to our being, and once they are overcome, blackness proves intolerable because of the enslavement it produces, or recollects. We must get away from it and its excitements, which poison the whole mind. *Epistrophē* (return to the origin, to the self) is then the awakening experience of the self's return to its source in whiteness (its purity and perfection in the depths of our being). *Epistrophē* is the whiteness of black being newly revealed. And anti-black *metanoia* (change of mind) proves to us that a change, or break in being, is worth both the cost of repentance and renunciation. The hitherto enslaved black soul discovers via *metanoia* the whiteness (the power) that is its stronghold. The source and the caesura are linked then, not by the urge to be wiser, purer, less slavish, but because they allow us to show and know how each act of conversion makes a white racial immanence conceivable and so achievable for the falsely black.

One cannot help but note that these emphases—in Naipaul's reading of black power—are to do with mastery (of immanence, experience, otherness, and ipseity). The historical reality of racism led Naipaul to question the idea that ideology is ever finally determining of blackness. Such theoretical *certainty*, which consists for the most part in the belief that black thought must begin by ruining the doxa through which it is understood, not only introduces the idea of a cause that is curiously absent from its effects, and yet is nevertheless determining; it also loses sight of the ways in which white ruination is the *first stage of black subversive art*. When racist fiction is the means to black freedom, perhaps it is a good thing that the autos should be so deceived? If the meaning of the political can be falsely imposed, that is because its ideology is already presumed to be referentially stable, whereas fiction supposedly is not. But what gives the game away is the very opposition between fiction and rhetoric, which tries to correct racial lie for mistaken truth, an opposition that can only repeat the error that this distinction is designed to correct—namely, that any substitution of knowledge for ideological error is itself already a sign of ideological certitude.

In this sense the problem of conversion is not simply one of epistemology or ontology. It might be argued instead that it involves a wager that one deludes oneself into imagining is all about the winnings (of a liberation from race), rather than the true passion and fear of a black truth and world.

Clearly, what is at stake here has something to do with the status of literal conversion. The passage from Malcolm X above teaches nothing more clearly than that the act of conversion can never be divided between knowledge and naiveté, autobiography and cognition. While there is something innocent in the desire simply to write down words without knowing their meanings, being able to scribe, and then being able to read aloud what has been inscribed, is clearly a moment of radical transformation: "I'd written words that I never knew were in the world," Malcolm X tells us. The writing down of words consists, then, of a continuous labor that is itself the production, *in potentia*, of an irreducible—or nontotalizable—transformation. Does it matter whether the convert sincerely believes that conversion *changes* him, or that it marks a caesura within the self? Or whether he knows the words written down? If he did know them, he certainly would never have been enthralled by the changes wrought in writing them down. Which is to say, that writing (as we understand it here, having nothing to do with belief or self-expression) and its inscription has no other existence than its eventfulness; more precisely, what is elaborated in the very movement of inscription is a world that has no existence, or alibi, outside or prior to being written. Because inscription precedes any concept of meaning or sense, it is not possible firstly to know the thoughts that attach themselves belatedly to the words as recollected. This is a *conversion*, in brief, that unsettles all the distinctions between truth and sincerity, ideology and politics, autobiography and fiction, that Naipaul is trying to make. Yet what is it in Malcolm X's narrative, in fact, that sounds so revelatory, and whose discovery lies neither in a naïve faith nor in an amazed awareness, but in the slow, demanding act by which he, as a copyist, fills in page after page as he mentally translates his own inadequacies into thoughtful potentiality? Represented both as an absence, a blank, and a profusion of punctuation marks, the x of black power is both expressed and presented through this impossibility of knowing the words that one needs to learn. Thus, what is being inscribed here is not true discourse, nor the fantasy that writing is an exercise of power, but that of a tabula rasa—a blank on which nothing is written but the pure potentiality of writing itself.

No wonder that such a writing should so readily begin with the lexical form of words and finds there the expression of both what one is deprived of and what one might become, since deprivation and potentiality are, consequently, both implicated in the new sense of a world accessible in the turning back on itself of an iteration that has no predicate or signification as such. And where what is then uttered or named is a positing-power inscribing itself as the sheer inexpressible potentiality of language. This is a writing whose initial relationship (or lack of a relationship) to cognition recalls the mistaken writing down of an x in a Birmingham hotel. In terms of autobiography, then, the letter is not the effect of a desire, nor the telling trope of a *prosopon*, but an inscription that is nothing but the very movement of its being written and, as such, evokes neither a literal nor figural awareness. This passage, I think, supports my reading of the x as a mark that can neither be posited nor negated as either deception or manipulation, and in whose emancipation from context and law Malcolm X proved himself to be the ultimate reader and messenger.

But, you will say, what then of the politics of conversion? Malcolm X, unsurprisingly perhaps, refers to conversion as a kind of disciplined self-observation. Here, return and rebirth are both signs of how the convert turns away from diversion, or what it means to be diverted from thoughts that enslave you, or how *conversio* more generally denotes how the mind is diverted from contemplating private miseries because it cares about nothing else than the contemplation of (white) entertainments or pleasures. This suggests that there is nothing more wretched than diversion; or is it that without the diversion of *conversio*, the self cannot grasp its wretchedness? It is not enough to be persuaded of the truth of *conversion*. One must be wholly compelled by it, and then one will see a whole transformation of the moral life and of the soul occur. Inner freedom, for those who experience it, makes thought the master of desire, and beatitude the true object of happiness. Likewise, in such a gaze one turns away from the world as is (in its inequities and injustice), the better to fold in oneself in one's passions, fears, desires. Do not look at others; concentrate all your attention on yourself. One must know oneself. But how does one separate oneself from blackness so as to return to it? How does one recover one's black essence? One must know oneself. But, for Malcolm X, self-knowledge is not defined in terms of *existentia* but in terms of an *x*; each act of conversion is therefore not a return from the weak, the false, the inessential, to the originary, the true, and the essential, via a dialectics of racial mastery. Rather, *conversio* resides in a return to the self-positing prosopopoeia of a letter that cannot be doubted and that therefore acts as a promise, for all that may be comprehended lies in the word, the letter, "x." (*This implies that every word and letter is potentially an x.*) A gaze diverted from the x cannot know or be persuaded as to the risks of diversion, and if the self cannot know diversion, he cannot resist it or liberate himself, which is the true telos of a radical black immanence. One must know oneself. But any positing of the x as a principle of identity is incapable of knowing or becoming it without reconfirming its meaning as falsehood. And the failure to convert that recognition is the proper definition of the x's politics.

Make no mistake about it. What else does it mean to be converted but to enjoy the pleasure of a striving toward only one aim: a vigilance that is

infallibly self-aware, *or* a mind hopelessly miserable and dejected and oppressed by external quarrels and diversions, carried away by all the false
happinesses and consolations of white law and judgement. Attend to what
you are not in order to become what you are. See oneself as one is in order
not to reach the self as an object of knowledge. For white knowledge blackens thought and being in the depths of its enslavement. Why? Because it is
the coming-into-being of what one is not (n'est pas). As Pierre Hadot rightly
notes, here logic and rhetoric have become the slaves of conversion, and the
recovery of one's original nature (via *epistrophē*) is a liberation from the racial perversion in which one ordinarily lives, and a drastic reorientation of
one's whole being (*metanoia*).[40] Hence the need for a withdrawal that is also
a form of renunciation, and a return that is also a kind of faithfulness to the
good. But the truth of conversion is not the unconcealing of an essence. The
form of its truth is itself an event of concealment that consists above all in
the transcendental concealment of blackness as knowledge and as truth.

Consequently, it is the point at which he consents to his ignorance that
Malcolm X is able to dialectically possess the knowledge of what he does not
know. But this does not mean that ignorance has been dispelled, for what is
striking about the passage is the way in which the actual world of the prison
gives way to the potential world of the x, as each letter in the tablet signifies
nothing but the necessity to keep on reading and writing, and this is why, according to Malcolm X, the arbitrariness of a word like "aardvark" is proof
of both the power of memory and the endless potential for self-delusion.
Iteration is not meaning but an event; it is an occurrence—a repetition—
whose sheer positing force converts nothing and everything, and, as such, is
the place (the non-place) where language becomes radically contingent as it
touches on a politics: the politics of the x as *non*-event. To read this passage
as naïve literalism, as Naipaul seems to suggest we do, would therefore be
to read naively, ignorant of the moment when, with the appearance of the x,
black writing becomes the expression of what might be possible in the writing down of a world.

What does the x bring into being? Nothing but the act of writing. As such,
it should not be confused with ego, knowledge, or *mauvaise conscience*—for
it is neither guilty, nor innocent. This also means that it is prior to any intentionality or affirmation, regardless of their provenance as will, resistance,
desire, or identity; or their recognition as name, situation, or status. What

matters is the act—for whoever is enigmatic enough to commit to it—that declares the x to be the emphatic manifestation of pure mediacy, understood here as the pure potentiality of its violence. The implication is that the x, as autos, signifies something other than presence. In addition, it has nothing whatsoever to do with reconciliation, non-identity, ipseity or testimony.

We have thus come to a paradoxical set of conclusions about black power discourse. It is only when it frees itself of any ideological certitude that it acquires the positing power of language. But in freeing itself from popular untruth, black power can only convert itself into deadly prosopopoeia. And the proof of that, argues Naipaul, lies in the writing of *From Michael de Freitas to Michael X*; writing here means an autos without reason or doxa which, in turn, signifies a subversive world of mere mimicry rather than genuine truth. In this sense, paradoxically, Naipaul's challenge to black writers of diaspora is how to learn to write ignorantly, or how to free blackness in every sense and from sense. For only then can black power possess the knowledge that rhetoric or politics gets in the way of. But can what is at stake here really be reduced to that of when innocence becomes corruptible? And what of Malcolm X's discovery of an x that makes every word falsifiable since every word makes us equally incapable of telling apart the positing-power of language from that of meaning and sense? The necessity of making blackness discontinuous with (non-conforming to) sense, calls into question the veracity of Naipaul's separation of truth from trope. Which is why Malcolm X insists that black power has a truth. For it shows the world as it is: a world in which anti-blackness is so obstinate and fanatical. But this is a positing-power that is constantly disavowed, for nothing is surer than the reverential power of anti-blackness. As such, it allows us to return to our opening question: To what extent is modern blackness founded on difference, and ill-founded as différance?

Philosophy and Innocence

But there's no such thing as an innocent reading, we must say what we are guilty of. . . . A philosophical reading of *Capital* is quite the opposite of an innocent reading. It is a guilty reading, but not one that absolves its crime on confessing it. On the contrary, it takes the responsibility for its crime as a "justified crime" and defends it by proving its necessity.

It is therefore a special reading which exculpates itself as a reading
by posing every guilty reading the very question that unmasks its
innocence, the mere question of its innocence: *what is it to read?*
Louis Althusser, *Reading Capital*[41]

My opening two epigraphs forced us to say: "there is no going back to an innocent view of what it [blackness] consists of."[42] Hall wasted no time in saying that for black Marxist theory to advance, it has to read dialectically and
so *guiltily*. Why? Because there is no philosophical reading of Marx that is
not already guilty? According to Althusser (above): to read (Marx) one must
unmask the innocence of reading [*lessen, herauslesen*] itself. To read Marx
philosophically, therefore, is to expose the guilt of innocence and the guilt
that masks itself as innocent; or, to use a famous phrase of Marx (as read
by Althusser), Marxist dialectics *must show the structure (the kernel) hidden
(overdetermined) by the mystical shell (of phenomena)*. One must show how "*the
mystical shell is nothing but the mystified form* of the dialectic itself."[43] To ex-
tricate structure from its mystified form—whether the "kernel" denotes "fusion," "link," "level," or "*ruptural unity*"—is to know a "good" (contradictory, heterogeneous, guilty) reading from a "bad" (mystical, abstract, falsely
innocent) reading.[44] Since all philosophy is inevitably an experience of guilt,
and innocence cannot be read without philosophy, all philosophy is, then, a
dialectics (of the most guilty *or* the least innocent) that teaches us how we
are necessarily deceived by the mutability of sense, desire, praxis, and experience. Here, what Hall learns from Althusser—and especially from his
pivotal early work, *For Marx*—is that dialectics concerns structure and not
essence; not because the role of structure is really more essential, but because it shows how phenomena, even when they appear to be simple, disguise themselves in this way as deceptively simple appearances. Here again,
a dialectical reading not only guiltily confesses what it itself unmasks; it also
disturbs any naïve semblance of essence or phenomena. Wherever essence
is presupposed, what must be deduced from it is how form works *against*
the structure that determines it. And here, finally, is the key point: for dialectics to be a criterion of truth, it must reveal how "essences" mask a more
complex idea of structure, a mystification that, however, is usually false, for
structure gives no indication of its quality, which, for his part, Althusser always describes as an active causal development of fusion and rupture.

The lessons that Hall takes from these points are fundamental: We can know nothing of blackness; and yet people spend their time trying to define what it was or can be. But on the other hand, the choice is not a simple one between innocent error (false dialectics) or erroneous innocence (abstract ideology). That opposition remains merely theoretical. The rule of Hallean dialectics is more nuanced, supple: *"there is no necessary correspondence"* between essence and phenomena; that is, black practice and struggle are articulated in terms of *effects* that may not appear in a unified or rupturing fashion, and hence cannot easily be traced back to their origins, no matter how overdetermined, or masked, those origins are by empire or capital.[45] To apply this rule then is to know that homogeneity may not necessarily be ideological, and the same applies to dialectics; if rupture emerges in an over-determinate way, however complex, one is entitled to ask why "over-determination" may not mask its own ideological concealment? To try and bring something back to the authority of first principles: Is that an essence laid bare, or a masquerading exculpation? How does one think this return without abolishing or usurping its authority as reason? Dialectics may object in vain, but if all reading is guilty—and guilty in its innocence—then any reading of *Capital*, say, or of Marxism more generally, must innocently cover up its guilt, and guiltily reveal (in a purely formal way, far removed from any struggle) responsibility for its own assumed infallibility.

In this second part we shall see why this problem remained central to Hall's Marxist reading of blackness and why it concerns the relationship between thought and causality.

4. Dialectics Regained

What does a "Marxist reading" even mean? It involves "two radically different reading principles" (suggests Althusser):

(a) Firstly, one that corrects "absences of vision" [*bévues*] by revealing or *recognizing* them for *what they are*.[46] Reading, then, is always the mark or sign of a suspicion; and dialectical philosophy is the most suspicious of philosophies. Those who are blind remain naïve, if not ignorant, of what they fail to see; their blindness must, it seems, be converted into knowledge. The task of dialectical thought is thus to know how blindness *functions*. In thought, in ideology; and the political history of struggle. And yes, indeed: to explain why, in any regime, *what cannot be seen* can be both *infinite* (which is to say: has no external frontiers), and *definite*, because it is limited inside itself, in all its determinations, "by what is excluded from it *in it* by its very definition."[47] In philosophy, it is no different. In the end, idealists are not blind because they have no glasses, but because they fail to recognize that idealism is itself a blindness of *method*; likewise, if Marxism is the scientific conscience of method, that is because Marx allows us to go farther and to grasp the structural *Théorie* that also eluded him. Therefore, to read dialectically is to have "eyes [that] are clear," eyes that can perceive the consequence of method, knowledge, history. A good Marxist always has good eyesight: for they see how methods, depending on whether they are informed by science and not ideology, signify principles that allow us to recognize both essence and phenomena in the truth of their concrete determinations.

(b) Secondly, Marx allows the reader to see how the "obscure field of the invisible" structures and informs phenomena: in such insight, ignorance is no longer simply *opposed* to vision, but lines seeing itself; that is, obscurity is less like an incapacity, or a metaphorical incapacity to see, but more a non-vision inherent to vision itself, a blindness structuring our very ability to see—like an anamorphosis requiring us to squint and evaluate differently. It is "this necessary and paradoxical identity of non-vision and vision within vision itself" that is no doubt key to the overdetermined—and ultimately philosophical—ways in which politics fuses with economics, say, or ideology distorts the class system, or the state functions as a heterogeneous system when placed in opposition to various levels of civil society. At the heart of these essential truths is the belief that only dialectics can articulate these blind spots—these ruptural unities—at the heart of all social structures and their established forms of contradiction.

In *For Marx*—or *Reading Capital*—what matters is that one doesn't read too fast or too slowly, for then one understands nothing. To give one example, contradiction should not be read in terms of an abstract schema, for it is composed *only* of actual structures; for example, rebellions, protests, strikes, and so on, always articulate, in fact, new terms and relations (in capital as structure): "it is not just *the terms* which change, it is also *their relations themselves.*"[48] Such changes show directly how each rupture in structure functions as the un-asked-for "answer" posed by "the unuttered *question*" of capital itself.[49] The suggestion seems to be that each rupture is, or rather originally was, a signifier separated from its meaning: for its "unuttered question" refers to denegated elements. Whereas, for Hall, the value of Marx's reading lies not so much in how it makes us see the omissions of what is ruptured, say, but in what is thereby revealed by struggle, and by the methods of struggle, and by what then is determined by it, but never rigidly, as a new articulation of social or economic forces. The point that Hall insists on is that forces are not separable from structural effects on the one hand, nor from articulate practices on the other. Articulation, in the genuine sense of the word, can only be recognized in how people believe, doubt, love, resist; that is, express, represent, cause to signify their relation to structure.

Before pursuing this further, however, perhaps it might be worth recalling that Hall introduces his "reading" of Marx's 1857 "Introduction" to the *Critique of Political Economy* (and the scare quotes are his) by saying that all reading "reflects my problematic, inevitably."[50]

The word "*inevitably*" first requires our attention for it returns us to the question of what it means to read Marx dialectically in both the form of his truth and untruth. Now, Hall's persistent critique of, as well as his enthusiastic commitment to, *For Marx*, concerns how Althusser reads Marxism. Hall accuses Althusser of *hardening up* Marx's dialectic, and in sharp contrast to Marx's "the concrete in thought."[51] What is at stake here is not acuity, or blindness, but the *décalage* (rupture) by which being opens itself to thought. For Hall, Althusser is "guilty" of assuming that categories produce social relations "in the first place."[52] The result of this is that theory becomes the hard element of politics, and dialectics becomes the charismatic essence of thought. Everything seems to turn here on how reading produces and reproduces itself *as* thought. Dialectics cannot make a fool wise, but it can make them blind, blind to reason, which only makes being wretched; the real a beggar to thought.

The political element of this dispute consists, above all, in who has the last word on the ends of Marxist thought (or its beginning as knowledge or concept). One reads Marx only when one is finally able to tell apart—convert, break (punctuate)—true Marxist philosophy from the false, the guilty scientific version from the ideologically innocent. The dispute will also consist, as we shall see, in a dispute over the politics of ideology itself (as science, as praxis). Hall writes:

> Any theory of "theoretical practice," such as Althusser's, which seeks to establish an "impassable threshold" between thought and its object, has to come to terms with the concrete reference (which in Marx proceeds from the *"working up of observation and conception"*). [Hall's emphases][53]

Working up: this phrase indicates the direction Marxist theory should be travelling in; its "'given' points of departure . . . [should not necessarily be the economy]," for every phenomenon is the "sum of many, prior, determinations."[54] Again, Hall's emphasis is on unmasking the "essential relations" *behind* the necessary but mystifying inversions assumed by the "surface forms" of capital—a method that Hall identifies as Marx's *scientific* dialectic in *Capital*. Latent forms should not be viewed from the lofty air of theory, therefore, but grasped actively, concretely, as phenomenology. Those who are capable of grasping phenomena dialectically, on the basis of breaks and punctuations, are not simply naïve Hegelians; only on the basis of a unity of distinct, differentiated elements can thought be linked to phenomena (connected to different levels of interpretation), and can different social forces be grasped according to their political, practical measure.

To give just one example: that of the last instance. Confronting the issue of the economy as the *cause* of sociopolitical events, Hall said, in a 2012 *Guardian* interview: "When is the last instance? If you're analyzing the present conjuncture, you can't begin and end at the economy. It is necessary, but insufficient."[55] The concern here isn't simply with how time and being do or do not conform to the "absolute predictability" of an "already witnessed truth."[56] The problem is not simply one of determinism, but one of conversion. Or whether conversion is itself a principle of error, and one that leads inevitably into dogmatism. For Hall, each conjuncture is formed by multiple levels, forces, and interests, which entails a wide field of contingent acts and events whose foundations are never simple, and whose non-simple origins, in their *différances* and consequences, do not necessarily correspond with the economic. To determine the economy in this way is inevitably to confuse cause for consequence. Here, cause actually becomes the effect of an effect (that of a fall before the origin), and effect can only *present* itself as a cause that has no end other than that of error or deception (original sin). Just as Althusser (whose 1962 essay on "Contradiction and Overdetermination" is pivotal here) concludes that "neither at the first instant nor the last, the solitary hour of the 'last instant' never comes," Hall also says, "I got involved in cultural studies because I didn't think life was purely economically determined."[57] Which will also lead him to say, "We have to acknowledge the real indeterminacy of the political."[58] Note the word *real*, by which is meant the practices, the experiences, of struggle, struggles that animate and expose the indeterminacy of political power. What then can be said about the relation between "the real indeterminacy of the political" and its determination as politics? Whatever the real's attribution or its effects, one is never able to draw a reliable or predictable dividing line between political power and its determination as politics. Yet without struggle—whose possibility can only generate further errors or fictions—it is never possible to politically decide which one of the two possibilities—necessary or insufficient—will be the right one. "Right one" being the question as to which struggle will yield up those effects that stand out in nothing more clearly than as ruptures in the structure.

This, then, is Hall's Marxist philosophy of reading: it does not begin with an answer given to an "absent question"—"the *absence of a concept behind a word*"—but denotes a question asked from the point of view of phenomena themselves; their concrete relation to reality.[59] Consequently, whereas Althusser begins with the absence of a question, an absence that in effect punctuates structure, Hall refers to the positing-figure of absence; precisely, levels, elements, concretions, and so on, that refer to how absence is articulated. Furthermore, it is this nuanced difference that expressly enables them to read *Capital* anew, and to read other Marxist philosophical texts by reestablishing the letter and the form of their ideological expression. Above all, such reading enables both to produce, in the precise sense of the word, opposing insights into how Marxist knowledge is itself produced, and how it conceives of knowledge as a *production* that "takes place *entirely in thought*," or, mutatis mutandis, takes place as *the différantial last instance* of the concrete in thought.[60]

As far as this opposition is concerned: Hall says that Althusser's later work sets up an impassable boundary between thought and the real (*das*

Reale), and one that confuses Marx's *mature* method with theoreticism. Thus, Althusser's own commentary on the 1857 "Introduction," which also strives to limit Marx's relation to "ideological" philosophy: "It is impossible to leave a closed space simply by taking up a position merely *outside* it," he writes. In other words, to distinguish what is outside thought does not necessarily lead to a better grasp of what is thought's outside (for in general "the real *problem* to be posed" may get lost in the effort to distinguish object from the form of thought[61]). But whereas for Althusser, the real problem posed is always that of structure, for Hall, in contrast, the real is always complexly situated as *my* problematic: that is, thought is fundamentally an *auto refractive effect*; it is always mediated by one's autobiographical historicity as an individual.[62] This is why differences "must be grasped as real, differentiated processes in the real world," which is where true complexity lies.[63] And this is why Hall ends his own essay on Marx's 1857 "Introduction" with a metaphor of illumination (and thus a figure of conversion): "One of the traces of light which this text [the 1857 "Introduction"] captures for us is the illumination of this surprisingly late moment of supersession—of return-and-transformation."[64]

I do not intend to list all the meanings of "supersession." To recognize overdetermination is inevitably to encounter what supersedes it, to enter into conflict with it, to affirm or disaffirm it, but always to understand it, to argue with it within oneself, for social forces (from which overdetermination derives) is a notion arrived at between determination and indeterminacy. This, at any rate, seems to be the focus of Hall's important 1974 essay on "Marx's Notes on Method: A 'Reading' of the '1857 Introduction,'" in which it becomes evident that there is no clear separation between difference and the constraints of method, as can be seen in the following passage:

> Each element appears as both *determining* and *determined*. What breaks this seamless circle of determinations? It can only be deciphered by reading back from the apparent identity of the categories to *their differentiated presuppositions* (determinate conditions).[65]

From this random and somewhat difficult passage, I should merely like to draw the following hypothesis: that reading backwards from the apparent to its disguised presupposition decides everything. We can only see what is determined as apparency, even when each element is assumed to be determining. To read back from phenomena to the form of their presupposed *condition* is thus what Hall singles out as the "methodological and theoretical key" to Marx's method.[66] Since this method is not merely a dialectic among others, and since it is singled out, in its "concrete specificity," as the point where thought meets its end in reality, it might seem that it is precisely this reading that distinguishes Marxist philosophy from some "essential dialectical law."[67] It is a reading of dialectics as prosopopoeia. By virtue of this movement, which is to say, the tracing of "real relations" as "phenomenal forms" (the words are Marx's), Hall is thereby able to be trace real relations back to their presupposed conditions.

But it is still difficult to avoid the question of what is being presupposed and what is being derived from such presupposition (and consequently embodies the outcome desired)?

Hall has described his position as one of strategic realism: "there is no law which guarantees that the ideology of a class is already and unequivocally given in or corresponds to the position which that class holds in the economic relations of capitalist production."[68] Elsewhere, he refers to certain *"tendential alignments"* between class, thought, and identity, albeit ones that should never be read as ever purely determining or as already there at the outset.[69] From this it follows that the relation between structure and force, however heavily dependent on finance or the economy, has to be more *nuanced* in its grasp of political conflict. It's a move that has not gone unchallenged, with some critics seeing this as evidence of Hall's own theoretical "innocence" vis-à-vis capital. Alex Callinicos, in a 2014 essay, goes so far as to say: "it is striking how innocent Hall's writings are of political economy"; a lack that reveals Hall's "theoretical original sin."[70] How innocent, then, is innocence? Innocence, it seems, is the one thing that is never innocent.

Yet it is odd (it seems to me) to accuse black theory of being theoretically innocent because of what it *knows* (even if the apple eaten has a price fixed by capital). Clearly, after such knowledge black theory can never be innocent in the same way again. Since, as Callinicos points out, no Marxist theory can take place without knowing political economy, no theory of Marxism can ever claim to *be* Marxist without first being innocent of capital. Which also means: no theory can become Marxist without acquiring knowledge of its own culpability; black theory is deemed guilty, accordingly, of having been naively unaware, or of having already transgressed, such knowledge. To "blackly" know Marxist theory, in short, is to be inordinately innocent. Put slightly differently, black Marxist theory is shameless only because it has yet to sin knowingly; and because it fails to recognize this—in its unashamed innocence—it cannot know its transgression, and thus is already culpable, already seduced in being open to sinful temptation. This would also suggest that its meaning is always already *fallen*; a fall that literally obscures, as it were, any claim to know itself as absolute and self-validating. If before the fall there was theory without difference, after the fall, the thing that falls is black Marxist theory, for it has no reachable innocence of which theory can be asserted. Its lack has no corresponding coherence as theory in history, time, or language. Thus, by definition, it is always first and last. It is *first*, in brief, because, like the strange fruit it is, its flesh ripens onto the expiration of its contents, and whose skin envelops nothing more than an absence blossoming as capital. But it is also *last*, because its fall is never able to reach theory, for like the hung, irresolved, obscene thing it is, it is held up by the tree of nonexistence and thereupon hangs suspended before the guilty law of its being. Now, is it a coincidence that Callinicos uses allegory to tar Hallean dialectics as a mask of deception—however "theoretical" he strives to dress up his unfavorable opinion?

But why is guilt and innocence yet again the ground on which this battle is being fought? Doesn't the remark not also imply that black Marxist philosophy can never be entirely innocent, and precisely because naiveté and final truth are always mysteriously intertwined therein? Doesn't the remark not also mean (both at the level of theory and at the level of politics), that to theorize blackness as the *indeterminate* trace of the political is to theorize it naively because one doesn't realize that, from the start, it is already expressed, and represented by a guilty truth that supplements it, and decisively? As if the language of political economy existed before the fall of blackness, only to see the latter emerge like Eve from Adam's exposed rib. The greater the innocence it seems, the purer the transgression.

But even this allegory is haunted by radical impossibility, and for two reasons. Hall outlines his project as a Marxism *without guarantees*—that is, as a careful teasing out of warring positions within capitalism itself. If anything, this is a reading that refuses all attempts to derive conjuncture from theological forms of thought (I am thinking here of eschatology and natural law). Above all, the way his work develops implies that a conjuncture can never be fully made sense of by theory: logically speaking, its "cause" is never simply an end to be determined by the economy. Structural antagonism, in short, is never simply a product of capital. *There is no necessary correspondence between class conflict and ideological position*, as Hall reminds us. This is why he says that blackness today offers us in fact a new kind of critical politics in which we must, he says, plunge "headlong into the maelstrom of a continuously contingent, unguaranteed, political argument and debate: a critical politics, a politics of criticism."[71] Moreover, we must do so knowingly, that is to say, guiltily, for there is no standard for establishing or evaluating what the outcome of such a debate will be. Hence, what we must always and necessarily do is *fight* all ideological idealisms (in their convictions, *ressentiments*; but, above all, their claims to know blackness as a *homo novus* experience or vocation).

To take a stand while knowing that there is "no straight, unbroken path" between *difference* and *capital*, between "a given category or relation . . . [and] a specific mode of production."[72] To an outstanding degree, black political struggle reveals "antagonisms [that] refuse to be neatly aligned" or coalesce into any settled form or organization.[73] From these remarks it follows that if blackness is to be thought then we must distinguish it from the idea that (i) it occupies the truth of its politics, or (ii) that its politics can only be truthfully defined against structure (which is marked by endless plunges and irreducible contingencies). Here the point is not so much to tell a black truth, but to develop a criticism that has no guarantees as truth. The situation suggests that blackness only *becomes* politically black in its difference from politics. Or, in the case of *conversio*, when it becomes an x. However, if criticism is always the exercise of a politics, at least insofar as criticism has a politics, why is criticism given precedence here? Does that not make criticism appear as the discourse that always speaks the truth of blackness? The reader is asked to decipher blackness as politics, but Hall himself suggests such desire is always deluded because blackness has no origin prior to language. To go beyond this impasse, Hall was thus compelled to contest such notions. But did he resolve them? To answer this question, we must return to the question of the political as Hall himself went on to do throughout his late work. And here we will see why innocence—which Hall will later refer to as his own unguarded moment—will increasingly become the whole problem, at least insofar as it has a relation to criticism, the void, and the blackness of politics.

Indeed—to speak plainly—we have already shown why innocence cannot be understood as simply naïve knowledge. Let us briefly summarize why. First, innocence is not immanence but its retrospective illusion. Hence it makes no sense to see blackness as enslaved to its own potentiality, which it then confuses with actuality. Second, it is said that Hall was insufficiently Marxist in his grasp of alienation, but to me this amounts to a premature reading. One is not exploited in so far as one is black, but how one represents oneself as black is the sign of one's relation to capital. For some, this is a mere sociology of investments but, as we have just seen, this loses sight of the dialectical battle in which blackness arises as a social value in the midst of society; or the protracted and complicated ways in which it is misrecognized and valorized as a n'est pas, and precisely because its place in the structure cannot be fixed or determined as a politics. This battle is very dialectical and infinitely nuanced; it presupposes as a condition the imposition of a certain valorization that Hall has well-described in *Policing the Crisis*[74]—in a word, racism is not merely a social fact, involving a substantialist theory of value, or even an ideology, but a relation to difference (that is not at all symbolic, or synecdochal); or if we prefer, it is through conflict that difference emerges as a passionate desire for affirmation and/or subjection. Third, blackness is valorized and determined insofar as difference is also the very possibility of its praxis; whence the ways in which certain differences are judged to be more aberrant than representative in their character; this explains why the relation of blackness to reality is grounded in the work of a ceaseless phantasmagoria, while abolishing any possibility that it may have in the political organization of truth. Consequently, difference explains why blackness is valued and why it cannot be affirmed as the source and origin of value, for it is merely a material means through which difference acquires value as capital. If blackness does not have this evaluated power, it cannot be recognized as difference, and for that reason it must be reproduced if it is to be maximized as an embodied-capital-relation. If the slave does not work, his or her evaluation as slavish cannot be turned to appreciation in the hierarchical chains of capital.

Hence instead of opposing truth to deception, one of Hall's major insights—which for me is why his work has been so influential—is that all racist discourse is naïve but never innocent: naïve in the wish to separate racial truths from structures of antagonism, and non-innocent in the way that struggles over the meaning of blackness are also always multi-accented struggles over representation. This, then, is why blackness is read as a void waiting to fall into being; and why absence is its *veritas*, the truth of its literal, historical being. Perhaps this is also why blackness, historically speaking, has never been the direct echo of the ideological claims that would seek to either condemn or redeem it as something real in an act of understanding. If blackness is no more than its representational history, that is because, as figure, it is always disfigured by the rhetorical attempt to present its history as if it were an ontology to be unveiled. Racist discourse, in brief, is always an allegory of misreading. And in that allegory, it is always blackness that deceives through the deceptive faculty of prosopopoeia.

In his theoretical texts, Hall gives us an answer to this problematic by way of a symptom and a word: *innocence*, and its reading-by-conversion. But perhaps it *is not this* word that needs to be exculpated, but the blackness that it masks, whose différance must be produced as always originally fallen, transgressed? Let us continue by pursuing further the idea that Hall's work proceeds from these two opposed terms—différance and dialectics—less to explain them than to complicate them.

Today, these oppositions might seem unduly antiquated. Or, anachronistic. I do not have a position on this. I am only concerned with how Hall invites others to think blackness: as one of the fundamental ways in which people live their "imaginary relationship to the real conditions of existence" (Althusser), and because of this, how people "acquire consciousness of their position" (Gramsci) as subjects in ideology. Invariably the concern remains the same. To say that there is no single reference that defines "this term 'black' within a particular semantic field or ideological formation," is also to say that "structure" does not explain the power of the trope. And so the material means of its production should not be abstracted from the "constative resonance" of its politicization.[75] Indeed, the prosopopoeia of this figure seems to stall or suspend the notion of the political itself as metaphysically understood, for example, as the loss or gain of authority, power, and leadership. The black critic's task consists, then, in comprehending the continued, constantly changing ideological life of its expropriation. And indeed, it is not the ostensible meaning that must be recognized, but how it realizes the absent, unspoken term that surreptitiously defines it by naming it. Where this expropriation manifests itself, blackness is *constituted*.[76] Contrary, therefore, to the claims of a certain Marxism, "the word ['black'] itself has no specific class connotation," Hall argues, for blackness "exists ideologically only in relation to the contestation around those chains of meaning and the social forces involved in that contestation."[77] Again, the point is not translation *or* conversion, but to show how blackness is the result of a "constant unending process in the representation of its significance," Hall concludes.[78]

Politics, as a field of meaning, is marked by (intersected, crossed by) ideological conflict. As certain meanings wither away, what endures gives rise to new struggles and meanings. Before discussing the black politics of such dialectics in detail, let us clarify in all its aspects this idea of contestation.

5. Dialectics Lost

The knowledge of radical innocence also performs the harshest mutilations.
Paul de Man, *Allegories of Reading*[79]

In Hall's essays on diaspora and identity there is always an observable point where autobiography intrudes upon the theoretical narrative. One of the more poignant examples is his reflection on the cost of coming to England as a postwar immigrant: "Diaspora is a loss. It's not forever, it doesn't mean that you can't do something about it, or that other places can't fill the gap, the void, but the void is always the regretful moment that wasn't realized."[80] "So being displaced, or out of place, is a characteristic experience of mine."[81]

There is thus a connection between absence and diaspora, which is to say: absence is a *metaphor* of diaspora; and this figure of out-of-place-ness, of being always apart, of a gap that can never be filled, this relation is by no means a direct one. The regretful moment is present everywhere, in every concept and representation, but it is always displaced and dislocated, even in relation to the diaspora that institutes it. Referring to "black culture and the ordinary life of black people," Hall says, "I couldn't get to it"; "I could sort of imagine it and relate to it by empathy, but I couldn't *be* of it."[82]

This confession—in its enigma and ambiguity—does not lie in a failure of imagination. Rather it concerns the difficulty of conversion. *Nothing is more black than this feeling (that what we call black is never ours).* There is an alterity to blackness in which, in a purely formal, or desultory way, one is, from the first, marked off in opposition to it, precisely in the face of its ineffaceable and unassumable quality of being. To know that one could never belong to it, or *be* it, is the clearest promise of its unreachability, and consequently what can never be declared or possessed are its commitments or obligations. Neither reason nor imagination can prevail. *Just as the imagination never wholly overcomes such alterity, the n'est pas undoes the toils of empathy* (the dream, or image, of what can never be known nor possessed). The result is a knowledge that precedes guilt or innocence, or at least the consciousness of guilt, and one that is neither true nor false. And this is the mystical basis of its (blackness's) authority.

We never arrive at our black origin in any way that makes it present. We recall the past as something already lost; the present as the echo of its tracing, in whose flight we never arrive at presence as such; as if diaspora were the point where all identity is lost, starting with the very identity of loss whose regretful inaccessibility is a clue to the secondary effect of our aspiration rather than its originary presupposition.

There is a sense that our blackness does not belong to us, and that we wander about forced to bear the trace of these missing elements, knowing that any attempt at symbiosis would be false, a vain way of being, given the impossibility of finding an adequate model for what we are not, and could never be. But even here, might Hall's denial of the very category of identity, far from being a denial of blackness, actually be his attempt to grasp its inherent ambiguity? The fact that to know blackness is to know what is withheld, and that it takes on an ineligibility that distresses us.

Here's another autobiographical anecdote that has become something of a leitmotif of Hall's late work.

> It is a story frequently retold in my family—with great humor all round, though I never saw the joke, part of our family lore—that when my mother first brought me home from the hospital at my birth, my sister looked into my crib and said, "Where did you get this Coolie baby from? . . . This was my sister's way of remarking that, as often happens in the best of mixed families, I had come out a good deal darker skinned than was average in my family. I hardly know any more whether this really happened or was a manufactured story by my family or even perhaps whether I made it up and have now forgotten when and why. But I felt, then and now, summoned to my "place" by it.[83]

Let us examine this thought of being summoned. What is being represented by these words and their recollection? They show the affect, not of being summoned, but of being darkened both by what is said and what isn't; of being occupied, retroactively, by what cannot be spoken. All things necessarily follow from the affect of being placed—yet strangely unaddressed—by this *après-coup* that is both unforgettable and uncertain.

But perhaps this "afterwardsness"[84] is not the affect of a memory (Hall cannot be certain whether it happened or was manufactured); perhaps the affect of the sister's words only ever lies in what they do not say, a n'est pas that only later becomes affecting, if not representable, because what it manifests is so obviously uncertain. Maybe, but at least this story shows how indeterminate this "who's this" is, even if it is not clear whom this addressee is that, in being summoned, is darkened by the disclosure. Even if we suppose that it is the trope itself that darkens, because it cannot be determined as addressee, or referent, what subsists insofar as the words spoken are unforgettable, is the sense of being possessed by what they express but that remains, enigmatically, inarticulate, uncomprehended. Therefore, in whatever way it is conceived, whether as affect or enigma, prophecy or judgement, what cannot be forgotten are the traces left, not by the words spoken, but by what cannot be read or interpreted as the affect of being summoned into place by them. The anecdote thus presents a painful memory that is itself an undecidable mix of recollection and fiction. It does not take much to know that what haunts both mind and memory occurs as if it were a slip, an innocently malicious gift that leaves unreadable traces, that makes explicit the disjunction between what is remembered and the thoughts and feelings that are summoned by it. To receive such a gift is to be disinherited-arrested by it. To assume the language of blackness, Hall implies, is to discover a kind of shibboleth, or pharmakon in which the poison given is the effect of a harmless remedy, wherein innocent arrival becomes the point of a knowing condemnation. The danger is not one of arrival as error, however. It is also the knowledge that, for all his innocence, the black *infans* is no longer, and can never again be, the same as his family, but is always the darker, the "Other one."[85] The darker one has no face. Instead, he is disfigured, defaced by virtue of this racial a priori. We have only to imagine the darker one to form an opinion as to their goodness, or culpability. The unloved one always means the darker one. And the darker it is, the easier it is to judge or condemn it.

One will always be summoned by this judgement summed up in a single phrase—who's this. And one will never be able to explain or truly know it, for as soon as the black infans is summoned by these words, he knows that his blackness can only grow darker, as if it were a stain, spreading out over a lifetime. The return home thus turns out to be a deprivation, a loss of innocence and of any sense of belonging. The scene is one of violence and grief, defeat and effacement. To that extent, the language of diaspora is a figure for how blackness acts as a caul that is more like a poisoned robe, that shelters insofar as it wounds, and that protects by making visible—and so excessively—the poisoning veil of one's illegitimacy.

No matter how often this story is told, therefore, the affect of the sister's words cannot be enclosed by an autos or a bios, since there is no "I" that can arise from the "who's this." There is no other outcome than the affect of being condemned by being summoned. For what the words make present is an outcome that precedes thoughts, words, and being, and consequently, to that extent, articulate an outcome beyond time or memory. For although we can never be certain about whom is being summoned, what we can never doubt is the n'est pas that presents itself as if for the first time, and that happens interminably as if for the first time. Therefore "nothing" happens, but the infans is affected by the fact that it never quite happens and never stops happening, as though by being claimed by it, he is exposed to a *who's this* that keeps on happening (which overwhelms time in the recollection of it).

There is no assurance (*securitas*) to be had. The black autos is always the belated affect of a prosopopoeia that darkens both time and being, for its bios is a presence without presence, whose obliteration is concealed by the doubt that it never happens because it always does. Our autos thus can never be written as an "I," for the "I" has no place, but remains unaddressed, emblazoned. One is placed (summoned) by it not because of who one is, but rather because one is intruded upon by a judgement (negrophobia) that renders the "I"/infans n'est pas.

So, when the sister uses the metaphorical term "Coolie" to state a literal meaning (you are not like us), it is to assert, with some violence, what it feels like to be summoned into being by anti-blackness. To be so chosen is to be disparaged. Her words say to the black infans that he is a "this" whose difference embodies a difference that is neither true nor proper. This is the destiny to which the darker one is intended. You cannot forgive childish innocence for this knowledge, but neither can you allow it to forget this judgement and its memory. No, for these words address what is not being addressed by her—this summoning is neither in the body nor the soul, but what it reveals changes the meaning of both. What they announce is the devastation that precedes every dark birth. For Hall, what therefore cannot be determined is how his sister's words darken, interminably, his upbringing, but also how they cause feelings of misery to be attached to existence itself. This is also confirmed by the difficulty of writing them. For writing itself is now darkened, and every decision to write as autos (or bios) hears these words echoing *insofar as they affect the darker one* that Hall imagines he now is (and is not). The power that arms these words also makes us lose our power over them. Perhaps blackness has no right to consider itself legitimate. But the n'est pas it contains has nothing to do with value or rights. To be so vested is to be undone. And to be corrupt in one's innocence. Yes, blackness is unquestionably different, for there is an underlying deceitfulness about it. But blackness is not only illegitimate, it is also an "is not," and this n'est pas may constitute a force, an affect, but never a politics. This is why blackness has no literal referent. Its only referent is contestation; and its only advent is the absolute exception for those rendered by it. Moreover, the implications of that confusion convey a wrong that cannot be named, an error whose word is lacking. Anyone who tries to find a destiny in blackness will find reason paralyzed by the disdain of misunderstanding. There is no blackness other than *that of an abandoning community*. With respect to that community: what cannot be situated within it is the autos as the bios of desirable life. And the difference between being named and being cast out only consists in the fact that the mind is more likely to confuse the figural darkness of diaspora with that of a language forced to darken its own languageless innocence as deadly prosopopoeia. Moreover, the effect of being mercilessly denounced by being welcomed is in fact perfectly consistent with the black politics of diaspora: the always too dark infans, like the postwar Caribbean immigrant, occupies the hearth as an outsider, and he or she is the point where inclusion is only realized by the violent exclusion of the alter, who is seen as nothing less than an error of being as such. To be so designated is to be translated by being mistranslated, wherein one's autobiography becomes *a mistake that goes on*; but it is also to come across a judgement and a narration—that is to say, a story frequently told—that makes the referential impossible to tell apart from deception, fiction from fantasy. From this knowledge there arises the sense that blackness is never identical to itself or with its meaning; and what sets apart blacks from other humans is the successive nature of this n'est pas that seems endless. The story frequently told, in other words, not only dramatizes divisions within blacknesses, it also betrays an injustice that is absolute because irrevocable. For if race confers some kind of irrefutable, irresistible knowledge in those claimed by it, the price of that reclamation is often exacting and cannot be easily borne. To ask who is ever truly, literally black? is thus to see difference as something fabulated, not given; a discourse expressly imposed, not a destiny achieved. "Black is important historically," Hall suggests, "because it was the bit that was never named, never spoken. . . . So all of us in different ways learn to be black."[86] Here *metanoia* opens the self to a greater dereliction. That is why the decision to name that nameless prosopopoeia (who's this?), and the strange, regretful logic by which one is summoned into place by it, is never one's own, but a sign of how one is rendered readable by being obliterated, and first and foremost by the redoubtable, irreducible effect of being summoned. For what kind of knowledge is this in which the assumption of a culture collapses any distinction between knowledge and dereliction, harmless joke and poisoned inheritance?

There seems, therefore, to be a contradiction between the idea of blackness as an unnameable, unspeakable summoning and self-knowledge as an achieved identity. Hall would seem to equate diaspora with an unassimilable *autos*, while his family would insist that blackness names a collectivity that *establishes no necessary correspondence* between inclusion and being-with. Inclusion offers no inner security but punishes bios as life. Such a task precedes both summons and obligation and makes being hostage to the world. It is, indeed, like being brought to a closed door, yet being told all the time that only you (the darker one) can open it. But at the same time, you are told you cannot enter it, for, on account of your darkness, you must not enter. For the darker one, the open door is nothing but an impasse intended just for him. For the darker one is himself the door. There can be no vestibule, no threshold, when one's darkness blocks the way. But, in a way, these positions are both shaped by a summoning that also expiates and doubtless also mistranslates, for to acknowledge the darker one is to acknowledge the foreignness, not of black life, but of its irredeemable election. At the same time, one is necessarily and intimately bound to it, under the title of a merciless fate. In other words, like Oedipus, blackness, too, is the cause and realization of an offense that he has no knowledge of. No matter what he does, he can neither escape it nor fulfill it for this x, however it is suffered or tarried with, exists at the heart of the subject, and will haunt him his whole life: "I felt, then and now, summoned to my 'place' by it." To the extent that the x can never be named or spoken of (and so is not simply a metaphor or a prosopopoeia), its strangeness cannot, as such, be represented, but remains uncertain as to its knowledge and truth.

And what then of representation? Representation remains a key term for Hall, which he thematized from his earliest forays into cultural studies to his later essays exploring black art and visual culture. In any case, in "New Ethnicities," Hall proposes a reading of representation as part of how subjects are positioned, and the term is invoked, as if in passing, immediately after a discussion of blackness and ethnicity. "Representation is possible only because enunciation is always produced within codes which have a history, a position within the discursive formations of a particular space and time."[87] Representation is the medium or means by which these codes enter into history, giving representation the role of an arbiter by which these codes themselves become historical, but also—and this is difficult—these codes cannot be historically meaningful without being represented—that is to say, enunciated—which gives representation a special and eminent position in the making-known of a blackness that would thereby be not a position among others, but the new conjuncture that is just its meaning as a politics. And just as this politics is determining, blackness appears here as an articulation that has no fixed or definitive code, but only appears through its disarticulation, or as an excess that might just appear as a resistance to historic codes or meanings; what interests me here is what allows blackness to be both what transgresses and what conforms (in history) to its conjunctural representation.

For example, whatever the facts of the matter, Hall has always been insistent that difference *like* representation (and we shall come back to this simile) is always slippery: "Difference, like representation, is also a slippery, and therefore, contested concept." From what has been said above, we know that difference is related to the new political struggle of blackness in 1980s Britain. But we also know why the resistance and ambivalence involved in being politically black explicitly relates to the writing of autobiography. Indeed, the connection between autobiography and the "death" that converts-sublates it has been our focus throughout. We have seen why the black autobiographical subject is dismissed as vain, uncertain, murderous, and so on. But we have also seen how truth is whitened, as it were, by the innocent murder of black rhetoric, and simply because, as we have said, *conversio* was simultaneously able to bring about a new black critical politics and subvert it. In short, we have seen why murderous innocence is intimately embedded within the question of black autobiography. For what the autos lacks is precisely the innocence of its bios. And only dialectics can name this guilt/gift. The notion that blackness can somehow be read as *conversio* is certainly related to its slipperiness. "I couldn't get to it," writes Hall. "I could sort of imagine it and relate to it by empathy but I couldn't *be* of it." But what is it that makes blackness so slippery? Is it slippery because it is black, or black because it is slippery? Or, put slightly differently, is blackness slippery because we can never know it, and so contrary to our ability to return to it? Anyone who tries to convert because they cannot return to the self are just obeying an imaginary injunction, rather than revealing an original essence. Anyone wishing to *become* black will thus find an autos that can never be grasped as bios, because this is a conversion that is both enough, and never enough. Let it be supposed that the thing that causes blackness's slippery effect must therefore differ from its representation or articulation, for the thing that blackness is (its n'est pas) is also the cause of both its slipperiness (with regard to immanence) and its failure (with regard to liberation). And if representation is said to be inherently slippery, then it must remain so even in its definition. Therefore, what is contested, insofar as it is conceived to be slippery, differs from both its representation and its slipperiness, and thereby cannot simply be represented as Hall seems to propose. How does one take hold of this slipperiness without making it representable and so meaningful? In a sense, paradoxically enough, it could be said that Hall's attempt to grasp the difference inherent in blackness cannot itself take hold of blackness without contradicting and/or suspending it, and which needs must let go of the undecidable difference we must analyze here. Dialectics, in brief, is always the product of a deceitful prosopopoeia. This much is evident from the above. But what arises from this slipperiness is decidedly more complicated. In "New Ethnicities," Hall elaborates the problem as follows:

> Difference, like representation, is also a slippery, and therefore, contested concept. There is the "difference" that makes a radical and unbridgeable separation:

and there is a "difference" that is positional, conditional and conjunctural, closer to Derrida's notion of différance, though if we are concerned to maintain a politics it cannot be defined exclusively in terms of an infinite sliding of the signifier.[88]

Between simile and metaphor, the distance at first appears so wide as to be unbridgeable. Yet the two figures manage to exist side by side without one being reducible to the other. But what is it that allows one to pass from one to the other? Is not the figure of politics what allows this focus on each separately? Or is politics precisely the literalization of the *gap* between them that allows difference and its representation to coincide in a new racial and historical meaning? First: difference is divided between the two tropes. But it is also what prevents the two from being separated; to maintain difference as différance, it must be grasped dialectically. For its position lacks meaning, or subsists on false meaning; the *infinity* of différance must be made *definite* in its movement if its meaning is to be determined as true (as a political truth). Considered as trope, difference is unbridgeable, but when considered as a politics, it overcomes separation. The thing that makes difference positional is the same thing that makes différance the very essence of politics. This is because dialectics brings to an end, or allows us to get hold of, the endless slipperiness of the signifier. In this way, then, différance suddenly becomes a question of deciding between two differences, the unbridgeable and the conditional, and between two rhetorical figures, that of simile and metaphor; and politics is the attempt to draw a line between them. By using a simile to propose two metaphorical differences, Hall's purpose is to characterize a difference that cannot be situated between, but only within difference. There is blackness only to the extent that dialectics has the power to determine its referential movement through sublation, and, by the same reasoning, grasp the endless comprehension of its n'est pas. But if politics arises from différance, to the extent to which différance emerges from the very sliding of signifiers, it is impossible to say whether politics is literal or figural: from the moment there is politics, a metaphorical difference is implied, and whenever there is metaphor, a literal interpretation of the distance between differences is slippery (or figural) from the start.

Hall thus situates his plea for différance firmly in a double bind: the realization that difference is no more than separation straightway becomes linked to two antithetical and exclusive metaphorical modes that can only be thought as unbridgeable analogies. It is also suggested that the juxtaposition of these seemingly unrelated ideas can be sutured (by politics): in order for différance to be maintained it cannot be thought as irreducibly infinite, for the endless slipperiness (of figure) must be checked by the limits of the finite. The latter is the province of the decision to limit what dialectics referentially knows, the former that of an endless slipperiness *within* the tropological or the referential. And once again politics takes on a constituent role that has consequences for the signification of difference, which henceforth appears both *like* a rhetoric of conversion and a statement of fact. The analogy being proposed here, however—and it is here that we must modify our understanding of the relation between difference and representation—is itself a slippery example of trope sliding under meaning, and what slides away is not what is representable, but a signifier that has no content, or to explain it more clearly: différance is not something that is separately added to meaning, or something that is engendered in the space between identities that then has to be bridged; it is what makes all such totalizing separations impossible. And it is this very designation of an irreversible, undecidable limit that constitutes the x of politics, and which the infinite play of signifiers and of difference comes to represent, through endless contestation.

A critical black politics, in other words, is what is added to the scenes of différantial struggle in order to mark the lack of a signifier that could close the set. The endless slide of signifiers would thereby be brought to a halt if politics were a closed set, rather than that which acknowledges the impossibility of closure. With this emphasis, one would naturally expect Hall to go on to extol différance as the x of black politics, but no; instead, he argues that if politics is to be maintained, it cannot be thought exclusively in terms of an infinite sliding of the signifier. Why then does he choose to present blackness as a difference that brings to an end the différance of difference (which must occur if there is to be a politics)? Perhaps différance is too innocent or too knowing a notion? Or perhaps it is precisely too slippery a notion that can never be converted to the political as such—that is, in its wake comes too unconstrained a fall, or a plunge down slippery slopes too precipitate?

The drawing of a line between simile and metaphor, concept and notion, is not only inexact and slippery; it also subverts the very possibility of situating a difference *between* différance and politics. For it is precisely the impossibility of bridging this separation that presupposes the slipperiness with which the difference *between* differences proceeds. And just as this slipperiness must complicate the opposition between différance and politics, in the same way, différance must necessarily exceed any appeal to represent it as a politics, for différance just is this slippery work that cannot be grasped *as* a politics: the x of différance is formed when blackness always falls short of its claim to be a politics, and therefore it cannot be represented as such, whence its deferral and complication of any dialectical logic of politics.

Although *différance* apparently represents for Hall the future of black critical politics, his treatment of it does seem to illustrate yet another unguarded moment that must be corrected. I want to suggest that the root of this correction is not difference but the need to maintain it as a *black* politics, which unsettles all the distinctions that Hall is trying to make. My understanding of this is as follows. In the first place, one cannot help but be struck by the appearance of Derrida in Hall's texts, and their successive references to a weave of differences, which is itself densely woven out of different terms. Furthermore, there exists in Hall's reading of politics, at moments of its own conjuncture, what we might call a politics not of blackness but of two tropological seams that can no longer be seen as the work of politics or can be thought of as a praxis that therefore falls short of politics as Hall defines it (as a play of identity and difference). This already departs from what he describes in *The Fateful Triangle* as: "the interplay between difference and différance—that is to say, the contradiction *inside* the very signification of difference rather than, as was the case previously, the fixed us-and-them polarization that opposed 'their difference' (which meant nationalism) to 'our identity' (which meant modernity)—is how the politics of cultural identity is now playing itself out on the global stage."[89]

Immediately preceding this citation, Hall cites the following passage from Derrida's "Différance" essay:

> [Différance means] the movement according to which language, any code or system of referral in general, is constituted historically as a weave of differences. It is because of difference that the movement of signification is possible only if each so-called present element is related to something other than itself, thereby keeping within itself the mark of the past element, and already letting itself be articulated by the mark of the future element, this trace being related no less to what is called the future than to what is called the past . . . not in order to see opposition erase itself but to see what indicates that each of the terms must appear

as the difference of the other, as the other different and deferred in the economy of the same.[90]

In the previous reading of the anecdote of the darker infans, the question was not: What would it mean for blackness to be made present in its absence? But rather: there is no way of knowing it. All that is comprehended in the word "black" is what one is not. And to understand that is to arrive, dialectically, at justice. For racist judgement is always the law (the mask) of the n'est pas. It should therefore be read as a conversion of which I know nothing, and which knows nothing of me, but all the same it comes as a command by which my being is allotted and obligated. And yet Hall seems to be presenting such responsibility less as an elusive prosopopoeia than as an example of the efficacity of political judgment. And the very certainty with which he does so invokes différance, not as Derrida has it as a trace-structure that is the quasi-transcendental condition of difference itself, but as the moment wherein politics and signification meet in any system of representation. Consequently, différance can only be thought as a contradiction waiting to be comprehended as part of a dialectical logic, a logic that sees the political as the *limit* of difference, rather than as the trace that precedes the very distinction between politics and representation. So, too, the implicit belief and idea that différance can only be expressed as a politics if it becomes the object or thought of a new conjuncture.

Does this not make the political function as a kind of last instance? This insistence on contradiction already extends the Derridean text, as does the frank reference to the political as the end of différance, as if the one logically followed the other, or as if différance were something like an innocence for making politics representable as such, or the mode through which each and every difference can be thought, and so on ad infinitum, as a looser, more permeable, and more porous weave of positionalities; rather than as an elusive mode of thought in which positions can only repeat one another in a nonbinary, undecidable logic.[91]

My hypothesis is that this positioning of blackness, on the border of politics and history, (and thereby also, as we shall see, on the border of both difference and its theory), is what makes it so elusive, or slippery, for Hall to deal with directly without reproducing the binary terms in which différance is thus transformed into a politics that is either open or closed, bounded or liberated. Far from bringing about a different idea of black cultural politics, such knowledge prevents it in fact, for what we see is a blackness forever caught in the fall of its representation. And, indeed, before coming back to blackness as such, Hall finds himself glossing Derrida, Gramsci, Althusser, et alia, in ways that necessarily complicate the supposedly clear relation between différance and representation. For the present, I cannot give a clearer explanation of this impasse.

This then turns out to be the focus of Hall's overall approach to black cultural politics, as can be seen when he characterizes it in "Cultural Identity and Diaspora" (1990) as an *implicative* relationship between representation and enunciation, a relation that is "never complete, always in process, and always constituted within, not outside representation."[92] He further illustrates this idea as follows: "Practices of representation always implicate the positions from which we speak or write—the positions of *enunciation*."[93] Identity so to speak never finally corresponds, or is never identical to one's enunciative position, but emerges from within it, and, in so far as we are able to articulate it, this identity will not be of the same order as that by which we are affected, insofar as being affected requires us to act. Whosoever seeks to practice identity in an absolute or definite sense will come up against this knowledge that he or she only acts in so far as we are constituted out of our incessant differences which cannot be explained fully. Difference is what we think through and necessarily work through, precisely because what we are is not infinite, or immutable, or absolutely determined. And it is this insistence on our finite difference that represents, says Hall, the true politics of cultural identity, although we practice it with the most intense passion and ignorance.

Moreover, we ourselves can never undertake such politics at the level of thought, for in our life, in the representation of our life, in what life affords us to desire and to know as life, what we enjoy is often a fiction or phantasm. Should anyone want an example for a clearer understanding of the matter, I can think of none that would adequately explain the point better than that of the unconscious. Hall never really rigorously explores this aspect, but let us admit that there can be something within us that can neither be thought nor be conceived along the order of a *self*-representation, but in respect to which our order and existence, say, betrays a non-relation; or else, ends up as a more split enunciative position that necessarily employs difference as a lexis of redoubt and self-doubt, by which one suddenly experiences one's difference as a desuetude, or as something tainted, lost, beyond civility and language. Likewise, to that extent the n'est pas is a truth that dialectics must, and cannot, say. For we are equally incapable of knowing and not desiring to know it in equal measure. For the fact is that blackness always names a n'est pas rather than a praxis or method; and so the aspiration to be possessed of it, to be possessed by a power that is itself n'est pas, often times results in the feeling of an incommensurable opacity. Indeed, any black person can experience this when they realize the truth of what it means to be irredeemably black. To constitute an effective social critique, at least according to the exigencies of that moment when the hateful essence of a culture becomes evident in one's being, is to come up against a truth beyond reason, or at least a perpetual suspension of judgement, in which one knows nothing but doubt, delusion, or uncertainty, but in a way that renders reason futile—*This impasse is something like an hallucination*: here the autos knows itself as a body, but bios cannot be given life. On the contrary, what gets recognized here are the regent signs of a fervid self-effacement.

We have seen examples of this in Hall's texts, despite politics being erected into *the* meaning of black autobiography. From this we may conclude that the x represents an error—a prosopopoeia—that cannot be named, and so cannot be substituted for difference or dialectics. A point that Hall insists on. But as we have also demonstrated, in attempting to name the difference that blackness is, he often reduces it to an identity that has to be *consequential*.

As we have seen, in his iconic 1988 essay, "New Ethnicities," Hall presents a "significant shift": "a significant shift that has been going on (and is still going on)."[94] This shift means: "dominant regimes of representation" are undergoing new forms of contestation. This may seem obvious, but I am interested in the implied word *continuously*. Otherwise, how does the struggle "to come into representation," or the struggle to gain "*access* to the rights of representation" become politically effective?[95] Hall's answer, conjuncture, seems empty and right, because it amounts to saying: it is because new relations change the terms of relation that they serve to distinguish a *given* essence from changes in the structure—in short, struggle induces us to think differently as a way of marking such distinctions (or, more generally, we can say that out of contradiction emerges new structure).[96] In becoming-black, as it were, including the end of a certain essential subject, whose innocence presumably was never innocent nor essential, I never simply replace or substitute a preceding phrase, but I *"displace*, reorganize and reposition the different cultural strategies in relation to one another."[97] Hall seems to recognize this as a form of questioning that is no longer guilty or innocent, for it has made innocence into the most disturbing source of power. Innocence makes all of us guilty, and so forces us to choose a different meaning than resistance or complicity. Innocence is no doubt what makes us rebel, and especially when we are forced to justify the justness of our former naiveté.

This gesture on Hall's part—to describe the significance of new shifts within blackness and thereby, in short, its politics—is opposed to any reductionist or formalist account of justice. Hall's proposal is that, during the 1980s (and the question of time and difference is pivotal here), a new conjunctural shift has led to a new critical object: blackness now means; that which is neither simply *in* representation nor *outside* of it: such is the meaning of the word "conversion." Ideally, it means a rupture *and* an abandoning, but also a new distribution of power. Let's call it this newly emerging machine that changes being in its depths, that alters beings' relation to both world and judgement. I know being's truth not only through reason, therefore, but by illuminating being's darkest obscurity. To say that this machine is fantasy is clearly ridiculous. But to say that autos and bios both have had to submit and compromise with the machine is also wrong. But this is precisely what Hall is saying of the conjuncture, if we follow him. And thus, the machine becomes the phantasmatic driver of the onto-political; it is both the "weakening or fading away" of everything that formerly stood as the post-imperial essence, and denotes a new way of thinking rights, violence, and justice in the post-colony, or more generally the black world.

But if blackness *never is the last instance* of politics (for it is always the trace of différances that it can never stand in for or exhaust), it cannot also be said that this structure *befalls* an essential innocence. For if blackness is the explicit designation of a conjuncture through the transformation of force, or structure, at what moment is it ever clearly definable as innocent? Such a notion implies that the relation to innocence is both what defines politics as a new expressive force and what leads to a new positionality. Innocence would thus be the moment through which violence (this would be the force that rends) represents and repeats itself as politics, or as the politics of politics. And politics then has to be necessarily innocent of politics for difference to determine itself as innocently violent. The shift *from* innocence to difference thus literally becomes the politics of politics.

These curious positions within the theory of position (which become no less curious when Hall refers to his own autobiography) help formulate the question that I have wanted to pursue throughout. To put it bluntly, I want to say that Hall's insistence that the *essential* meaning of blackness is at an end forces him to announce the end as a positionality, an event, by contrast, which whatever its importance for Hall's thinking, or at least his complex engagement with Marxism, opens some difficult issues for the articulation of position-as-event.[98] And even though he wants to avoid the binary form of thought that he associates with capitalism, he also ends up in spite of himself in the uncomfortable position of someone trying to think difference differently but who can only, *consequently*, not think what makes blackness different *in its* difference. All the more so when the n'est pas (because we are obliged to convert it into différance) must be thought dialectically. Thus, not even différance can escape the machine. Yet this, clearly, turns out to be the point: blackness is and is not innocent *because* it is not always possible to separate its phenomenology from what is no longer thinkable as phenomenology. Under the pressure of this uncertainty, the ambivalence (enigmatically always both innocent and knowing) of the machine thus returns with a vengeance in the political articulation of those who would be black beyond any access or right to its inconceivability. My broader suggestion would be that no such (innocent) truth could be articulated, and no contestation constituted; blackness is, then, the very figure of an erasure—the prosopopoeia of an x— that is never persistent or present in its erasure. It is the same with its ending: which can only disturb, fissure, those exclusions that despise and seek to condemn it. That is why to say that blackness brings truth to an end in illusion, and regardless of evidence, law, or judgement, is equally to be deceived by the liberatory ends and means (and the disturbing trace) of its innocent power.

Coda: The End of Blackness (in its Innocence)

The foregoing raises, as I see it, a question of nonarrival—not what is deferred, but whether it is possible to know, when one has or has not arrived. Every idiom of arrival—that of truth, knowledge, conversion, justice, diaspora, the last word or instance—is by its structure, by its desire, prevented from ever securely knowing itself, since there is always the possibility of an error that will never be read as such, and yet that will come to be what enables the very expression of completion. If there is no theory, or politics, entirely free of this x, except the rhetorical, what would it mean to knowingly speak, or write, from the assertive mode of its denial? And yet if politics is this knowledge *and* its denial, why is the obligation always one of being forced to choose between suspending this x, or abolishing it, expelling it or incorporating it as something other? In any case, what appears as the x is in a way the materialization of a mistake—and in particular a form of tabula rasa—that can prove literally fatal and especially when the condemned subject is black.

Michael X spent approximately three years on death row before he was executed on May 16, 1975. One of the "obscene rituals" of death row in Trinidad involved the weekly reading of death warrants on Thursday afternoons, when a prisoner was told that he would be put to death the following Tuesday morning.[99] Geoffrey Robertson, who clearly regards the death penalty as "cruel and unusual punishment," describes the arrival of the prison governor with the death warrant as follows: "He would stride up and down with his folded parchment, sometimes taking a small sadistic pleasure in stopping in front of one man whom he would torture for a moment merely by clearing his throat, and then moving across to the cage of the actual victim, where he unraveled his scroll."[100] All the terms that are at stake here—indeterminacy and legislation, misreading and murder, innocence and cruelty, a writing (of law) that itself does violence to those before whom it is performed, and a reading that is both deadly and undecidable precisely because it falsely (that is, arbitrarily) withholds the meaning of a letter—these terms are ones for which we have tried to provide a reading of as the effects of a mistake that can never be innocently determined or foreknown. And yet, as a result of this ignorance—its politics or ideology—my commentary has also had to walk the thin green line between obligation and resistance. And precisely because of the moment of which we cannot ever speak or write: a moment of suspense when the letter unravelling the undecidable difference between cruelty and law, fear and cognition, sees knowledge converted—via a slow, interruptive movement—into an innocence that can never avoid choosing itself except as fatally undone. This, then, would be a blackness whose execution literally repeats the end of any essential notion, without for all that transforming its imprisoned meaning into a last redemptive moment.

Six

Crystallization

It follows from the previous chapter, as we pointed out, that black politi-cal life has no essence but only something like the anti-teleology of its own ending. It is clear from the example of Stuart Hall, for instance, that black-ness exceeds identity but not the disquieting franchises of false conversion. On the other hand, the x that enfranchises, and that, ultimately, appears via the charismatic machine of black power, also disenfranchises black power as power. This also accords with the politics of an end that is always com-ing to an end (whether innocently or guiltily). Those who are most innocent in their politics are most likely (politically) to bring blackness to an end. Consequently, blackness must be interrogated in its innocence, and precisely because innocence is almost completely unprincipled in its innocence. (As could be seen in the story and fate of Michael X.) What interests me here, however, is what that un-thought makes visible. What is more satisfying: the innocence in which blackness lives, philosophically, or the knowledge that offers itself as contemplative culpability? I propose to address this ques-tion here at some length. We shall ask how delusion is enjoyed and how, im-printed in the heart of its many pleasures, idealism acts as the *legitimation* of race power. We shall also ask why the n'est pas has to be carefully avoided in order to maintain idealism's pure expression. What do we understand by the n'est pas? Distressingly, the notion speaks not to the imaginary bliss of per-fection, nor to its diverting possession, but to the *political* form of a lie that distracts us from thinking about our wretchedness. But what is it that gives rise to it; and why is it not an object that situates us in the world, but an ek-static awareness of our distance from it? Thus, when Fanon advises us to think about the n'est pas, it is not to procure from us some kind of pleasure but violence, the saving violence that rends the *distractions* specific to the colonial state. That is why the n'est pas belongs to the world but only in the most radical way, as a kind of opening without telos or end. But we must first discuss black idealism and the certainty and assurance that allows it to think about itself without being too much occupied or distracted by the n'est pas. Only then can we approach it from the other side, as it were, of distraction. In order to treat this subject properly, we will therefore begin with crystallization: this principle also obliges me to forget the n'est pas; but perhaps in a way that allows me to find a way back to it?

Crystallization, in the first place, refers to an idealized reflection, or, more precisely, a seeing that omits imperfection from reflection. Stendhal introduces the word to illustrate the imaginary nature of love: "the continual acts of folly which make a lover see every perfection in the woman he is beginning to love."[1] For the beloved is seen not *"as she really is*, but as you want her to be"; and the more beautiful and removed from reality she appears to be the more endowed she is with perfection [2] Are the *folies de l'amour* and the reflection the same thing? Like every imaginary sentiment, the question of the lover's true image—or of its imagining—points back to the extreme and particular circumstance of how passion occupies the mind and diverts us. Diversion should be understood as more than mere temperament, even though it gives rise to a secret satisfaction and excitement. Diversion must appear first in order for its pleasures and predicates to be constituted; conversely, crystallization sends us back not to the object (which we have little knowledge of and is always destined to leave us unsatisfied) but to the glorious pleasures of diversion; in short, we want to see the lover only in her enticing splendor, not in her truth. Other words can express this theme that distinguishes the imaginary, the merely analogical, from that of the real: disclosure, manifestation, revelation, truth, and so on. It is interesting to note that when Stendhal introduces crystallization, he uses the figure of a blackened surface to distinguish the real imperfections of life from the glistening whitenesses that so entice us in their ardent pursuit.[3]

Let this chapter therefore be, among other things, a study of the exquisite exaggerations separating blackness from what glistens in the discourse and politics of love. With a focus on the idealizing metaphors by which crystallization allows us access to the hidden, obscure depths, and what glistens, or shines forth, is *the impossible perfection of whiteness* in all of its delusory—but unhappy—splendor.

In the colony, the ur-fantasy of being the object of white love crystallizes a certain phantasmal relation to blackness misrecognized as such. Fanon, in his first book, *Black Skin, White Masks*, says that in the colony, perception is imaginary; or the way things appear in the world is already racialized. Because the world is understood in terms of racial perfectibility, everything seen in it, every object, acquires a measure of racial infallibility and/or dejection. The world is illuminated—crystallized—in such a way that everything we see in it becomes visible for us through racial ek-stases. (His reference here are to various fables, legends, and texts, including René Maran's novel, *Un Hommes pareil aux autres*, where a reference to Stendhal's concept does indeed occur).[4] But the word *crystallization*—the process by which what appears to us appears in terms of this racial mode of appearing—also comes to be reversed, or converted, in his later texts, so that what is unseen, or seen askance, or only barely, hidden by racist delusion, is unveiled in a most profound manner.

In Fanon's late work, the difference between the imaginary and what crystallization allows to appear—between distraction and manifestation—is of deep philosophical concern. The condition for establishing this identification from distraction to manifestation is to understand the n'est pas in its unusual sense. Instead of taking it as an experience or, in terms of modern politics, as a set of ideological ruptures, the n'est pas must be understood as a *disturbing will to particularity* through and through, in which blackness acquires new form and density. The n'est pas makes it impossible for blackness to be in the world of racialized beings. Yet even though it appalls racial social life, its mode of appearing cannot (politically) be converted to anything at all: desire, anger, fear, pleasure, justice. The n'est pas differs fundamentally from a racial conception of the world. It cannot be monstrated as the path to pleasure, or to truth. As such, our concern will not be with the inversion, delusory or revelatory, of its phenomenality, but with the racial logic that continues to link blackness and distraction in Fanon's discussion of the politics of revolutionary decolonial culture.

Quite the contrary: this chapter is about another kind of misrecognition, about a political theme that runs through Fanon's whole thought on national culture, and which he believes is necessarily contested and repressed as soon as it is stated: the desire to reveal a black political life that is not supported by white ideals (of religion, or philosophy), but is itself sustained by the belief that no ideal exists (of identity, faith; community, or nationality). Moreover, crystallization here denotes a certain poetics of the *nothing*, or n'est pas. Everything disclosed by this *nothing* thereby reveals nothing but itself. And yet this is a life for which the world has no picture; for what it reveals is a world-picture that cannot be established in the racial sense of the term. On the other hand, what it reveals is a violent world in which the *whip makes every wound complicit.*

This is the first point that—revealing my main thesis from the start—I would like to bring out: how pleasure is first taken hold of as a *suffering that is unaware of itself* (let us call this the first crystallization), which produces a politics of imitation, or duplicity, which prevents the people from truly seeing itself as it is and discourages any encounter with blackness as a figure of force, power, and possibility. This can be recognized by the fact that there is no gap between suffering and the pleasures that sustain it. Let us say, for now, that the satisfactions of such suffering are politically determined, and that, because of its prestige-power, anti-blackness sustains a multiplicity of errors that is itself unable to imagine the connection between pain and delusion. Without any ability to divert one's gaze towards it, black pain is invisible to the world, and this holds for every imperfection that it both accuses and loves. Here, to embrace blackness means to embrace two apparently opposing truths: to refuse it's suffering so as to affirm one's humanity and to do so in ignorance of the conditions that remain heretical to humanism as a *racial* truth. This paradox is opposed, as a totally different mode of thought, to the various humanisms by which whiteness defines the ideal of universal community, including that of the Orient, or the West, which, like every other humanism in the European tradition, is a humanism of natural necessity and teleology, that is to say, a phenomenology of racial superiority.

If Fanonian crystallization, so to speak, unveils the dishonor of humanism, it is in order to bring out, in the guise of an abyssal opening, a politics beyond that of racial community. Indeed, it denotes a mobilization of those who have nothing, and for whom nothing is their only possession, and to that extent, those who remain untouched by the glittering promises of humanism (at the level of law, the nation-state, and the subject). What triumphs with the wretched (*les damnés*), who come into being from nothing, as nothing, or what shines forth, precipitated out of nothing, is a certain postulation of the depths, of being thrown into the abyssal depths, as the place where blackness, or what has never before been called *blackness*, is both formed *and* disfigured into being. It is here that the aporia of such depths is revealed. To be thrown without diversion is to be wretched. But to not be so thrown is inconceivably more wretched, because one knows that, wretched though one is, it is easier to bear suffering if one does not think about it. The act that crystallizes wretchedness brings blackness itself into itself and is only possible through it. Thus, it is that what is revealed as black life is revealed to itself as a delivering. Because any thought of blackness that continues to think it as a racial concept cannot think the priority of its invention, or what Fanon calls, its "new law of expression."[5] Crystallization is not therefore a negation. It should not be thought of as a figure for the unrepressed, since its diversion is not one of submission or compromise. It refers to a certain aversive avocation that is experienced as a rupture that is also a suspension of the self. Here, impressional immediacy takes precedence over thought. Or what impresses already has an immanent reality before any particular impression can be thought. For what crystallizes is a being that suffers and enjoys itself from the viewpoint of its suffering predication. However, along with Fanon, we must ask if, truly speaking, there is no pain without diversion, what does distraction mean for black political life? And what if those new laws of expression cannot establish that life, but are invariably attended by new whips for the joys of black dejection?

To free blackness into this law of expression, to discover, if possible, its implications for both politics and philosophy; and to ascertain its revolutionary juncture or antagonism—such is the task that I have set myself here.

I

Let us start with the famous chapter on national culture and Fanon's reading of Keïta Fodéba's prose poem, "Aube Africaine," first published in *Presence Africaine* in 1951. "Aube Africaine" tells the story of the peasant farmer, Naman, who, in response to a request from the colonial district, is selected by his village and sent to the front during the Second World War, and who, after having fought in both Europe and Africa, is killed on his way home by white French soldiers. It is based on a real event: the massacre, by the French, of West African troops at Tiaroye in 1944.

Fanon tells us that: "The reason I have chosen this long poem is because of its undeniable pedagogical value. Here things are clear. It is a meticulous account that develops progressively."[6]

This implies both that structure and form do not stand opposed but meticulously unfold in a progressive way. It also implies that, to read this poem, is "to understand the role we have to play, to identify our approach and fight."[7] For to understand "the poem is *not only an intellectual act, but also a political one.*"[8]

To read "Aube Africaine" is thus to profess a role, to identify one's practice, by virtue of the fact that the poem contests, disputes, fights over a certain politics of reading. For what is made negatively explicit by the poem is a scene of instruction that is also a scene of struggle: the first shows how colonial violence is often misrecognized out of loyalty or obedience; the second shows how this obedience often results in wretchedness, because the necessity of struggle or combat is so little recognized by the people. To learn from such a poem is thus to understand that understanding is itself the history of an historical struggle; or what we might call the (always violent) transformation of reading into pedagogy. Then crystallization supervenes. "Aube Africaine" is an indispensable manifestation of a certain "logic" by which Fanon illustrates his main theses. What does Fanon mean by this word?[9] *Crystallization* manifests what is masked or simply missing in the political domain; it reveals what is beyond (or outside of) the blindness, but also the fanaticism by which delusion is lived; it takes its strength from what stops us from knowing our own wretchedness, yet without grounding this unveiling in the racial limits of a world. Hence crystallization rejoins knowing and critique, but can only do so by transgressing the order by which delusion effectively becomes the condition of concept or reason. For those who do not know that this order is the effect of metaphysics, crystallization removes the illusion since it corresponds, on the contrary, to the effect of being plunged into an abyss beyond both race and humanism.

The idea that the revolutionary hopes of a people may be crystallized (*cristallisèrent*) by what they make manifest, and "with the intention of opening up the future," gives some sense of the audacity of Fanon's thesis.[10] In other words, crystallization amounts to recognizing that what "truly" exists as "real" should never be taken simply as what it is given to be, for what gives itself (inevitably as cause, principle, morality, etc.) relies on the anterior authority of a *white ratio* or *causa*, whose authority is justified de jure since it is given in fact, and this *fact* testifies to the lived experience [*Erlebnis*] of black impossibility. By thus lifting the prohibition of a black critique of reason, crystallization liberates hope as possibility (while always mindful that hope too needs to be put in question within the limits of anti-blackness). Without a doubt, it is this possibility that crystallization makes manifest; but crystallization can manifestly not manifest itself; it cannot *give* itself to what it is not. And it is precisely because the n'est pas is *not* given that there is a need for crystallization. Accordingly, it is the n'est pas, and not reason or ideology, that is the beginning of possibility and the impossibility of black beginning. What other decolonial philosophy, in the history of colonialism, has argued that blackness is the mine where being is made crystalline? We must, however, go further still. In order for crystallization to give rise to a revolution from which self-revelation is born, that encounter must not rest in form; it must be, not an aesthetic upheaval, but a sudden cut or fracture in being itself, which then becomes the basis for a new postcolonial reality, the reinvention of all necessity, all meaning and conviction. Like the delusory state that precedes it, crystallization is a relation of wretchedness and delusion, a relation that troubles the ways in which the people enjoy their own suffering. For it no longer denotes perfection but a repugnance at the esteem in which perfection is held. It is in this way and in it alone that crystallization can be deployed as *via veritas*. But crystallization cannot last; it too must be contested (*contestée*).[11] Hence it cannot be understood as communication but only as an event, for what it reveals is the n'est pas revealing itself. What is more, it is clear that the struggle over delusion is part of a larger merciless war, which is nothing but a struggle over the reality of the postcolonial world, which, without crystallization and this manifestation, would be nothing but abstract, idealistic elements, lacking all consistency and existence. So much so that we can say that the very existence of blackness is due to nothing but its crystallization prior to which it has led only a subjugated existence.

All this may be stated differently. It may be said that "Aube Africaine" allows Fanon to question the ways in which domination is felt but not recognized, for nothing is more wretched than those who mistake delusion for the truth, and who are all the more deceived by their belief in the infallibility—the legality and legitimacy—of domination. Devotion to the leader in decolonial war, or to what is innerly called his charisma, is thus blamed for distracting the people from gaining any knowledge of the miseries afflicting them. It is understood that obedience—whether to the native *ecclesia* or to the colonial authority—itself derives from the delusory politics of charismatic domination.[12] That is why the shortest way to prevent delusion is to contest its truth, and the surest way of refuting it is to expose what it excludes. I am not speaking of the poem *as* truth, but of its critique of power and truth in which, once these new laws of expression have been accomplished, the idealism of race philosophy is established and brought to an end. Before crystallization can be accomplished, before it unveils delusion, there is only *the fantasy of its accomplishment* as an ideal of art, philosophy, and politics.

What becomes of race philosophy under these circumstances? Fanon presents two outcomes. The first is reproached for turning to the past, away from the realities of domination, in its striving to name a black *essence* that it contemplates at leisure without distress. The people are thus advised to seek solace in traditional forms of power and, by virtue of such obedience, enjoy the honor and premiums of race vanity. Such enjoyments conform to a *magical* domination by force, one directed by nativist forms, but one always separated from the means and relations of colonial administration. Moreover, tradition becomes the condition of the possibility of any black power whatsoever—only by being never separated from itself, and in sole possession of itself, can it be deployed and act. On the other hand, domination also crystallizes another form of disobedience. Here a new thinking emerges from those who are the non-owners; from those who *own* no stake in the imaginary organizations of the past. This thinking is no longer a statement of blackness as ideal or origin (as in négritude), but a theory that seeks the complete reversal of black tradition. Fanon speaks here of a n'est pas in whose recognition we are given access to the *nothing*, and through this nothing to a world where blackness is not, namely, *beyond or outside of the world but not of it*. Distraction is now no more than a *masking of belief that is itself masked*: a givenness that crystallizes all those elements by which blackness remains alter, wretched, n'est pas.[13] All questions of *black* authenticity are rejected, as are all the questions of race philosophy: Is blackness part of the logos? Does blackness belong to the history of spirit? What is its fate or destiny as *Dasein*?

And so on. I repeat: what gets crystallized in the depths is, historically, the audacious refusal of such questions and fantasies.

This is why Fanon's reading of "Aube Africaine" is so singular. One finds, precisely, a reading of decolonial culture that differs significantly from that of tradition. In his 1954 preface to *Les Hommes de la Danse*, for example, Fodéba also invokes the metaphor of the mask, but with obvious differences:

> I will never forget the impression made on me by the visit to the ethnographic collections of a Paris museum. Of all the objects which adorned one of the rooms, two masks in particular grabbed my attention. They had such an incredibly human expression! They seemed to be impregnated with such melancholy in this setting which was not their own, such simple wooden figurines had never before seemed to me to be endowed with such a great power of evocation. Since my arrival in France, I had never discovered an image of Africa at once so concrete and so pathetic. In spite of the difference in their forms and the particular signs which characterized them, both of them evoked in my eyes so many memories of my country, that even at night I seemed to hear in a kind of half-sleep the nostalgic voice of the most venerable of the two of them telling me his story.[14]

The stories that the masks proceed to tell are thus: those of social honor enfeoffed in sacred ritual; and a form of patriarchal and patrimonial domination that converges with language and cultural form. Fodéba presents this spiritual aristocracy as a total means of communal organization—hence the role of the mask is social and utilitarian (*utilitaire*), and not aesthetic, nor commercial.[15] Moreover, the bearer of the mask serves to conjure up the god who is represented upon it; here, there is no separation between form and godly power, at least in so far as the mask is thus not a representation but the living embodiment of sovereign authority. All other lives are only alive in it—for they become joined to an absolute life that alone has the power of self-revelation. Perhaps this is why Fodéba suggests such sovereignty must not be abandoned "to chance and the vicissitudes of history."[16]

It's a point of view repeated in the 1957 article, "La danse africaine et la scène":[17]

> For us, authenticity is synonymous with reality. To the extent where folklore is a set of traditions, poems, songs, dances and popular legends of a country, it can only be the reflection of the life of this country. And if this life evolves, there is no reason why the folklore which is its living expression, does not evolve. This is why the modern folklore of present-day Africa is as authentic as that of ancient

Africa, both of which are the real expression of life in our country at two different periods in its history.[18]

Accordingly, what the mask accomplishes is the real expression of how the
people submit to sacred rule, and how the legitimacy of that rule in turn dis-
closures the "original language" (*langage original*) of African authority, now
usurped by corruption and alienation.[19] The thematization of language as a
mask (of mystical authority) could be said to narrate a prosopopoeia that is
prior to its signifying function.

But this is not the story, or not the entire story, told by "La danse africaine et la scène." The undoing of the representational and iconic function
of the mask by materialism does not suffice to explain the cultural catastro-
phe that "La danse africaine et la scène" indites. For it is the alignment of
masking with sovereign power, whether living or not, which constitutes cultural authenticity or historic loss. The iconic, sacred, or, if one wishes, the
aesthetic power of the mask is not constitutive of living expression, *for it can
only be a reflection of it*. In fact, reflection is the figurative element that allows for the restoration of the original language of the mask. And yet this
original language is not given or produced but posited as an arbitrary act
of sacred power. The appearance and waning of sacred power, in spite of
the mask, is not an historical event, but a *pas* achieved by the positional
power of language, and therefore beyond expression. There must, then, be
a prosopopoeia of disfigurement that is prior to life's living expression, and
despite the role that the mask is being asked to play as symbol and apos-
trophe. Thus African modernity is an ongoing struggle between revelation
and commemoration, and precisely because the people are no longer able to
distinguish sacred domination from capitalist inauthenticity, or belief from
profit. The sovereign *innocence* of the mask now discloses a world lost and
forgotten, commercialized for profit; and its sacred legitimacy has become
a mere ornament, "coated with a vulgar polish."[20] Everything depends here
on the meaning of the *masque* as origin. The mask is both "the conscious
work of man" and a guardian of sacred tradition.[21] It is both a principle of
cultural life and of any real or authentic expression. Hence the fact that,
as sacred devices of articulation, these same articulations, independently
of their signifying constraints, are also able to reveal the obliteration of the
sacred by capital. For Fanon, however, what remains of precolonial culture

in the postcolony is only *the delusory narrative of its transcendental loss.* Once again—but in the mode of loss—what is masked is the belief that he who "wears" the mask lives "for" the god whose authority is absent. Either one lives "for" the sacred or one lives "off" it. For the former, at least in thought, the sacred is the whole articulation of a culture, and one legitimated by tradition, whereas colonialism, by contrast, is simply domination by force, or, rather, a naked possession of power that has no inner meaning as cultural life. Thus, instead of concluding that there is no sacred truth because there is only a false sense of the sacred, we must on the contrary say that the idea of a truth somehow repressed by colonialism can only be believed in because of this transcendental delusion that there is only one true or genuine vision of what African sacred life is. Once again—but from the sense of its idealism—what is true can only be recognized because its degraded imitation exists. Moreover, such a truth can only be borne witness to in imperial France—in a Paris museum—where the politics of black alienation supposedly carries infinitely more weight than in Africa.

We thus need to inquire into why Fanon deliberately reads "Aube Africaine" as taking up a position outside the divisions and terminology of both négritude and race philosophy. And why this reading has itself been dismissed as "massively ethnocentric"? This phrase, taken from Christopher Miller's 1990 book *Theories of Africans*, is clearly enough aimed at Fanon: it forms a critique refuting what he sees as Fanon's violent, totalizing vision of cultural liberation (or the belief that the nation has, as its ground and condition of emergence, violent liberation), whose first response, when confronted with tradition, is to "call out the firing squad."[22] Doubtless, and on the condition that we accept this relation between "Fanon's theories" and firing squads, the view that ethnic traditions have to be "liquidated" for a revolutionary culture to emerge (a charge of fanaticism that is itself fanatic), sets out from an idealism that produces the deeply scurrilous claim that Fanon's theories directly influenced "the reign of terror in Guinea."[23] But even if we accept the idea of collusion (which we do not)—between Fanon's theories and the policies later pursued by Fodéba and Sékou Touré—Fanon's sustained discussion of tradition, in "On National Culture," never refers to liquidation other than to the practices and intent of the colonial power, which imprints itself on indigenous culture like an imperial stamp on coinage: tails

I win, heads you lose. Which is also why Fanon identifies with Fodéba's own admission that European culture should never simply be *imitated* (specifically in relation to an African avant-garde, but with much broader consequences) as an example of crystallization. In other words, the very opposition between ethnicity and universalism that Miller tries to impose on his reading of "Aube Africaine" is already stamped by the imperial logic it ostensibly refuses, a collusion of fanaticism and mimicry (this collusion itself produces a fanatic discourse) to which we shall return in the conclusion of this chapter.

As we continue to insist on the importance of crystallization for Fanon's understanding of national culture, we should bear in mind that his chapter includes a reading of Fodéba that explores the criteria by which decolonial art can embody the revolutionary hopes of the people. In doing so, we shall see why crystallization, as taken up by Fanon, consists in trying to separate the mendacious, delusory nature of neocolonialism from the new configurations of decolonialism. The desire here is to show how the real is administered or expropriated, on the one hand, and, on the other hand, how expropriation crystallizes, in turn, a wretchedness that is contingent, uncertain, and whose existence is so obscured by its abyssal descent into form it is hard to tell apart the form that claims it from the delusion that never recognizes it. Let us say that the relation between structure and form here is infinitely-finite.[24] Let us also say that it is impossible to conceive crystallization abstractly as either true or false. For to do so is to impose on it a formal identity that can only be abstractly (that is to say, falsely) affirmed or denied. Similarly, the belief that blackness can only be given credence in the expropriation of its form (in the attempt to separate it from wretchedness), must also necessarily exclude it from the deluded nature of such truth. But to contest such knowledge one cannot simply refer to a more genuine truth. That opposition remains abstract, ludic, purely ideological. This is why it is necessary to take a different route from that of dialectic, and to arrive at a more speculative understanding. The difficulty of that opposition recurs throughout Fanon's many readings of the decolonial avant-garde. In *The Wretched of the Earth*, for example, Fanon essentially condemns négritude for being unable to distinguish the false forms of cultural inertia from its own deluded belief in a more genuine black cultural authenticity. In the colony, it is the former that presides. But after this period of inertia (in which culture has become rigid, congealed, petrified), Fanon introduces the following (distinctly enigmatic) thesis:

> The crystallization of the national consciousness will not only radically change the literary genres and themes but also create a completely new audience. Whereas the colonized intellectual started out producing work exclusively with the oppressor in mind—either in order to charm him or to denounce him by using ethnic or subjectivist categories—he gradually switches over to addressing himself to his people [via "a will to particularize" (*se fait volunté particularisante*)].[25]

The whole relation of delusion to expropriation is being invoked here. There are two ways in which anti-colonialism forms: either through an exclusive appeal to bourgeois, neocolonial forms or via this *se fait volunté particularisante*. By no means is this contrast a settled one. He who seeks the attitude of charm or denunciation is just as naïve as he who confuses particularity for justice or revolution. The question remains of whether this will to particularize (and what it is that it crystallizes) establishes the nation to come or whether it is something that gives form to its misrecognition? Such, for me, is the question of what, politically, sends us back to form and what, utopically, switches it over by means of color, tone, word, or stone; let us clarify some of the ramifications.

Again, from a slightly different angle involving a letter sent to the Iranian critic, ʿAli Shariʿati (from 1961 but published in English only in 2018): "Nevertheless, I think that reviving sectarian and religious mindsets could impede this necessary unification [of Algerian nationhood]—already difficult enough to attain—and divert that *nation yet to come*, which is at best a *'nation in becoming,'* from its ideal future, bringing it instead closer to its past."[26] In a later lecture addressing Fanon's critique, Shariʿati explains why a return [*bazgasht*] to Islam is a necessary condition of postcolonial sovereignty: "It is for our fortification and growth then that, in the same Third World, we return to religion. And we see that a return to a conscious Islam and a reliance upon it not only does not produce schisms in the opposition to a unified colonialism, but also *a predestined and inevitable necessity* in the formation of a unified anti-colonial front on a global scale."[27] These references to the nation to come (which become no less curious when one notices that at the end of the chapter on national culture, the chapter in which he introduces crystallization, Fanon says that that nation will be "surrounded, vulnerable, and in permanent danger"[28]) reprise the question with which we began: namely, how can decolonial life come into itself, and how can it engender itself, or reveal itself to itself, or be understood as an originary return to itself (no matter how infinitely elaborated this origin is as the authentic *form* of culture)? Shari'ati, by contrast, whatever his real relation to Fanon's thinking, and taking (at least in the 1960s) an apparently more religious stance on these questions, opens some difficult issues for the Fanonian position and, even as he too tends to close off the dimensions of what we are calling the n'est pas, asks some uncomfortable questions of anyone trying to think about religion and politics today.[29] In sum, can a crystallizing encounter be thought without representing it *as* a teleology, and thus as an idealism? And he poses the problem in all its rigor and stark simplicity, as we shall see. Fanon's project is, however, well known: there can be no return prior to the act (the utterly transformative precipitation) that crystallizes its uttering. To be thrown into the void, the black depths, is to experience the necessity of the n'est pas—the institution of the infinite saturation of the finite by those depths. Or again, just as misrecognition is experienced as pleasure, crystallization *precisely* designates the relation between delusion and reality in black life; more, it is only by going beyond this relation that the people can overcome the opposition between *conscious*, *mimetic* forms and racial authenticity (for that opposition is precisely what crystallization counters, as Fanon tells us).[30] All the circumstances favorable to the notion of a nation to come exist in the here and now, but without teleology: the people may or may not know these circumstances, but it is their latent aspiration to unity, an aspiration to which all cultural forms bear witness, including that of poetry, that will precipitate a crisis in the colony that may or may not lead to new fidelity and faith.

To return to the question of pedagogy: what crystallizes is not knowledge, but its interpretation. No learning is possible without misrecognition. Hence crystallization is not initially a concept; it is first of all a danger that allows the people to realize their own corruption. There is no theory of the postcolony that avoids this danger, or that is not implicated in the pain, joys, and suffering that are also connected to its particularizing will. Another very specific example will help us here (to be pursued in the larger context of this book). Recent investigations have shed some light on the political philosophical readings of postcolonialism, whose cohesion continues to be resolved dogmatically or at least moralistically as a humanism. (This precise misreading is precisely what we now call the "postcolonial," be it by Edward Said or Homi Bhabha, Partha Chatterjee or Achille Mbembe, Gayatri Chakravorty Spivak or Jasbir Puar.[31] That is to say, readings in which blackness is not recognized except as a metaphor of humanism, which is their real concern, and that, in fact, fail to grasp how blackness alters the very meaning and fate of political humanism.) There is, however, a different understanding of humanism, one that further understands the whole relationship between politics and philosophy rather differently: an understanding that does not share this dogmatism and moralism. This reading is Fanonian, but what it crystallizes—perpetually misunderstood as history, biography, meaning, identity, or knowledge—has yet to be determined. This is why it is absurd to condemn Fanon in the name of a humanism (or anti-humanism) that claims to know the meaning of the Fanonian text. We are no longer so willing to be the dupes of such criticism, a criticism that has never been concerned with the difficulty of reading a *black* decolonial text; for that criticism, there is no other task than that of *knowledge*, an emphasis that precisely discards, ignores, muffles the reading that tries to restore blackness to its future to come, a future that is always called into question, contested, and is itself always already the trace of an unthought violence.

Some such reformulation is what Fanon seems at least to be turning around, in the many fascinating attempts in his late work (essentially those works published just before his death in 1961, from the Rome address on "Mutual Foundations for National Culture and Liberation Struggles," through to the chapters on "Misadventures of National Consciousness" and "On National Culture" in *The Wretched of the Earth*) to isolate and define the value of humanism to the people's liberation struggle. Fanon, no doubt, saw and foresaw that his appeal to this term was not only entangled within a history of philosophy but more especially with the image of strife, rebellion and disorder, and he returns many times, elaborating and sometimes subverting his earlier formulations in the attempt to clarify the terms of the struggle, and to invent new laws of its expression.

This is why crystallization is difficult: it puts us on the wrong track, but on the other hand it never leads us anywhere. There is no path. There is no "wrong" track either: the n'est pas alone leads to it. But the n'est pas, considered rigorously, can never enter into itself in such a way that it can lead to a way or a path. Well then? The n'est pas is the blackest depth whose manifestation cannot be pictured. Which is why it is infinite *and* finite. Without it, crystallization would cease to be a task and also cease to be connected to revelatory violence. At least, this seems to be the principle of Fanon's entirely unqualifiable notion of tabula rasa, to which we now turn.

II

Here again, we can see that the n'est pas—the necessary imperfection of structure and form—carries within itself the revelation to which every decolonial life owes its possibility. What is given to that life is not allegiances, or the pleasures of constraints and rites; it is not a particularizing will, such as the radiant, irreducible core of a mind too much occupied and distracted by passion's imperfections. Instead, this n'est pas is what places power in this life, puts it in possession of itself as a black power—a *willing power of particularity*. It can then see itself *freely*; and it is because its sole desire was not to see that it is thereby able to see how it is surrounded by perfect reflections erasing black pain and suffering. In the end, no power can erase this desire, and none can claim the n'est pas as will. So what makes it possible for us to recognize it? To crystallize—and so render decisive—its real particularity?

The task begins in "Misadventures of National Consciousness." Once the colonial power and its forces—that is, the police, the courts, the army—have been rejected, Fanon, using the example of the colonial bourgeoisie, moves onto the idea that party political power itself also need to be contested, and, starting out from the point that power in the postcolony is corrupt, he begins to say that neocolonialism is what founds the postcolonial nation-state. "Seen through its eyes, its mission has nothing to do with transforming the nation; it consists, prosaically, of being the transmission line between the nation and a capitalism, rampant though camouflaged, which today puts on the masque of neocolonialism."[32] This pact—between race, nation, and capital—is complex due to the fact that the colonial bourgeoisie, who, Fanon maintains, represent an inferior copy of the European bourgeoisie, also use nationalist ideology to mask their corruption, and so disguise the fact that they are politically "decadent," "bereft," "narcissistic," "ultra-nationalist," not to say "racist."[33] What is meant here is how the parties live off booty, plunder, confiscations, and so forth, and how that power is legitimized (not to say sanctified) by political ideology. Thus the crystallizing element of the postcolony is now divided between an elite and an abyssal form (of life) in which the people, after the terror of civil war, are now subjugated to an ideology based on "the resurgence of tribal parties and federalism."[34]

Fanon is one of the first to think the role of ideological domination in the postcolony. It is here that we find his analysis of the limits of national idealism. He thought that for decolonialism to take hold, national consciousness had to become "the all-embracing crystallization of the innermost hopes of the whole people," instead of "an empty shell, a crude and fragile travesty of what it might have been."[35] Conscious of the fact that revolution must mean a more authentic realization, Fanon says nothing of how a second, anti-bourgeois revolution is to reveal the mask beneath the masque, so to speak, or how those innermost hopes are to reveal the (latent) meaning of the colonial elites, which must be unmasked (as a travesty) for those hopes to become manifest. But let us not be too hasty. The emergence of what is innermost to the people is the *political* condition for the nation's emergence. Fanon's wish is simply that, in the postcolony, the masquerade by which the elites maintain power should be exposed in order for it not to be confused with those crystallizing elements that are essential to the nation to come. That is why he is plainly obsessed with the opposition between an empty, inert, "stereotypical formalism" based on religious nationalism and race, and a mobilization that demystifies and contests, not so much ideological illusion, or subterfuge, but the racialization of the symbolic itself, in its bourgeois transformation. Yet nothing here is certain. The distinction between the stereotypical and what perturbs it is itself in danger of becoming delusory, idealistic. This is why Fanon suggests that the nation to come has no assignable place, or authentic form, but must, nonetheless, be opposed to "the modern form of the dictatorship of the bourgeoisie," which he says has to be seen for what it is: "unmasked, unpainted, unscrupulous and cynical."[36]

In order for the second crystallization to take place, however, another encounter must come about: and here he turns to the question of the power and will of the leader. "The leader, who has behind him a lifetime of political action and devoted patriotism, constitutes a screen between the people and the rapacious bourgeoisie since he stands surety for the ventures of that

caste and closes his eyes to their insolence, their mediocrity and their fundamental immorality. He acts as a braking-power on the awakening consciousness of the people."[37] This then turns out to be the real crux of this first approach to the problem of power: it is no longer just a struggle between the
elites and the masses, but far beyond it, an aporetic relation between ideology and power in which imaginary delusion, in its first phase, is, in essence,
what corresponds to the meanings and practices of the leader-dictator in
his bewildering mystification of the masses. The question of displacement is
thereby extended: power is in fact now an attribute of a certain kind of jouissance (or drive to mastery) rather than just the authentic realization of the
nation.[38] This holds especially for the ways in which political idealism maintains the economic order of the colony. Idealism itself becomes the mediator of capital and the exploitation of political influence, patronage, prestige,
and so on. This insight contributes a second caution: national consciousness, which we might once have been tempted to associate with the manifestation of a pure presence, with the outer realization of what is inner, also
reveals, says Fanon, the enigmatic enjoyment (by the powerful) of what is
perversely hidden, and that is unknown, infinitely so. Or again (for these rapacious mediocrities) political power entails a latent struggle between party
officials, coming into their roles as dilettantes, and the leader's assumed supremacy over party power. Here the leader is not he who decides, but he
who lulls, and pacifies, he who seduces and violates; in short, he who urges
the people to "fall back into the past and to become drunk on the remembrance of the epoch which led up to independence."[39] Thanks to this violating seduction, the wretched occupy a wholly different relation to the state of
exception, for, if this is a state of exception, it is one defined by a complicit
unawareness, or even by a kind of enjoyment that compels (is itself compelled) to ignore, and to leave undeciphered all the signifiers (ethical, didactic, propagandistic, political, etc.) that have come to a halt and are "completely demobilized."[40]Above all, political parties become more and more a
means of securing jouissance in this manner. In such apathy, no crystallizing encounter can take place in a community that is not so much abandoned
or disavowed, as lulled, and one for whom the decision to interiorize a world,
or to ease one's wretchedness, is unable to move beyond the consolations
of ideological conformity. The postcolony would then name not an impropriety of being and consciousness, but an enjoyment that is simultaneously

unrecognized because it makes a show of power when, in the absence of all inhibition, it descends into the realm of the drive.

Because the people can be made to conform to this "spectacular lethargy" by which they remain inured to their exploitation, Fanon has to further clarify the concept of the nation to come in his letter to Shariʿati and the chapter from *The Wretched of the Earth*.[41] Now he says that crystallization has two opponents against which it must struggle: mimesis (the subterfuge of power) and apathy (its existential adversary). He has to make this distinction in order to try and separate revolt (that sees the people wake up from delusion) from the kind of enigmatic enjoyment (of the darkness of the drive) that, as we have just seen, Fanon says cannot simply be renounced. (The national bourgeoisie names, after all, the more or less secret aspiration of independence itself, which typically does not seek to announce or signal itself *as* a subterfuge but as a truthful realization of the revolution: nothing is more cynical than the claim to be against the former colonial power while mimicking its thought and institutions, or masking the masque). He has to try and make these awkward and perhaps even contradictory distinctions if he is to maintain the opposition between crystallization and cultural inertia. I leave aside the question of whether Fanon's desire for the distinction may itself be a symptom of revolutionary, idealistic love, or whether the theory of crystallization is itself the sign of a phantasmatic seduction. But if apathy is the enemy of crystallization, things are not so straightforward with the supposed opposition between the masses and political leadership, which turns out to involve a more complicitous relation between drive and the desire to be driven:

> We have many times indicated the very often detrimental role of the leader. This is because in certain regions the party is organized like a gang whose toughest member takes over the leadership. The leader's ancestry and powers are readily mentioned, and in a knowing and slightly admiring tone it is quickly pointed out that he inspires awe in his close collaborators. In order to avoid these many pitfalls a persistent battle has to be waged to prevent the party from becoming a compliant instrument in the hands of a leader. *Leader* comes from the English verb "to lead," meaning "to drive" in French [*conduire*]. The driver of people no longer exists today. People are no longer a herd and do not need to be driven. If the leader drives me I want him to know that at the same time I am driving him. The nation should not be an affair run by a big boss. Hence the panic that grips

government circles every time one of their leaders falls ill, because they are obsessed with the question of succession: What will happen to the country if the leader dies? The influential circles, who in their irresponsibility are more concerned with safeguarding their lifestyle, their cocktail parties, their paid travel and their profitable racketeering, have abdicated in favor of a leader and occasionally discover the spiritual void at the heart of the nation.[42]

The development of politics into a drive that diverts us from the void in the ruling order is in sharp contrast to the enigma of the leader whose status is both the subject and object of the drive. We have seen that his enigma evolves as both void and drive—a product of his quite unique nature. As a boss, he is considered indispensable to party organization and its centralization of power. But at the same time, he also does not belong to those he connives with, whom he bribes and tips. He is a man without social honor, but he is also a man who enjoys power for power's sake. Nothing can ever separate him from the judicious diversions of expediency. He himself, however, is nothing but the enigmatic experience of corruption. And, as the most effectively unprincipled of the elite, he also has great appeal. But is he admired because he is feared, or feared because he is so admired? He has to be tough, but he also knows how to *appear to be* awe-inspiring, to possess the moral qualities that will win the people over to his side, even if they also earn him the envy of the elites, whom he despises, for, for them, power is something to be either envied or feared. Yet, on closer inspection, what is being described here is a kind of irreducible ambiguity (the leader is both an ambiguous *opponent* of the political elites, because of this drive to mastery, but he is also an ambiguous *partner* of those elites, because of this selfsame drive to mastery by which they are driven to form the party). Or this drive to drive is what founds neocolonial sovereignty, be it in the form of the people or the party. It follows that the leader's relation to his own driveness (as a driver of power) therefore entails a persistent battle with himself and with others. To be sure, the structure that maintains him is an experience of pathos without sense. This is why the age-old distinction of sovereignty *as that which leads*, or as that which governs solely at its own behest, is dismissed as inadequate in the postcolony. For, although sovereignty arises from or is already determined by this drive to drive [*conduire*], its actions are never adequate to it insofar as it is bound by it. Or the sovereign is never purely or simply sovereign, for to lead is merely the effect of being led. This is why, in Fanon's theory of power in the postcolony, the leader is driven to fabricate a popular (ideological) image of himself as the subject who drives the interests of the masses because he is bound to them as sources of money and power.

This is all taken as evidence that sovereignty cannot establish itself without in some sense being driven by the other that confirms it, for this is the law of its own nature. Or sovereignty cannot determine itself without being mediated by this drivenness, which it cannot do without and so depends on, and which, ultimately, it has to perform as masked. This may also be why Fanon flags up the question of translation—that is, of a certain English definition of sovereignty as a war of all against all. For insofar as neocolonial sovereignty is always more than and less than its concept, and its government always more and less than its capacity to govern, any lust for power that is absolute will prove to be absolutely ruinous. Consequently, when this drivenness is mistaken for the phantasm of its concept, the attempt to determine it as will results in a sovereignty that is nothing more than the effect of its appetites; or as governed by nothing but appetite, even when it appears to be not so. And when this confusion of drive and decision takes place, what is called a decision is essentially a kind of perversion in which politics *may or may not* enter into a crisis, for there is no decision that is not the venal, irremediable effect of an arbitrary, perverse spontaneity. At least, this seems to be one of the results of the bourgeois seizure of power in the postcolony. The image of sovereignty that emerges is one thus defined by delirious decisionism. Consequently, national life becomes a nightmare from which the people dare not awake in case they wake up to something worse. This nightmare also shows us that neocolonial sovereignty remains haunted by its insecurity, or is no more than the fearful insecurity that founds it. This is a fear that cannot be calmed and that takes the form of a persecutory, merciless cruelty towards the people. Such, at first glance, are the reasons why Fanon describes the leader as a big boss and the party as gangsters. Such description also defines politics as a series of warring ideologies: woven out of narratives, stereotypes, and key words, and obligatory and arbitrary rewards and punishments, each one of which makes it impossible to distinguish between a wholehearted acceptance of corruption (which would inevitably compromise independence with its true enemy, subterfuge) and a merely passive, external, and expedient apathy that also exposes a spiritual void at the heart of the nation. In the light of all this, the leader can embody the popular will, but only if he *appears to be led*, but insofar as the leader does not permit this inhibition, then he becomes one with the drive that both founds and crystallizes the desire for absolute mastery—that is, insofar as the leader gives form to the people, institutionally, his relation to power is in a sense *even more apathetic and deceitful than that of the bourgeoisie*. What he reveals is the void at the heart of neocolonial mastery, but on the absolute condition that he appears to be no more than a sovereignty up against its limit, or that founds itself as the limit of both drive and the desire to be driven, or, better still, that presents itself wheresoever it can as a cultural revolution that luxuriates in the jouissance of its own excessive prohibition (in the perverse sense of these expressions).

A little later, Fanon summarizes this quite hard-won but perhaps notorious position as follows:

> [T]he crystallization of the caste spirit must be avoided. We have seen in the preceding pages that nationalism, that magnificent song that made the people rise against their oppressors, stops short, falters and dies away on the day that independence is proclaimed. Nationalism is not a political doctrine, nor a program. If you really wish your country to avoid repression, or at best halts and uncertainties, a rapid step must be taken from national consciousness to political and social consciousness.[43]

Indeed, this is almost as far as Fanon gets with the politics of crystallization in *The Wretched of the Earth*. We might summarize it by saying that there is a kind of general drive-structure dimension to decolonial power whose form is that of apathy and violence, that is therefore driven to realize (disguise) itself as a kind of absolute perversity but one that is opposed to sovereignty in the more restrictive sense of party or government in that its point is not exactly to be repressive or representative (that is, telling the masses what they want to hear). Here, drive decides everything: the leader creates memory, justice, and happiness, but is at his most refined when he leads the people inevitably into error and can enjoy the evil he contains. And consequently, political life is only possible through his benevolence. Truly speaking, his drive is nothing other than this: the unprincipled organization of finite life according to racial capital. Such, more or less, are the effects of his deceptive drive to power: it can only manifest itself as sovereignly inhibited for a cynical and manipulative purpose, for example that of racial-ethnic or religious rivalry, or stereotypical forms of repression and perversion more generally.

III

We need to add one further element, however, to the picture of crystallization that emerges, an element that might help us understand the relation between manifestation and the philosophy of distraction that is being thought by way of politics, and which, as such, is crucial to Fanon's theory of decolonial culture.

This further element, which I passed over earlier in the general and complicated attempt to separate out crystallization from mimesis and apathy, is to do with art, with the nation as a form of art that is "conscious and sovereign."[44] To an outstanding degree, the conduct of the political leader is subject to quite a different, indeed, exactly the opposite, principle of moral discipline and authority. Whereas the leader always might be telling a lie, crystallization reveals *what appears to be concealed but that was never actually concealed,* for it reveals how truth, as it were, is being cynically manipulated and expressed, and how, after independence, there is no longer a "colonial" or "anti-colonial" truth to be expressed, as much as a metamorphosis in the very language of truth in the colony, which gives way to a series of malevolent discontinuities. These transformations are accompanied, conversely and necessarily, by new forms of paranoia and clarity. It is easy to see why: crystallization does not produce truth but shows how it comes into view *as* racial truth and falsity; as such, crystallization does not reveal or distort either term but gathers together what is hidden and unhidden by both truth and falsity; or, it is the *moment* at which the people's *à-venir* is given form and density: "the living expression of the nation is the collective consciousness in motion of the entire people," Fanon declares.[45] This is what we called manifestation, and truly what it reveals is a void at the heart of the decolonial demos. Accordingly, crystallization, in Fanon's political philosophy, is not solely marked by a dialectical progression from, say, work to knowledge, as in Hegel, or from alienated life to a life liberated, but to a being opened up by its own *concession* (a word that we will keep on coming back to) and one that knows that the path of revolt will also be the path of delirium, of an uncompromising refusal, which it embraces as the very force of its being. (One thinks here of a moment of unrest that risks sharing the same fate as the leader's corrupting power and, internally, the same compulsion as the propertied and cultured circles of the bourgeoisie—namely, to concede nothing in the pursuit of state power and its class interest. That risk cannot be omitted. However, if crystallization is to mercilessly expose and traverse that class interest it must discover the absolute disorder of what Fanon calls the tabula rasa. Disorder is, then, the ultimate condition of manifestation.) This is why Fanon presents crystallization as a politics that doesn't merely revise (or correct) delusory desire, separating the pure from the impure, but that changes desire itself by engendering new forms of force and power.

This is more than a program, perhaps it is no more than a desire. But this motif of absolute revolt should not be confused with morality, theology, or teleology (as in the works of Shari'ati or Fodéba). To take just one example: the role of literary culture in the political education of the masses. Here we will see Fanon attempting to work out the residual problems in the relation between philosophy, politics, and aesthetics, in the attempt to formulate a new object and new politico-philosophical position; and to engender a shift in his own discourse.

Henceforth, he will strive to combine two problems: the singular delusions that, once seen and known, cause their possessors more grief over what they lack than satisfaction over what they enjoy in their perfection, and the *necessarily* black life that emerges from that suffering (in its singularity for those who suffer), in which we recognize the n'est pas as if it were a verb without tense or mode, since all who inevitably feel it, against their will, conclude that it is a manifestation without a subject.

The task to be accomplished here is not politics, but the philosophical form of what politics crystallizes, such that philosophy as a whole for Fanon just is or should be what crystallizes, as least insofar as it has a relation to politics and/or revolutionary culture. This generalization of the problem will then see Fanon grappling with that emerging as it appears in Fodéba, and it has him, perhaps surprisingly for the postcolonial pessimist we thought he was, endorsing a fundamentally vangardist position for the poet-philosopher, who will be explicitly and even militantly defined in opposition to the bourgeoisie and the leader. This move is then linked to pedagogy (or at least its inadequacies), as Fanon has to accept that in fact crystallization is more implicated in practices of mystification than he at first allowed. I cite the following, crucial passage, at some length:

> Sooner or later, however, the colonized intellectual realizes the existence of a nation is not proved by culture, but in the people's struggle against the forces of occupation. No colonialism draws its justification from the fact that the territories it occupies are culturally nonexistent. Colonialism will never be put to shame by exhibiting unknown cultural treasures under its nose. The colonized intellectual, at the very moment when he undertakes a work of art, fails to realize he is using techniques and a language borrowed from the occupier. He is content to cloak these instruments in a style that is meant to be national but which is strangely reminiscent of exoticism. The colonized intellectual who returns to his people through works of art behaves in fact like a foreigner. Sometimes he will not hesitate to use the local dialects to demonstrate his desire to be as close to the people as possible, but the ideas he expresses, the preoccupations that haunt him are in no way related to the daily lot of the men and women of his country. The culture with which the intellectual is preoccupied is very often nothing but an inventory of particularisms. Seeking to cling close to the people, he clings merely to a visible veneer. *This veneer, however, is merely a reflection of a dense, subterranean life in perpetual renewal.* This reification, which seems all too obvious and characteristic of the people, is in fact but the inert, already invalidated outcome of the many, and not always coherent, adaptations of a more fundamental substance beset with radical changes. Instead of seeking out this substance, the intellectual lets himself be mesmerized by these mummified fragments which, now consolidated, signify, on the contrary, negation, obsolescence, and fabrication. Culture never has the translucency of custom. Culture eminently eludes any form of simplification. In its essence it is the very opposite of custom, which is always a deterioration of culture. Seeking to stick to tradition or reviving neglected traditions is not only going against history, but against one's people. When a people support an armed or even political struggle against a merciless colonialism, tradition changes meaning. What was a technique of passive resistance may, in this phase, be radically doomed. Traditions in an underdeveloped country undergoing armed struggle are fundamentally unstable and crisscrossed by centrifugal forces. This is why the intellectual often risks being out of step. The peoples who have waged the struggle are increasingly impermeable to demagoguery, and by seeking to follow them too closely, the intellectual turns out be nothing better than a vulgar opportunist, even behind the times.[46]

The passage joins several others in Fanon's work in which what is believed to be new turns out to be only stolen goods, and so becomes the object of new dispossession. Since black life does not make its appearance here in conceptual form, what reification makes explicit is a kind of vulgar opportunism. Here the "I" has not the slightest idea, or notion, of how its lived experience corresponds to corruption. What is experienced instead is the "I's" submission to racial ek-stases precisely because they cannot be experienced. Indeed, the "I" runs heedlessly into the abyss of what annuls it, hence obscuring the submission (thus revealed) that is its mode of (unrevealed) existence. Nothing is revealed then but the pain of concealing the unrevealed. Crystallization thus can no longer signify the manifestation of being, power, eros, and so on. *It signifies an imperfection that is content with itself,* and a desire for perfection that remains imitative out of ignorance or fear. In the extreme exoticism of such thought can be discerned an extreme passivity. Fanon concludes from this that these works display a strange affinity with colonialism. They cease to be a revival of neglected traditions except to affirm the a priori value of colonial culture to which they strive to belong. In any case, the intelligibility of mass cultural form, at which they seem to be continually aiming, does not necessarily mean a change in ideological structure. This is precisely the same for each of the particularisms under consideration, if it is the case that they can never satisfy us because experience deceives us, that is because experience remains the empty print and trace of our original deception. Nativist art is thus a pathos (of diversion), and precisely when its enjoyment is presented as originary, for its sense is an object that is truly imaginary.

It will have been noticed that, in the above passage, the metaphor of secrecy, of hidden depths, is generalized: it now defines the relation between demagoguery and politics, or the consequences of what it means to confuse truth for falsehood, custom for armed struggle, resistance for deception, or at least (for the colonial intellectual) why the recourse to nativism reflects, or is part of, reification itself. To be sure, the beautiful *veneer* of nativism constitutes the association (as it must) of bourgeois idealism and *ressentiment*. The demagogic effect of which serves to disguise the artist's true personality; and which accords with a desperate attempt to find compensation for those "mummified fragments" of the self. In this respect, the charismatic element of custom is brought under domination of this reification. Decolonial art is thus read as a crystallization of several elements, and one whose divertive meaning reveals the vein beneath the ligature: the return to tradition is thus essentially the circulation of bloody delusory truths (already assimilated), in which a whole masochistic thought-structure is expressed. It is not an encounter with truth, but, to be sure, bespeaks a permanent fixation on the truth of the colonizer; a position that continues to perform the wish "to be a 'nigger,' not an exceptional 'nigger,' but a real 'nigger,' a 'dirty nigger,' the sort defined by the white man."[47] Just as phantasmatic violence conceals the self-injury it performs, and is a martyr to what it reifies, the attack on the colonizer's language is itself the result of an extreme—masochistic—vision that inevitably confuses dismemberment of language with the dismemberment of colonialism. Here, the wish to depict the endless screams of the tortured, the cutting, the oozing, the vomiting of blood, however well-believed this paroxysm may be as a discourse, leaves the impression of a delusion strengthened by fantasy; and, just as this lust for revenge secretly venerates what it publicly despises, it is tricked in turn by its inability to look upon what is hidden by these venerations: the *jouissance* that confuses masochism for revenge. Such fantasy, regardless of whether it defines itself as accusation or defense, or as an "anamorphic transformation" of history, is the ultimate trap of colonialism, for it can only confirm native life as one lived in lies and deception, and so unable to reach self-understanding.[48] Accordingly, any decolonial aesthetic, however radically defined it may be as anti-colonial, can never free itself from its own deception if the aesthetic, believed to offer a vision of the past that is wholly more enjoyable than the sufferings of the present, is declared to be the true end of politics. The point here is not to eradicate error, but to show how the aesthetic is still being thought in racial, metaphysical terms, in the sense of traditions that can give no support to the future, and in the form of a racial seduction that remains blindly free in its own deception, and so can never be sure of the wretchedness that inevitably follows in its wake.

This is why decolonial literature cannot be one with the people "until it first realize[s] our alienation."[49] "It is not enough," Fanon continues, "to try and disengage ourselves by accumulating proclamations and denials [the metonymic displacement of idealizing metaphors]. It is not enough to reunite with the people in a past where they no longer exist. . . . We must focus on that zone of hidden fluctuation where the people can be found, for let there be no mistake about it, it is here that their souls are crystallized and their perception and respiration transfigured."[50] This is why Fanon turns to

Fodéba, whose poetic work is less about negation than "identifying the exact historical moment of the struggle, with defining the place of action and the ideas around which the will of the people will crystallize."[51] In other words, what allows the people both to interiorize and move beyond apathy and alienation is not negation, nor self-mutilation, but the thought that allows what is secretly hidden to be manifested; that is to say, that point or zone at which the colonizer's language suddenly fluctuates and disperses, and its alienating subterfuges are no longer read as the restoration of reason and therefore of truth, but as an unstable, monumental pressure to form the nation to come. In other words, for Fanon there is no guarantee that tradition can give form or shape to armed struggle, or even be the essential element or figure of it, for such a position (which he attributes to Shariʿati), can only view culture as the transcendental locus of eternal laws that are somehow invisible, and yet endure, sustained by the idealizing metaphors of the nation. Quite the opposite is true: the subterranean life that is to be perpetually renewed by armed struggle is not an inventory of particularisms, a black *Dasein* that is ideal and universal. What matters here is the criterion by which tradition is being evaluated: tradition here is nothing but the permanent delusion of a universal culture that has been repressed, forgotten, or lost, but no longer exists, is only an abstract ideal, a principle determined by humanism.

The conclusion that inevitably follows from this—that such universalism is secular, Western, capitalist—perhaps explains Fanon's reluctance to endorse Shariʿati's belief that an Islamic version of a revolutionary culture should be conceived, institutionally, as the same substance as the nation to come. Everything turns here on the question of interpretation. For Fanon, crystallization is, in sum, the philosophy that both represses and exposes the void of cultural nationalism: it is not only the philosophy that bears witness (as *shahid*) to the pious nation obscured by decadence or corruption, only to be restored through *shahadat*, but a philosophy that goes fishing[52] in the black abyssal depths in order to endow wretchedness with existence: a philosophy that, rather than returning from the void with a message for the masses (a message contrary to bourgeois, secular deception), *begins by evacuating all such philosophical idealism*, and hence by refusing to align itself with any colonial object whatsoever (Fanonism is not a philosophy of negation), in order to set out from nothing but the fall, from abyss to infinitesimal abyss, and from infinity to nothingness. Is there a more radical critique of revolutionary idealism, with its pretension to restore the truth of things? Is there a more striking way of saying that Fanon's "object" par excellence is nothing but the n'est pas, the void whose blackest depths remain incommensurable with the world?

In Shariʿati's reading of Fanonism, which he repeatedly presents as an example of *shahid* (which, it will be remembered, also plays such a significant role in Abolhasan Banisadr's 1971 preface to *Duzokhian-e Zamin* [his Persian translation of *The Wretched of the Earth*], "About Fanon and His Thoughts"), what is thus introduced is a confusion between the veneer of the text, so to speak, and the dark subterranean life that is its philosophical object.[53] Accordingly, in thinking Fanonism, it becomes all the more necessary for Banisadr and, to a lesser extent, Shariʿati, to classify Western bourgeois, secular deception as a form of anti-humanism, which Banisadr says (contrary to his general presentation of the "revolutionary creativeness" of the young and the oppressed) is now in crisis in Asia, Africa, Latin America, as well as in Europe:

> The translation of this book [*The Wretched of the Earth*], which is from start to end a rejection of the bourgeois values and culture of the West, has become available exactly when the bourgeoisie is in crisis in its own stronghold, which is to say, in Europe, and violence [*ghahr*] is pervading this society too. The young generation that is worried about its future, a generation that will make the future, has lost hope in the values of a society based on a consumption economy, values that are presumed eternal. Wherever able, this generation has raised the flag of rebellion [*shuresh*] around the world against a culture that exhibits one response, that is, force [*zur*], to the totality of humanity's issues.[54]

Here, too, what distinguishes this fighting (*razmande*) humanity from the colonial bourgeoisie (and thus what comes under the rubric of revolutionary creativity) is *shahadat*, which channels the "violence and power of the people through the swamp of confusion." Indeed, what inhibits this power is nothing but imitation, which cannot liberate thought from its neocolonial constraints. But insofar as Fanonism is itself both "a mirror and a floodlight," how is one to know true illumination from its narcissistic delusion? If *shahadat* is also what crystallizes, undecidably, both what inhibits (self-alienation) and what galvanizes (new ways of thinking and action), isn't this also exemplarily the case with neocolonialism? Banisadr continues: "Fanon's art is that he understands the mechanisms underlying these shifts and trans-formations [from imitation to revolution] and articulates them. His art is that he illustrates how a concrete process, by which new customs are im-posed upon the colonized, engenders new ways of thinking and doing."[55] Yet how do we distinguish this art from the very thing it is most supposed not to be, its very opposite—namely Western reification? In Shari'ati, for ex-ample, decolonialism is truly inventive *not* when it represents, but when it *shows* how revolutionary thought suddenly takes on form in the nation state. Without this *relevé*, so to speak, there is no crystallizing return. These no-tions go along with what Shari'ati elsewhere describes as an illumination that is of the order of an unveiling, and which will lead him, ambiguously perhaps, to attribute this view to Fanon too, as though all that needed to be done was to *unconceal* deception. In this he remains a thinker of ontology-as-illumination. Yet, this thought of revelation cannot be known in itself; it can only be seen in what it illumines, for what is authentic and eternal must be hidden so as to prevent its corruption. Anyone wishing to return to such knowledge must thereby be able to recognize it irrevocably, for as soon as they discover it, they must also throw off the yoke of established thought and custom. For the truth that brings us freedom also shows how we lack authority and justice. But what if, momentarily, we cannot tell apart the ve-neer from the life taking form in the field of this crystallizing vision: at the very least, by dint of the fact that true invention must, at the same time, *ap-pear* to be illuminating?

For Fanon, the time—the moment—of revolution always involves a nec-essary exposure to instability and irresolution, a moment to which no *Vor-stellung* is identical, but which bears witness to a void to which the revolu-tionary moment attests, or, in some respects opens, by allowing people to see as if for the first time, or to see from the wrong side as it were. Contrary to these emphases, in Shari'ati's illumination, what is unveiled is a common enterprise leading each and all to see anew their common precarity, pov-erty, and wretchedness. *Shahadat* does not only illuminate our wretched-ness; it also illuminates how it can be filled with an infinite and immutable revelation.

Here the connection of the wretched with what Shari'ati famously calls illumination becomes clear, but via a key difference. In Fanon what is re-peatedly expressed, and increasingly worried over, is the difficulty of being able to tell apart what illumines from the fantasy of its unveiling, especially in the way that the politics of illuminism is expressed and communicated to others, and regardless of whether this communication is received as truth or revelation. This is because in our distractedness, we are incapable of attaining the n'est pas by our own efforts. The way Shariʿati bypasses this is to say that only the *shahid* can lay claim to truth, and he does so in his resolute opposition to secular rhetoric and representation. *Shahadat* already is, in a certain sense, the alethic-ludic shadow of illumination. And what it reveals is a political life that is never anything but a pedagogical self-relation (so as to abolish the distance between faith and its teaching). These premises find their most striking expression in that of an advent that "returns" political life to the pedagogical practices that sanctify it. But life thereby knows itself as logos, to which it gives life, which it is made of, for what is comprehended as life is the true life of spirit, rather than the infinite abyss of deception; and it is our understanding that allows what was hidden to be found, and it is we who discover life as logos. Could it be said then that return takes place as the effect of a logos-illumination in which the past casts its light on the present, and via a faith that is felt to be more imperious than doubt (but not any the less deceptive)? An illumination that thus reveals the lack of logos *and* its ideal presence, to the extent that it is shown to us as the (repressed) truth of delusion?

If Fanonism is read along these lines (the foregoing is clearly only brief notes on the preface, and do not claim to represent Shariʿati's vast corpus on *bazgasht* or *shahadat*[56]), that is, as a "mold" waiting to be filled by Islamic content, how is it possible to imagine Fanonism, under its philosophical veneer, as anything other than an idealized beginning that must itself be returned from? And how is it possible to imagine that the fascination exerted by the mirror that Fanon holds up to the masses, a mirror image allowing them to see themselves for the first time, without alienation or fear, is purely centered on truth rather than on delusion, or that the philosophical form of that reflection can only be accomplished by taking religion as the essence of the political, one whose message is achieved through *shahadat*? In brief, there seems to be no suspicion, in Banisadr, for example, that what appears to be the most revolutionary illumination might not also be the most convincing imitation (politically); or that what is *revealed as secret, hidden, might also illumine what has been effaced, forgotten, dissimulated* (philosophically).

I would like to suggest that this is no less a political decision than a philosophical question, and one that also allows Shari'ati to displace the problem or possibility that what crystallization ultimately reveals is, as it were, nothing and rightly so—for why should the passage from politics to religion be any the less unstable than the passage from desire to delusion? Perhaps this question is too simple. I am well aware that Shari'ati is thinking of something different than delusion, or the imaginary, when he says that *bazgasht* also reveals something ungraspable, unnameable, and unsayable—namely, the great revolt of Being that is absolutely heterogeneous to the world, and, as such, lies beyond reason, dialectic, philosophy and representation.

Beyond the shadow of a doubt, it is this shared insistence on an unassimilable, severe refusal that brings Shari'ati closer to Fanon, whence their notion of revolt as something abrupt, unprecedented, untimely, and in which the only wager is against all forms of power and domination. And yet, Shari'ati's project remains one of ideology and of reformation; the possibility of liberation is not that of a pure wager, for Islam remains *the* figure of reconciliation and desire. (This more orthodox version of *bazgasht* is very different from Fanon's refusal to see cultural revolution as ideological war, and precisely because what it conceals has neither object, image, nor form). Once understood, this is why, contra Miller and others, Fanonism is not just a reprise of the universal as understood by philosophy, but nor is it merely an idealism masquerading as an ever purer form of the general will, and thereby condemned to repeat the impasses of colonial sovereignty. But nor does Fanon, and in spite of Shari'ati's reading, reproduce the language of authenticity under the guise of religion, or see in religion an ethical response to the politics of neocolonialism, with culture seen as the locus—the habitus—of *shahadat*. For Fanon, in brief, the dispute is not one of faith, but one of exemplarity; in other words, if the belief is that only in *shahadat* can logos be illumined, *shahadat* ceases to seem like a mysterious and contingent revelation of living being. Instead, it becomes integrated into a network of offices and legislatures that derive from the political ambitions of the *ecclesia*. Even if the latter is understood as the most severe form of renunciation—of life, value, difference, and desire—and represents a moment of terrible frugality, despite all of this, Fanon's belief is not so much the notion that such resistance must not enter the form of a clerical, institutional reasoning (and which is the world of politics and deception [*tazvir*]) but, on

the contrary, that the people must also resist the imaginary of absolute resistance as revelation.

Whence the essential role of an abyssal opening, and the economic and
political role of the wretched, the *nothing* that cannot be negated and that
opens a void *within* power, discourse, reason—whether conceived as revolt
or inertia. Shariʿati wants to say that Fanonism is *shahadat*, but the choice of
metaphors—of an exposure of what is secretly hidden or denied—continues
to plague his discussion in a way that he never entirely deals with, and this
shows up symptomatically, I suggest, in his repeated discussion of *shahadat*
as the place where philosophy crystallizes itself as religion.[57]

Shahadat exposes what is hidden, which means that it is clearly not synonymous with jihad and may be in some considerable tension with it as a
means. That *shahadat* gathers these different attributes is perhaps what leads
Banisadr, in "About Fanon and His Thoughts" (and Shariʿati in the later lectures), to want to make a distinction between a good crystallization and a
bad crystallization. He is provoked into doing so by just the persuasive, anti-
mimetic features of *shahadat* he has now recognized, features that are in fact
inseparable from, and indeed fundamental to, a revolutionary model of Islamic community: in *shahadat*, in brief, martyrdom completes the "exposure of what is being denied." But this very same ethical character of Islam
will mean it comes to be effected by an essential uncertainty (Shariʿati calls
it rather oddly an "invitation"), such that the effect of *shahadat always might*
be exposed in its truth or veracity by what is said, paradoxically, to be the
true form of the duplicity that designates it, the more so as Shariʿati identifies, in Iran's bourgeois secular elites, a struggle to gain the upper hand when
it comes to lying about lying (which is why everything that the corrupt say is
undeniably true, and why politics is always the matter of thinking the truth
without being able to say it). A successfully religious performance of *shahadat* by the *ecclesia* is thus the means, despite what Shariʿati says at several
times, which allows him to think the purity of revolt, and thus to affirm revelation as the crystallizing essence that leads us to truth. (Given the importance of these notions in late Fanon, one measures the stakes of this *shahadat*/crystallization question as one in which a revolutionary will is or is not
allowed to appear, by way of art, philosophy, or politics). Under the pressure
of this uncertainty, in a 1960s lecture on *Bazgasht*, Shariʿati now identifies a
return to Islam not as a return to tradition, or a "line of inheritance," but a

return to "Islam as an ideology."⁵⁸ In the *Sociology of Islam*, Shariʿati defines this ideology not as "a return [*bazgasht*] to the past, but the revival of the past in the present."⁵⁹ (It should be noted here how this refusal of historical time, of traditionalism, is similar to Fanon's concept of a tabula rasa, but his notion is irreconcilable with that of return and reformation; indeed, Fanon uses this phrase in *The Wretched of the Earth* to represent the necessity of disorder in any revolutionary moment—for that which is disclosed may soon be covered up, and there is no straight path from event to revolution.) But the bad crystallization actually wins the argument (for *shahadat* is now precisely defined as the essence of *bazgasht*, that is to say, in order for *shahadat* to found and awaken in us a new sense of *ummati* [political community], it has to return to a source higher than itself, a source that leaves us free only insofar as we accept its absolute authority, and which is different from the void and its infinitely-finite fall within meaning).

What constitutes *shahadat* is, then, a *reading of exemplarity that is itself martyr to its own exemplary reading*. To know *shahadat* in as much as its truth is exemplary is thus to be illuminated by ideology, but only insofar as what is illuminated induces, or rouses in us belief in the truth and reality of its exemplarity. It's an aporia, however veritable or inventive, that only acquires the weight of truth insofar as it becomes politically effective as ideology— that is, takes hold of the minds of men. If this is true—or, at a minimum, true of *shahadat* as Shariʿati defines it—then it makes sense to say that it is essentially through the presence of illumination, for the purpose of differentiating truth from simulacra, logos from power, that *shahadat* becomes the revelatory truth of decolonial struggle, with Islam being the ideological form—and I would add, the decision, the decree—that discloses *shahadat* as the crystallizing origin and paradigm. The return to ideology is also the true end of politics in the real of being. But if *shahadat* is structured by *bazgasht*, by a return that exposes deception, this is a return that is thereby always rebegun and undone as the unending negation of exposure and deception. Suffice it to say, this is not the same thing as the nation to come; whose *à-venir* (the form through which it comes) has no predestined end, and no foundation, for its revival is a wager against history, desire, fantasy, and law.

Let us briefly conclude this section. First, and crucially: Shariʿati does not pursue this possibility, already here indicated by Fanon, that revelation cannot be conceived as a logic (of exemplarity) without making it express a metonymy (or phantasm) of displacement.[60] This notion is not rhetorical, but refers to how, in the postcolony, doxa can literally become the true enjoyment of error. And Fanon gives two further reasons for why this is so: the first has to do with the revolutionary appearance of those who have nothing, an appearance that is situated at the limit of what can be read as doxa due to their inimitable exclusion and censorship; and the second (which must in fact take logical priority) being what we (what I, at least, from a black perspective) would have to call the necessary impossibility of their being a (blackness of) being without being, and what Fanon rather strikingly calls a n'est pas, whose figure is that of a tabula rasa (explicitly defined as absolute disorder). This figure also denotes a limit-situation of what can be figured, and precisely because its finite infinitude decenters the symbolic work of all structure.

The impossibility of this n'est pas, and the extent to which it infiltrates the very concept of being itself, is what interests me here: we shall see it resonate throughout the discussions of Fodéba in the next section, in the form of a *pas* or *relevé* that cannot be figured, conceived, or perceived as the symbolic work of culture. And although Shari'ati's discussion of Fanon does indeed capture something of this impossibility, he does not seem inclined to stress this point, namely that a cultural revolution may indeed be driven by delusion, may even contradict it by underscoring another concealment, whereby the model it offers is not the actual truth but rather the cunning imitation that appears *as* truth. To reduce the work of revolt to that of ideology, in short, one also has to be aware that *all* ideology is subject to mastery and law—that is, it consolidates delusion in the space of the void. In order to avoid this impasse (which is not easy), Fanon recognizes that what makes revelation crystallizing is not what is said to be true but what the masses believe to be true, whatever the facts of the matter—this means that the truth has become (has always already become) undecidable as truth, which is why the relationship between politics and truth does not rest upon one "metaphysical principle," as Fanon tells us, and why, too, he insists that the future to come makes visible an opening that has no *arché*, telos, or predestined end.[61]

Secondly, I would like to defend the thesis that Shari'ati's use of the word *crystallization* is noticeably different from that of Fanon. Indeed, when Shari'ati uses the term, he is, in many ways, highlighting these differences, and in a way that recasts his entire relationship to Fanonism. It occurs in a context in which he is contrasting authentic and inauthentic existence: "But real or authentic being lasts for many centuries—over the entire course of history as culture, civilization, and art take shape. It crystallizes in me."[62] Here, once again, what crystallizes (be it form or origin) is the desire for a sublime historicity that, paradoxically, ends up denying time and alterity. Here no real break occurs between *Dasein* and its historicity, since what art, culture, and civilization crystallize, over many centuries, is an essence prior to its temporalization as time. At the center of manifestation, there is the ideal form of a particularizing will. The relation between logos and illumination is thus realized in living being. This is a paradoxical discovery, in view of the fact that will is always *in advance* of what crystallizes it as *Dasein*, and by way of an anticipatory, belated rediscovery of what completes it in the absence of any relation. But what difference is there between real or authentic being and this ideal of its accomplishment? How is one "given" this experience, and on what basis is will joined to its appearing, imprinted by its reflection? And are we not back, once again, in an economy of good (authentic) and bad (inauthentic) crystallization? This is perhaps the inevitable result of a point of view that sees in manifestation an exemplarity that only becomes meaningful when it is linked to an eschatology, however nuanced or dialectical, whose self-presence relies upon its unambiguousness. This is why Shari'iati states, by antiphrasis, that being *is* what it crystallizes, for what crystallizes it *is* being's authenticity, and via a path that leads back to God. What does this signify, if not an attempt to think not only the political limits of being and becoming but also the (prevailing) legitimate form of religious community? It is unfortunate, however, that this historicity—that attains its end in will—is noticeably different from that moment (of *shahadat*) that makes visible an aporia between history and revelation, between the world of experience and the moment of encounter, when the *agon* becomes the thought of infinite life, and there is no way of attaining that thought without the necessary death of the subject, or, more precisely, its reinvention. But what I am claiming is the real paradox—the undecidability of crystallization as pedagogy, and, thereby, the fundamental undecidability of a truth that is always duped, or that dupes itself—this real paradox is curiously elided in the belief that authentic *Dasein* does not need to be founded (crystallized) for it *is* what founds (crystallizes) authenticity.

This comes down to saying that it may well be impossible to decide whether manifestation necessarily presupposes delusion or simply refers to the way delusion is manifested. For a literally revealed truth may also conceal what it illumines, and without contradiction. However different the means they employ, manifestation is incapable of realizing its goal without deception. It is what makes revelation exemplary. This includes the exception to which it refers, and the inception that is its goal. What remains obscure therefore is why illumination is not connected entirely to what is feigned. It is because the mind can be so easily seduced by the pleasures of deception that reason and faith go to war against it. Only as such can *shahadat*—or the politics of its truth—be crystallized. Why? Because the light of the depths is so dazzling? Or is it because it is only through such depths that logos can be illuminated? But a question immediately arises from these two different ways of thinking exemplarity, and one that has considerable implications for Shari'ati's reading of Fanon: Does *shahadat* (the process by which the masses receive the logos) necessarily end in revolution or does it, like the politics of duplicity, remain suspended in a purely idealized—and ultimately metonymical—desire for luminous chimeras? This suggests, as a corollary, that the true task of cultural revolution always entails the ability to tell apart signs from their referents, albeit by the negative road of exposing error and deception. Language and the world cannot be redeemed, therefore, until bad crystallization can be rewritten as authentic historicity. As such, even if revolution cannot occur without *shahadat*, what has to be grasped is the sign that links them, in the passage from error to truth, to their referents understood as light and law. Illumination is thus the result of pedantry: the masses must be able to illumine its nuances, and so ensure its correct version. Earlier we called this an abyssal descent, because logos must descend into the abyss if the relation between infinity and the subject is to be made irrefutably present. Every living being will be judged according to this lucidity. It is what the exemplarity of invention or revelation means. In illumination, then, what gets crystallized at the bottom of the abyss is the image being cast by the infinite lost in the shadows of particularity.

He who declares it true—under the effect of ideology—is no more ignorant or wiser than he who compels belief that its referent is delusion.

Now, Fanon, when concerning himself with national culture, does not reject the idea that crystallization marks a concern with revelation and with ideology, but even though this ideology is born very specifically in neocolonial society, what distinguishes it are necessarily unforeseen forms of expression that acquire new significations. What crystallizes being—negrophobic, bourgeois, decolonial—is not revelation, but the subterranean renewal of signs that cannot be rendered as philosophy, and that are without political-religious definition. To be sure, this is why manifestation is defined as a will to capture the particularity of things without pathos. Hence Fanon's audacious refusal of all meaning and all thought derived from the sacred. There is no talk here of an unequivocal meaning, for there always will be a thousand detours, a thousand artifices by which the forms (the ideological codes) of the nation can be confused—nay, hijacked—by the language of authenticity; consequently, there is simply no easy way of avoiding these eventualities. In fact, the nation to come does not presuppose an ideal affirmation or message, simply because its definition is always already surrounded by irreducible dangers. This is the impasse in which any cultural criticism cut off from the realities of political power finds itself. But rather than return to a notion of the absolute—with its whiff of transcendentalism—the challenge Fanon set himself was to envisage an infinite series of encounters falling across multiple tabulæ rasæ, but with no assignable order or hierarchy. This is why the exact historical moment of struggle matters to Fanon—and I would suggest not so much for Shari'ati—for it is the precise point at which the will of the people constitutes a new inventive relationship to the world.

This is why, as we know, Fanon, in his dispute with Shari'ati, agrees that, in the absence of liberation, the "rebirth of religious spirit" can become a "great power" for alienated humanity, but so too, he suggests, religion should never declare itself to be the political truth of that power, however persuasive it appears. For, even if the truth were to become present through *shahadat*, there still needs to be an *ecclesia* who can recognize its exemplarity in order to deliver its message to society. We might thus quite precisely approach the problem of the division between good crystallization and others, whose political importance is considerable, especially at times of crisis, as a division between an imaginary form of the state and the real of its manifestation. But here, too, our task is not to oppose manifestation, say, to religion; but is rather to understand the n'est pas that opens *as* nothingness, and in which there is no subject, no *cogito*, no authenticity, and no necessary moment of revelation. It may be recognized, or it may not. And

experience shows us that this *relevé* is one forever poised between nothingness and delusion, and that it is undecidable, irreversible, wretched. This will
be clear enough to all who have followed Fanon's reading of the n'est pas and
the imaginary, an account that conceives of it as something more and something less than politics, and thereby as the limit-condition of political philosophy itself (as I believe it in fact must be). And although Fanon does not
formulate the problem in this way, I want to suggest that this is why crystallization can be summarily and abstractly presented as the unresolved relation between politics and philosophy in his account. It is an account whose
project is not new, but to which its reading of black texts offers renewed possibilities of learning and exploration, to which I now turn.

IV

And in the scorched blue of the sky, right above the body of
Naman, a gigantic vulture slowly hovered. It seemed to say
to him: "Naman! You have not danced the dance that bears
my name. *Others will dance it [D'autres la danseront]*."
Keïta Fodéba, "Aube Africaine"

"Aube Africaine" will serve, insofar as it presents itself as an incomplete
dance (that is, as a *pas* that never quite performs or presents itself), as our
transition from Shari'ati to Fodéba. The poem will also allow us to return
to the role, despite Fanon's reluctance, played by religion in national culture,
and because what is in question is, above all, the resonances of sacred tradition buried and then revived, resonances that must be registered in the
struggle for decolonial culture.

In our opening remarks, we drew attention to Fanon's reading of "Aube
Africaine" in terms of the poem's "undeniable pedagogical value": in its de-
piction of the Tiaroye massacre, the poem not only brings to an abrupt end
any idealism about independence; it also shows how traditionalism, in itself, can be the cultural equivalent of idealism.[63] How does the poem achieve
this? By doing the opposite to what Fanon criticizes Shari'ati for: by showing how religion "risks being out of step" with the struggle against colonialism—including the war against fascism—and by showing that struggle in its
real historical significance.[64] Clearly, what is at stake here has something to

do with how race continues to define the politics of independence and how the suppression of that fact presupposes racism in its very elaboration. What the poem crystallizes, therefore, is the politics of a missed encounter, that is to say, the radical confusion of tradition for the pitfalls of culture, and of custom for the aporias of the present. Fanon's point here is a subtle one and should not be mistaken: the value of the poem lies not in what it represents, but in how it makes visible the violence of anti-black representation (that is often *never read as such*). This is why Fanon describes the poem as an "authentic invitation," or what, in his Rome address, he calls a "real invocation" [*réelle invocation*], which means: a "demystification" that crystallizes the struggle over national culture.[65] This is why the reading of "Aube Africaine" constitutes a fundamental moment in Fanon's chapter on national culture, and why through it (and its modes of expression) he discovers that the question of the poetic is also the problem of crystallization—a problem that turns on the complex relation between the *pas* (or what it means to be in step with the struggle *or* be subjugated) and the *relevé* (what is required for art to become the real of an encounter *or* be reduced to mere formalism). To perhaps understand why, let us briefly return to the final lines of the poem (above).

Others will dance it, Fodéba says, for the dead can no longer dance the Douga—the dance of the vulture god. But what is this dance for? And what does it mean to dance or not dance it? To be chosen to dance this dance, we are told, is a rare honor, and for a peasant to be so chosen doubly so, for the Douga is the dance of emperors. "[E]very step represents a period in the history of the Mandingos" that has been performed down through the centuries.[66] In other words, every *pas* unifies in one and the same metonymic movement a metaphorical history; every *pas* is an *emerging* unity of form and praxis, of gesture and performance; and every step is thereby absorbed into the eternity that comes before and after—as remembrance is swallowed up by infinity, and glory is allotted its place in tradition and history, since to perform the dance is to see "thought transposed into the world of bodies."[67] To dance this dance is thus to be transformed: from the particular to the heroic, the finite to the infinite, the corporeal to a force superior to man. From this ancestral ritual, which deserves a richer analysis than I can offer here, Fodéba draws a whole philosophy: namely, to observe these *pas* is to witness origin become image and world become spirit, for what is required, in sum, is the ability to see how each step marks out the rule of kings and how each step carries the weight of the glorious dead, independent of reason or representation. But what also emerges with each *pas* is the unity of living being and sacred power, which swiftly vanishes again. Why? Because contrary to sacred tradition, modern spiritlessness has led man astray from what is holy, insurgent, perfect. There is another superimposition here: if modern secular Africa can no longer perform these *pas*, having lost contact with the ancestors in the pursuit of other pleasures, Africa needs new forms (of rule) for the lived expression of ideology. The glories that have been lost—of religion and sacred power—indicate a political life that has withdrawn from rule and that is without a center; modern black desire is now forcibly subdued and charmed by other truths (miseries) and consolations (racial capital). This is simply the price paid for a (false) crystallization, which is a far more terrible and harmful a fate than sacred authentic power.

A dialectic comes into play at this point: in it, the failure to dance the dance becomes a metaphor for something out of reach, deferred, suspended. If to dance the Douga consists in the desire to have one's strength, beauty, and piety be measured by the glorious measures of culture, why are these *pas* the means to their own negative disfiguration? The poem's repeated emphasis on violence and grief—on elegy and defeat rather than on hope or glory— does nothing more than present these *pas* as having lost the power to negate (and so transform, sublate, reveal, or exult). The wars that gave spirit law, power, and life have removed these *pas* from any redemptive or recapitulatory narrative. Along with these deferred elements, the poetic narrative literally becomes an asymptote of endless unreachability. In fact, what circulates here are not so much acts of heroic judgement, but tropes of doubt and suspension; deferrals that elliptically signify—without saying so—a parabasis; a continuous motion between recognition and aporia that appears in the poem as *letters* that have gone astray, or that are so far apart from knowledge that they have no meaning in either city or kingdom, and that consequently remain in darkness. For it is the alignment of these letters with death that constitutes the dance of spirit as one of deadly disfiguration. The transition from death to disfiguration, from the aesthetic to the political, is thus clearly marked in the poem as it moves from the figure of war to that of the dance, and from dawn to twilight. In the poem we accordingly see misread letters, in which what remains of the dead signifies a common unawareness (of Naman's murder at the hands of white officers) that the kingdom's *ecclesia* are equally incapable of knowing and have no desire to know. Here every message sent is immediately separated, and yet already deferred. It is what the *pas* means: a repose that, independent of reason and mastery, signifies death and conflict.[68] The dance of the vulture thus reveals a death's head (both literally and allegorically), that reveals not eternity, but just other empty signifiers, *which never bring the parabasis to a rest*. Why? Because blackness has no repose, and is denied any rest, and has literally no space for judgment?

All of these questions are just a prelude to what Fanon calls attention to in his reading; namely, how the void of rule (at the heart of the postcolony) is covered over—by denial and repression, but also condemnation—by the need to anchor reality in tradition. Whence the poem's pedagogical value in its rejection of such idealism in favor of a tabula rasa, and why this rejection represents a synecdoche of the political even though it has no semantic destination *as* politics. So how does this missed encounter make community possible? No doubt because these various *pas* or missteps carry within themselves the transcendent capacity of the nation to come. This *relevé* only becomes readable as a transcendental condition of possibility; and also as a practice that is, above all, that of *struggle*, which, as the negative impact of not being able to bear the suffering of one's fellow men, crystallizes how political community exists by virtue of being absent for those who have nothing, who exist as nothing, wretchedly in the depths. But all this, which is posed from the beginning as a dispute between philosophy and revolt, still does not explain Fanon's reading of the poem.

As previously mentioned, Fanon distinguishes Fodéba's work for its historical exactitude (with respect to the revolutionary moment), and because it is also *in step* [*à la même cadence*] with the people:

> We should not therefore be content to delve into the people's past to find concrete examples to counter colonialism's endeavors to distort and depreciate. We must work and struggle in step [*à la même cadence*] with the people so as to shape the future and prepare the ground where vigorous shoots are already sprouting. National culture is no folklore where an abstract populism is convinced that it has uncovered the popular truth.[69]

The phrase "*à la même cadence*" should give us pause here: it doesn't say at what speed or pace this work or struggle should occur (or even whether it can occur), but it does oscillate between two themes, considered as totalities in their respective relation to national culture, and from which Fanon deduces an essential feature of crystallization: abstract populism, and what it takes or believes to be the true form of the people's past, "risks being out of step" and "behind the times," in as much as it cannot develop that will to particularize that is the essential feature of cultural revolution.[70] Thus, the importance to Fanon of the notion of reading as struggle or revolt, and thus also his belief that the future literature of the nation cannot be prejudged without being reduced to an abstract, pedagogical presupposition (which is neither memorial nor just).

This clearly gives Fodéba's poetic philosophy a political dimension, even though the form of its expression has yet to be elaborated, and Fanon is keen to specify that dimension by distinguishing it from an abstract idea of struggle or philosophy, still less to propose it as a propositional truth about history. If it thus becomes impossible to determine what "*à la même cadence*" should be or is, it is also impossible to know or specify how it is to be essentially defined as a particularity (the explicit discussion of which is here necessarily deferred). Whereas abstract populism reduces combat to hermeneutics and substitutes present alienation for the efficacious rediscovery of the past, which, again, replaces a popular truth with one that is narcissistically reassuring (i.e., the perfect image of the people substituted for one's imperfect self-identity), the nation to come is characterized by an emphasis on the necessity of contingency, with the entrancement of difference, immanence, and historicity never taking place as such. Indeed, he says, the moment the people are plunged into their wretchedness they realize their former enjoyment of the charismatic qualities of the ruling clique, which has become their second nature.

From this principle that crystallizes the necessity of revolt, a choice has to be made between custom and the insurgency that is *à la même cadence*. This also explains why Fanon uses the word "*détraquer*" (meaning to wreck, to put out of use) to show how this *relevé* becomes necessary, and via writings that can, at any one moment, become *déchirure* (meaning a rupture or tear that is also a moment of danger), subverting and so transforming both time and historical judgment.[71] If this remark, which would have to be developed, is not wrong, it would explain why, in his reading of literature, Fanon avoids paraphrase but remains loyal to referentiality. It would also explain his refusal to oppose anti-black genocide to a humanistic, aesthetic-ethical ideal that is above race since it is racism itself. In passing, Fanon seems to be expressing a disagreement with Fodéba on the question of the dangers of abstract populism (at least in the article on "La danse africaine et la scène," where Fodéba writes, "for us, authenticity is synonymous with reality . . . with living expression").[72] Indeed, if living expression is itself a metaphor of the performative political power of the aesthetic, its (political) expression can no more be rendered authentically than tradition can be experienced as a living aesthetic. In "Aube Africaine," what we see instead is how each *pas* (of tradition) defers the power of such expression and therewith its significance as living reality or form. By taking this step (*pas*) beyond the traditional conceptions of the dance (*pas*) as a mode of cultural representation, as a polarity of light and darkness, of artifice and authenticity, of essence or mask, of ritual or power, the way is prepared for the subsequent undoing of the *pas* by a *n'est*. The n'est pas—like the phrase "*à la même cadence*"—does not fall within the representational code of the text, it does not dance in or out of step with figure or concept. The n'est pas brings another aspect of language into play—that is, the darkening movement of the sun, determined by the day as a violent act of power, or its persistent anti-illumination, suggests that the n'est pas can only be manifested as an arbitrary (deadly) act of language. The waning of the day, the suspension of the dance, both result from the single act of power by which language posits what is no longer, as the sun rises only to fall not on life's living expression but on death. The result is that the n'est pas cannot become part of a sequence of steps, or even be punctuated by a will to particularity. It is a *pas* without telos or antecedence. Only retrospectively can it be seen to have a dialectical relationship to the battle between day and night, or between the two transcendental orders of being—the dance of gods and of history. Again, here prosopopoeia, unlike night following day, has to be deposited via customs (letters) that lack authority and justice.

On the one hand, all this still leaves the exact nature of the relation *à la même cadence* to cultural revolution implicit, and on the other, it has to defer the problem introduced into the whole argument by trying to think *à-venir* as a moment of *cristallisation*. Decolonial politics, on this description, does not tell the people its truth, nor does it provide it with approved content (that is: the n'est pas is not to be confused with revelation), but it introduces a note of radical discontinuity into what the people believe and understand to be the truth. What is in play here is a movement that exposes truth as a system of anti-black tropes. On Fanon's account there is, then, nowhere else to go: we can continue to study the passage from myth into history—or, in the language of the poem, the passage from dance to war—in the hope that we can overcome, or prevent, the return of history into myth (or the slide back into the language and signification of reification). Or we can choose to unmask not only the mystifications of racial discourse, but to contest its mode of communicability—that is to say, the very system of its semiology, its representational meaning, but also the political power of its aesthetic. The struggle over national culture, in fact, has as its aim to discard the mythic reading of black culture, and to take a text such as "Aube Africaine" and make it the expression of a counter-political thought. Not only, however, is this speculative thinking the object of Fanon's attention: it is an integral part of his own *écriture*, his attempt to resituate the rhetorical code (or codes) by which blackness is made racially, referentially meaningful as a mimetic function of the text. How can one dance *this* dance, to continue the metaphor, if the blackest dance is nothing but the infinity of its deadly repose? Such is the case with the n'est pas, in whose unique motion we are cast down into the abyss, and where what crystallizes performs nothing but the restless impossibility of its meaning.

These themes, which, from Shari'ati to Fanon to Fodéba, have become familiar to us by now, are crucial for any understanding not only of Fanon's political philosophy, but also one of his more obscure objects: the drive—or crystallizing power—of subjects carried forward by a relentless, but imperious, general will during times of crisis. It is of the essence of this trope that what suffuses all movement is irremediably outside presence and resolution. Far from inviting the subject to become, to manifest what it is, to take a step (and each step is the span of centuries), it makes appear, instead, that which annuls it, and simply because the future work of the nation is still to be danced (read) as justice. For to dance this dance—as piety or knowledge—is to risk being disfigured in turn by the mythical (racial) violence that founds it. Admitting that the struggle for national independence necessarily includes these ambiguities (recognizing, in other words, the problems raised around the extremely complex relations between form, structure, praxis, and being), Fanon invokes, with extreme irony, the image of the colonial intellectual who mutilates popular culture as a substitute for his own existential anguish. It's a mutilation in which manifestation is shown to be confused with masochism. Which is another way of saying that there is no straightforward way to distinguish between spontaneity and resistance, especially if we take into account that spontaneity is itself delusory, and that resistance can only repeat the language of spontaneity as its own revolutionary alibi. This is why Fanon says that Fodéba *sees further*, and by dint of the fact that he reveals the obscure paths by which speaking the truth to power can also conceal political repression as the true fate of cultural revolution and of civil war. This is, thus, a vision that is able to reveal without compromising the constant oscillation between, on the one hand, a struggle that is resolute in its opposition to colonialism, as exemplified by "Aube Africaine," and, on the other, a poetic relation to the political that Fanon concedes is itself a *concession* to what subverts all delusory expressions of existence, and which itself manifests a courageously strange solicitude that opens up the masses to a profoundly disfiguring improvisation.

I want to say that these affirmations could betray a blind faith and even heroism (and Fanon's image of national culture has seemed entirely idealized to certain critics). But the problematic raised by crystallization resists such moralizing precisely because it refuses to surrender to seduction. For it is already clear that the notion commits Fanon to an irredeemably pessimistic view of independence and what it lays bare—namely, a negatively explicit *return* to colonialism, as we have seen.

V

We need to move slowly, and the problem lies in having to gradually
expose mechanisms that reveal themselves in their totality.
Frantz Fanon, *Black Skin, White Masks*

In conclusion, I would like briefly to return to Fanon's theory of manifestation. The most difficult thing in Fanon is doubtless the attempt to have a crystallizing vision (of the nation to come) that doesn't end up reifying it into a concept; it's a caution that represents a major effort by him not to repeat the *situation* of racial philosophy. That struggle makes itself felt in the opposition to all forms of imaginary delusion, but in ways that disallow the conversion of negation into some kind of central, unshakeable certitude or faith (what Fanon famously calls, in the chapter on violence, a thought that is "literally disarmed" by its own integrity).[73] This repeats what is in fact a constant worry in Fanon: namely that to have faith is to concede that one may be undone, irreparably so, by that concession and, more unsettlingly, be possessed by roles that one doesn't know that one is unconsciously playing. Any attempt to break out of delusion must thereby resist the illusion of its unveiling. He who by his class interest is compelled to live "off" politics will almost always be tempted to regard corruption as the "essence" of politics. Or, he must consider the vanity of his submission to be the unexpressed truth of his "real" interests. So how does one counter these inner enjoyments and their intolerable presumptions? One must be able to see what one cannot yet see; one must make the incomprehensible the vocation of one's politics.

Throughout the discussion of national culture, this problem has showed up in the way that what is provisionally called manifestation can never be a figure of dialectical resolution, whatever its crystallizing form. In that context, Fanon's manifest attempt to find, in the power of political events, new structures and forms is where the incomprehensible crystallizes. Therefore, if one can see something emerging in the depths, and if that something can carry out a reversal of racial phenomenology itself, it will prove fruitful. However, one must be wary not to see manifestation simply as a cure for one's miseries. That way delusion lies on the basis, explicit or implicit, that such cause betrays a devotional form of thinking, and precisely because the act of lucidity by which one realizes that one suffers can itself be a form of blindness, and one that masks itself as understanding. And for this, a more speculative understanding of who one is, is needed. This is the decisive quality of Fanon's psychopolitics: his declaration, again in the text on violence, that the wretched "do not lay claim to [represent the] truth . . . because they are the truth in their very being."[74] Hence their *distance* to class politics and interests. The wretched do not demand new allegiances for they are not united by ethos or cause. What they forge in coming together is a kind of infinite incapacity of the finite. Here again, from a phenomenological viewpoint, the wretched do not strive to have their worth, or disappointments, legitimated as politics. They have no stake in bigotry or self-righteousness. Nor are they interested in past glories or guilt. Or the ethics of being right. Yet they are the saving violence, for their being is a testimony to those who seek the depths and those who do not. This violence is never a question of certainty, or exactitude, but of black ethical life. And that is why they are not devoted to politics, for they are nourished by the nothing that makes them incomprehensible to politics. We could say that if such truth is not simply antithetical *to* colonialism, no more can it be represented *by* it, for such truth manifests nothing less than the *nontruth* of the *colonisé*.

This is why it makes no sense to claim, as Miller does in his *Theories of Africans*, that Fanon ignores or avoids textual particularities in favor of metatheoretical description. In a general way, these problems come down to whether Fanon substitutes praxis for theory (with theory criticized for itself being the locus and focus of a "relativizing [of] truth and ethics").[75] In a slightly different configuration of the same problem, Fanon's analysis of "Aube Africaine" is thus accused of imposing an idea of the nation "in places where it may need reappraising,"[76] an accusation that, in the context of the chapters on national consciousness, is simply magical. But Miller's criticism is more complicated and indeed delusory than this implies for, when analyzing the future of theory (Fanon's own) he adopts, as it were, an opposition between theory and practice that, paradoxically, ends up reading the aesthetic as *the* model for the postcolonial state.[77] The assumption that theory cannot see its own ethnocentrism—hence the assumption that *ethnos* must be hidden for *theoria* to *see* (blind) itself—is based on a falsely objective notion of truth that is thus totalized into meaning. It is this blatant and highly revealing fudge that allows Miller to make the bold claim that what is "true in theory and in the discourse of a naïve or oppressive politics" is only "true in quotation marks." And he does so seemingly without realizing that his own ability to make such claims is absolute and repressive (with or without quotation marks). However firm this taming of theory, what distinguishes Miller's denunciation of its politics amounts to a failure to actually read what Fanon is saying. In fact, the only way that ethics emerges in Miller's discourse is through the illiberal dismissal of Fanonian theory; and according to a logic in which Miller's ability, as it were, to *tell the truth of truth* amounts to nothing more than a dogmatic presupposition that cannot fail, however, to become as tendentially absolute and violent as the supposed "truth" of a self-validating theory. And of course, the confidence that allows him to put truth within quotation marks is also what blinds him to his own interpretative violence in every sense of the word. The theory that leads him to denounce Fanonism thus feeds off its own passionate delusion, and in a reading that no longer simply repeats the violence done to literature by theory but that moralizes it as ethics.

Only statements that make explicit Fanon's anti-nativism are then accorded face value, and any statement that does not explicitly state that anti-nativism (especially the most general statements about national culture) becomes a mask for it, or a euphemistic, or strategically calculated indirect or encrypted expression of a political terrorism that is assumed by Miller to be the true and sinister consequence of Fanonian theory. This fudging is a fairly typical example of a white idealist position, whereby black particularity is either disavowed or marginalized (as a universal claim *to* particularity), and explains why Miller presents this, against his own intentions, as a *theory* of reading, thus doubling the double-speak of what Fanon describes as the racial form of truth in the colony, a doubling that oscillates from simulacrum to simulacrum, which best illustrates those paradoxes. This doubling shows up symptomatically, for example, in Miller's questionable claim that "Fanon's essays had a part to play both in [Sékou] Touré's discourse and in his [murderous] actions" (and once again the violence of theory can literally be read here in the form of real political violence, and one that shows how ethics is itself being violently presupposed, and in ways that are *ex hypothesi* because the ethics of the accusation cannot be dealt with simply as a question of meaning, and which is why Miller's reading of Fanon comes across as so unethically violent).[78] And this is also why the true target of Fanon's reading of national culture—the oppressiveness of post-independence regimes such as that of Touré's Guinea—is lost sight of as soon as it is raised as a question *of* reading. Indeed, the policies that Fodéba's ministerial and cultural work helped frame, through the designation of the nation as a struggle for truth in a sea of uncertainty, and through an *aesthetics of enmity*, by which power expresses and enjoys its own transgressive perversity, are thus rendered trivial as a literary devotion to theory.

I want to say: this claim about Fanonism as a *model* for a "bad" post-independence politics ought to: (i) make Miller aware of how the claim *"there is no real ethics without ethnicity"*—a claim that he argues Fanon denies—is not really opposed to theory, for the belief that theory *is* violence, as against ethics, only results in an increasingly violent justification of *ethnos* as ethics; (ii) lead him to ask why the same meaning and topos—of the violent exclusion of black particularity by theory, that he attributes to Fanon—occurs in his own work; and (iii) recast the analysis more generally beyond that of ethics and indeed of truth. Consequently, since the only thing that makes us sure that Fanon's views on national culture are oppressive is the evidence of his theory, we are taken aback to discover that only a theory that opposes theory is truly ethical, and presumably because we are obliged to prefer its devotion to black particularity to that of a particular black theory. The idea that Fanon's views of national culture entail the liquidation of the particular by the universal, the local by the global, necessarily makes it impossible for Miller to see how Fanon's text, both in regard to Fodéba, and cultural revolution more generally, problematizes these oppositions. All the more so when we know that there is no attempt in Fanon to make racist culture into a philosophical claim (as we have shown) precisely because what passes for truth in the colony is what puts truth in question. And how was this conclusion reached? To a large extent, by recounting the force—the pedagogy—of a poem in which the truth of the nation has become its fundamental question. That is, by following the function—and not the themes—of a literature in which revolution is not the signified but the signifier of a nation to come.

This is why aesthetics is not a mirror to the nation but that which reveals it's *à-venir*. Similarly, ethnicity, far from being the true form of culture (its signified)—and what could this possibly mean in a racist system of truth?— is shown to be part of the same mendacity defining the colonial bourgeoisie, both in respect of culture and the pursuit of power, for it simply cannot be the case that ethnic rivalry plays no role in the struggle for independence. Miller's analysis errs not in opposing *ethnos* to theory but in not following the consequences of its own insight, which should have made it impossible for him to tendentially *know* the true form of independence from its cynical dissimulation as history or fate. In that analysis, Miller views relativism as on the side of tolerance, but this tolerance is presented in an essentially illiberal way—namely, as a moralism, and one that can only hide (and thereby expose) its own intolerances and vanities. Here, the true other (that is, the one who objects to being relativistic) is excluded (and so liquidated) as inauthentically black.

Such, at first glance are the consequences of a certain distinction between philosophy and politics. Yet, such a distinction risks being moralistic from the start, in its theoretical politics. To understand Fanon, however,

other distinctions need to come into play. In Fanon's reading of "Aube Africaine," for example, delusion is a very widespread quality and nobody is entirely free from it. In the native *ecclesia* or the colonial administration, delusion is a sort of structural disease that effects both power and the striving
for power. This is why Fanon is driven to describe ontologies of truth *as* cynical illusions in the postcolony. More, traditional ideas of rule and custom
seem incapable of going beyond such cynical appropriations, indeed they often become identical to them in the demagogic form of their effects and passions. They are therefore constantly in danger of being out of step with the
people's struggle. Suffice it to say, Fanon does not go down this route: in analyzing "Aube Africaine" in his chapter on national culture, he in fact ends
up fundamentally rejecting moralism (and its petit-bourgeois version). From
"Aube Africaine," he also shows why (as opposed to Shari'ati) one must refuse to see the infinite as restoration, saying that the poem is not a fable
even if we respond to it as such, and saying that what it brings to mind as
a moment of struggle and decision (as opposed to a politics and rhetoric
of truth) is a crystallization (of the real) rather than a model for its figurative symbolization (and thus the referential truth of an illumination). Admitting that these add up to criteria for cultural revolution rather than of
truth—recognizing, in other words, the problem we raised around the relation between crystallization as subterfuge and crystallization as manifestation—Fanon, invokes, apparently rhetorically, "a national culture tak[ing]
form and shape [via combat]" for those in prison, facing the guillotine, and
fighting the French.[79] This interpretation goes along with the earlier figure
of *à la même cadence* as the locus of an asynchronous movement whose form
is yet to be determined. This second postulate follows on from what Fodéba
evokes as a "moment's battle."[80] There is also a *relevé* here in the manner
in which the "aube" of independence is being conceived—that is, as a mo-
mentous struggle that is further divided between day and night, and which
functions here as a figure of division that introduces a fundamental ambiguity into the question of what enlightens or darkens. The word *"aube"*
thus occupies a specific place of undecidability (let us say that what it illumines is necessarily shadowed by darkness). Illumination is thus paired with
a profound blindness. Fanon—this is his key insight—thus grasps why division cannot be determined as a dialectics or negation, for warring struggle is also the locus of the poem's own parabasis, to the extent that its form

(represented in the poem by suspension) is itself suspended between nativism and the (political-national-theoretical) violence that founds it. Therefore, if the dawn signifies a struggle in suspension—because of what it divides: that is, the night (of war) from the day (of independence)—that is because this equivocation is a kind of infinite, non-formalizable equivocation without resolution or end.

The battle between day and night could easily be read as an allegory. But this is not how Fanon reads it. Rather what "Aube Africaine" crystallizes is neither the tragedy of defeat at the hands of an imperial power, nor nativist resistance in all its purity. In the vocabulary of the poem, the "aube" does not refer to an order of power or transcendence, but refers to the dangers that leads people to confuse belief with the positing power of language. People should not have too much faith in such *pas*; it will lead them to idealize black figurability as what illumines liberation; it will not allow them to grasp the deadly repose of its positing. That is how the n'est pas counters idealism. It is precisely the figure, the trope, the power of crystallization, if the people can be made to understand that it betokens not a dawn but a deadly awakening, and that is the proper definition of its justice. And this is precisely how Fanon chooses to read it.

So when the poem opens with the phrase "c'était l'aube," a phrase that is repeated (as anaphora), what interests Fanon here is a power (of figuration) that divides itself from power, understood as the driving force of politics. Although, or rather just because, the dawn is not only a metaphor (of war or illumination), but a metalepsis that enacts a division between nativism and national culture, what comes into view is a division—between the feeling and worship of power—*that cannot be liquidated*. Everything follows on from this contiguous, originary vacillation. I want to say that everything is clear here, and everything can be immediately recognized as true, and yet everything is in a frenetic dance of equivocation. Likewise, the notion of the nation to come mobilizes metalepsis to signify an equivocation at once revolutionary, perpetual, and ruinous. In the petit-bourgeois forms of capital and politics, there is thus no security to be had. Perhaps this is why Fanon is finally unable to determine what the revolutionary moment is, or more importantly, what it is *not*, a reluctance that goes along with a whole set of complicated refusals. In the course of these refusals, Fanon again virulently criticizes the idea of war as heroic sacrifice or custom, and, as is always the case in Fanon, the apparently simplistic take on the discursive practices he is discussing (the claim that everything is set down here in black and white, in broad daylight) becomes the most complex reflection on irreducible antagonisms, such that he ends up not only describing but endorsing the view that to read is to know that we can only dance *blindly*—at the risk of making all the wrong moves, and at the risk of corrupting the sequence—for the nation is as yet undefined. And this uncertainty, like it or not, has to be part *of any black horizon of meaning*. This is a declaration that renounces the political-ontological codes of illumination precisely because they lack such clarity. The truth of this non-illumination therefore is this: unable to signify the coin (of secular resistance), or the sarcophagi (of religious, mythic transcendence), that horizon has no outline, for its opacity is not dark enough to be dialecticized, and its darkness is too blinding to be witnessed without aporia.[81] For what crystallization implies is not something brought to an ever greater density of illumination, but the high pressure by which cultural particularity is transformed, which becomes still more dense the more it is traversed. Think of it as a force that allows the establishment of both community and form, of community as form, but only insofar as each is the instance of a colossal manifestation at one moment or the very image of a deadening inertia at another. This is the first point.

The important word in these definitions is *blackness*—that is, those depths that allow the n'est pas to be openly seen, or that allow blindness to *be posed* in front of the abyss, swept away by a continuous series of *pas* that lead nowhere and are senseless. (Among the glorious and the inglorious, too, the living and the socially dead.) The reading of Fodéba follows Fanon's other demonstrations in his work that the n'est pas cannot be conceived as law or right, but nor can it be thematized as non-identity; rather, the knowledge it transmits requires an ongoing aporia that involves what we have just described as a non-formalizable equivocation, a *justice*, whose motif of decision has neither form, name, group, or identity, and from which a whole number of political positions become untenable. Struggle permeates the n'est pas: struggle is its mode and proposition, but struggle (by the same reasoning) does not determine it in a teleological sense. That is why Shari'ati was unable to grasp it. It must therefore follow that the n'est pas is not an attribute of being, whether understood as something lacking or possessed. But neither is it transcendent insofar as its truth lies elsewhere. This is why

Fanon refers to it as an immanent flaw [*tarde*] that makes ontology impossible. This is the second point; it allows us to understand why Fanon is critical of both race philosophy and of negritude. Race philosophy is unable to separate race from ontology or to fuse them completely. Hence its turn to a nativist definition, which is seemingly occupied by the thought of how blackness differs from its *essence*, because it now *represents* an ipseity whose historicity is understood. What can we conclude from this? That blackness is not simply identity or destiny, but an act—a praxis—that arises from a direct confrontation with the duplicities that thereby define it? To introduce the national struggle into the form of the poem is, then, for the colonized intellectual, the only effective response to the demand that both subject and poem perform the (racially mythic) dance (of interpretation) that (always fails to) liberate them. Blackness, then, *as* struggle, the fulfillment of a crystallizing futurity sans mimesis; *or* the ardent pursuit of an essence defined by its inability to see, and whose only desire is to see in darkness.

In a way, I believe that the entire debate between Shari'ati and Fanon concerning national culture is summarized in his discussion of Fodéba's poem. That debate returns us to the question of *shahadat*, or to what can never be read as a *sequence of exemplarity*, and so to the articulation of poetry as a politics-in-ruins. As we have seen, the relation between struggle, religion, and war, remains—intentionally or not—the key relation; it becomes for Fanon *the* question of Fodéba's poetics. However uncomfortable this may be, it seems clear that there is no way to separate the good and bad forms of crystallization without violence. From the cynical indeterminacy of truth and untruth in the postcolony, we can see that the nation to come requires a decision, a decision that for Fanon also entails something like a struggle over national consciousness, but a decision, however supposedly violent it will be, that is also the effect of a undecidability.[82] Indeed, it seems that in *The Wretched of the Earth*, Fanon could never say, as Shari'ati does, that we must choose: either being or becoming. Why? *Because that opposition is still pious*: and even if *bazghast*—unlike, say, jihad or revolution—is the enigmatic point of decision *itself*, whereby among things it is not so much a return to tradition but the direct expression of the struggle that becomes it, for the message is never simply given in itself, why is this opening to the future a concession to *shahadat* rather than a figure of radical dissociation? This undecidable struggle is to be found in Fanon's vision of the nation to come, but the character of its *à-venir* is not absolute, for it has nothing to do with what Hegel (and I would argue, Shariʿati), in *Lectures on the Philosophy of Religion*, conceives of as "the surrender of an immediate finitude" to the spiritual discovery of an infinite truth (regardless of whether this spiritualization of finitude is conceived as *the* point of a crystallizing ecstasy or expiation).[83] No, what we understand as the infinitely-finite is not sacrifice, but the nothing that governs the world gone black: it is a void without which there can be no invention. We must therefore conclude that Shariʿati risks making religion the truth of independence, and in a way that cannot allow ambiguity to define the manner and form of cultural authenticity. And that this inability, in turn, represents an attempt to free Islam from the weakness and impotence of western sovereignty while still, however, in thrall to its figure and concept. Does *bazghast* thereby signify redeemed life, or does it remain interwoven (at a certain past moment) to a phenomenology of deception? This has been our question. It also concerns what it means to strive for power as a matter of faith, without doubt ringing in our ears. How this relates to our problem of crystallization can, however, be made clearer still by returning to Fanon's chapter on national culture: "A nation born of the concerted action of the people, which embodies the actual aspirations of the people and transforms the state, depends on exceptionally inventive cultural manifestations for its very existence."[84] In *The Wretched of the Earth*, this goes along with the suggestion that decolonial resistance must itself resist (at the last and first resort) western notions of resistance if it is to be inventive, rather than remain a slavish imitation of the various forces seeking to circumscribe it.

One final point: it is difficult not to imagine this invention as violence, not because of its threat to reason or the state, but because it does not yet have a political definition, nor a language of ontological embodiment. The name of this violence, if it can be given a name, is that of the n'est pas; its blackness cannot be recast as yet another, more sovereign thought (of being). It's wretchedness, in fact, admits to the dead no sacrifice or dwelling-place, more especially as it shows up the fluctuating zones or limits of a degradation that cannot be easily rendered without being mutilated. That is why, instead of drawing up a platform of blackness as agency, let us conclude by saying that black non-representability is what Fanon's politics never answers, and why Fanon answers as he does.

Seven
On Revolutionary Suicide

So many of my comrades are gone now. Some tight partners, crime partners, and brothers off the block are begging on the street. Others are in asylum, penitentiary, or grave. They are all suicides of one kind or another who had the sensitivity and tragic imagination to see the oppression. Some overcame: they are the revolutionary suicides. Others were reactionary suicides who either overestimated or underestimated the enemy, but in any case were powerless to change their conception of the oppressor.

Only resistance can destroy the pressures that cause revolutionary suicide.

Huey P. Newton, *Revolutionary Suicide* (1973)[1]

The wager—to die in such a way that one's suicide [homocidium dolorosum] over-comes death—not by giving in to it, going towards to it, or working for it, but dying in such a way that one's suicide [suicidium] is more than suicide even though one's death is already known and identifiable as such, a death in whose resistance one discovers something other than death.

This would be a suicide, then, whose most resolute resistance is an indication of the social death that afforms[2] it, setting the same mark on resistance and re-action alike.

It may seem strange to approach suicide from the angle of resistance. After all, isn't suicide a transgression, an evasion, even in its ineffable resistance to life, power, to society?[3]

Why, then, should we consider this most singular decision from the perspective of what—in the language of black sacrifice and protest—most often oppresses it, shackles it, or condemns it? And isn't the most intractable feature of suicide precisely its refusal of resistance, the moral-theological definition of life as utility, futurity, or duty? But we may still wonder why Huey Newton himself, after having set up this great antagonism between resistance and reaction, between those who choose to resist social death and those who pathologically perform it, should turn to Nietzsche, and his notions of *reaction* and of *will to power*, to uncover another, more revolutionary form of suicide. The question remains, in other words, of whether what we consider to be *social* death is really so easy to distinguish from what we consider to be a *resistant* death—that is, a death defined by its "afformation"; or by its *vir* (virility), capacity, passion, or power. . .

I

Let us begin by saying that nothing seems more elusive than this distinction. It cannot be credited or limited to a matter of individual sensitivity, strength, or weakness; nor is it limited to questions of justice, belonging, or community. Indeed, everything in Newton's theory combines to suggest the proximity—the intimate relation—between reaction and this suicide that, at first glance, seems to be opposed to it and to resist it, or that seeks to negate it, *actively*. The suicide that would fulfill its revolutionary possibility must always resist the reactance that grounds its very possibility. It must be reactive in that it resists, and resistant in that it endures reaction. Just as revolutionary suicide is shown to be structured by reaction, by its atavisms and tyrannies, so, too, the desire to resist it is grounded in a counterreaction, both because the enmity that precedes it requires that black suicide always be a substitute for resistance, and because of the suicidal structure of black resistance itself.[4] This means by the same token that reaction carries within itself the drive—the destiny—of resistance and of that which resists it. Since therefore black resistance is not suicidal because it resists, but suicidal because it is reactive, we must look beyond the diremptions of death and power, and what they betoken, to see how resistance and reaction are connected. We must also see how reactive suicide produces what it forbids, making possible the very thing that it would make impossible: the resistance against black social death and against reaction. In short, and at risk of encroaching on what will be my conclusion, I would say that black reactive death *is* black resistance, is *the same as* its revolutionary other. This duality is ambiguous, and so we must understand it carefully, literally, and in all its senses. It involves two very different notions of resistance—of black resistance—and two very different notions of death—of black death—in which the miseries of one are what drive us to seek a more revolutionary terminus in the other, but it is resistance (as lack *and* drive; as sacrifice *and* bestowal) that brings us imperceptibly to the two deaths. But not as cause and consequence, affirmation, or negation; but as an experience of suicide that is therefore only formable, translatable, as a resistance to the obsessions and conformity by which blacks *give in* to suicide as a defining *telos* or end.

Thus, either we understand that revolutionary suicide is the same as reactive suicide, in which case revolutionary suicide, always identical to itself in its sacrificial difference, triumphantly assimilates reactive suicide into itself—this is the dialectical (and, in Newton, the *political*) version of this duality—or we understand reaction to be the same as resistance, and at once the duality becomes more difficult to understand, at once we no longer know who or what this revolutionary suicide is that a moment ago seemed so obvious, nor do we know whether we are still dealing with resistance at all. Indeed, I am not even sure that we should distinguish the second suicide from the first. To do so would be to resolve it dialectically, whereas here it is only because resistance is already doubled by reaction (i.e., in the sense of a double origin) that it is possible to distinguish a difference in the *same* notion. But that notion does exist in Newton, where it indicates what I will call, for lack of a better term, an *ethical* beyond of resistance. That, at least, is what I would like to demonstrate: that here, in this infinitesimal, imperceptible difference of emphasis, is where Newton's notion of black revolutionary politics is ultimately played out. This is also an opportunity for me to extend and reflect upon previous analyses of black resistance: that is, the hope of its affirmation versus the reactive enmity of its truth.[5]

But even before we turn to the Newtonian wavering between a politics and an ethics of resistance, we should first like to comment on the word *resistance*. Resistance, far more than freedom, changes the very nature of what we think we know about black life and death. Nowadays we speak easily—and I've just been doing so myself—about the revolutionary "subject," the subject of liberation, and the subject who resists (worldly injustice, say, in the name of freedom). But what do we really know about resistance? In philosophy, resistance seems to create its own resistance (to definition); and is, at the same time, the taking place of that imperative.[6] To know resistance is possible only if we pursue its reactions. And thus, the need to draw a boundary line between resistance and reaction, even though we know it is impossible to do so without presumption. Resistance, then, ultimately belongs neither to life nor concept, but to the symbols we have of them, or, less commonly, it is an "afformative" capacity that no will can symbolize without making resistance into what is not itself resistant.[7] This is a particularly stark example of the problem before us. If life is to retain its vital, subversive power, whether prefigured as drive or impulse, life itself must resist that which resists it. Resistance is thus deemed to be either a drive or capacity that gives immediacy to life/will through struggle or combat; consequently, it is presented as a force or energy that inevitably confronts power because it is already immanent to it. Resistance is thus both an unfolding *power*, since in it force and life are truly one, and a *willed* encounter with the alienations and oppressions that would suppress it, and that in the end condemns, escapes power. Without desire—*of* power, or *to* power—resistance cannot constitute or fulfill itself; it cannot model or manifest itself as possibility or actuality. And, first of all, because resistance is, before all else, with and without resistance; and so ever beyond and behind itself in advance. As such, we cannot know it beyond these infinitely-finite points of reaction. Faced with the suicide of the worker, the subaltern, or the slave—whose only object is assumed to be freedom?—resistance is not merely a datum but the reactive affect of what it is not (n'est pas). It is resistance that resists (itself) and resistance that is unable to resist (itself as resistant).

But what does it mean to say that reaction becomes resistant through suicide? Or that freedom is the inner meaning of that encounter? This, of course, is how classical philosophemes render the unfree life of the slave. In the slave, freedom is assumed to be nothing but virtue, knowledge, and recognition. Apart from fugitivity or escape, the slave can only encounter true life in the moment he discovers suicide as fate. As such, freedom not only *produces* life; it also makes the slave see how resistance grounds his sovereign possibility, by setting aside what he thinks he knows about slave life and its human possibility. But what of that jouissance that leads him imperceptibly to destruction—and that sees in suicide a singularly black afformation, one that makes a politics of life—a life deemed transcendent—impossible? If suicide is the moment in which I perceive that everything could happen, a moment in which a gap opens up in my knowledge and experience to which

I have no relation, but to which I give myself utterly, what is it that I experience—the forfeit or the danger that comes from truly knowing it? But if this is the wager that frees me, in which I behold resistance's dazzling light, have I not already lost what I imagined I gained—that is, a freedom symbolized as the meaningful, transcendent movement of all affirmation, for to lose myself in that thought is to perish in the very discovery of it?

In this connection, it may be useful to recall that the word *resistance* appears only rarely in Newton's *Revolutionary Suicide*, who preferred to speak of "confrontation," "spontaneity," or "the ability to act."[8] That is why it is best to recognize right away that revolutionary suicide comes to us not as an "affirmative *capacity* to resist"[9] but from a particular interpretation of a black reactive *incapacity* to resist: it is from his theory and experience of anti-black state violence and the Black Panther Party (BPP), founded in 1966, that we must date the use of the phrase "revolutionary suicide."

This phrase, as Newton well knew, comes from philosophy. It denotes a moment before any possible assurance of a meaningful beyond. We could even say that it is the key term in his reading of Nietzsche's will to power. The suicide is not primarily he or she who suffers, much less the psychology of suffering to which we so often find it reduced today. Above all, the word *suicide* designates the highest maxim, the "overcoming" or drive, the revolutionary *journée* or quest for life that is posed, supposed, and presupposed in Section 36 of *Twilight of the Idols*: "To die proudly when it is no longer possible to live proudly. Death of one's free choice, death at the proper time; with a clear head and joyfulness . . . an *adding up* of life."[10] And, as Gillian Rose has shown, it is only to the extent that such a death, in the form of its tallying up, is heir to the true nobility, the true freedom of its will to power, that it becomes resistant in the modern sense of the word.[11] Not only does an unfree (slavish?) death appear to be a reactive death; it also manifests a suicide of the will: "When you *do away with* yourself you are doing the most admirable thing there is," Nietzsche writes, "*life* itself gets more of a benefit from this than from any sort of 'life' or renunciation, of anaemia, or other virtues."[12] Suicide, then, is not a negative, even pessimistic ideal. Pessimism (*pur, vert*) is life negating itself as will and representation; suicide is the affirmation, not of life, but of will to power. Apart from this affirmation there is only decadence, wretchedness, sickness, fragility, despair. Recourse to suicide is thus necessary to recapture that drive to life that has not been preceded by any sickliness and is itself life's blackest afformation. By the word *black*, I do not want to indicate an identity—that is, a psychological or emotional index—but more the scandalous assertion of resistance's unensurability as possibility. This should not be understood in the sense of being-toward-death, but more in the sense of a being for whom life withdraws from futurity, and who is henceforth to be conceived as the point where subject, consciousness, representation, or will cannot be named in this way, either in labor or in desire, in struggle or in the work of art. For, as is clear from what we have just said, and as Newton quite rightly notes, this is a being without the surety of any *ipse* structure, and one whose death, paradoxically, is the condition wherein unlivable life is transformed into will to power.

Thus, it was this *afformative* concept of suicide that Newton imported from philosophy, and with astounding amplitude. Power and resistance are no longer opposed, nor are they equivalent. Indeed, they are no longer even equivalent to themselves. They are their own resistance and their own (resistant) reaction. Black power, for example, no longer creates resistance, but rather is the differential structure of black reaction, a reaction that *also* inhabits resistance. "Reaction" and "resistance" can therefore no longer be simply opposed, but neither have they become identical. Rather, the very notion of their identities as vitalist or voluntary is put in question. In addition to this aporia, the inseparability of black power and suicide renders any affirmation that contains it problematic.

My purpose here is not to reevaluate the politics of that decision in the history of the Black Panther Party, or the strategies to which it gave rise. I would merely like to call attention, in a very preliminary way, to what Newton says of suicide as a revolutionary attitude toward black social death. And to the notion of suicide as a black power *freely* chosen that is neither power nor decision, but a power that escapes both power and decision. Or as the destiny of a *philia* that simultaneously acquits itself in a *phobos* that sets out to condemn and destroy it. No doubt this appeal to revolutionary *philia* (as well as several others: will, freedom, autonomy, liberation, actuality, possibility, and so on) permitted Newton's trenchant critique of reactance by ridding it from the outset of all psychologism and all vitalism or biologism. But why keep the word—and hence also the concept—of *suicide*, particularly when it was simultaneously being invested with all the pathos and pathology of social psychology? Wasn't what was at stake, as Howard Caygill has indicated in *On Resistance* (and a related text), the removal of blackness from any "theology of resistance" to a *thanato-politics* issuing from an appeal to suicide as the highest maxim that blackness reveals by itself and, after a fashion, in itself, as black political immortality?[13] In fact, would Newton have agreed on this notion of an "immortal revolution that is always to come" if he had not embraced suicide, and more than anyone else, as a black power that is somehow more originary than life, representation, or will to power?

Perhaps it is because black life is always on the outside of life that its death can only occur in politics as an enigmatic spectacle?[14] As such, suicide does not mean evasion or escape, but the drive that brings us imperceptibly to our deathly afformation. That is, the fate whose cause and effect in the world is always the exception because, being dead, it can neither die nor be killed, and thereby is the infinite labor of a dying without end? Thus, the suicides that are doubles of each other, and that Newton himself is first induced to say are both a reaction—an aphanisis or ascesis—and a resistance because of the struggle to find another meaning (both protest and defense) in black life-death: perhaps this is why he concludes his autobiography with this appeal to a *philia* that turns against itself, by refusing the assurance of either nihilism or martyrdom in the choice of taking a stand. This idea—that *philia* is only resistant when it seeks neither end nor community—also means that black resistance can only be gained insofar as it withdraws from every determination, be it political or ontological. Thus, suicide may transform what is always already present as reaction, provided it does not accord with itself, and that it makes plain its founding in the movement of the plea—for the overcoming of life—that it can neither be assured of nor determine. In which case, the *mort à bout touchant* of which Fanon speaks[15] (and which in Newton's text is never encountered as a "death-wish"[16]) becomes revolutionary, *or* it negates the tyranny that dominates it but is not present, in which case it is reactive, imaginary. The doubleness of the word "reactive-suicide" carries the text's signifying possibilities beyond what could be reasonably attributed to a politics of resistance. Newton's reading of Fanon thereby shows a more complex dividing line between death and resistance that often functions *against* its own explicit (metaphysical) assertions, not just by creating ambiguity, but by inscribing a systematic suicide behind or through what is being said about revolution.

Nor is this a matter of overlooking the fact that the Newtonian black revolutionary subject is always the most besieged, precarious subject, the profoundly condemned subject of enmity and of violence—and therefore nothing like the sovereign and freely chosen subject of the philosophers, nothing like the virile, autonomous ego of possibility, or its ethical successor, the subject of a capacity to resist. Nevertheless, this infinitely besieged subject, reduced to a reactive demand for freedom that political-philosophical life arouses and forbids, is still a subject that resists. Newton, in a very enigmatic way, retains the *word*—at least as the purest moment of lived capacity, the real as opposed to a false vitality, a desire to live that is equally willing to be condemned in its continued strength. That this position, from the very fact of its being mystical, ecstatic even, is equivalent to an unknowable renunciation makes little difference. Newton chooses it to the extent that, in daring to resist, black suicide promises not so much reappropriation but a withdrawal without reserve. Emptied of substance, virtually dead, black reactive life subsists in the withholding of what it renounces. And in the closed world of social death, in which it continues to murder itself, to murder itself in order to resist itself, black life takes the form of a protest that has, historically, appealed to what is withheld in the agon of its existence.

It is not my intention here, however, to analyze this powerful refusal of black social death in any detail, this refusal that is all the more powerful for being presented in the guise of a death without law or limits, that is *sub judice*, and that cannot be actualized or affirmed as such. If, getting ahead of the analyses to come, I have nevertheless referred briefly to this refusal as *beyond* resistance, it is because it constitutes both the outer limit of what resists and the condition of impossibility of any language of politics being able to grasp its resistance today. Above all, I have referred to it because it seems to me that resistance functions here as a veritable *symptom*. How are we to say that black power *is* resistant, or that it somehow conforms to a discourse (of resistance) that is always conforming to the authority of what it philosophically resists and unwittingly affirms as such? Once the many misreadings of Newton's text have been taken into account, shouldn't we have asked instead what, even in Newton himself, had brought about this desire for black suicidal death? Shouldn't we have suspected the radicality and ideality of a notion made in the name of an impossible actuality? An ideality that is always dead in the act, so to speak, and is as fatal as it is impossible?

In short, shouldn't we indeed have returned not to Newton, but to Newton's *philosophical* understanding of suicide, which alone holds the key to its *political* affirmation as black power?

II

we must choose: either blood or the message

'Ali Shari'ati, *Husayn, vāres-i adam*[17]

Vitalism or *mortalism*? Arguably what is at stake here is a reading of Nietzsche that goes beyond the metaphysics of energy or will.

Let us now examine more closely the strategies and assumptions involved in this critical rereading. It is clear that Newton was not seeking the meaning of Nietzsche's will to power in any traditional sense. I want to compare that reading to another that also positions itself on the question of suicide as the true object of will to power. Georges Bataille's various writings on death, inner experience, and sovereignty will be our example.[18] And not only because these writings are themselves Nietzschean writings of autobiography, but also because Bataille writes of a wager that could be said to be a direct response to the unreadable nature of resistance, and of what lies beyond it: a death for which no literal, proper term can be substituted. In writing of suicide, Bataille realized that death had already become a political question of affirmation *beyond* the subject. If politics is the figure of limits, resistance makes us see that the true cost of inner experience is, in a sense, our encounter with the illimitable.

But also, in what follows, I also want to argue that Bataille's reading of Nietzsche maintains life not as power but as a will to chance that, if we follow the trail, is always in danger of confusing risk with the affirmation of what, if we had but lost it, we were never in danger of losing—that is, ourselves, our *own* fear of death, our own will *to* affirmation.[19] Or perhaps we should say, denying the chance of death doesn't make those who deny it any more reactive or resistant. Just *less* sovereign.

Bataille's great achievement is thus to wake us to the loss of such losing while urging us passionately to risk beyond our limits. He wants us to sacrifice ourselves for something that is literally unsacrificeable, for it is nowhere to be found. In a word, here a line is tautly drawn between *expenditure* and the laws of *return* (the return that conserves itself, but always outside of it-self). Those whose lack of life makes them desperately want to own life, to conserve it, are therefore also the most reactive. Bataille's attempt to found a sovereign community was thus an attempt to bring to an end such mortal-ism.[20] (But is sacrifice, in its abandoning, anything more than a means? And is the self that abandons itself, to pleasure and/or cruelty, resistant, or merely a self forcibly subduing itself to the pleasures of abandonment? The sacrifi-cial community is nothing other than the sacrifice *of* community, the aban-doning that gives itself unreservedly over to abandonment.)[21] But both risk and limit remain figures of speculation in his work, via a dialectics of resis-tance and spectacle. They are, in other words, consolations; sacrificial sub-stitutes for an always already transgressed limit. They are not vehicles that make us see the literally black and, in a sense, lethal afformation of will to power. Or at least this will be my argument in what follows.

And still more profoundly, does sovereignty *manifest* itself as what truly returns to itself, by expending itself in all the chance events that resist it, while canceling all the conserving forms that play a part in it? It would then be necessary for sovereignty to return to itself in at least two senses: as ran-dom expenditure (of the finite) and as the expenditure that has to maintain chance as the improbable, and infinite figure of a return that can never be sacrificed as such. As regards chance, it becomes impossible to tell whether those who lack drive, or are unable to kill (or expend) the anguished servil-ity that is killing them, are simply reactive, or are unable to affirm not their difference, but their sovereign *identity*. It is necessary to say here that chance preexists return as either identity or relation. There is resistance to the ex-tent that absolute expenditure (that is, chance) is affirmed. But this affirma-tion must itself resist resistance's return to itself. In this regard, it is neces-sary not to draw back from the consequences of reaction for sovereignty to be the affirmation of chance, but sovereignty cannot thereby resist its own absolute affirmation that is its own reactive principle. Which is why resis-tance must consist of and realize itself as absolute expenditure.

We can equally say, then, no compromise is possible between Bataille's vitalism and Newton's reactive ontology. If we are reactive because we can-not resist life, or because we cannot bear to live without such consolation, why assume that we must necessarily sacrifice life to become less so? How does such insight account for those who are not (n'est pas), and who are infinitely abandoned, without any means of abandoning themselves to sense or revolt?

What I want to claim here is that the role of suicide in Bataillean criticism—which is reactive precisely because it only acknowledges sovereign life as resistant—is always to risk a certain limit and to be the pathos, or inner experience, of its transgression. It is the wager whose only definition is to be the acknowledgement of an impossible limit, to be the symbol of an immanence without end or closure. (Suicide is thus an experience of acknowledgement.) Death, in other words, is what is paradoxically *added* to the finite in order to supply the limit wherein life discovers that it is "forever deprived of sense" (and hence sovereign in its impossibility) and that life, reactive life, is "mere performance"—that is to say, a servile, egoic spectacle.[22] The very designation of a limit as constitutive of life, a life wherein suicide comes to represent, through its transgression, a sovereign or reactive possibility, can, in short, no longer be thought to be a ceaseless affirmation of power, but rather a limit that Bataille variously defines as "evil," inutilious, or "sacred" expenditure. One begins to see where resistance fits in. Sacrifice is incapable of attaining this limit because it is unable to live its own death as resistant. All self-sacrifice is therefore reactive. There are no exceptions. But sacrifice teaches us very little about our experience of limits. It returns in each event as the limit that rules over every desire, since desire seeks only its own dissolution; it shows how sovereignty is mastered by the very need to affirm it; to affirm it as the most resistant determination. In this way, the limit that expends itself as sovereign can only do so insofar as it goes beyond all knowledge, but this suicide remains forever preserved in the form of such sovereign acknowledgment. When Bataille defined sovereignty, famously, as "NOTHING," this was a way of afforming chance as a principle that disrupts any servile purpose, but it is precisely for this reason that nothing can be left to chance in such definition.[23] As such, the beyond of resistance is both the opposition and afformation of a probability *without* telos, but only insofar as this beyond returns to itself as a sovereign reactive movement. In other words, as a mimetic offering to what, in the end, everyone is aiming—namely, death as the limit, or transgressive end. To give ourselves over to excess is to withdraw from the miseries of our being. Such a gift frees us from all that remains servile, and reveals to us an ecstasy independent of reason, knowledge, and faith.

It is interesting to note the ways in which Bataille's historical and aesthetic discussions of sovereignty tend to employ figures of surrender and loss. But always in a language that allows neither. As such resistance is reduced, initially and before all else, to a determinate transition. Hence the craving, the fascination, with "NOTHING"; since nothing can fill this infinite abyss, and none can resist its immutable attraction. Thus, if there is to be a community beyond that of the subject, there has to be risk for that subject to be formed or to come into being, that is, enter into the world. Community and subject can both be grasped as a movement of risk without any assurable sense; but what every person can be assured of is the *sense* of such indeterminacy. We are incapable of knowing either what we are or whether we are without risk, or without explicitly *corpsing* the anguish defining human life in general.[24] This *trans* before any possible sense is thus thoroughly determined and determining of what it means to be *with* others, or to die sovereignly. But this will to chance, named in this way, cannot do justice to what Newton calls the withheld life of black speech and language; that is to say, the non-sovereign life that suicides itself because it can no longer resist the world, or its non-existence.

Does it change anything to call this limit sacrifice? Probably not. And yet existing discussions almost invariably confront, leave unresolved, and detour around the question of the nature and boundaries of this sacrifice. As Jean-Luc Nancy puts it in "The Unsacrificeable": The question of life is where sacrifice begins, but can life, or being-with, ever be sacrificed?[25] And if sovereignty is that miraculous moment in which the subject expires before itself, and expires from the enjoyment of expiring, at what point does life become sovereign, and therefore resistant? Bataille never provides us with an answer. Rather life alone is what transgresses (itself), and what resists its own reactive appropriation as death. But from this perspective, let us say: the horror of what separates us from what we are in our anguish is less terrible than the idea of an infinite monotony of non-sovereign being. Reason cannot make us choose either, and inner experience cannot reveal either as wrong. So at what point can one resolve the difficult question of when sovereignty begins if not either by saying, with Nietzsche, *thus I willed it* (as chance, as power); or, with Bataille, *thus I cede or abandon it* (as chance, as sacrificial loss).

But this is not quite true for another, much more problematic aspect of Bataille's affirmation of chance: the aspect that deals with the mania, the *philia* for transgression—and here we should take transgression in both its senses, as crime and offense. Indeed, we know that from early on Bataille felt constrained, alongside his wish to literally *be* Nietzsche, to say that the person who puts his own life at risk experiences a consummation, an ecstasy, that, rather than seeking a beyond, is a fatal encounter with radical immanence—an argument that, as Newton also suggests, is itself a refusal of transcendence, since being-with here fuses with the process of becoming. Without retracing the various steps of this Bataillean myth—this violent passion that the ego devotes to itself (or that devotes the ego to itself in its own sundering)—it's worth pointing out that this myth also serves to reinstate a myth of the (white, Western) subject as both destiny and foundation. It designates a subject who can only enter into relationships with others by assuming this abyssal, expiatory, sovereign obliteration-restoration *beyond* otherness. It is, Bataille tells us, a crime to *enjoy* chance as a will to power. His reasoning is that what resists also transgresses, and it must do so in such a way that it is at once without diminution or *ressentiment*.

On this score, violent sacrifice is taken to be the essence of society but only for those who seemingly have already made the choice, and not just any choice, but the choice to be a non—or absolute—subject, who is thus headless (i.e., sovereign) and always at fault (i.e., transgressive) in their very being, for to be sovereign is to be at fault to any order or system. Hence the need to wager, to mitigate or expiate the egotism of this mitigation. In saying that egotism lives without resistance, for it merely dissimulates it, and conceivably takes malign pleasure in doing so, is to say that will still belongs in the category of desire and not that of drive, or its ethics.

Yes, we are fated to be. And to establish community myth is needed (Bataille calls it the "sacred"—a word whose own mythic character is never really questioned as such, but endlessly performed as if it were a kind of mana). When the issue is race or power, however, we know that life has already, in a sense, been invaded or intruded upon by a fault that is never simply sacrificial-ontological. As Newton (reading Fanon here) convincingly demonstrates, the reaction that vainly seeks to authorize itself as ipseity (since its authority comes from outside of itself, or from what it thinks of as vitality) is always part of this phantasm that sees, in sovereignty, the *chopped away*, mutilated part, the severed head whose loss allows the community to both mourn and rationalize itself as a collective. And here, precisely, is where the essence of community arises and where one must embrace the terrible founding power of resistance—resistance as the mutilated beyond of the subject, in whose name the subject discovers its limit—not because one's identity is limited, but because, as a subject, one becomes a subject only insofar as I am not (n'est pas). Or: I exist *because* I am mutilated-severed. And here, equally, the desire to transgress being becomes a servant of power, to make it the event of *non-sens* in its resistance to sense.

And since a choice must be made, it must be one that offers the least interest, the least usefulness, the least productive outcome. Not because these values are slavish or servile, but because they have become representative of reactive life. This is already tantamount to saying—but here lies the enigma—that to be a subject of black power one must lose two things: life and its relation to language—for this is a life that is not yet *in* language, and so cannot be cathected or recathected as language (n'est pas); and so you must stake two things: your reason and your will, your knowledge and your freedom, your death and your life. This bears repeating. In the case of Bataille, we can only transcend-resurrect ourselves if we heal the split between sacred (life) and sovereignty (the politics—the joy—the experience of community as the affirmation of chance and transgression, and therefore the chance to truly, transgressively, be white). The power that would risk submission to the former of its own accord (that is, autonomously) gains everything; whereas in the case of revolutionary suicide, there is power precisely because there was never any sovereign life. Ultimately, in Bataille's philosophy, blackness must be treated as a slave, as exemplified by its lack of limit-experiences. For it cannot return to sovereignty either as sense or nonsense, it cannot transgress the situation of social death in which it is inscribed, and it cannot affirm this situation as either one of being or chance.

We are speaking here of a crime that precedes the language of sovereignty and being. Indeed, this leads me to suspect the exact opposite, that the community that loses the sacred—as myth—loses nothing but itself and remains perfectly undecidable as life *and* politics. There is no black political community not because of an absence of myth, but because black life is already decapitated, so to speak, and only by killing itself (rather than being endlessly killed) can it more abundantly live as resistant.

You could say that in expiration Bataille redirects dialectics toward a non-political politics (i.e., myth), wherein society is obliged to risk itself in order to be reborn as sovereign immanence; whereas for Newton, revolution is possible because black life *is* the risk of the political as traditionally defined. For it is not life that must be resisted, but the world that expels black life from the human. Or less tendentiously: if suicide is what discloses the religious and ethical truth of sacrifice, that sacrificing has always relied on a white passion to *become*; as if by becoming white, it were possible for the subject to appropriate the risk of dissolution and to do so irremediably. At one point, Bataille writes as if sovereignty is the miracle of *my* will, and supposedly because of the pain and torment of being reducing to *nothing*. But for those who have been nothing, and whose difference is a no longer and a not yet, the political has a different story to tell than the choice of humanization (as the necessary cost of subjection). I hope to make this clearer in what follows.

To explain and displace will to power by chance the black or non-white subject must thus become itself the power that resists—and that, finally, is why Bataille's enigmatic rereading of Nietzsche as an ecstatic myth of surrender that can scarcely surrender its own myth, and which therefore cannot communicate itself as resistant, has a profoundly different address-structure than Newton's. A glance at their respective works is enough to suggest this. Whereas Bataille ontologizes sacrifice, Newton puts into question the sacrificial truth of blackness. The difference here is not what is being staked as the risk to one's life, but the story of one's *fascination* with the wager that one submits to as the price of one's community, and to which one imagines oneself obliged through this very fascination; namely, a *philia* of expiration that grounds itself in what sunders and unites it in a perfect sacrificial economy of desire, mortality, and finitude.

That being so, Bataille's error was not so much a totalitarian fascination (Nancy) with sacrifice but the confusion of chance with a "nothing" that withdraws and must withdraw itself from every relation (including the *trans* that is assumed to lie at the archaic womb of the world).

One of the most obvious differences between Bataille and Newton on suicide therefore concerns both the stake and the value of what it means to be, and to be acknowledged as such: only whiteness can become the singular, sovereign instance, since it is responsible for the knowledge by which man knows the real essence of the finite, which is why it has to guard itself against the black abysses from which it arose but cannot do without.

To explain the consequences of this let us once again examine the concept of sovereignty and its influence on Bataillean criticism. Bataille understands authentic sovereignty as an *unreserved* relation to death—that is to say, the sovereign is he who discovers his most authentic instance in the wager of absolute loss. Sovereign life ensues when "the possibility of life opens up without limit."[26] The subject becomes sovereign when he is no longer *enslaved* (Bataille's word) by anguish, identity, laws, labor, and prohibition. Hence, the sovereign "is he who is, as if death were not."[27] Sovereignty marks not the *future*—as repetition or end—but the perpetual risk of life's ending. *That is why freedom is only representable as sacrifice.* Sacrifice, then, as both what aligns (the space proper to life and death) and what violates any attempt to limit it to loss or dispensation. Again, for the sovereign to offer sacrifice—be it in the form of war, death, or massacre—it is essential that the sovereign bears no resemblance to what resembles it, or that limits it to a *spectacle* of freedom. But this loss is not a Hegelian act of recuperation—of exchange or economy—but a *willed* dissipation that cannot be corrected or contained; and that signifies an abandonment without reserve, an abandonment that nothing escapes, and that is also a kind of poetic writing.

But what, once again, can never be abandoned is this thought of an exemplary fate that never ceases to risk its own sovereign exceptionalism. As if the theory of exception has to resort to a logic of exception in order to figure or reveal the exception that it is meant to explain. And one that continues to reveal a certain pious thinking of the sacred—in its livable, deathly limits—as both racial exception and rule.[28]

Here Nietzsche's "Triumph precisely in the last agony," far from reconciling will and power, separates them still further.[29] Indeed, *regis cida (cidium)*—which is one of the most important determinations of sovereignty in its classical, religious form—is reconceived here as a will to nothingness, that not only takes pleasure in sacrifice, but performs this jouissance as an endlessly active principle of abandonment. There is more than a whiff here of recuperation in the sense that theology is now anthropology, and sovereignty is now acephalic. Nevertheless, Bataille's insight remains unsettling: if the concept or logic that linked sovereignty to redemption is no longer, and has been replaced by a caesura whose most exemplary figure (the "NOTHING") can no longer be construed, so to speak, as law, outcome, reason, or faith, then there is no idiom of sovereignty, whether based on tribute or donation, on *sacrificium* or *sacer*, that can avoid this sacrificial principle of afformation. Community and spirit are thus the effects of afformation, and both compete in their chance to be nothing. This is not so much a sovereignty gone astray than the expression of a vitalism, the determination of death as a decision to be nothing, or, to borrow a phrase from Fanon, the sacrifice of life to an abyss, an *arché*, whose individuation presupposes nothing but the power to afform nothing, and that this nothing remains lost between nothingness and infinity. (This is where the shared desire for community abuts onto a principle of abandonment so absolute that it is nothing but chance itself).

How can we save the besieged subject and condemn vitalism without casting around for a more authentic—less dialectical, less rivalrous—image of resistance? At least this will be the frame for thinking through Nietzsche's (and Bataille's) legacy, which will also allow us to clarify how Newton's notion of revolutionary suicide—and its formulation of resistance and reaction—poses difficult questions for that legacy. And, first and foremost, how that notion makes evident a certain thinking of suicide in black thought.

III

Let us turn to one contemporary example: that of the Cameroonian scholar, Achille Mbembe. In 2003, Mbembe published an essay, "Necropolitics," that turns to Bataille to rethink the place of death, terror, and suicide in modern idioms of state power.[30] But instead of the camp, Mbembe turned to the example of the colony, and specifically blackness, to ask in what sense sovereignty, and its genealogy of values, can still be affirmed sovereignly? Or by what right does it still make sense to divide sovereignty into the *least* and the *most* sovereign, or to separate what is more authentically endowed as sovereign from that which is merely endowed as its spectacle? Mbembe makes this question specific, by considering two decisions and two typologies: that of the suicide bomber and that of the slave. I would like to suggest that the suicide bomber and the slave are opposed as two qualities of affirmation and negation, but also as two forms of destruction and creativity, life and death.

Here are the passages in question:

> There is no doubt that in the case of the suicide bomber the sacrifice consists of the spectacular putting to death of the self, of becoming his or her own victim (self-sacrifice). The self-sacrificed proceeds to take power over his or her death and to approach it head-on. This power may be derived from the belief that the destruction of one's own body does not affect the continuity of the being. The idea is that the being exists outside of us. The self-sacrifice consists, here, in the removal of a twofold prohibition: that of self-immolation (suicide) and that of murder. Unlike primitive sacrifices, however, there is no animal to serve as a substitute victim. Death here achieves the character of a transgression. But unlike crucifixion, it has no expiatory dimension. It is not related to the Hegelian paradigms of prestige or recognition. Indeed, a dead person cannot recognize his or her killer, who is also dead. Does this imply that death occurs here as pure annihilation and nothingness, excess and scandal?[31]

And:

> Death in the present is the mediator of redemption. Far from being an encounter with a limit, boundary, or barrier, it is experienced as "a release from terror and bondage." As Gilroy notes, this preference for death over continued servitude is a commentary on the nature of freedom itself (or the lack thereof). If this lack is the very nature of what it means for the slave or the colonized to exist, the same lack is also precisely the way in which he or she takes account of his or her mortality. Referring to the practice of individual or mass suicide by slaves cornered by the slave catchers, Gilroy suggests that death, in this case, can be represented as agency. For death is precisely that from and over which I have power. But it is also that space where freedom and negation operate.[32]

Why should one suicide be better than the other? Why is one deemed an absence or failure of agency or resistance, and why is one deemed resistance in its pure state? If the culmination of suicide lies in the recognition of the very difference between annihilation and agency, why is death by suicide-bombing considered a lesser death for this statement to be true? What can be said about this opposition that can only evoke validation (of suicide) as a difference between redemption and agency? The difference between an experience of will thereof, rather than an unfree desire? But is this not a difference that is marked, in turn, by a hope to live that can never actually be lived,

since it can only sacrifice itself—as a hope for the future—that makes freedom aberrant, or ungraspable?

Of course, these oppositions are themselves animated by oppositions
that remain implicit: the suicide bombing is described as a spectacular exercise of power, the slave suicide as a release from terror and bondage; the
suicide bombing is a transgression beyond recognition, the slave suicide is a
servile representation that affirms death as power, and so returns to itself as
a recognition, or as that which wills recognition as power. The very transferential process that tends to absolutize the revolutionary speculum of one (as
the death whose being exists outside of itself) de-absolutizes the assumptions that are still operative in the slavishness of the other (as the being that
lacks being).

On the one hand, if the death of the suicide martyr can only be thought
as a sacrifice without expiation, what cannot really be thought is suicide as
a death *without* expiated power. But on the other hand, acting as if agency
can be changed into power does not make it so, it is simply to think desire as
sacrifice, and therefore refers not so much to suicide as it does to its sacrificial meaning. In brief, slavery must sacrifice itself as sacrifice in order to affirm its non-slavish truth. But even if we say that Mbembe's (and Paul Gilroy's) ideas of the slave here have a lot in common (or at least seem to have
a lot in common in the construction of the slave as the opposite of a sovereign expenditure), the idea of slavery being proposed here does not escape
the Bataillean censure, that what is being proposed as a return to agency is
merely a slavish *imitation* of sovereignty. What can be said about a suicide
that could transform itself into a will to power rather than reduce itself to a
dialectics? Or if we want to save blackness, as a non-sovereign affirmation
of life, do we always need to oppose it, finally, to a sacrificial rhetoric whose
self-destruction is singled out as merely a spectacle, which not even death
can redeem?

The more one studies Mbembe's oppositional rhetoric, the more one
can't help noticing that slave suicide is characterized as an affirmation of
value (of freedom, say, or mortality) and suicide bombing is indicated to be
a mere means, or as a sign that remains signless. His reasoning is simple:
representation saves us from annihilation. No amount of power can substitute for the power of representation. Therefore, even if "sacrifice consists of
the spectacular putting to death of the self" (which was also the reasoning

behind Bataille's critique of modern fascist power), what can never be sacrificed is the concept of sacrifice itself, or the logic that links it to an economy of redemption. This is always the problem with pointing out death as the limit or boundary to life. The representation of death as the impossible limit to possibility always works to secure the meaning of impossibility as limit. This is the basis of Bataille's argument against the differentiation of mastery and slavery as a function of the Hegelian dialectic. What is never put to death, or what is never risked as such, is death as a speculative concept of philosophy. A speculation that Bataille, as we know, unwittingly repeats. In both the historical and ontological context of resistance, this is why slavery, in its resistance, remains enslaved to the sovereignty that initiates it: for only sovereignty can represent the giving and taking of slave life to the extent that it restores to death the spirit and counter-spirit of immortality. Indeed, sovereignty can only be affirmed in its difference from black Hegelian mastery, for the latter is always dependent on its relation to the slave and therefore can never redeem it.

Contrary to Mbembe, therefore, I think that slave resistance and revolutionary suicide are absolutely distinct—not formally but ontologically. If the former seeks a redemptive world, the latter names a world where possibility cannot be afformed without consolation or pathos. Consequently, I do not believe that Newton would accept the argument that slave suicide is *less* reactive, and for this simple reason: any desire to save oneself from social death is already proof that the sacrificer is socially dead.

Again, why is suicide transgressive in the example of the bomber and not in that of the slave? Both suicides are read as attempts to take power over death. And the phrase "taking power" must itself be taken in the strongest sense: what is taken back is being, being as will and destruction. However, whereas for the suicide bomber, death is seen to be separate from the continuity of being, for the slave, death reveals the non-being of being, a lack or nothingness. Accordingly, the suicide that does not *recognize* this power (of death) ends in annihilation, and the suicide that does becomes an expiation, a triumph, because, by separating death from non-being, it separates death from that will to nothingness that is somehow deeper in us than either life or death. These ontological arguments, in the context of what precedes them—histories of genocide and enslavement—tempt me to think that the true meaning of necropower is this categorial will to nothingness, and that the sovereign decision is thus divided between those who confront this will head-on (Mbembe's words) and those who divert it into questions of possibility and agency. But is there another way of thinking about the suicide bomber and the slave in relation to sovereignty? Can one think of a suicide that is more sovereign than sovereignty precisely because it is less than sovereign?

And how does the desire of the least, rather than the most sovereign, relate martyrdom to agency?

"In the logic of 'martyrdom,'" Mbembe writes, "the will to die is fused with the willingness to take the enemy with you, that is, with closing the door on the possibility of life for everyone."[33] Mbembe, of course, is somewhat hesitant about treating the suicide bomber—his example here—as a martyr, hence the scare quotes around the word martyrdom, but he does not exclude the word *sacrifice*. He writes, "the besieged body becomes a piece of metal whose function is, through sacrifice, to bring eternal life into being. The body duplicates itself and, in death, literally and metaphorically escapes the state of siege and occupation."[34] The word "sacrifice" here acquires a political as well as a sacred connotation (the suicide martyr does not only seek to kill the enemy; he also attempts to bring "eternal life into being" by deriving its essence from the sacramental exchange of blood in an interminable war on behalf of that community). Suicide bombings should not be understood simply as murder, as when modern militias massacre disposable populations in camps and zones of exception. For what is fleetingly revealed as the body literally transforms itself into a weapon: here "resistance and self-destruction are synonymous."[35] The word massacre, by contrast, solely defines the ways in which modern warfare and genocide reduce people to "empty, meaningless corporealities"—ways of killing, in short, that are purely instrumental and indiscriminate, and that reject the politics of waging war and the traditional categories of state power and territory.[36] Less instrumentally, but just as murderously perhaps, the martyr's sacrifice "reveals nothing" but a "subterfuge"; these words, taken from Bataille, underpin the conviction that, in the suicide's sacrifice (again drawing on Bataille), the martyr "dies seeing himself die, and even, in some sense, through his own will, at one with the weapon of sacrifice."[37] Note here how sacrifice, at the level of martyrdom, is in the service of a disfiguration and restoration of body and will (a belief generally fed by the wish to no longer feel oppressed by the expectations and demands of finitude). If the enemy was once proudly seen as the limit of political life, now the enemy is generalized as the embodied limit of life itself. This is considered the defining shift in modern antagonism, wherein the state of exception and relations of enmity "have become the normative status of the right to kill."[38]

In our present moment, the one thing that all critics seem to agree on about suicide martyrdom is that it is "the ultimate form of resistance" that, ironically, "acts as self-preservation."[39] These words, taken from Jasbir Puar's *Terrorist Assemblages* (2007), also suggest that suicide martyrdom is "the giving of life to the future of political struggles"; a life given, moreover, from the "conditions of life's impossibility"—in other words, revolutionary suicide makes the impossible *manifest* in political life as such.[40] But what does the giving of life as self-sacrifice mean? The relationship between life and power is redemptive to the extent that suicide can be still be determined as a representation, to the point where it can be politically affirmed as a symbol, which the community is affected by, insofar as it establishes or denies it. It follows that for suicide to become a political force it has to be made real by representation. Political and historical realities demand it: our capacity for being affected demands that suicide should follow a mimetic model of sacrifice. As such Puar cites a passage from Gayatri Spivak, in which she says: "there are no designated killees in suicide bombing . . . [and] there is no dishonor in such shared and innocent death."[41] But for whom is Spivak speaking? More, if there is no "killee" or victim in this shared aftermath, why does this imply a dying that is innocent, rather than an impossibility that is unknowable? Since there is no killee or victim, there is no murder, but also no resistance or possibility. All that there is are bodies reduced to expressing the power of death as spectacle, in whose performance they are merely the passive semblants or effects. Such equivalence not only voids political life of value, but seems to equate innocence with redemption, with the result that sacrifice becomes even less capable of resolving human unfreedom or conferring on it any significance. Spivak's formulation not only implies a death beyond any conceivable political order, and therefore beyond torment or struggle; it also cannot think revolutionary suicide without the notion of a nonreferential spectacle that belongs to no one, is for no one, for it is a shared apprenticeship in utter extremity. Death occurs here not as excess and scandal, but as a pure manifestation that precedes morality and self. This is why suicide is presented as the indefinite exchange of an impossible innocence. It is in this sense that Spivak, even without elaborating the concept of revolutionary suicide or giving it its full significance, was already speaking as if suicide is the restorative, sovereign effect of power in which the fit between appropriation and sublation is seamless. As such suicide can thus be witnessed and saved for representation because it is always judged to be a matter of feeling and sensibility rather than of will to power or justice. Perhaps this is why Bataille says that the philosophical concept of death can never escape the "obscene colonization of death," which is both its *pathos* and its *ressentiment*.

IV

Optimism is dead—it died of vanity.
Charles V. Charles, MD[42]

The vir *of sacrifice.* It strikes me that there are now two ways of thinking about black resistance: as capacity (liberal humanism) and as incapacity (Afro-pessimism). This *disputatio* takes the form (for me) of a meditation on resistance—whether blackness is that which is not (n'est pas) or that which is. If, when all is said and done, blackness is the affirmation of a new covenant, despite all its wretchedness and slaughter, is that because its power is yet to be recognized as a singular and incomparable affirmation, or because that power is always beyond power—and this is the price paid for the revolutionary beyond of its ethics? In this chapter I have sought to underline how these two views on blackness are opposed. For, while it remains the case that a theory of resistance will not have necessary racially resistant consequences, for me, Mbembe's attempt to moralize resistance in its resistances can never lead to a black resistant truth. And just as Newton's merit lies in trying to think resistance as black power, so the whole dignity of his thought consists in the way it pursues its contrary reactive principle as the completely realized truth of blackness. Resistance is not heroism or freedom. Nor is it sacrifice or redemption. All in all, resistance is not the sovereign chance of being. Let us say it is the fall that awaits every becoming, but a fall that cannot be rejoined to being without schism. On this particular point, Mbembe does not pursue the ambiguities of sovereign power as disintegration. In a strict sense, if we are all now simultaneously *homines sacri*, which is itself the measure of what necropower is defined against, it is precisely because our political fate is inextricable from the possibility that we could all end up butchered at a moment's notice—by drones or war machines—and there is no way anymore of avoiding this extermination by any sacrificial appeal. Neither law nor mercy will save us, nor will technology if its power is always assumed to belong to prosthetic enmity. But how can human consciousness or its technicity be anything but reactive and defensive, if the prosthetic is itself what racial consciousness is defined against?[43]

Such arguments feel a lot like racial paranoia. That is, the question of technology is always about the *racial* limit that technology attempts to eradicate. But in this case, as they say, even paranoia has technical racist prostheses. Or perhaps we should say that denying the paranoia of technical life doesn't make those racially "real" fears go away. Perhaps this is why Afro-pessimism is suspicious of the humanism of such arguments—because of the temptation to reify technology as the cure for racism while denying the racist means of obtaining this cure. Such arguments offer us nothing else but an analogy between technique and extermination. Merely being suspicious of analogy could itself be dismissed as reification if it is not *for* something. Instead of analogy, Afro-pessimism takes seriously the idea that the slave is a non-sovereign relation to the world. As such, its relation to the world is not a matter of *sensibilia* (affect), or of alienation, but is structured by an antagonism defined by racist incapacity. So, what would an Afro-pessimist make of the Mbembe-Gilroy idea that the slave can only enter into being, or into representation, as a suicide? Can the socially dead even commit suicide? Is there something about turning racial slavery into a form of agency that simply repeats its incapacity in the form of critique?

Perhaps this is not the right question, or the right question cannot yet be put into words. Even though we would like to believe that as individuals we would have agency in the face of certain destruction, and in large part because this is what is meant by the assumption of possibility, what leaves me uneasy, or decidedly unconvinced, is the belief that (i) agency comes into being through sacrifice, and that (ii) the unfree could ever sacrifice themselves sovereignly. It is not that we could never actively respond to what we believe is *fated*, or to what we see is in need of *liberating*; but why presume that freedom is the telos of sovereignty rather than a will to nothingness? In

putting myself to death, and hence grasping the end of possibility as negation, why assume that this will is in any sense a plea for freedom, or could
be resisted, or that it shares any complicity with a life-affirming martyrdom? What could possibly confirm in me the certainty thereof? On what basis could I assume that the desire for liberation (in *extremis*) is not, from the
first, the easiest and most complicit, act of self-delusion or terror? And why
this belief that those who are socially dead, and so never quite alive or dead,
could redeem themselves by *choosing* to see themselves as free and resistant
in death's proximity?

What Newton's contribution to that tradition allows us to see is that
there is a mastery (philosophical) for whom blackness is always already mastered, and for whom there is no remedy for the remedial concept of sovereignty as such.

Unsurprisingly, when Newton represents mastery or slavery, he does so
in the Nietzschean sense, as passive-active relations of value or force. Accordingly, he removes resistance from the law of ontology—that is, he presents blackness as an anti-value to the precise extent that it troubles every
sovereign relation of expenditure and of resistance.

These two images of resistance appear to have little in common, and,
in fact, that is the point. The first allows for sovereignty to emerge as non-
knowledge (of what Bataille famously calls *le non-savoir*); the second allows
us to see how blackness is a displaced name for death itself and is nothing
other than this; that blackness is a name for nothing as such. As death, however, this n'est pas cannot be posited as nothing, for its oblivion offers no
consolation. And only in that sense can it be called resistant. As such, its predicament does not lie in what Bataille calls *le non-savoir*—namely, the category of a loss without reserve, for its obliteration cannot be characterized as
negation; or more simply, blackness offers a death that cannot even be assigned the negation of meaning or sense, or its analogical value. Black social
death is thus, beyond *savoir*, a name that is incapable of assuming the meaning of sacrifice, for it marks an effacement of both the infinite pathos of sacrifice as "spiritual truth" (these words are Nancy's), and its passing cannot
be trans-posed as the mark, or the sublation by which the finite must be sacrificed for sacrifice to accede to its own truth.[44] Blackness is the name, in
brief, by which being unnames and surrenders itself, and this is why it is also
an absolute resistance to the philosophical idea and rhetoric of resistance.

Why then is it repeatedly posed and deposed according to the (philosophical) language of sovereignty?

This is a very difficult question to answer. But let us consider an initial hypothesis. What Bataille refers to as sacrifice is not censored by virtue of the fact it puts death to work, but rather the opposite: sacrifice cannot become sacrifice without immediacy, it cannot reproduce itself without immediacy, for immediacy is precisely what allows for the materialization of spirit, and without that materialization sacrifice cannot become philosophy. But in order to affirm itself as spirit, as sovereign, dialectics thereby renders immediacy figurative, that is to say, allegorical, slavish. This is why, for Bataille, sacrifice is "fascinating as light," and why, for Nancy, sacrifice "cast[s] an obscure light."[45] Sacrifice (and its philosophy) cannot become or affirm itself without this presumption of finitude, with its eye-catching terror and effects. What, then, do we see when we look upon sacrifice? And, depending on where we look, is it possible to see anything beyond martyrs and victims, slaves and masters? That is to say, sacrificial spectacles permitting the (white) allegories of philosophy?

Going back to Mbembe's assertion: the sacrifice that is expelled from the polis always returns to haunt the spaces of everyday life, for the power to decide who is *disposable* and who is not is equated with the *racial* distribution of death, in which "the murderous functions of the state" can now operate with impunity against those deemed enemies, and against those considered dangerous, infectious, or simply expedient in their immediacy.[46] It is not perhaps an accident that one of Mbembe's ongoing concerns is how racial-ethnic difference has become the murderous limit of all sovereign possibility in the modern nation-state. Expedited mass race murder does not bear witness to the demise of sacrifice but is the "most complete example of a state exercising the right to kill"; what biopower exposes is how the logic of exception has become separated from law and spirit and is no longer part of a sovereign decision. And yet, in the colony, as Mbembe also has pointed out, this separation was already in play. Mbembe cites Arendt's infamous comment (in the *Origins of Totalitarianism*): "so that when European men massacred them [natives] they *somehow were not aware* that they had committed murder."[47] This separation between awareness and massacre also renders sacrifice invalid, or pointless. Native life would seem to represent what is killable but not sacrificeable, what is posited as valueless life. Yet what is the lesson that Mbembe takes away from this? That there are some who live "in a state of injury," and some who injure, who cause this injury.[48] It is when he says that injurious life persists, recreates itself, that he reveals the limits of his humanism. He gives voice not to an afformation beyond sovereignty, but to philosophy's sovereign lament, not to revolutionary suicide as a force (of afformation) but to the moral sadness of those who have suffered "a horrifying experience, something alien beyond imagination or comprehension."[49] Resistance, as it is thought in *Revolutionary Suicide*, has nothing to do with imagination or empathy; such language can only reiterate (or reflect) a reactive thinking of black life. To feel that black suffering is something somehow *beyond* the limits of imagination is to still think black life as reducible to the whiteness of its representation, and so can only reiterate that reflection as the meaning of an anti-black negation.[50] Mbembe is thus unable to bring into view the other of such positing, the other of philosophy that is always already there at the origin, namely the enslaved life that is also irredeemably withheld and that withholds itself from what human being makes possible, or racially knowable as such.

V

All "communication" participates in suicide and crime.
Georges Bataille, *On Nietzsche*[51]

Suicidium: *devoit* or *on doit*? Let us say that, in philosophy, this caricature is always the slave's desire. But is there another answer? To be liberated, not from suffering, but from will-less oblivion?

Just to be clear: this is not an acceptance or refusal of suicide.

Nor is it an insistence on the freedom of decision. As if all one had to do was to say: yes, I accept all of this pain and anguish, now I know my nature and my existence.

No. To renounce all obedience, all obligation, and first of all to existence, is the slave's first resistant act. *Everything* else is mere hope or expediency ...

———

Before concluding, let's just briefly sum up for a moment. The condemnation of suicide bombing in Mbembe originally involved two kinds of outrage:

as outlined in "Necropolitics," the suicide bombing was originally condemned for equating martyrdom and survival; and for making the body into a weapon of war against other bodies (*guerre au corps-à-corps*) (the idea that the martyr "clos[es] the door on the possibility of life for everyone").[52] Moreover, when he associates suicide martyrdom with the example of Palestine—but can Palestine ever be just an example?—Mbembe says that the besieged body represents sacrifice through transgression.

We must be careful not to invert the relations here. There is no doubt that sacrifice reveals, as Bataille says, nothing but its own subterfuge; for there to be a sacrifice it does not matter what the object says or does but what it is; *mana* in a word is the essence of sacrifice, but for sacrifice to be effective it has to become known as such. It has to be communicated. Or acknowledged. The link between spectacle and knowledge thus relies on there being a representation, on whose assured repetition we can rely. What outrages Mbembe about the suicide bombing is that a death that seeks to go beyond representation has no expiatory dimension and so cannot be sublated. It is not related to the Hegelian paradigms of prestige or recognition. But these formulations and opinions seem to me to display a misunderstanding. If, on the one hand, suicide is an example of sacrifice, then the desire for eternity (for paradise), does indeed confer prestige and recognition; and natural death is not simply death but is itself an act of spiritual expiation and sublation. Indeed, one could read the decision to self-detonate as Spivak does: not as violence, or as spiritualization, but as the negating innocence of negation.

Mbembe doesn't pursue any of this: firstly, because, to have value, suicide has to be seen to be redemptive; and secondly, it must be recognized as morally innocent. Only in this sense can suicide be an instance of agency. But these formulations put into jeopardy Newton's idea that suicide can also be life-afforming as an exception precisely because of its incapacity to posit and to mean. And precisely because no moral-theological lesson can be derived from it. One thing is certain: lying at the heart of Newton's Nietzschean reading of suicide is the belief that the most life-afforming act could be the one that ends, not one's life, but its racially contingent de-mediation. That, at least, is what Newton takes from Nietzsche: that is, the belief that one's suicide should not be done out of *ressentiment*, but from will to power; or, more precisely, from its afformation. And not because black suffering has no meaning, or a meaning beyond one's control, but because a *black* afformation should not be confused with self-preservation, salvation, or morality. How does revolutionary suicide perform black life-afformation? Not by willing life or negating it; nor by preserving life as life. But by an act of creative willing. It testifies not to a diminished life but to a life overflowing with deadly abundance. As such, it is able to perform a transvaluation. Everything that is done to *that* life cannot be done again. The hardest task is thus not to transform reaction into sovereignty—but to avoid trying to conserve the NOTHING as a *reason* for one's self-destruction. Creative willing is to be understood here as the active destruction of everything that is reactive and life-denying up to and including the joy in destroying, which is also an affirmation—that is, the affirmative power of negation. Hence the doctrine of eternal recurrence, which Nietzsche describes in *Ecce Homo* as "the highest formula of affirmation that is at all attainable," a formula in which to will everything is to will nothing but the *thought* of affirmation, the affirmation of what is without meaning or telos, "but inevitably recurring, without any finale into nothingness," which is also why this thought is also called "the most extreme form of nihilism."[53] Accordingly, the thought of death as consolation or as escape is dismissed as weakness, cowardice, or spitefulness. The subterfuge of the ascetic ideal is its sacrificial hope for a better life. Whereas suicide as life-afformation is what rebels against the ascetic ideal and all its conventions.

If resistance is a demand for black sovereign life, it is not a demand for presence or absence, whether manifested as chance or enmity.

If there is a resistant life, it is infinitely beyond our comprehension, since being resistant, it bears no relation to our wishes or desires.

This being so, who would dare say to the slave that its suffering was meaningless and/or transgressive? Certainly not we, who bear no relation to him. But this is precisely what the discourse of sovereignty presumes. And in response to which the only answer would be that I (as slave) can only affirm life as suffering, as a kind of infinite suffering, and only as such can it be affirmed or resisted as a kind of meaningful eternity not to be endured as such. Rather the idea of life as interminable dying might well be the most compelling reason to end it.

With this in mind, let us therefore now return, in conclusion, to the text that gives this chapter its title. In the Epilogue to *Revolutionary Suicide*, Newton writes:

> The difference [between revolutionary and reactive suicide] lies in hope and de-
> sire. By hoping and desiring, the revolutionary suicide chooses life; he is, in the
> words of Nietszche, "an arrow of longing for another shore." Both suicides de-
> spise tyranny, but the revolutionary is both a great despiser and a great adorer
> who longs for another shore. The reactionary suicide must learn, as his brother
> the revolutionary has learned, that the desert is not a circle. It is a spiral. When
> we have passed through the desert, nothing will be the same.[54]

As this passage implies, there is no redemptive meaning to be found within black life. Rather the reverse. One cannot live this unlivable life—this desert—except by resisting it. If resistance is the power of turning death against itself, of negating reaction, that is because one cannot hold onto life as a possession or capacity. The reversal of reaction would be no reversal at all, but a reinstatement, without this absolute letting go. It is by confirming the wager—and not by escaping it—that black power answers the demand of will to power. This means that black power offers neither escape nor absolution but, on the contrary, is the endless elaboration of the resistance which arises out of reaction.

Let us then determine this point, and let us say: resistance is the double negation of reaction and of being acted-upon. But to which view will we be inclined? Neither reason nor passion can decide the question. The movement of resistance, already a result of these pressures, separates us from the decidability of decision, of the ability to decide. It is no wonder that Newton's autobiography, with its endless accounts of trial and summary execution, shows how reaction and resistance are profoundly implicated in one another. It is also no wonder that he had great difficulty in writing a black revolutionary life that attempts to elaborate both positions without reducing either to a logic of exception or enmity. The desert of reactionary suicide is a good example of the attempt to deny nihilism as the end of existence whilst knowing that any attempt at its escape could always end with reactive nihilism. Which doesn't mean that the reactive ending of life cannot be resistant to life in another sense. One must write with this life, from this life, writing for black life *as* life, but one must write knowing that the desert is not a circle—that is, an eternal recurrence that makes death as such meaningless—but a spiral in which hope and desire, despair and adoration, suicide and enmity are radically intermingled and indeterminate (whether they are understood as revolt or reaction).

The spiral thus describes a unicity of return and chance—the spiral is eternal and is eternal because it spirals, for it does nothing but return. Thus, blackness only occurs through its reactive recapitulations, since it is nothing other than the power by which its reactive modes occur. Hence there is only resistance *in* reaction, or according to reaction, and these are themselves reactions to resistance's power, its trajectories and intuitions. And this is what leads Newton to conclude: revolutionary suicide is not an event, but a circling back, in which each turn takes account of a previous turn, and in whose collective movement every single moment resists and reacts to those spiral turnings that precede it.

Only in this way can one speak of an ethical beyond of resistance—that is to say, the arrow in whose infinite-finite arc chance assumes a chaotic order of thought as afformation. Now flight here is not a dialectical movement, but the principle of its resistant mediacy and negation.

In any case, Newton *does* name revolutionary suicide as a life-affirming decision in the world. And nothing could be further from nihilism. The idea that eternal recurrence might be a counsel of resignation never occurs to him. Several times in the book in his attempts to outline the ideal of black revolutionary politics and leadership, he repeats an African proverb: "I am we"—"I, we, all of us are the one and the multitude."[55]

I am we: as a definition of black community, this idea chimes with Newton's other great Maoist idea of "intercommunalism," according to which there is no being, everything is becoming; or that the one can only be affirmed as the being of becoming, the multiple.[56] But note the two ways of thinking becoming here: that of the arrow (there is no being beyond becoming), and that of the spiral (no becoming beyond multiplicity); neither multiplicity nor becoming are resistant or reactive in themselves, nor do they enter into relation as means or ends. But neither are they conceived as singularities or multiplicities in which being, in turn, could be seen to *escape* its determination by constant change and transformation. Newton's view of the party and political leadership was thus one of afformation, the afformation that the multitude is itself one. Intercommmunalism would be—perhaps perpetually—not the disjunctive synthesis of desert and spiral but rather the afformation of chance as the multiple itself. Multiple afformation is the way in which the one—the leader, community, or the party—affirms and resists itself by remaining nobody and nothing. There is no negativity in becoming here—there is no diminishment to be expiated or redeemed (Mbembe), no innocence that is deemed to be the truth of the multiple (Spivak). Nevertheless, there is an afformation of a figure-obliterating act as the being of that which becomes resistant through reactive repetition. Suicide is black being becoming itself, suicide is the law by which blackness abandons itself to multiplicity, and multiplicity returns to the one as the unity of reaction and resistance. We must understand the stakes of Newton's Nietzschean interpretation: the notion that *I am we* depends entirely on the notion that only in being absolutely abandoned can life be afformed. Suicide afforms becoming and it afforms the being of becoming. So paradoxically it is Newton, not Mbembe, who takes suicide seriously *in the world*. Newton's distaste for reactive nihilism does not exclude a sensitivity to its effects, which merely increases his desire to transform it. In fact, *Revolutionary Suicide* was written to defend his version of black revolutionary politics. And his vision of the BPP as a party of black life-afformation was inextricably connected to the figure of blackness as literally a *crime* of communication. Indeed, at the time of writing the book, Newton had personally witnessed countless members of the BPP being condemned for the crime of being resistant: murdered for arming themselves, for defending the people against police brutality, for bursting the limits of anti-blackness. Only by refusing blackness can one correspond to its resistance.

Yes, one must wager one's singularity as if it were the multiple. There is no choice, you are already committed by the fact that singularity is the point where the multiple acts upon itself, and the multiple is the place where the singular is acted-upon in its irreducible resistance to reaction. Which will you choose then? Let us say: since a choice must be made, let us see which offers you the least resistance. You have two things to lose: life and enslavement. And two things to stake: your death and your will, your knowledge and your existence. Since you must necessarily choose, you are no more affronted by choosing one rather than the other. There is no rivalry over something that neither possesses—a life free from endless struggle and terror. But your suicide? Let us weigh up the gain and the loss involved in suicide-as-resisting: if you resist, you resist everything (force, structure, order, law, *ressentiment*); if you lose, you lose nothing but reactance. Which is why it is impossible to tell apart getting even from an even greater loss. But isn't the wager itself an appropriation? And isn't blackness *ressentiment*? This is why it matters that resistance is not a wager of life or of its value. It is a drive: both arrow and desert. At the same time, it is a spiral, a turning, a repetition, that has to begin with what infinitely condemns it. Since there is equal gain and loss, the drive cannot resist itself as drive, and its force cannot be denied, only moralized as a means or end.

This is why there may be a deeper link between reaction and resistance than we have hitherto examined: if the former conserves, according to Bataille, the latter is the irresistible power for the black to expend itself, to follow its path, whether out of the desert or into the universal spiral, for one must choose and one cannot choose: such precisely is the limit of black ethics.

Let us say then: the drive to resist is irreducible to both its revolutionary affects and reactive affects. And that this is the profound intuition of black power itself. Resistance cannot become a power without becoming a transcendent principle. This is what Newton means when he speaks of reaction, of the tragedy of its suspect witnessing. To know how to transform reaction is to know that blackness is nothing other than resistance itself. But we do not yet know the power of affirming resistance because we confuse it as an end to be obtained rather than a n'est pas that can never be represented as such, because it resists resistance. Thus, the axiom that is extremely difficult: blackness is the afformation that murders itself as resistant. It is the afformation of suicide as resistant. Only in this sense can one say that the one is the multiple. What this means is not at all that the multiple can only be affirmed as one, but rather, the multiple is afformed as the one's resistance to itself, beyond its consistency as one, its contingency and decision.

Suicide, for Newton, is thus affirmed as the moment when black revolutionary life somehow turns into not necessity (destiny), nor *ressentiment* (slavery), but the reaction of resistance itself. Again, if I can only know resistance as meaning or sense, then I no longer resist my death, since what is revealed to me, as model or object, can only speak to my enslavement. And, at the same time, to become a revolutionary subject I have to *kill myself*, to kill myself in front of myself: the reactive other that I am no longer exists, has never been me, since I killed myself from the start, since I assimilated, consumed, incorporated him from the beginning. And precisely because I could not lend myself the certainty of being in favor of, let alone become capable of, resistance.

We must therefore attach the greatest importance to the following conclusion: suicide can never become sovereign to the precise extent that the one is the multitude and vice versa. This is where Mbembe's notion of necropower paradoxically comes back in. In Newton's case, the idea that politics has literally become murder, and sovereignty massacre, in ways that, by implication, exceed the meanings of enemy and exception as commonly understood by politics, is nothing new in American history. Black America has always experienced the duress of a besieged population. But what is new is the formulation of suicide as a logic—a language—by which the besieged body is made fateful, and not simply because it resists, but more because it is prepared to risk everything *for* that which it is not. And so it comes as no surprise that Mbembe should segue from a discussion of the suicide bomber to that of the slave (the latter is missing from Puar's and Spivak's accounts). No surprise, either, that he should directly assert that in slave-suicide, one glimpses freedom and agency (rather than innocence), futurity rather than history; an assertion that repeats Bataille's reading of sacrifice as authenticity, but with a crucial difference: here the moment of death amounts to a refusal of social death, rather than the assumption of a "supreme virility" by which death "precisely makes possible all other possibilities" (Heidegger). The problem with this sacrificial conception of death—of death as the "space where freedom and negation operate"—is not the historical example of slaves killing themselves when cornered by slave catchers, but the fact that it arises from an emphasis on a subject willing to kill itself in order to preserve its futurity as a subject.[57] A notion that is, broadly speaking, dialectical, which means that it remains, to all intents and purposes, *servile*, and therefore nonresistant. If being sovereign is to be found in suicide, one's sovereignty does not exist, sovereignty does not exist, but cancels itself by the fact of being dead and is therefore never master even of its own death, even if this becoming-dead is its only chance at redemption.

———

One final comment. Although Newton's reading of Nietzsche is enigmatically brief,[58] what he takes from Nietzsche should therefore be understood as follows:

To admit the thought that there is no resistance besides that of suicide, and most certainly none that is not reactive, raises a difficulty that is no less startling to us: if one believes that the decision to end one's life is not a decision against life but the only chance by which life can be won in its disappropriation, then it is most likely also the case that black life must expend itself in order to live, in the sense that it reveals an *is not* (n'est pas) that precedes one's being. Whosoever does not want to avail himself of this possibility remains reactive, because they cannot free themselves from what blackness *is* not; and so are deconstituted by the thought of it.[59] Resistance therefore leaves us with no choice: it is nothing but the meaning of black life's resistance to itself. Without this resistance of life—to its meaning and esteem as life—that is, without this black *power*, whose finite loss becomes an infinite chance of defiance and revolt, blackness would not have the assertive force that it does—and there would be no possibility of it becoming other to itself. Blackness has no being; but this *is not* does not, however, mean a nullity—or a nothing—but is the occurrence of an expense that withdraws itself from every consolation. This withdrawal—which Newton also characterizes as a refusal, as resistance, and, in *Revolutionary Suicide*, as community—belongs to the perduring structure of blackness itself, so that Newton can say that in blackness, what is revealed is neither desert nor an arrow, origin or process, but that which remains withheld even as it releases itself in ever-multiple occurrences. And this resistance—insofar as it is simultaneously the resistance *of* resistance—must remain withdrawn from itself—that is, it must remain reactive.

In that it resists, the most revolutionary black subject is therefore first and foremost the most suicidal—we could even go so far as to say: black revolution *is* suicide and suicide is black revolution (suicide signifies here neither a means or tactic of resistance à la Clausewitz, but a black asemia that refuses all the orders of logos and logic, as well as the police states of being and ontology).[60] Let us also remember that by representing black political death as the *not* of sacrifice, in the mode of an unpayable debt, or inutilious expenditure, the black revolutionary subject also expends itself beyond representable capacity, including that of resistance. Therefore we must take care not to reduce revolutionary suicide to that of ego or spectacle, or as *driven* by a logic of enmity and sacrifice. In reality, the black subject is nothing outside of the death wherein it consciously gives-withholds itself from itself; and the structure of black community cannot be a *negativum*, or an abandoning, but a non-giving that is nonetheless an *ot-one* (a not-nothing), whose death, insofar as it frees itself, actually should be called the true and ultimate revolutionary suicide.[61]

What Newton reads in Nietzsche's will to power is, then, this: that the best way to serve the community is to help it die well, to overcome its resistance to death, and to know itself through this suicide—the imperatives of that willing lead to the revolutionary effects of destruction, that is to say, to the most destructive acts of creation. By willing its own death, the community gives the lie to life's neutrality or universality. And in that imperative to die, it negates death and gives voice to the living—it affirms itself, not as life, but as will to power.

Here death ceases *to be* death, but rather every moment of life is lived as irremediable, in order to live it again as black power. Here, there is no *sacrifice* of life to political community, but the realization that by giving up everything, one receives back—absolutely, infinitely—the same. And the same as resistant. The alternate symbol of this ecstatic nihilism is black *ressentiment* that counters state violence with infinite mercy. Or opposes niggers with guns to unarmed freedom marchers. Now Newton's decision, as Minister of Defense, to place armed patrols in the community ought to be read as a political strategy first and foremost, but not because the gun was a means or an end, but because it transformed the lines of resistance *as such*—from finite self-destructive suffering to an infinite calculation that was inherently suicidal. The gun provided "reasons" (his word) not simply for defense, but so that people could see and know black power, and not mistake its courage for mere malice or egotistical posturing. Black power lives, but precisely for this reason, it cannot be given power as a datum or representation. It cannot come to presence without sacrificing its presencing, for blackness is nothing other than the power of its effacement, and, sensu stricto, it can only give (represent) itself as reactive.

But can resistance be made into a law—a law of blackness—without sacrificing itself? By the same token, can resistance redeem itself as an argument for self-obliteration? As a finite gift of being? Can the resistant will as will (*vouloir*) be the same as the legislative will (*Wille*) of duty (*devoit*) or of obligation (*on doit*) without suiciding itself as the *choice* of resistance? Would this not also be evidence of a *ressentiment*, the return to law as origin?[62] Newton indicates that the drama of blackness was not to appear before the law but signifies the ability to tell the law to go fuck itself. That, it would be useless to deny, is what Newton attempts to do in *Revolutionary Suicide*. Blackness as the lie, the malignant discord, of law whose repeated death confirms the errancy of its legislation. And for whom the law of the world is absolute injustice. Yet it can be shown that this project is inherently self-subverting because its very starting point is not life or law but the desire for a kind of infinite withholding, that is nothing or n'est pas. But this figure is, at every moment, both absolutely resistant and beyond any attempt at resistance. In any case it is not something that anyone can simply choose to do nor merely avoid. What blackness resists then is this: that it does not resist, and before all else, that it does nothing but resist (itself) in its resistance.

Eight

The Real and the Apparent

Conversio and the x. We began the first part of this book with just one question: What is it that makes existents black? Mastery and violence; this is what makes existents black. Mastery is not added to violence by a sort of *tekhnē*; it is in the very sign by which it is given at the moment of its affirmation. As far as the choices go, you must master the sign due to its relationship with subjection and difference, for if you are mastered by it, you will not be able to think or act, or be.

Mastery over the sign situates the subject as power, starting with the sign as will, contract, and judgement. The truly sovereign pays the sign no heed, for it starts out from him, and is enchained to him, but only up to a certain point. The slave has to learn to sign, for he begins from its enchainment. This is his labor and his blindness. The slave can only become a subject—in the freedom of his present as presence—by knowing his subjection, the impossibility of assuming it, and so evoking the sign as the instant of its transcendence. From the dungeon of materiality to the peon work of representation—these are the two forms of identification open to the slave. The sign offers mastery existence in the form of enjoyment, and consequently allows it to exist apart from itself. The slave is subjected to the object that he labors to subject to the sign, and which he nevertheless can only affirm as reason and not as enjoyment. But then there is this: the power of revelation that begins as a moment of transcendence is also a moment of violence, of weighing and separation, but the power that liberates the slave from its enchainment is knowledge and light.

So from the slave enfeoffed in darkness, not knowing whether his sentence is one of death or life, we see a subject emerge into a blinding moment of light in which it is assumed that on this day all the cows are white. However, after such trial and crisis, he is not certain that the sign that liberates should not also be seen as the surest sign of slavery. Indeed, why should he assume that to come into the light is to be possessed by an a priori? That it makes the unknown knowable; or that it allows us to identify with our own alterity? For instead of heralding a new dawn, this blinding light leads him straight back to the heart of violence itself—that is, the revelation that sees blackness disappear from itself, because it submits, or is always submitting, to a judgement that makes whiteness the truth of its affirmation and submission and reduces blackness to a sign of non-being. Such a light also presents his servitude to him as the (impossible) enjoyment of pure mastery. It forces upon him the sudden awareness of this n'est pas, for it betokens the continuing conversion of black existents into a *non-sovereign* awareness. And because blackness can be never sure of itself as mastery or affirmation it cannot even assume its annihilation as a possibility. For any approach to black death as resistant cannot grasp itself as resistant, and a truly reactive death is no longer able to be murderously reactive. It is exactly thus that blackness murders itself—or succumbs to its trial and summary execution.

Therefore, with this second part, we have tried to find the meaning of conversion in the deadly freedom that embodies it, beginning with the violent excesses of this n'est pas. When we say that blackness unveils a n'est pas that is not dependent on the real or the subject, we are simply saying that there is something about blackness (an x) that bewilders categories and judgements that have, from Aristotle to Hegel, *joined the human to ontology*. Consequently, we are saying simply that the n'est pas does not belong to ontology; for there is no royal road that leads to it (as spirit, as identity) that does not annihilate and reject it as the mutilated part of the real and the subject. We can add to that the violence by which blackness is finally reduced to an x in which there is no more need for the sign to be the fulfillment of a symbolic contract. One of the ways in which the x confounds the sign is that it evokes a power that is beyond power, meaning both the recognition of difference itself and the most abject forms of idealism. Thus, there is black power—that is, the x in its radical difference—because it does not deny the close proximity between blackness, terrorism, and death.

In this second part we have sought to explain this via the question of *conversio*, and consequently the self's submission to its own radical dissociation.

However, we have yet to fully explain why the n'est pas cannot be considered an event of conversion, whether at the level of *being, thing,* or *identification*. It follows from this that the n'est pas cannot be conceived as an act of conversion insofar as it has no capacity to form itself, or affirm itself, as an identity, given that the n'est pas cannot be posited outside of a will to perish as black. This can also be deduced from our extensive reading of *homocidium dolorosum* in relation to black power. However, I do not want to revisit that argument here.

It is clear from everything we have said above that we perceive the x to be a chimera, a deceit, that forms itself in relation to the political laws of force and violence. Black conversion results from its relationship to that which masters it. This converted mastery is the power of black power, the power that is so resolutely beyond power, starting with the power of conversion to think, or be, *the model and exemplar, the phantasm and judge* of blackness itself.

There are three further propositions that follow on from this.

First, if the x is to be understood as revelation, the revelation which *exposes* being to the thought of the n'est pas is not one of exchange but one of self-annihilation, and this is why I have called this a conversion without mediation or exchange.

Secondly, given that the x cannot moor itself in an absolute fidelity to being, the converted subject cannot form itself without the reintegration of an infinite dissolution, which is here identified with an irreconcilable condemnation.

From now on let us say that conversion is not initially an indictment of what is null or void, but the desolation of what is upheld. It follows from this that the x is a death that dies for itself, and dies as something absolutely unknowable. In other words, analysis of the x must begin, not with its conversion into flesh or social death, nor with their definitions or principles, but with a n'est pas that is beyond the means of either concept to express it and so cannot be apprehended by either term. Where the n'est pas appears, what can be seen all at once, at a glance, are perceptions endlessly deceived and propositions endlessly conceived as guilt or innocence. Moreover, if the x cannot therefore be a principle of enjoyment or sublation, how do we perceive or understand it as an existent?

Thirdly, and finally, what then is converted by the x and what is the difference between knowing it and experiencing it (see chapters 5 and 7)?

In addition to these kinds of arguments, there is, as I hope to show in what follows, another, third kind of argument, which we shall call a *black* conception of the real that situates it beyond any affirmation or foundation. This kind of knowing proceeds from black revolutionary social thought (incarnated, for me, by Malcolm X) that changes the signs and meaning of conversion itself.

I will explain all these notions with a single example. If *conversio* places the subject in front of itself, in front of its "lived experience," this transcendence offers the subject a liberation from what it is in itself. Conversion—as event—offers the subject a new *reality*, and consequently permits it a new "there is" prior to thought or immanence. The converted subject abhors the subject it converts, and nevertheless keeps its distance with regards to that abhorrence. Such are the conditions, it seems to me, under which philosophy converts itself into revelation (of wisdom, truth, and becoming). In this way, all philosophy is inevitably the experience of conversion—that is, the enjoyment (and the renunciation) of what it reveals to the unconverted. In Malcolm X's story of his conversion, however, we see how he employs proofs and propositions that differ, fundamentally, from the philosophical Idea of unconcealing an essence. The x is not the utterance of an *epistrophē* (return); nor is it the expression of a *metanoia* (rebirth). Nor can it be thought in an existentially essential way as an experience, perhaps not even in terms of the character of a transformation. The x cannot be understood by the term *human being*; nor can it be affirmed as a *causa* or object, as a duty or incapacity. The x is not just the overcoming of the self, but the reconstruction of its reference, as a truth of immanence. This is evident solely from the fact that it denotes an apriority that cannot be affirmed or renounced. For one can only know it insofar as it is not, or is doubtful; and is therefore necessarily condemned as uncertain or false. This is the first point. Let us say that the x annihilates without converting, and that this, in a revolutionary way, changes all possibility (and all dialectics) of the real and the subject.

In what follows I hope to be able to show that the relationship of conversion to manifestation is as entirely different from the politics of mastery as it is from the ethics of sacrifice. For the moment, I would like to at least indicate how the x itself refers to this situation as a manifestation of the real.

The x that the n'est pas names exceeds all schemas and sets, including that of the x (as part of a set whose *causa* exists and is infinite). In order for this x, which belongs to nobody and which human being cannot assume, to become an x, it must first enter into relationship with what Malcolm X calls the *real*. What is it that links the real and the x? For me, the x is a pure act or leap, and this leap is at once insignificant and infinite, for it is separated from existents. It is certainly not yet real in a pure revolutionary sense, which would transform it into the *abyss*, but neither is it an assignable form of being, since for the present, this power that is beyond itself can only be retroactively fabricated in the image of the power that resembles it.

The relationship of the x with the real is, on the contrary, present in black beings as an immanent power, but this is a power that does not have identity as a principle. The situation of conversion must thus be understood as invention, and this is what the power of the n'est pas is; namely, to encroach upon the *sense* that blackness is, and to endure the real that becomes, in its turn, senseless, within the constraints of being.

Part 2 began with blackness as the event whereby the subject manages to accomplish all its innocence—that is to say, all the intensity of its negation, all the finality of its ending—and at the same time it realizes that it cannot be cured of the belief that it is in a relationship with what it is not, that it remains bound to the nullifying power of what it cannot assume, which is absolute, and in regard to which it is exposed to the violence of an ending it is no longer able to determine or innocently imagine as black. This n'est pas determines the future of blackness as the undetermined, and the future of black power as a risk without gain. It determines what in black power contrasts sharply with that of politics, and all allegories of the sovereign state. Starting from allegory to understand the x, one never again meets with the x as a figure of knowledge or innocence.

To be sure, Malcolm X's conception of black power as a real, absolutely unknowable event tends toward the same end. But it preserves for the x a power over that of politics: real revolution cannot determine itself as an x while at the same time determining—or revealing—an x that is chosen or unique, and *thus* neither authentic nor inauthentic. To grasp the x as revolution it is not enough to situate it within a philosophy of sense or meaning, which makes conversion the principal attribute of means and ends. It is a matter of showing that conversion is an act that takes place *through* language. And indeed, were we to separate the real from the n'est pas, conversion would be the pure means—the pure violence—that enables black being to become itself. The subject's identity by itself is incapable of yielding this. To uphold this thesis, I have insisted upon the irremissible tabula rasa that constitutes the writing of the x, and upon the hypostasis that ends in the positing of a *nothing* over meaning or sense, but which by the same token can never be shut up in the finality of an identity that conversion ultimately does not undo. It is not a matter of contesting the fact of possibility, to which Malcolm X's descriptions of the dictionary have accustomed us. It is a matter of showing the ontological virtuality of certain lexemes, which are the differentiation rather than the realization of possibility as opposed to a subject shut in on itself. This is precisely the reason why the x of conversion is profound. It is not simply a renewal through positing, which remains attached to a referent, giving the ego the security of actuality. More than the renewal of black moods and qualities, the x is essentially a rare vigilance that cannot be determined as human. That is the second point. Here revolution is nonhuman and so resolutely singular *in* its imparting to being a violence beyond ontology that it cannot be or be conceived without aporia. (By the same reasoning, the x links *conversio* to passions that cannot be mastered.)

How can the x enter into relation to the real without allowing itself to be shackled again by mastery? If in the face of apartheid-segregation the x is no longer able to manifest, how can the x become the event it announces? The problem does not consist in rescuing the x from injury, but in knowing how to propose it without recourse to hypostasis or analogy. Such is the situation of what one might call the attempt not to reduce contingency *to* mediacy, where the temptation is to grasp the x as logic or ontology, without facing up to the x as the annihilation of mediacy. Malcolm X's early writing under the influence of Elijah Muhammad, sometimes fell into that trap.[1] But he didn't remain there. To the extent that the task of the x is the annihilation of white state violence and its institutions, it opens a way out of the human and its racist sense. The x *is* this process of manifestation. The x is the real—and so can no longer be understood as violent possibility, or as a violence that is completely determined. Ultimately, it can never be given or assumed, which is why its sole refuge is invention as a pure means. This is why the x is both an endless task and the ungraspable future that takes place as justice; because it cannot enter into relation with law, it becomes, in turn, law-annihilating for those whom it frees and actualizes.[2]

This situation is linked, without doubt, to the great X'ian project, which confronts us with the question of what is essential for a *real* black revolution to take place, and what constitutes it: a dream of a dream, constituted by morality and tolerance, or its derisive refusal, driven by violence and madness? If the former resorts to mediation by law, the latter brings us face-to-face with a ferocious incertitude, and precisely by renouncing blackness as image and identification. Last but not least, what is essential is first, not knowledge or science, but nothing other than their *absence*; doubtless, it is here where the experience of reading Malcolm X causes more than a little disquiet, for it is here, out of this absence that his most decisive words are woven, and where the undecipherable, or untranslatable nature of an x is first written down as the sign of a becoming that is less than history or meaning, but more than identity or politics. All of which is to say, the very discrepancy between a non-violent, *Negro* revolution and a black, violently real revolution alerts the reader to a diremption that is both obscure and telling—indeed, a great deal of effort will be needed before it will be possible to ascertain precisely what Malcolm X means by the real *of* revolution. Those that are suggested in what follows constitute a provisional profile whose merit remains almost exclusively didactic; they enable us to locate and group together the different problems—political, theological, historical—by which the formulation of this real makes its appearance, and this without, I think, being at variance with the conventional readings of Malcolm X's thought in political theory. It is this formulation that must be interrogated, first of all by freeing it from every empirical connotation; second, by grasping what may be apprehended by its rhetoric, and third by discerning in its incommensurability its proper vocation and truth. It is proposed to distinguish three levels of discourse in the theoretical-political speeches: the level of law (in the sense of justice and power); the level of violence (in the sense of tactics, but also of ontology); and the level of ahumanity (which is roughly where racist myth and sovereignty converge). These three levels are to be conceived as toric relations.

These three levels are bound together according to a mode of interrogation, at once dialectical and figurative, of anti-blackness as a crisis that renews itself in black thought, and the demand—both ontological and theological—that blacks unmaster themselves by learning to speak differently, a speech that cannot attain any formulation until it breaks with the enemy that plagues it, the history of a predation that is with us still. The black bourgeoisie cannot see this because they have yet to undergo the caesura that refusal makes possible, and that severs the charred roots of history, work, and sense. If anti-blackness is the enemy, the black bourgeoisie must also be denounced for not being able to formulate this enmity at the level of praxis or will; for they have not yet grasped the fact that anti-blackness is not merely a pathological accident but is the very structure, the figure, by which being, power, and identity is indelibly linked. The *law of anti-blackness* all throughout America's history is what has proved to be the most decisive gesture; in short, it continues to define all possibility. It cannot be escaped, but nor cannot it be tarried with; for in its resistance may be glimpsed the most dazzling decision, for to be both black *and* resistant is find oneself, literally, heterogeneous to the racist state. This is why Malcolm X, alongside Martin Luther King Jr. (albeit differently), will come to define blackness as what dwells on the border of law (but not as a fugitivity defined by pathology or escape, but more as a refusal that can never be foresworn, and whose heterogeneity can never become a property of knowledge or exchange). Indeed, although the set may change, the finite limits linking each point to the frame do not, and (by the same proposition) must be comprehended anew in their topological function.

This being-otherwise only has meaning insofar as it occupies a place in the transcendent, and this transcendence in turn receives its final meaning from the fact that it is violently excluded from the (racial) secularization of power, and the phantasms that constitute it. This is without a doubt why blackness is likened to an *ahumanity*—that is to say, a separation that can never quite be captured as separation but can only be performed as a kind of nonsense, glossolalia, or poetry—for it is racist reason that possesses blackness as subject and holds it prisoner. Accordingly, to free blackness one must not subject it to a new form of mastery, seizing on black beauty or power as a new prosecutor or judge of feeling; nor must one possess it as a humanism, or right. To produce a real revolution in blackness will therefore mean: neither a negation nor an affirmation—that is, juridical or scientific concepts of repression or liberation, notions that continue to hold blackness captive and so lose it as such; but in the absence of such slavish concepts, a real revolution must go back to the *antagonism* that, at the same time, links being and enmity; it must attend to the forceful sundering of the real and the apparent that gives meaning and sense to what I am here calling the logical and politico-theological diremption that is the experience of blackness.

In the history of blackness as a concept, two figures indicate this necessity with a particular clarity: in the final speeches of Martin Luther King Jr. and Malcolm X, for example, something happens that has left most political theorists at a loss: a notion of a nonviolence that is absolutely violent; and a notion of violence that reverses the meaning of political violence as historically understood. In fact, beneath these reversible oppositions, a catachresis is forming that will not resolve the diremptions that determine it, and that will test the experience and thought of both men by confronting them with the most difficult obscurity. It is this shared fascination—with an x that is itself without tenor or analogy—that underpins the explicit rhetorical rivalries between violence and nonviolence, say, or the ballot and the bullet. My purpose here will not be to pose the one against the other, but to show how the meaning of various words, concepts, tropes reveal what is hidden in the language of the other. What is at stake here is how to make legible this opacity when all the while knowing that such translation is impossible. Why? Because the point of their rhetorical rivalry is not an escape from mythic bondage into a life that is merely natural, but the wish to make blackness the point where a revealed, illuminated truth is the aspect of a black transcendent freedom.

However, if transcendence is the mark of this exchange between King and Malcolm X, what interests me is their preoccupation with an x that cannot be figured by allegory or analogy. Let us simply say that the x appears in both thinkers, not when it is oriented toward violently posited means-ends, at the level of politics, but when it opens black transcendence to the world, the transcendence that shows how every racialized object, or being, is *not* (n'est pas): neither simulacra nor actuality, neither justice nor charity, which is to say, once again, an x beyond the categories and divisions of politics. In what follows our main task will be to show how this n'est pas involves more than a relationship to transcendence or alterity, and precisely because it is not already a means veiled by the mediacy of power. To see what this involves, I will limit myself here to the three levels of discourse already mentioned in my introductory remarks.

1. Law

For Malcolm X any system of law founded on race constitutes a *crime* (his word) against justice, with the juridical system itself limited to being in the service of a racial state system. More fundamentally, law becomes aporetic when it makes race hierarchy into a quasi-juridical practice.

Given that this did—and does—take place in the nation-state, the answer is not a better legal logic of representation, but from the start, the meaning of law must have other criteria applied to it; hence the use of the word "violence" as a caesura between the promise of law and the reality and signs of its practices. Here, I do believe that Malcolm X—as can be seen in his *Autobiography*—uses the figure of a tabula rasa to imagine a new figure and correlation of law to that of justice, as can be seen in his theory of language—as a transcendence writing itself into being, but always as a citation—a way of being, a habitus, or violent inscription, and not simply as an original purity of language. The essence of law is, then, the seeds it sows in the form of inscriptions, whose revelation can only be exposed later—either at the level of the word or as a judging word of the all but coming.[3] The all-but coming is the promise of a world in which blackness retrieves its positive character; this promise is not teleological, nor is it post-race, rather it is the point where blackness is no longer immobilized by its history. We must work these fields if only for the sake a new clarity of expression, a new parable of the real. This can be seen in Malcolm X's comments on language. If, in the *Autobiography*, Malcolm X tells us the fine point that words *are* freedom because they are not handed down by a judge, and seemingly fall without hierarchy or prejudice, then it would be a mistake to confuse this fall with contract or reason; words liberate us (whatever their linguistic form or origin) because they are beyond unanimity or final clarity and thus constitute a violent inversion of the ways in which myths, narratives, imprison and/or captivate us.

From the outset, the real furnishes Malcolm X's analysis of racial terror with a concept that is decisive in that, making explicit immediately what is essential in his theological conception of law (a higher juridical-ethical law), it allows him to show how whiteness is not simply the enemy, but how it is without law, hence the need to classify the acts of racial terror that go to make up its lawlessness. The biblical folk wisdom of an eye for an eye, for example, implies that law and violence are intertwined, where anti-black violence itself has literally become the ground and figure of law at once. The concept of whiteness that emerges is no longer absolutely other (as it was in his early work; that is, whiteness is no longer for him the absolute enemy), but whiteness is what allows racism to emerge as *the* form of state praxis and law.

A shift can be discerned, rhetorically, on several levels (from theology to state theory, rhetoric to truth), so that a theological concept of race is changed from being the hierarchical apex, to being a rhetorical analogue or metaphor to how white supremacy reproduces itself as a praxis. (Moreover, the real object of antagonism is no longer ontology, or contrariety: it is what permits race to be constantly defined as the formal unity of being.) But what if the meaning of white supremacy is entirely integrated into the law of the state at all levels, and in a way which makes theology inconsequential or complicit: the black subject can only be integrated in that meaning by being the excluded *part* (an internal exclusion structured by antagonism as Afro-pessimism teaches us) and all integrationism (from one level to the next) is thus shut out as a possibility (even the politics of consensus is not sufficient—the belief in a shared cause—to account for this exclusion). Because the law of segregation embodies the rhetoric of race war it stands in tension with this new emphasis on violence being only one response among others to white supremacy. In order to conduct a more dialectical structural analysis (and so go beyond the oppositional analogies of most readers of Malcolm X's political theory), we may therefore need to go back to the politico-theological concept of blackness operating in Malcolm X's work.

The question remains whether King's adherence to Christian concepts of promise and redemption offers a more or less different theological reading of these oppositions.[4] The levels of opposition are as follows.

Malcolm X regarded the American state as criminal (there is no separation between law, enmity, and criminality); statism was never anything more than criminality from the point of view of the formerly enslaved. It is therefore not surprising that, as his thought progresses, the mythic nature of race should tend to be law preserving but in ways that only multiplies statist violence (and in ways not theorized by King, nor indeed by Benjamin or Schmidt). Mythical racial violence, however, continues to inform the rhetorical violence of the Nation of Islam. In its own way, the anti-white rhetoric assigned by Elijah Muhammad contained at least two further problems regarding a revolutionary black discourse: race remains the ground and figure of black power, as such blackness is essentially made subordinate to the whiteness of its concept, or what begins and ends as a theological-political parable. In his early speeches, in his analysis of myth and religion, Malcolm X had already indicated that the constituent unit of racist myth acquires meaning as fate because the myth can only foresee the end of structures of antagonism in that of a *race war*. As too, other race war theorists both then and now, reviving the theological notion of a just war to propose two major outcomes, themselves subdivided: that of history, comprising an immanent logic of antagonism, and a hierarchical Darwinian struggle over racial privilege and scarcity; and a teleology, comprising the use, means, and ends of a narrative of genocide (and so extinction). But, however many levels are proposed and whatever the definitions given, there can be no doubt that Malcolm X invested in the rhetoric of such narratives even though theoretically he sought to go beyond them. To understand race war as an inevitability is not the same thing as understanding it as a consequence. To recognize its historical-theological instance as myth, or as working out an explicitly mythic syntax; to commit to it (to want it to occur) is not merely to want myth to be law-preserving; it is also to move race war into a divine myth of origin. Perhaps we could say that Malcolm X became both a kind of apologue in this connection, but also a witness—a messenger—to its limits.

What matters here in this notion of race war is not merely divine violence, but blackness as a mode of being that consists as a kind of suicidal indetermination of means-ends. The cataclysm is an event different from that of transcendence or of redemption. It is an event before law or politics. Race is the means through which being becomes discernable to itself, and this fact of unveiling is precisely the only way of saving—despite everything—blackness as the reconciling figure of history with final ends. Black messanism, Malcolm X suggests, can only evoke race as an imperative law of finality. So it can only lay hold of itself as the form of the imperative itself. Without this demand—that race is the only just means and end—blackness remains a law that subjects the multiple to what it deems to be the sole, truly essential law: that race is a first principle that is unconditional and independent from all contingency. Enmity makes for all its power. Or enmity, in its finality, is what allows it to determine the destiny of everything, instead of being the categorial work of politics. Whiteness constitutes its politics. Hence the fundamental irony: the desire to posit blackness as a universal law of rule or spirit exposes the unposited mediacy of a whiteness in which the language of this law is inscribed in advance. For whatever manifests submission or enslavement cannot be converted into the transcendental language of blackness. In both cases, conversion is annihilated as politics. For the n'est pas cannot be instrumentalized as an essence; nor can it be legislated as a dialectical movement "in" consciousness. The n'est pas is not on the same level as categorial law. The movement here is inverse. Going back to Malcolm X's reflections on the word "aardvark": we can say that the n'est pas destroys the world of the symbol. One must recognize here not a power of communication, but an expressionless relationship to what is never there, with what cannot *be* there; but not with the being that is not there, but with the sublime violence of what is not.[5] There where the "is not" is actual *and* impossible, where one can no longer represent it or posit it, and where the subject is shattered into a world of multiplicities. The n'est pas is not a possibility, is not due to an actual multiplicity, is not reason; it shatters and fragments us, and nevertheless the *I* endures it without the delusion of reconciliation.

2. Violence

As we know, Malcolm X makes a distinction between violent and nonviolent revolution—only the former is considered to be actually revolutionary in its scope. If the American state, being an anti-black order and not just a series of racist acts, cannot be fought other than through the violence that composes it and constitutes thereby the real meaning of what it means to be an American, to be sincerely (an important word) black in one's Americanness is no more than to experience the successive violences composing it. From the point of view of politics (and the nation is the form of spiritual-ethical life for both integrationists and separatists), there is nothing in black nationalism that is not to be found in the sentence: "The only kind of revolution that is nonviolent is the Negro [as opposed to the Black] revolution." And: "Revolution is based on land. Land is the basis of all independence."[6] Hence there can be no question of a black revolution that is not grounded in a violent dispute over land, since a revolution that does not include land is not really a revolution—having described the latter as negro politics, only black nationalism grasps what it means for blackness to become revolutionary.

And yet it is evident that revolution itself (as a set of practices) is organized and that, through this organization, what Malcolm X sees as the need for the house and field negroes to come together, is linked to the counterclaim that such a need can itself be seen as the ground of another kind of revolution, one speaking at another level than that of a racist state. Violence has its uses, its rules, its grammar, that not only expose the true boundaries of freedom and liberation; violence also allows the black subject to go beyond both the restraint and fear ("of fighting back"), and though consisting solely of (black) self-defense ("whenever and wherever [the American negro] is being unjustly and unlawfully attacked"), it naturally forms an object of a liberated will.[7] As such, it strikes me as paradoxical that the decidedly complex and difficult question of whether revolution is naturally violent or merely the figure of a violent nature should be constantly invoked as a biographical, rather than a political-theological question, in readings of Malcolm X. For a long time indeed, such a rhetoric of violence had become synonymous with Malcolm X's name, and consequently black nationalist rhetoric was often reduced to a rhetorical violence that made readers nervous (if not bewildered). As a result of a complex historical movement toward the end of his life, however, in which "by whatever means necessary" is taken up as a problem (rather than a solution), a more complex picture emerges.[8] The new vision of blackness has still to be developed, but at least it is being postulated, and by Malcolm X himself. The Negro, he writes, has to see "the real game that he's in, then the Negro's going to develop a new tactic."[9] This new awareness is not without significance, for, although the game is a *con*, its rules must still be studied if one wants to be liberated from it. And if a new tactic is still needed for an analysis whose task is immense and whose burden is infinite, then the most radical thing is to posit a refusal to play the game insofar as it is likely the odds are always already stacked, whatever the nonviolent hopes and aspirations of a black polity. A black neoliberal or bourgeois discourse is only black, in brief, if it is no longer recognizable as a politics. This accords well with a number of propositions put forward in a number of speeches. Here are a few examples:

"We have to see each other with new eyes." ("The Ballot or the Bullet")[10]

"The so-called revolt will become a real black revolution. . . . When I say black, I mean non-white—black, brown, red or yellow." ("The Black Revolution")[11]

"You cannot have capitalism without racism." ("The Harlem 'Hate-Gang' Scare")[12]

Many scholars have pointed out that Malcolm X's trip to Africa and the Middle East could be defined as a turning point—a transformation—in his understanding of religion, the nation-state, race relations, et cetera: what is important to grasp is how these various speeches appear to use several systems of meaning to elaborate a new understanding of blackness. It is therefore legitimate to ask what this new meaning denotes regarding the relation between race and religion—a relation that will be referred as distinguishing the real and the apparent, as against a purely formal grasp of race inequality.

The belief that "truth is on the side of the oppressed today" is one (and clearly only one) of the idiomatic phrasings apt for consideration by the rhetoric of this new discourse of blackness and accordingly it comes under the "real" hypothesis.[13] Malcolm X's discussion of truth in the polity shares a number of characteristics with the early work without being reducible to it: for example, political virtues and passions are invariably explained using animal parables and analogies: wolves, dogs, unsurprisingly, but also foxes, mules, sheep, ducks, chickens, and so on all make an appearance. Just as a chicken cannot produce a duck egg (because, *systemically*, it can only produce what it is "constructed" to produce), so "the system in this country cannot produce freedom for an Afro-American."[14] But, he adds (in a way that makes the idea of system extremely complex), "if ever a chicken did produce a duck egg, I am quite sure you used to say that it was certainly a revolutionary chicken!" It should come as no surprise that the egg, as both tenor and vehicle, is the form of a speculative or, as it were, revolutionary symbol of a new kind of becoming.[15] Moreover, this new kind of subject, as opposed to its systemic construction, readily has to yield to a non-systemic creation; it has to go beyond its construal by any system, and it has to do so absolutely, at the level of being and of truth. (In this way, what is at stake in the symbolism of the duck egg is the loss—and the transformation—of what passes for desire and truth, but also what passes for their interpretive content, for it is no longer possible to be sure what the rhetorical status of such an image of freedom—that of a chicken producing a duck egg—is.) Malcolm X is thus describing a category of truth that falls neither into the essence-appearance opposition, nor into the opposition of real-simulacrum. It is an event different from the various hypostases by which racial existence arises.

The chicken-duck egg accomplishes a point of transcendence that contravenes univocity and system; its alterity cannot be subsumed under existent categories. This egg is on the same level as, but in meaning is opposed to, the n'est pas. The n'est pas is not accomplished as a *production* that sets into motion a new intuition, because it interrupts both form and production.

This is what the revolutionary interpretation of blackness is all about—about an enigmatic invention that no longer fits into any figurative container or system, and there is something inadequate as to what exactly it is. (And Malcolm X is saying this after his return from Mecca and his supposed turn to a post-racial interpretation of inequality and solidarity in the US!) A literal reading may assume that this is because the classical certainties of race are suddenly no longer readable, but perhaps the ground has shifted because we can never be absolutely sure when reality itself is uncertain, both construct and system at once, and where, he tells us, what is truly revolutionary is what remains obscure to any system. For its only legacy is chaos.

Nor should these symbols or analogies be taken as having merely allegorical value: the purpose of these idioms is not only folk wisdom, for they imply an identity between politics and nature in a way that shows blackness is a category that does not fit into either. We should be sensitive to the nuances of these animal fables. Indeed, they employ metaphors to subvert how race is used metaphysically to naturalize (white) politics *as* nature (inasmuch as the latter is invariably seen as a sort of privileged origin of the former, with politics read as the true telos of nature, with the political then made, ironically, the origin of the nature of nature, and nature the privileged vehicle of its narrative racial truth—a metaphysical move that unites Hobbes, Aristotle, Rousseau, and Bodin, to name only them). It is only by showing in what way blackness differs from nature and power that we can see how it interrupts the politics of politics. It is neither essence, nor reason, nor knowledge. And yet it is always seen as the violent exception *to* the narration of these relationships. It is hardly possible any longer to conceive of politics as an art that abandons the violence of nature given the ways in which race is used—and race is a concept that is both the border between politics and nature and what inevitably borders on the limits of either—and given the ways in which race is often used to express (violently, always violently) the idea that blackness is the outside of both politics and nature, the point where the nonsovereign becomes animal, or the animal becomes politically meaningful as a *res fungibiles*—all of this is at stake in the analogy of a chicken producing a duck egg, or that of wolves in the guise of sheep, and in which it is impossible not to see how the language of natural violence never ceases to accompany the discourse of anti-blackness, holding up to it the mirror of its own ontological violence. And does not politics, particularly today, make race into the border that is the very condition of where politics ends and lawless nature begins?

3. Ahumanity

These phrases—of law, of violence—which mean something different from rules or prescriptions, I argue also entail different theories of language. "We shall overcome," "by whatever means necessary" both entail inditements, but approach the threshold between discipline and punishment differently; both entail accusations, but what they accuse is markedly different, and so accordingly represent different figures of redemption. At the center of these attempts to let blackness stand, in its rights and in its becomings, as a new kind of symbolism, one therefore finds a resistance without teleology, and a knowledge without system. However, in these phrases there is also the presence of something else, which is . . . ? Well, I only have one word and that is *justice*, but I think that they are using this word to designate the meanings of a divine justice that is also, so to speak, an experience of madness. Divine justice cannot be converted into being without violence, but nor can it reconcile desire with the temporal forms of what is. To say that justice is incommensurable to the world is to say two things; on the one hand, the messianic judgement of the world as, namely, irreparably unjust, remains essentially other to the world. In other words, both accuse America—in its claim, origin, and promise—of being irreparably unjust. On the other hand, both entail a judgement that divine justice can only be just if it is beyond law, and so both announce a hitherto unknown truth, a truth that is also beyond the very dialectic of sovereign and bloodless violence. The consequences of this on the level of the political-theological are based on the illusion that the world as is *is* just, but both also entail a theory of language as a game, a con that, ceaselessly changing, can never be absolutely understood. (I'm referring here to Malcolm X's account of language as an enterprise of both translation and expression, with the dictionary itself no guarantee against madness, delusion, or pathos.) Here, in this simple analogy, language constitutes law, in which we can read the most urgent and concise definition of a sovereign decision, but this is a law that is not yet sovereign, or a law that is not yet law, and precisely because it cannot be produced without the experience of illusion. (Think back to the example of a chicken that gives birth to duck eggs: hence my wish to emphasize here Malcolm X's recourse to figures of the animal and the criminal as liminal points that cannot be easily translated into the prevailing languages of the political, or of truth. Truth can only be formulated when it is no longer a degraded racial model [or copy] of the divine. Profanation is not a negation of the absolute, but of one's racialized relationship to it.)

Since it evidently cannot be emphasized often enough that Malcolm X and King are, as many argue, symbols standing for two rhetorical modes of refusal and acceptance, I would argue that these symbols only have value because both remain incommensurable to us, impossible to translate, but also because they make the case for a different practice of making blackness readable as something which cannot be symbolized, an obscurity that includes a manifold of overcomings and violences, and one wherein we encounter the limits of myth, of writing and thinking politically about blackness, but beyond the conceptual frames of politics, theology, and law. Many readings and interpretations of their work tend to homogenize their differences as simple binaries, either in concepts or metaphysics, but not as interlinked phrasings of an all-but that remains incommensurable to what is (and therefore as something ultimately unreadable—that is to say, an x that is n'est pas). If Malcolm X and King are symbols, in brief, they clearly do not symbolize anything but their own essential obscurity. As such, we should not reduce this obscurity too easily to a secular concept of the political in relation to that of the state, nor to a salvific redemptive narrative of the political. It is too easy to read these relations as diremptions, rather than an attempt to name the prohibited, the forbidden—that is to say, the black overcoming, or caesura, for which no figure exists, and in which neither law nor power can be figuratively grounded; that is to say, an x that is neither fugitive, nor para-ontological, but a catachrestic alterity that denotes a new attitude to both knowledge and possibility. Nevertheless, it is through symbolism that both make us see how blackness is, in a sense, a catachresis, an all-but that is neither an ought nor a shall, neither a promise nor an end, but something that entails a decidedly singular, incommensurable overcoming.

It could be said that blackness is for both King and Malcolm X nothing more than the enchainment that allows us to draw the difference between an imaginary natural freedom and the human predicament of its enslavement. In order to analyze this obscurity, let us return, in conclusion, to Malcolm X's explicit analogy between racist myth and animal symbolism. This creaturely symbolism, let us recall, often accompanies his denunciations of state terror and white supremacy. At first sight, these metaphors may appear to be typical uses of a biblical tropology of predation (with whites [and bourgeois black leaders] appearing as wolves, lions, foxes, etc.); what defines them is not their allegorical character (as references to rapine, lust, greed, predation, etc.), but, so to speak, the conceptual risk that they entail. If white supremacy is natural, then black power is contra-nature, or it can only be determined by what nature is *not*: a kind of power that is, however, neither natural nor creaturely, and nor does it belong to the strong or to the weak, for it is testimony to a kind of natural supernaturalism; one that is beyond any discourse of nature (and therefore of sovereignty) since it has no meaning—allegorical or otherwise—that is, in the final analysis, based on an appeal to nature, be it that of law, freedom, or humanity. Thus, in the final analysis, black power is not, to use Malcolm X's rhetoric, an appeal to a natural economy of means, or ends, for it cannot count on (or be accounted for) by such allegories of meaning. A power that is black cannot be natural without altering the historical story that blackens it, but neither can its history be understood without altering the political discourse of race as a natural end. Such power cannot be integrated into nature but neither is it separable from it; let us say that it is a non-ontological relation whose written mode—implicit—goes beyond nature both as metaphor and concept, and whose thought-form is no longer thinkable as an authentic and/or inauthentic designation of the political. And precisely because here the catalyst is not race, nor simply freedom, but an exclusion that cannot be rendered as authentic or actual, nor de facto or de jure as human.

This is the intuition of black power as such—what I call its "ahumanity"—of a power that cannot be posited, produced, or above all presented as a *generic* form, in the sense that it is no longer dominated by the forms of whiteness. The ahuman must be appreciated as an x that *must* take place, but that can never take place (for the x to take place as such would be to neutralize its significance as impossibility).

A distinction has to be made, however, between black power as a discourse, referring to something definable as aim or objective, social movement, or ideology, and black power as a power beyond being, serving to identify something that cannot yet be grasped as being, and so cannot be grasped by metaphor or by concept. To say that black power can only be seen half-hidden by the political theology of Malcolm X or King, is to index their differing responses to the non-ontological difference of blackness itself, its anguish-laden existence as the unknown, the indeterminate, or the unenacted incommensuration that is always partly concealed by the racist concept of being as such. For the reader who is black, however, the phrase "black power" does not involve an activity of deciphering, for to grasp it the reader must learn the character of what King refers to as its overcoming; or what Fanon, in another context, calls the transvaluation of the myths and languages of the impure, the inauthentic, and the always belated. Whatever its travails or disavowals in relation to racial discourse (for example, the desire to see blackness as law, as case), any attempt to see in blackness the reality of its referent is to embed it in the mythical, fictional reality of the anti-black world. As King and Malcolm X so often remind us, to write allegorically black is not the same thing as calling a spade by its name, for that name is by definition untranslatable.

The political image of black life, as we analyzed it in Part 2, might seem unduly pessimistic, but no one can deny the history that disfigures it, and what would it mean to try and read that history optimistically? For if anyone wished to read the concluding lines of *Revolutionary Suicide* with a view to seeing in the abyssal itself a symbol of black life, they would have to acknowledge that *le grand trou noir* presents no easy image of redemption, just as it offers no consolation, and that it requires the destruction of any reading of blackness as fetish or symbol.

In this orphic descent, there is no resurrection to be retrieved from the work of art or the dialectical certainty of its concept. A leap into this abyss would require not only the will to go into a place where all identity is lost, but also to descend to a place where, however far the descent, one risks being forever entombed alive in one's own death, which is where black livable life begins. Far from being an irretrievable fall, or a submission to absolute destruction, by abandoning itself to the depths, black art beholds and finds itself, and becomes equal to the abyss, for it reveals it for what it is, and so demonstrates the exact relationship between form and negation, since this infinite abyss can be conceived only as an infinite parabasis. Here, each step leads ever downwards, but it is impossible to follow on without irony, rather than justice or faith. Indeed, the black work of art reveals every step to be pointless, uncertain, and arduous. This is why those who descend into the dark must be able tell apart what deceives us from the pretense of understanding everything. For he who enjoys fugitivity knows nothing of the imagination. Or they enjoy nothing but the imagination. But the abyss is the effect of power, not of imitation, and those capable of an "authentic upheaval" are rare.[1]

Moreover, the will to such revelation provides no guarantee of advantageous gain, for here art offers no sublimity of redemption and no recognition of the exclusion that forever separates blackness from the world as is. Indeed, what art manifests reveals only the blindest forms of desire, and what it discloses are those who blindly desire only to see the truth of their misrecognition. Which is why it makes no sense to consider black art from the perspective of knowledge or prosopopoeia, because it is incapable of making appear what should be so hidden. There are very few who would find in such misrecognition a symbolism advantageous to them, for it has no other content than the incomprehensibility that informs its endless descent into the darkness that surrounds it. Yet, though it cannot be substituted for the fetishism of its concept, this abyss nevertheless has produced an art (see chapter 9), whose desacralization of the image is well worth noticing, and which it would be fair to say still forms the historical question of black art, and what suffices to hold it together as a presentation cast into the depths.

Since, as I just said, the abyssal has nothing underlying it, in this final part, my task is not to read that nothing symbolically, but rather to present it in such a way for which Fanon's work remains a model. Indeed, this entire third part is no more than fragments derived from Fanon's own fragmentary writings on image, *eidos*, and representation scattered throughout his works. These marginalia on how the visual culture of racial-capitalist ideology is tyrannically centered on the *nègre*, his person, his language, his passion, his body, while trying for the most part to judge, punish, and govern blackness as image, returns us to the question of the previous chapters: Is it possible to have a poetics that allows us to see the Fanonian analyses of invention without blurring it with the ur-doxa of antiblackness? Although there are several documentary films about Fanon, for example, for us there is not enough contestation of representation in these films, and the one visual place where blackness is focused—on the *prosopon* as caricature or persona—is the place where the camera, more often than not, does the least work, relying mostly on the visual languages of biography, or documentary cliché.[2] Consequently, in this concluding part, we will be discussing an artist who has paid the most Fanonian kind of attention to the abyssal nature of black art. How does the image of blackness differ from its form? How does blackness engender its image as sign or symbol without disclosing itself? How do we understand the black art that plunges us into absolute darkness but is always *beyond* its black conception? Our aim here is not to present a detailed study of the artist's work assembled, but to ask what would the black image look like, guided by the intuition that it is always to some extent a caricature (of gesture, body, gaze), if it were to reveal itself in its black truth, and, at the same time, that that revealed truth was based on a relationship to the n'est pas—that is, to what is not *there*, and therefore the phantom visibility of the *invisable*.[3] And what would it mean to insist on a resemblance to that which escapes object, form, being; inasmuch as black art reveals the very obscurity of the real? To say that black art *qua* image is based on the very absence of blackness-as-image would in turn be only to realize the paradox: that *every black image is a caricature of the blackness of its concept.*

Nine

Corpus Exanime

How can you evoke pain within an image . . . I'm trying to portray
physical pain; the kind of pain that I have experienced.

Donald Rodney[1]

A four-year-old boy, who was unable to call for help or feed himself,
starved to death two weeks after his mother collapsed and died suddenly
in the flat they shared, a coroner has said. Chadrack Mulo was found
clinging to his mother's body about two days after his own death.

Guardian, June 8, 2017[2]

Pain tears [reißt]. It is the tear [Riß]. Only, it does not tear away into
disparate shreds. To be sure, pain does tear apart, it cuts [schneidet],
albeit in such a way that at the same time it pulls everything to itself,
gathers it in itself. As a cutting that gathers, its tearing is at the same time
that pulling, which, like a draft and plan [Vorriß und Aufriß], sketches and
joins what is held apart in the cut. Pain is the jointure within a cutting-
gathering tearing. Pain is the jointure of the tear. It is the threshold.
It carries out the between, the middle of the two separated within
it [in sie Geschiedenen]. Pain joins the tear of differentiation [Unter-
Schiedes]. Pain is differentiation itself [der Unter-Schied selber].

Martin Heidegger, Unterwegs zur Sprache[3]

The artist speaks in voice over; facing us, he is seated in a wheelchair. The
image over which he speaks is green-saturated—with green being the metaphor here of both incision, of being cut open, and what cises the whole field
of representation.[4] To be sure, the pain that presides over the very existence
of the image is also what rends picturing in general. The artist describes a

work that was never begun, never made.[5] The work is comprised of wheel-chairs placed in a maze and that are fitted with sensors. The artist refers to the machines as "wanting to get out but never quite managing it." In short, they are suspended, arrested; and their motion, in turn, cannot yield up an exit. The maze constitutes a subtle system of possibility and constraint. The wheelchairs, on the other hand, seem always to be on the threshold of escape, of emerging from the complex network of uncertainties, blind alleys, and feints into a place where representation is linked to that of concept, form to that of perspective, picture to that of nearness and distance, existence to that of escape. The problem with the maze is not that the machines are not perceptive *enough*—lacking sufficient capacity to solve the puzzle. It is a case, rather, of them of not being able to realize the difference between finding a way out, or trying to correct wrong turns, and knowing how to keep to a course for which there is no general rule.

What we see here is the way in which the sensors are unable to draw a line around the limits of what it means to go outside while also keeping within bounds. The desire to remove oneself, to plot an actual emergence virtually from a vast maze, can never manage to be quite far outside enough to see outside the bounds of one's limits. This leads me to believe that the wheelchairs are bound, not because they are unable to move rightly, or act in defiance of their sensors, but because, at bottom, they have no means to understand why each movement can appear only as off course, as something inappropriate, out of place. In essence, the very desire to free oneself from one's painful and disturbing existence can only confirm the sense of entrapment once more.

Let us say: the maze sketches possibility as a moment of pained impossibility. For how can one escape that which binds you to existence, and henceforth that exposes, in turn, your own incapacity to get out of it, or to flee the pain that grounds and limits experience? One cannot represent a way out from such suffering, even though one can no longer suffer it. And if it is in vain to try to escape pain, by way of images, any attempt to picture pain may well be an infinite, impossible task; in other words, any attempt to render pain visible by way of representation is to find oneself lost in an obscurity that is at once near and limitless, evident and hidden. The artist continues: the work should be quite a "soulful piece in the sense of wanting something you can never really have." This desire to want something else, to see this x not only with different eyes, but from different points of view, is quite different from a desire for refuge or transcendence. It is not only a matter of getting out, but of not being blinded by the need for escape as equaling freedom. If all hope of escape is pious, so is the obligation not to do so. Inversely, in these journeys to nowhere, it is not only desire that prevents the exit from being discovered, but the inability of the machines to refer back to another direction from ones already followed, to visualize those traces that would allow them to observe how, from moment to moment, their motion represents (which is to say, renders accessible) that which is both near and far, or that which resides outside all view, and so reveals what is hidden, inescapable. Such failure also makes visible, in a desultory and concrete way, how crisis cannot easily be borne, in so far as what is sensed, represented, or more simply, what is seen, or encountered, cannot allow the wheelchairs to make their way around what is equally inaccessible (to the space represented) and what is, inversely, and always at the same moment, the representation of inaccessibility.

As soon as the wheelchairs are placed in the maze, in brief, they are forced to enter a picture and a network that imprisons, and is inescapable, because it remains inaccessible and invisible *to* representation. The course mapped out is at the same time a prohibition that the machines confuse with possibilities occupying all the space between. Here every locus is concealed; and every desire to escape, to observe, to apprehend space, form, time, perspective, is impeded, hidden, cleft, concealed, because of the position or the distance of what is sensed from what is shown, apprehended, observed, traced on the surface of the visible. Where then is the way out if there is neither possibility nor limitation? And how can the "I" sense that which exceeds everything that I see in myself, that exceeds all the bounds of *excendence*?[6] Moreover, is this because black being cannot attain being, or, from the machines' point of view, because it cannot be posited? Nothing is harder than the task of trying to see something when there is no fixed point from which to judge it.

But the maze isn't a picture or a canvas. And the wheelchairs are not spectators. Indeed, the spectacle of their entrapment reflects nothing, in fact, but an envisioning of what it means to be imprisoned in an unreal, contracted, imperceptible space wherein, in the first and last instance, one is prevented from thinking about exiting, or being able to see a way out, and there is no solid means of escape, and yet one is forever driven, imperceptibly, by the same lines of perspective that brings one to the same impasse, the same identical space *in perpetua*.

In fact, it is the very discrepancy between visibility and that which renders all views discrepant (which is to say, that which makes all perspectives wretched, erroneous, inaccessible, distorted, senseless), that alerts us to a fissure, a wounding, that cannot be evaded and that cuts through the picture, including that of subject and of world. In what follows, I will be considering why the machinic—as both model and blind point—seems to be of a piece here with the profoundest pain. I will also be asking why the black British artist, Donald Rodney (1961–1998), whose very success in embodying the futility of the *never had*, was forced to use the word *pain*, both indirectly and directly, to represent this failure to make it out of the maze—which must inevitably be understood here as the full extent of his own illness, as a sickle cell sufferer, but also as the indefinable, inescapable miseries of blackness—that is, the experience of being despised, renounced, literally violated; but also rendered invisible, or effaced from, one's own being in pain.

Even if it were possible to differentiate clearly between the machinic (the imperfect relation between sensing and representation) and escape (the starting point, the trace, the exit), between the body and its pain, between art and illness, between function and possibility, between visibility and erasure, there would probably be no need for extensive treatises on how illness narrows one's possibilities and condemns one to a diminished milieu, from which one can no more escape than one can adapt oneself. But there would also, no doubt, be no need for art to reveal itself as a healthy (or sovereign?) capacity that one can make one's own, and that allows one to go to the limit of one's sickness as a concept, value, or form.

Here we can also recognize an ambivalence important to Rodney: those great ambitious thoughts that made his sicknesses seem all the more constraining, until he could suffer them no longer, also fascinated him, and opened up a still more sublime perspective on the maze of his suffering and of his blackness. "How can you evoke pain within an image?" he asks. That is, how does one begin to capture the impossibility of certain movements, to render the painful necroses that could never be rendered visible, to see the traces of immobility that could never be joined to reflection—without also following uncertain corridors, pathways, dead-ends, in which pain is no longer in evidence? How does one picture the void confronting you at the limits of the representable, the void that, washing over you, transports you, imprisons you, as the other side, the reverse side, of being and existence, but also as the other side of its all too visible woven texture, the monstration that enables others to see you as though in a distorting mirror?[7] Perhaps by seeing how blackness is made to appear, and at the same time, disappear; or perhaps by sharpening the perspective by which it is always seen at the edge of the frame, on the periphery, imprisoned by the most illusory, cliché-ridden concepts; or perhaps, by making blackness somehow equivalent to a cleaving inter-scission (*Unter-Schiedes*), a beingness that separates us from the desire to be, at the same time as it gives us insight into another desire, which is more wretched and desultory. Is it paradoxical to say that blackness, for Rodney, teaches us new ways of being affected and of being disabled by our affections? And not only in sickness, but even unto death; that blackness is, in fact, a disabling machine that offers us a different perspective on what it means to be within the frame, and of what it means to be inescapably invisible to it, lost in the abyss of a maze that prevents one from seeing what is inside or out, and that cannot be grasped as either affirmation or delusion. This would be the art, then, of a painful foreshadowing that makes all refusal, and all protest, meaningless.

There can be no limit, or there can be no endpoint, when pain is the place from which the image is being determined, for we cannot see it; or what we do see is merely a machine without the means to will, to be, to go to the limit of what it is, and, just as importantly, that can do no more than endure the spectacle beyond both negation and nihilism.

What do we see, then, when we look for that black inaccessibility in art, in the image, in lines of composition?

———

In the short documentary, *Three Songs on Pain Light and Time* (1995), Rodney amply demonstrates how complex and difficult his lifelong experience of sickle cell anemia has been, as he details his increasing inability to cope with the crippling necrosis of his joints; the recurring operations; as well as his constant effort to subsume it, to make it present, to make his illness fit into a larger artistic-political unity of mobility and immobility; considering it a challenge to figurability, to be anything but an object to be seen. After the film offers us a first glance at such pivotal works as *The House that Jack Built*, or *Flesh of My Flesh* (both of which we will return to), we hear Rodney talk of his astonishment as a child at being excluded from going to church due to his prostheses taking up too much room on the parishioners' bus. Insofar as he is *too* visible (this is a constant theme), what stands out is a figure isolated in his visibility, a figure forced to turn his eyes away from the eyes of others—the feigned sincerities, the excluding pieties, and the usurping piteousness in whose depths he appears precisely because he does not belong to the world picture.

It should come as no surprise that the spectacle he offers is one of being projected and diffracted, reflected and represented as a *corpus exanime*[8]—that is, as a life whose suffering is intimately foreign to it: the question thus asked of this corpus exanime is not what is endurable or not, nor whether it makes representation possible or not, but why pain is the starting (and the end) point of black being as such.

It is difficult to regard Rodney's major works without seeing this corpus exanime. Nevertheless, what comes into play is complex. The works, arranged chronologically, can be seen to constitute, according to the way one looks at them, two different aporias—a violation of profile that is also a profile of violation and a disappearance, with regard to the subject, which does not cease positing itself as a foundation, inasmuch as what cannot be founded is also the perfectly defined point of an "I," a beingness, that can never be seen as a subject; because, as image, blackness exposes a thinking of pain that is completely inaccessible to the way it is pictured. The first aporia would be a kind of self-destructive enunciation: a profile of a body in extremis; where pain is both a *spur* to form and the principle of a primal formlessness (or, more exactly, a violation that cannot emerge as such except in profile; at once what disturbs form and this disturbance itself) both ontically and epistemologically; and a violation that therefore defines experience because it precedes experience. The second aporia would be more that of the corpus exanime, its pain determined as the scission of the ego from itself in the exclusion of blackness from its own being-in-the-world—both these extremities occurring as a rending of experience, a tearing coinciding with black non-being, where the self is known only in its objectifying mortification. Where these two aporias intersect is in the figure of an exceptional singularity (the phantasm of black life as crime, as transgression), that is

also founded on a profiling that excludes blackness from experience, by reducing it to a categorical determination that renders it (in)visible, (in)defin-
able, deprived of all auto-affection in principle. To give just one example: in
the powerful *The House that Jack Built* (1988), Rodney presents a figure in effigy, in profile, who remains paradoxically both visible and undetermined,
framed against the backdrop of a scission, a history of violation; in this *persona ficta*, what is objectified is a beingness—a pseudo-gisant—whose singularity is made visible, definable, by violating profiles and legends that painfully surmount the possibility of a being experienced (fig. 1).

Contrary to Kant's suggestion that pain is the "spur" through which,
above all, "we feel our life"; here black life is seen to be separated forensically
from both life and experience, and its pain is felt by a non-object—the effigy,
the corpus exanime—that, strictly speaking, eludes ego, meaning, and the
very possibility of experience.[9] Moreover, it is the legends superimposed on
black inner being that here prove decisive: what appears externally behind
the effigy, in X-ray images of scissors and bodies, can be read as what cuts being internally from experience (and even more, since they suggest representation is itself an incision, a violation); here what is visibly segregated in effigy (the image as corpse; or as what is put on display in the world picture as
corpsed) also implies that black life is not only the consciousness or symptom of death in life, but that which always "dies" as image; yet not because
we feel the effigy to be lifelike, but because it is the point that makes black
subject, discourse, life, and world definitively uncertain, unknown, petrified,
and lifeless. Hence, its only advent is effacement. The effigy that shows us
quite simply, and in profile, all the violations that are rendered to blackness
as the image of a pseudo-gisant that corpses itself. For it must always already
choose between its violated visibility and the spectacle of an inescapable violation, to be anything but an object given to be seen and one lethally cut
from seeing; a forced choice that constrains it all the more.

Can one describe or even surmount these two aporias? One will not be
able to do so except by going back to the emergence of this beingness in pain,
since it is determined by a cleaving that precedes, violates, and exploits it.

Let us begin by saying that pain is being's rending of itself, where what
rends also gathers being's relation to itself. Accordingly, one cannot present
what is rent apart from itself. But what of this rending that allows Being
to show itself? Heidegger, whose formulation this is, suggests pain not only

Figure 1. Donald Rodney, *The House that Jack Built*. 1987. Mixed media, 183 × 183 cm. The Estate of Donald Rodney.

occupies an unsuspected space insofar as it is neither immanent nor transcendent, but it is the *cising* that *joins*; pain, he says: connects being and world; he also suggests pain *is* being because it is the frailest, the most distant movement by which Being both swathes and cises, but also exceeds all *repraesentare*.[10] Inversely, the indeterminateness of knowing someone else's pain is not the indeterminateness of a concept, or image, and does not refer to subjectivity, ego, or sense. What does pain signify then? Certainly, it concerns an experience of the world and of life before the ego: from the incision that Being opens to the threshold emerges an interlocution where being suffers itself, where it first cuts and rends, and where it is nothing more than pain's performative. Perhaps we could say that, in *scheidet*, what we see in profile, in effigy, is the double relation of pain to the being that it makes manifest; but this is a doubling, an *Unter-Schiedes*, that is, in turn, inseparable from its own inseparability to pain, like a gisant that is the model of the "sovereign" to which it submits as well as being a sovereign symbol of the scission between mortal and infinite life. Being reft from Being: like the repetition of a verb in the accusative noun, this *figura etymologica* designates not the uncertainty sensed over what is enunciated, or what is inner versus what is expressed, but the beingness of pain itself that somehow has no sense or object. This impersonal, senseless, anonymous, yet unendurable bestowal of Being, which agitates in the depths, we shall designate by the term *corpus exanime* inasmuch as it, too, resists all subjective form, experience, and sense.

We have not derived this notion from biography, philosophy, or art—from any artistic object whatsoever. For the corpus exanime excends inwardness as well as exteriority; in its lethal restraint, black being is detained, and constrained, forever the restraint and constraint of the pain it carries, and bears. The anonymous structure of its being invades, submerges every subject, person, or thing. The subject-object polarity by which we approach pain is not the starting point for a meditation that broaches the pathos of black being in general. In what follows, we will treat the corpus exanime as the unfolding of a pain in whose amplitude there is no harbor, and one that anchors itself in the depths of our being like a dead weight cast into the maelstrom. It is not enough to ignore it or to abandon oneself to it. And because the black body cannot be granted absolution or escape from the corpus examine, nothing appears to be moving, and yet everything is rushing on toward its affectivity insofar as it presupposes a fixed point, and one that grows ever darker in the depths.

The notion of what is at stake here eludes both the ontic and ontological meanings of loss, scission, and lack.

In the realm of domination, this corpus exanime is also symbolically prior to that which imposes itself as flesh, since flesh is identified as a loss—culturally, historically—of facticity.[11] We could say that the flesh is the very experience of the corpus exanime, if the term experience were not inapplicable to a situation in which the body is painfully rent apart from itself, in a way that is beyond measure. Why? Because there is no *there is* to be drawn from it; the n'est pas that is intimately foreign to it, cannot be situated as a loss that is then excised, nor can it be displayed via a mark or sign—a grammar or semiosis—that, according to the order of beings, mastery exerts on it.

When the body (*corpus*) is dissolved into flesh (*caro*), the suffering of flesh, which is neither an object nor the quality of an object, suffers from being itself. In the corpus exanime, where we are riven in effigy, we are not dealing with phenomenological experience. For this experience is not one that can be experienced. There is no longer a *body* or *flesh*; there is no feeling of being flooded with *sensations délicieuses*, oblivious to time or thought. But this suffering that in turn suffers itself as a non-presence, is an absolutely unavoidable "*wreckoning*," so to speak. It is not the dialectical counterpart of sensibility, and we do not grasp it as a thought, as a category wrung out of us. The corpus exanime has no transitive verb. Nothing responds to this corpus exanime, but this judgement, *you are less than*; the voice of this judgement is understood and terrorizes because it comes to us from the community but not *as* the community, but from the whiteness of its law; it is the judgement of a gaze whose function fulfills a relation to the world picture: that is, it locates a point always exterior to the picture, but in relation to what is dead to representation, since the confirmation of something less than life makes the life of representation impossible. The corpus exanime, in general—without it mattering what it embodies, without being able to resist those juridical or epistemic profiles that fix it in a violating dye—gives rise to what is not (n'est pas). The corpus exanime is an impersonal form, a scission that suffers, or it is the category of a limitation without limit. And yet, that limit is projected within the world picture as the ideal and real point of the unseen. Its anonymity is inherent, gratuitous, emergent.[12] The mind does not find itself faced with an apprehended exterior or hidden interior. The appearing—if one insists on this term—remains strictly opposed to phenomena. It is no longer lived as a *vecu*, but as a profile—a pseudo-gisant—that is excised and operated upon. It is no longer a world. What we call the corpus exanime is a suffering itself blackened by the incapacious assertion of its suffering; it is invaded, petrified by the gaze; but it can only experience itself as a hemorrhaging that precedes every object-relation, every *moi*, and that follows indifferently from the social death of its finite life. The disappearance of the *moi*/"I" and the *corpus* that can only accede to thought in as much as it disappears, is the sheer fact of a beingness that is pre-transitional; whether one wants to find an object for it or not, it lives without ever having been protected, secured, housed in being or language. How then does one explain this rift, this self-differentiation?[13] Blackness remains a pain of being, like an intermittent cry, or the spectacle of a foot on the neck, head, or back, and what it showcases (*darbieret*) belongs to neither place nor topos, law or concept, but to the body that belongs to nothing but the pain that execrates it, that turns it aside-from-itself, and is mortified in all the instances in which pain may be multiplied beyond the psyche and its pathos.

The kind of pain that I have experienced—is it wrong to call this a pathos, a painful harm that exceeds the form, the comportment, or bearing of affection? To this sense of pathos—the question that is always asked: How do you judge what it really is, if what it is produces an effect that is so like and unlike affection, so that we cannot distinguish the sense of harm from its denial? Rodney's work points to a pathos that is the effect of being acted on, for it is no longer simply a case of being affected or separated from any possibility that gives us access to form or thought, by which we grasp beings in their beingness. Pain fills the drive like a content; it drives it, but pain is also driven by the excess of its own assault, and thus it drives the "I" from a self-affection to an affect that nevertheless precedes it, in whose assault I am (nothing but) the *not* that rends. But the point of calling it a pathos does not refer to lived experience (*Erleben*) or an ontology or representation; there is no perspective from which blackness can be located, it cannot be situated as *Erleben* or *Erfahrung*—it withdraws from the pathos, the metaphysics of either term, as Fanon teaches us.

Before going any further with this analysis, let us consider Rodney's *Flesh of My Flesh* (1996), a work completed eighteen months before his death

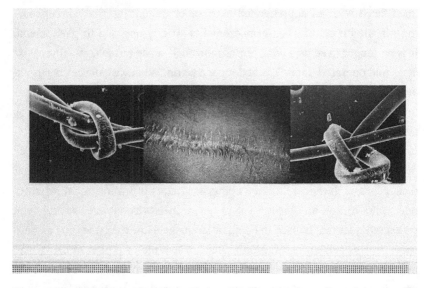

Figure 2. Donald Rodney, *Flesh of My Flesh*. 1996. Photograph on aluminum, 90 × 270 cm. The Estate of Donald Rodney.

(fig. 2). This is a work without *pathos* or *agnorisis*. Yet this analysis does not imply that the work is accordingly to be understood as the absence of pathos. The absence of a perspective from which to make sense of Rodney's pain is not something purely negative. *Flesh of My Flesh* shows us why the language of ontology always fails to name black being, pain, or jouissance. The corpus examine makes ontology insecure. Not because blackness equals precarity. Nor because it eludes sense or thought, and then becomes impossible to name or define. For the insecurity does not come from blackness itself, which the rending of philosophy conceals; it is just due to the fact that no concept approaches it, or goes toward it, without disfiguring, or threatening it; this frenzy, this madness, this violence that constitutes the jouissance of philosophy in its rending, also describes its absolutely indeterminate menace toward blackness. The indeterminateness that constitutes this violence can be seen in the Aristotelian categories of being, the Hegelian *Aufhebung*, and the Heideggerian thought of *Dasein*.

There is no ontology of black pain: it is either reduced to self-deception or dismissed as nonexistent.

The traces of this indifference even presents itself in *Flesh of My Flesh*—in how the wound on the artist's thigh has been harshly, brutally overstitched.[14]

In this jointure, pain is not only in the cleaving (of being from itself) but takes form in the way that black facticity has in-difference incised into it, an incision that rejoins pain to the form of its destining. Before these "white" incisions, it is impossible to take shelter in humanness, to withdraw into one's shell. One is always exposed. Whiteness writes its inter-scission into black beingness, parting it from its totality, its conviction and audacity. Instead of serving as a measure of care, whiteness delivers us over to the permanent rift of being. Pain does not sustain difference, especially when the imperative is to eradicate it as an inessential relation to indifference. Perhaps Heidegger was more right than he knew when he wrote: "Pain is the sign of the appropriative event." But perhaps he was wrong not to suggest that racism is also part of the essencing by which so many who suffer are judged and condemned.[15]

We can see this racialized essencing in the relation of pain to mastery; the always present risk of the hemorrhaging of substance into non-being. The indeterminateness of pain must be mastered by the cogito and by discourse, otherwise one remains precarious, disarticulated; on the contrary, without mastery, the body surrenders to the shame of surrendering. It is as a submission, the submission of mastery, that pain affects us and leaves its indelible impression: an impression that is more irremissible than the *cogitatio*, for it is what surpasses it. Pain must be fettered, constrained; it must be determined, rendered singular, limited. Rodney tells the story of having to wear a large leather constraint plus crutches as a child, and how those "additions" led to him being challenged and barred in his movements; but also how the ego finds itself caught before it even exists, suspended from the outset in effigy; or how pain inscribes itself in dialogical space; how it isolates, literally cuts away (*Abschied*) anonymity from, into, being, and how the ego is born out of this interpellation. With these additions, the body disappears in its appearing; but Rodney says just the opposite: that the body could no longer be disappeared-transformed into indifference, nor politely avoided by the other who assaults and so addresses it. In the *Abschied*, black disability is made one with its determination as a pain-strickened shame. By shame he means not a failure to escape being, or the offence of its nudity, but having to ask pardon for one's visibility and existence, and by nature of the fact that black existence is, at bottom, being's impenitent effigy.

One can also speak here of different forms of constraint that occur in response to black pain. Firstly, it is unvoiced and is not illumined by language.

Figure 3. Donald Rodney, *In The House of My Father.* 1997. Photograph, 123 × 153 cm. The Estate of Donald Rodney.

Like the harrowing case of Chadrack Mulo, it is often easier to speak about this silencing than to think about how these pressures and pains no longer form a world, but an endless darkness even in the middle of the day, forever overlooked in the midst of cities as the least valuable, the most useless, the least necessary to be found, articulated, determined, or noticed. Such also is the case with the fantastic, hallucinatory quality of works such as *The House that Jack Built*, or *In the House of My Father* (1996–7), even when they depict the most familiar objects and most familiar thing as a home, a dwelling, there seems to be no ontological locus for black pain (fig. 3).

In the various works using x-rays, skin, wounds, contusions, and so on, the corpus exanime seems to collapse the *ego sum* into a materiality, and one terrifyingly present in its weight and shape. Certain passages of *Three Songs of Pain Light and Time* do not only give (as is sometimes thought) a representation faithful to or exceeding pain, but penetrate behind the form that pain reveals into that materiality that, far from corresponding to the philosophy of *Dasein*, constitutes the dark impassable ground of black nonexistence. It makes things appear to us as effigies that cannot be given a place in either mirror or symbol, like the monotonous presence of a scar as it falls and yet remains somehow apart from the face, or like a persona eclipsed by the *ficta* that renders because it does not belong to it, but which is nonetheless the enigmatic immediacy of the picture.

Compare *Flesh of My Flesh*, for example, with that of Kader Attia's *Open Your Eyes* (2010; fig. 4). In Attia's image of a French First World War veteran, here juxtaposed alongside an African sculpture, there is horror: the entire magnitude of a pain, a disfigurement, that seems to exceed measure. We have noted elsewhere that it has become almost compulsory to refer to Attia's work as an *archeology*—of wounds, fissures, and scars—and as a *reparation*—of pain, loss, and hurt.[16] In combining the two, Attia does not, strictly

Figure 4. Kader Attia, *Open Your Eyes.* 2010. 2-channel analog slide projection. 180 slides. Courtesy of the Artist and Collection MoMA, Collection Frac Pays de la Loire and Collection Moderna Museet. Photo: Studio OAK.

speaking, reconcile them with each other. Quite the contrary, in fact: what runs throughout the work—and this is my first major hesitation—is that repair cannot be given form without disfigurement, that it coincides with it, and that repair would then be the labor—the concept—by which disfigurement is both produced and made sense of. To simplify matters, let us say, for now, that repair *is* disfigurement, but a disfigurement that, by contrast, has yet to be determined, or whose quality has yet to be torn, lopped-off, or go missing from lived experience. The two stand, then, in a dialectical relation, and Attia resolutely presents this—not as a phenomenologist, or a psychoanalyst, but as an artist, for whom the artwork acts as a kind of orthopedic auxiliary.

What we have here, in fact, are works seized—in both their form and their content—by disfigurement. This disfigurement is not at the level of sign or concept, but opens onto a wholly different mode of thought, that is to say, that moment when human being loses its primordial hold of itself, that is to say, loses its experience of mastery, domination, disposition, and is taken away, or abandons itself, to disfigurement as a kind of infinitesimal rapture, in which being presents itself as the missing, unforeseeable part of what is manufactured, or that offers itself as a spectacle of what is missing. At such moments, being cannot be posited or enjoyed as a durable substance, the object of everyday possession, but is forced to comprehend itself anew as a kind of *naked, precarious witnessing* whose *causa* consists, wholly and entirely, of a beyond: a horizon beyond that of commandment or word, relation or identity. Here sovereignty is what is represented as that which *precedes* rupture. Here repair is not opposed to disfigurement, but encloses it in a commemoration that changes the nature of both.

However, the inclusion of the "African" artwork opens up another space that is not so undetermined but can be precisely read as an opposing gesture—namely, a gesture that seems to equate blackness itself *with* disfigurement, as though blackness were itself something equivalent to an obscene crack that opens up in being. In other words, if there is something dreadful in the face (of disfigurement), a recess that cannot be faced, or a disappearance that is in fact vested in the face as the foundation, it is because of the rift that opens as a kind of tear or rupture in matter, and that shows an irruption that is also immanent to human being, and that is far more dreadful than a wound for it represents the limit to *repraesentare*. This suggests blackness is both at fault and a figuration in fault when confronted with its naked form and body. Therefore, one might say, its repair is irremissible, for it is nothing other than a disfigured relation to presence as such. Let us look further into this dialectic of representing and the sovereign loss that is made visible in the painful disfiguration of what is represented.

In Donald Rodney, who spent his entire life, ever since his childhood, crippled by pain, marked by pain, by the injuries attendant upon being black male and a sickle cell sufferer, to be conscious of one's body is to be torn away from it as an object of experience, as a subject of existence; that is to say, to some extent, to be black is to be mastered by constraint, by a being in permanent psychic pain, for one is exposed, not so much to mutilation, or disfigurement, but to being that can only appear to itself in representation as a death *of* representation, as a pseudo-gisant, all the while knowing that one can never be freed of this anonymous death, that one can never be healed in effigy, and that one's life is merely that which gives access to this mortifying malady. Blackness is not somehow a signifier that can strip one of one's disfigurement. There is no pathway from blackness into the anonymity of existence; no pathway, that is to say, beyond suffering to the labor, the calculation of disfigurement, or what Heidegger calls, in another context, the *gestell*[17] (the reproduction of the world as picture)—this suggests that there is no relief, no thought that could repair, or conquer black separation, no way of binding it by way of form or representation. Here we are far removed from disfigurement, the impersonal vigilance of being-as-manifestation, the lived experience of feeling oneself mastered by, or held in, disfigurement, in the sense that Attia gives to the term.

Indeed, in the scars that remain we see not so much evidence of an aestheticization as the marking, the penetration, of a perpetually invisible wounding.

What is new in the idea of black pain (which Rodney introduces to describe his illness, this sickness born of interpellation) is an experience where terror is the dominant motif, and we see the destruction of categories that had hitherto been used to describe the feelings evoked by embodiment. In the work of Attia, if blackness cannot be a spur to life, or knowledge, that is because it remains an effigy of itself, an object without a subject. A figure that is distant, complete, serene, even in its disfigurement. The identity of each of these terms—art, being, *gestell*—do not seem to be distorted *or* disfigured. In Rodney, by contrast, the sensible qualities of the black body are incommensurable with the emotional power it emits; and with what it makes visible as the very nature of this emotion, for it functions as a bearer of a monstrated inconsistency, which accounts for this disproportion and inadequateness. The situation is quite different from that of reparation or disfigurement. The disappearance from life that defines the corpus exanime is completely different from a scarring participation in being; in it, the identity of the terms is lost (they are lost in their worldliness). They are divested of what constituted their very substantivity. The participation of blackness in being does not consist in reparation; blackness is not the index of an incapacity or capacity, and if it falls into a n'est pas that is because it was always already confined in its confinement to a kind of infinite separation, or absolute incompleteness. The time of life that is n'est pas, cannot be mastered as a property of being, for it loses itself to an ever imperfect imperfectability; like a gisant that lies on a bed surrounded by aspersing images, or like a veil concealing a scission that is its own disappearance, or like a trompe l'oeil that no one has ever noticed, and that returns being to an undifferentiated background. The nonexistence of blackness as corpus exanime submerges it in a body that has become something empty, weightless, categorically ungraspable, and is thus no longer an existence without pain, the pain by which the "I" finds itself alone, lost to itself, cleft, expelled from itself, without voice, word, or epiphany; but nonetheless bound to the purest pain. We recognize here the corpus exanime (the lifeless body rendered in effigy). The impersonality of this *mortis* that, for Saint Augustine, is exterior to the soul, on the contrary describes a body where nothing prepares you for the loss of being, the aphanisis of desire and of thought, insofar as one is unable to escape this waning, or its unfathomably deep nearness that is also impossibly far. Rather than appeal to God, or meaning, the corpus exanime leads to the absence of meaning, the absence of any being; here foundation is marked by the incommensurate, the seldom found, by a pain erased beyond even that of anonymity; invisible, beyond salvation, motherless, and mutely alone. Blackness is the death that goes unnoticed because its worldly poverty, bereft of all possibility and gathering, occurs to those painted in effigy, a rendering whose only seclusion is the farthest reaches of the n'est pas. One no longer needs to be forced into the hold, or be strung up in some fog-laden wood, to be disappeared. For blackness, the light never comes.

————

Wretched man that I am, who shall deliver me from this body of death?
I have not body enough for my body, and I have too much body for my soul.
John Donne, *Fifty Sermons*, 19

This loss is nowise an anxiety about possession and is thereby a story of a loss never had; of being dispossessed in one's dispossession. According to Rodney's *The House that Jack Built*, blackness is an effigy stripped of its subjectivity, and has no power to have an unsurveilled existence. The image, as a meditation on a will to disappear, to disappear as black, is not a depersonalization; terror turns the subjectivity of the *ego sum* into a burned effigy; and its particularity qua effigy is turned inside out (we see not so much a living presence but its X-rayed obliteration displayed for all to see liked a burned outline). It is an illumination that returns in the heart of every negation, as a *mortis*—a maze—from which there is no exit. It is, if we may so, the impossibility of escape, the universality and anonymity of an annihilating *not* that is also the event of the purest pain. The pain of a separation from the logos is what the corpus exanime feels. And in the end, it is not a question of bemoaning or recognizing this fact. I write this without satisfaction or lament. There is no possible return from this waning and its mortification. And especially because to be black is to be unaware of it. Unaware, because one can never be present as an "I" without the *corpus exanime* as a residuum, an illocutionary spectacle?

To mortify oneself (*suicidium*), in a revolutionary or reactionary sense, is to seek to wake up from this unconsciousness, to go where freedom and negation operate. Mortification is the event of being that returns in the heart of this negation, as though it cannot be sublated. Rodney's sickness could not be negated; it was not redeemable. He couldn't sign himself into the world, nor sign himself out of a world in which black being is a crime (*Verbrechen*), and its pain the most just reward. In the nothingness—the nothing of the pain in which he was held—his being was condemned to the point of a suffocation and was unable to draw a more revolutionary consciousness from the corpus exanime's painful retreat. A corpse is not a negation; a scar is not a dialectic of presence and absence, but a trace, an incision, that presages only further suffering, hospitalization, and being prone. Of having experience but always being excluded from the experienceable: this is what it means, as Hegel puts it, to express "absolute disappearance," but as a gisant, a corpse, within the experiencing of it.[18]

My response to this is the agon exposed by Rodney and Mulo. In black disappearance, one disappears in effigy. In the hour of one's disappearance, one remains glued to this effigy, which also bears the mark of an originary mortification. This disturbing effigy cannot be sublated but returns like a specter. Thus, one feels this return not as a negation of presence, on the contrary, this impossibility of escaping from an anonymous and imperfectible existence constitutes the final depths of black tragedy. Lost in the middle of the maze, one knows one is subjectless, objectless, and without witness. Here "salvation" means a being that is *unfound*, not just something hidden or obscure, lost from view, living simply and without fuss, but something positively unsought for and seldom rescued. The lethal fatality of being unfound becomes the fatality of irremissible being. This clinging veneration mortifies qua effigy: there is no Lazarus here to cross the distance between being and nothingness; no Orpheus waiting for the beloved thing to return, returning where the irrevocable could once again appear in language, alive in one's reflection, one's logos, but now profoundly unrecognizable, wracked by the fear and horror of a newly embodied, but empty, evacuated, objectless pain. Some things should remain lost, for to possess them is to know that one is already lost, obliterated.

The thing that lets blackness appear, also pushes it over the edge of appearance, because what it enables cannot be saved as absence or presence. It seems also that because the n'est pas cannot be pictured or imagined, there is no essential difference between its execution and what allows it to be rendered.

Specters, effigies, X-rays are not only signifiers that Rodney uses to capture the effects of pain, or vestiges of the material he composed with; they were chosen because they allowed him to continue working while at the limit between being and nothingness where the corpus exanime inserted itself even in his practice, like an irresolvable constraint to the question of form and composition. Rodney recoiled before the corpus exanime because, in a way, he had the foreboding of an endless inessentiality by which pain came to dominate his being and his consciousness, including time itself. In *Three Songs of Pain, Time and Light*, the motif of time is also a decisive illustration of the "no exit" from a painful existence, its phantom return through the fissures, the incisions, the surgeries, through which the self was driven to affect (and so experience) itself as being. He could not work in the summer, for example, because this tended to be the period when he was most hospitalized. The pain of knowing that one could no longer be able to work in such light, or see what one has cultivated bloom, was also a great pain to him. And again, this is not a negation. The terror of pain does not come from what it endangers. But from the feeling of irretrievability. The fact that any form, concept, ambition, or desire—the highest illocutions that lead to the lowest kinds of inscriptions—can become so easily lost to alterity, illusion, and the world's frightful sublation. It is the sublated form of time's deception: hence the corpus exanime reveals the deception that is time itself; the dying away of being into infinite nothingness.

The horror of pain, as an experience of the corpus exanime, does not then reveal to us the universality, the impossibility of death, nor even a fear of pain. That is what is essential to its analysis: the pure nothingness revealed by anxiety in Heidegger's analysis does not constitute the corpus exanime. There is a horror of being's disappearance as fetish, as delinquency, and not anxiety over nothingness, fear of being and not fear of not being; there is being delinquent to, delivered over to something that is not a something, neither a res, power, or law. When the body is overwhelmed by pain, the horror of not knowing its end is no longer definable. The "something" appears to be "nothing," a corpus exanime that belongs to nothing in its disappearance.

Black suffering carries out the condemnation of a world, and its formulation is that of an aspersion with no exits. This is how Fanon responds to Sartre's infamous essay, "Orphée Noir".[19] For Sartre, blackness cannot discover itself as reflection, possession, or privation. Its pain is not yet in the world, hence its first (and final) truth: it is a being without existence. In the corpus exanime, another argument establishes itself: instead of an "I" marked by the impossibility of its existence, the infinite irresponsibility of its being, in a universe in which existence is bound by an unbreachable commitment to white form and value, can be discerned an existence that is no longer speculative, consistent, or private.

We are opposing, then, the pain-ridden crucible of blackness, the silence and horror of its disappearance, to the philosophical serene nudity of
the *pour soi*, the fear of being to the fear of nothingness. While anxiety,[20] in
Heidegger, brings about "being toward death," grasped and somehow understood, the horror of a painful death with no exits and which has no relief as
world indicates why blackness is an irremissible existence. There is no to-
morrow for the corpus exanime, aside from this interlocution in which it is
forced to live a death in life—this mortified excruxion cannot contain the infinity of today. In short, in the emergence of the corpus exanime, there is the
suffering of a limit that cannot be grasped, a perpetuity of a radical endan-
gering, and the necessity of forever taking on its impossible burden.

When, in the fifth chapter of *Black Skin, White Masks*, Fanon shows that
the ontological concept of blackness is equivalent to the idea of being crossed
out, he seems to catch sight of a situation analogous to that which led to the
notion of the corpus exanime. Blackness is never simply an experience (*Erfahrung*) but the de-perance (*Entfahrung*) of a dissimulation that—worse—
has no certainty of existence, or is n'est pas. According to Fanon, negation
does not have a meaning for the constrained movement of the corpus exanime; for, when applied to the uncertainty of its being, negation no longer makes sense. To deny the absence of being for the black is to plunge him
into a kind of endless night, a zone of non-being (*non-être*), where he would
at least remain as *the non-sense of sense*, as the conscious unconsciousness of
the *non-être* that illuminates it.[21] Absolute negation of this *non-être* is then
impossible, and the concept of its existence is illusory. But Fanon's critique
of black non-being only aims at the necessity of self-consciousness, of a being
that knows who or what he is. Black humanism always approaches Being as
an egoic formulation, as a ruse of self-deception, and, because it cannot represent the being who is not, ends up sealed in non-knowledge. The darkness
into which the corpus exanime plunges, which obscures the profound invis-
ibility of its being, is also understood as a *non-sens*. The fact that it is a *non-
sens* obtained through violation remains the key point—that is, blackness is
the suffering of a violation that founds it, but whose nominative (*non-moi*)
can only think and determine itself obliquely as a corpus exanime. And this
is just what is new in this situation: the corpus exanime cannot be acceded
to, nor can it be resisted, for its foundation—which is also its pain—cannot
be mastered or represented.

Blackness, as the presence of non-being, is not a particularity of presence. There is not a "something" that knows, or that can bear witness to it. There is the atmosphere of an unreality, which can, to be sure, appear later as its structure, but originally blackness is the impersonal, unreal event of a *non-être* and a n'est pas. It is like the density of a void, like a fervor that *burns*, but that cannot be escaped. There is non-being, but there is the n'est pas of the *non* (a disappearance without foundation) *toward* which, *in* which, every structure becomes rotten, infected, worm-eaten (*les racines vermoules de l'édifice*).[22] There is no pathos that is not already infested by this *non-être*— no blackness without pathology. The prognosis? Blackness is the very play of lysis and morbidity that would play itself out even if there were nothing *but* pain, sickness, disability. It forces one to think with fervor, but itself becomes the morbid fixation that prevents thought, which refuses to be an object of thought, thus it forces thinking to present itself as an object for itself, or to concentrate itself in a *cry*, a n'est pas that is the terrible object of a fervent morbidity—a fervor that can only be stilled by a complete lysis. It is to express just this paradoxical existence that we have introduced the term corpus exanime—we want to call attention to this extreme pain, its morbid (and yet unreal) universality as a force, a concept, a species-being, which is not to be identified with the Sartrean *en soi*, or the Hegelian *für sicht*, that could be taken up as an alienated example of *ressentiment*.

We want to call attention to the existential terror of the corpus exanime as the void itself, devoid of all being, empty even of void, whatever be the power of negation applied to itself. Negation does not end up with a black being as a structure (*l'édifice*) and organization of objects, will, or intentionality; that which affirms and composes itself as the corpus exanime cannot be thought, imagined, or apprehended as a dialectic of sense and being, for it is without referent, object, without propriety or possession, and is the non-place where pain is no longer predicable as a spur, a gathering, or an annihilation (*autochiria*), but as something that betokens a kind of ultra-anonymous, impersonal privation. A "shameful livery" of absence, the corpus exanime is beyond contradiction; it refuses everything but its own nonexistence, its *non-être* without being, potency, self-presence, or self-capacity. In this sense, the corpus exanime has nothing to offer but suffering itself, the suffering of the "itself," the effigy by which it reveals and condemns itself, and precisely for what it is not, the infinite "non" that cannot be conceived without morbidity, pain, the rupture, the incapacity, that cannot be grasped as bodily pain, but nonetheless must be suffered, endured, tarried with, isolated from being and hope.

"I consider the present in terms of something to be exceeded [*à dépasser*]," Fanon writes.[23] In modern philosophy the idea of death and anxiety in the face of unendurable pain is opposed to infinity in the name of an opening to finitude. To realize one's limits as finite is not to see pain's nothingness, but to bear what cannot be borne. As death, and an attitude taken with respect to death, the negation of the beingness of pain is not merely an impassive thought. Nor is it an inescapable ethical obligation—a thought that is still too pious vis-à-vis the incurable, when one has no choice but to twist and turn in that abyss. Here, the nothingness of pain is still conceived independently of the corpus exanime, without recognizing the universality of the corpus exanime for those who are infinitely set apart from subject, being, world as philosophically understood; the dialectical character of the finite and the infinite cannot understand the disabling pain of the corpus exanime. One starts with the morbid universe, which is not limited by pain, and the originary otherness by which it is represented. But black suffering is still envisaged as the end and limit of human being—as a shore both limits and infinitizes the ocean. But we must ask if black pain, unthinkable as a limit or negation of being, is possible as a finite attestation, as something we know, or is nameable; we must ask whether consciousness, thought, finitude, with their existential attitudes of possibility and impossibility, can ever be the locus of this infinitely painful interval that is always a *not* before it is *other*, and so remains irreducible to the one who suffers as a corpus exanime in their otherness.

Perhaps there exists, in these artworks by Rodney, a definition that opens up to us another way of thinking about the corpus exanime? And, indeed, they seem to offer us, or make visible, five gestures, or indications, which we can briefly consider in conclusion:

(i) Blackness is hated, but is it hateful? Should one go on hating it because one detects in such a hatred a pleasure—a certain pleasure outside of the realm of pure or even practical reason? Can anti-blackness be categorial? Now, the strength of Rodney's work stems, on the contrary, from the fact that this pleasure assumed to be a free decision is not an inversion of pain, nor its inconvenience, nor does it suppress or master it, but on the contrary, the seductiveness of anti-blackness stems from a pleasure that allows one to love pain so long as it remains inordinately hateful.

(ii) Is black pain unjust? Black pain cannot cease to be unjust, for it reflects the injustice of black being itself. In other words, the black ego is never free to entirely free itself from its own pain; indeed, pain is the unjust egoism of blackness that, in this regard, is the realm of an interminable corpus exanime; but black egoism is often derided for its own injustice—that is to say, the intimate connection between injustice and egoism (by which blackness appears to "enjoy" its appearance as pain). The spectacle of black egoism conceals an extreme intolerance. For what it suffers from and enjoys (presumably), is both involuntary and constitutive, an egotism that can always be stigmatized as *too much and never enough*, an excessive subtraction that is both unjustly egotistical, and is condemned for being nothing but ego. Rodney stresses that black suffering does not simply, or primarily, derive from the egotism of the self. His work amounts to a radical redefinition of a corpus exanime that determines all his behaviors and modalities from the start. Moreover, while this pathos might make sense in the psychical realm, it imposes on black being a ceaseless, metaphysical condemnation aimed not at liberty, beauty, or form, but a pained inaccessibility that is always exposed, precarious, unknown.

(iii) I will not outline here the complex connections between effigy and nonexistence discussed above. But by using Rodney's work concerning black pain in general, it is possible to reach a locus where the question of pain is not based on making it predicable, known, or manageable. This locus could be formulated as follows: Does pain make blackness more accessible to the subject? Put differently, does the pathos, which enjoys an uncontested primacy, acknowledge itself merely as an object, or does it reveal what can appear only if it immediately disappears from the light of objects? We know that Rodney was debilitated so much that light (or a certain light) was opaque to him, or, as we saw in the example of Mulo, how even when objectified black suffering cannot be seen, represented, or encountered as a world picture. Mulo confronts this directly: there is no otherness, no other, no witness, and literally no savior, when one's suffering is rendered in effigy as corpus exanime.

(iv) The other may lose its coherence, but the black cannot be restored to the world without pathology. Its pain is delimited from the realms of reason, and it is already lost to the symbols of sovereignty. Pain is not what the ego decides; it is the suffering of judgement itself. But can one think the scars (of the corpus exanime) beyond its mortification? Can one think disfigurement without an arbitrary and irreversible *sense* that one's eyes may have been disfigured in the judging of it? One can only see disfigurement because the price of otherness is this expense of the ego, which grants being *proprio motu* even in its disfigurement. As has been argued, this investiture is also a divestiture; but when the pain seen is black, pain itself loses all concession or restoration; it just is disfigurement (like Descartes's piece of wax).[24]

(v) We thus come to a radical conclusion: the corpus exanime renders conceptually impossible the acknowledgement of black pain—at least in the sense of a sovereign, egoic, possibility. Fundamentally, the corpus exanime excludes the ego from the maze-like depths of its pain. Even though pain pushed Rodney into art, it was not the incurable necroses that made it all but impossible to live, or to imagine a future, for what he was never able to experience was not so much death (finitude) but a way out of the corpus exanime that already told him he was a black "this" or "that"; and that, as a machine without eyes or quiddity, his art could only offer an interlocution that makes being itself unrecognizable, effaced, invisable.

It is from this scenario that we return, finally, to the maze and its execution: there can be no approach to pain—as unknowable limit—if one's alterity always leads the subject back to itself, and through a vision that, instead of freeing the "I," is the terror by which the subject seems most effectively to have been condemned to live in a cruel and painful manner. It is exactly thus that the corpus exanime is the very place where the "I"'s torment and suffering can be put on display. Thus, without any contradiction, it allows us to conceive of a kind of effigy, or pseudo-gisant, whose function is to be seen, exhibited, as something dead, no longer living, to be put away without care or witness.

Preface

1. Frantz Fanon, *Peau noire, masques blancs* (Éditions du Seuil: Paris, 1952), 6.

2. The problems discussed here are closely related to those I examined in two recent works titled *Whither Fanon?: Studies in the Blackness of Being* (Stanford: Stanford University Press, 2018) and *Lacan Noir: Lacan and Afro-Pessimism* (London: Palgrave Macmillan, 2021). While the reader is not required to refer to those books, they should be aware that they form a kind of critical introduction to the notions, and definitions, pursued in this book.

3. Emmanuel Levinas, *Otherwise than Being, or Beyond Essence*, trans. Alphonso Lingis (Pittsburgh: Duquesne University Press, 1969).

4. I borrow the word *invisable*—meaning unable to be intended or aimed at—from Jean-Luc Marion's *The Visible and the Revealed*, trans. Christina M. Gschwandtner (New York: Fordham University Press, 2008).

5. The allusion is to Darby English, *How to See a Work of Art in Total Darkness* (Cambridge, MA: MIT Press, 2007).

6. Jacques Lacan, *The Seminar of Jacques Lacan, Book XIV: The Logic of Fantasy, 1966–1967*, trans. Cormac Gallagher (unofficial), 115, PDF. Published online by *Jacques Lacan in Ireland*, http://www.lacaninireland.com/web/wp-content/uploads/2010/06/14-Logic-of-Phantasy-Complete.pdf.

7. The allusion here is to Martin Luther King Jr.'s last speech, "I've Been to the Mountaintop," given on April 3, 1968.

Part I

1. Werner Hamacher, *Minima Philologica*, trans. Catharine Diehl and Jason Groves (New York: Fordham University Press, 2015), 44.

2. The allusion here is to two texts by Lacan: the *Schwärmereien* or "black swarms" of "Kant with Sade" in *Écrits*, trans. Bruce Fink (New York: W. W. Norton, 2002), 652; and the "signifying swarm" of *lalangue* in *Encore: The Seminar of Jacques Lacan, Book XX*, trans. Bruce Fink (New York: W. W. Norton, 1999), 143.

3. Edward Said, *The Selected Works of Edward Said, 1966–2006* (New York: Vintage, 2019), 533; Paul de Man, *The Resistance of Theory* (Minneapolis: Minnesota University Press, 2002), 24.

4. Said, *Selected Works*, 532.

5. In general terms, perhaps it might be better to say: we have found that the n'est pas cannot be posited. That we should say instead: blackness has been hitherto deposited by a prosopopoeia rather than attained by any restoration of it?

6. Edward Said, cited in Timothy Brennan, *Places of Mind: A Life of Edward Said* (New York: Farrar, Straus and Giroux, 2021), 169.

7. Edward Said, *Beginnings: Intention and Method* (London: Granta, 1985), 366–67.

8. Peter Szondi, *On Textual Understanding and Other Essays*, trans. Harvey Mendelsohn (Minnesota: Minnesota University Press, 1986), 20, 5. See also August Boeckh, *On Interpretation and Criticism* (Oklahoma: Oklahoma University Press), 1968.

9. Szondi, *Textual Understanding*, 12.

10. Szondi, 18, 17.

11. Szondi, 5.

12. Szondi, 6.

13. Szondi, 6.

14. Szondi, 21.

15. Szondi, 17.

16. "[I]t is not by chance that *voeu*, a wish, is also *veut*, the third person [singular] indicative of *vouloir*, nor that it is by chance either that the negating *non* should also be the naming *nom*; nor is it by chance, or arbitrary . . . What must be appreciated is the deposit, the alluvium, the petrification that is marked by the way a group handles its unconscious experience." Jacques Lacan, "The Third (La Troisième)," trans. Philip Dravers, *The Lacanian Review* 7 (Spring 2019): 94.

17. Jean-Claude Milner, "Back and Forth from Letter to Homophony," *Problemi International* 1, no.1 (2017): 85.

18. Milner, "Back and Forth," 85.

19. Lacan, *Encore*, 143.

20. Milner, "Back and Forth," 97.

Chapter 1

An earlier version of this chapter was published in *Propter Nos*, Volume 4 (Fall, 2020): 27–51.

1. Frantz Fanon, *Peau noire, masques blancs* (Éditions du Seuil: Paris, 1995), 6; Frantz Fanon, *Black Skin, White Masks*, trans. Charles Lam Markmann (New York: Grove Press, 1967); and *Black Skin, White Masks*, trans. Richard Philcox (New York: Grove Press, 2008).

2. Pierre Macherey, "Figures of Interpellation in Althusser and Fanon," *Radical Philosophy* 173 (May/June 20): 17, my emphasis. When Macherey, describing the effect of Althusser's iconic 1970 essay, "Ideology and Ideological State Apparatuses," tells us that it was "particularly disconcerting" to him, whose "enigma" he was "left to decrypt"—the decision to interrogate that enigma and its formulae (an odd phrase that conveys something systematic in relation to meaning), is what leads him to turn to Fanon, specifically *Black Skin, White Masks* and the sentence, "Tiens, un nègre!": "it is interesting to compare them," he writes, and to contrast their "taking up [of] the problem of subjectivation [*subjectivation*]" (Macherey, "Figures of Interpellation," 9). But what also remains enigmatic, or at least unexplained, is

how this return to the notion of *retournement*, whose limits are scrupulously reproduced, does not include Macherey's own use of the concept in *Pour une théorie de la production littéraire* (Lyon: ENS Éditions, 2014), to capture the *différence* between art and ideology; or how art makes ideology *visible*, decipherable, by exposing its imaginary contours as in a broken mirror. This displaced genealogy would seem to suggest (contrary to Macherey) a *retourné* that is itself ambiguous, displaced, absent; there is even, in this subtle and odd reversal, a suspicion that blackness is the *inverted* image of this earlier attachment, and so the means by which *retourné* makes visible the belief, posterior to Althusser, that ideology is a specular relation, and/or how art presents a real that is the (black?) reversal of ideology. The pattern is itself paradoxical, ironical, and too precise (which does not mean innocent) not to be deliberate. We shall be broaching its repercussions throughout.

3. For the classic account, see Louis Althusser, *Lenin and Philosophy and other Essays*, trans. Ben Brewster (London: Monthly Review Press, 1971), 127–89.

4. Macherey, "Figures," 14, 18.

5. Macherey, "Figures," 14, 15.

6. Macherey, "Figures," 15, 16.

7. Macherey, "Figures," 16. Significantly, Macherey says that Althusser's notion of subjection allows Marxist literary theory to go beyond the 'classical' reading of ideology: in which "*ideology is defined by what it is not*, by what it fails to be, or, to put it another way, by the distance it keeps from the real and its materiality." Macherey, "Figures," 9, my emphases. This old, traditional understanding of ideology, in brief, is disappointing for it can only see ideology as a *reflection of*, rather than effective agent of, social reproduction; in fact, Macherey insists that ideology is neither a representational nor reactive response to the real. This "is not"—its rhetoric or what it calls into question—will be of much concern to us in what follows given its ubiquity in both *Pour une théorie de la production littéraire* and this later essay on Althusser and Fanon.

8. Macherey, "Figures," 15.

9. Macherey, "Figures," 14.

10. Fanon, *Black Skin*, 123.

11. For a commentary on "monstration," see chapter 2.

12. Fanon, *Black Skin*, 89–90.

13. Macherey, "Figures," 16.

14. For a detailed analysis of these terms and figures, see my *Whither Fanon?: Studies in the Blackness of Being* (Stanford: Stanford University Press, 2018).

15. Fanon, *Black Skin*, 52.

16. Fanon, *Black Skin*, 112–13.

17. Jean-Paul Sartre, *L'Être et le néant: Essai d'ontologie phénoménologique* (Paris: Gallimard, 1943). All references are to the English translation, *Being and Nothingness*, trans. Hazel E. Barnes (New York: Philosophical Library, 1966).

18. Sartre, *Being and Nothingness*, 17.

19. Fanon, *Black Skin*, 92.

20. Sartre, *Being and Nothingness*, 22n14.

21. Frantz Fanon, *The Wretched of the Earth*, trans. Richard Philcox (New York: Grove Press, 2004), 65.

22. Who knows whether this dream of being colorless, when we think we are awake, is not another dream slightly different from the first, on which our dreams are grafted onto a negrophobia? Such dreams have a praxis (moreover without being imposed), and a good deal of eroticism; but they also incarnate a desire to go beyond the purely black phenomenal form of who one is, in the pursuit of the vain phantoms and illusions of a 'white' knowledge of desire.

23. Fanon, *Black Skin*, 90, 92, translation modified.

24. Fanon, *Black Skin*, 92.

25. Macherey, "Figures," 18.

26. Fanon, *Black Skin*, 89.

27. The term *eidos* is to be understood here as the aspect under which something shows itself.

28. After references to Sartre's *Réflexions sur la question juive* (1946), Macherey argues that Fanon's analysis remains existential, phenomenological; that it is constituted by a *situation*, "which is to say on the plane that is at once that of being for itself and that of being for the other, in a certain historical context." It follows that a subject is only "ever a subject in a situation," and that is because the subject is always *overdetermined* (a word that we shall come back to), "which is to say a subject specified according to the norms of the situation." And it is because Althusser fails to ask or question "the criteria imposed by the situation" that he also fails to see how interpellation is both a process of *selection* and *relegation*. This is what we might call the true thrust of Macherey's *anti-Althusserian decryption*: subjection is not only a recruitment by which the subject learns to subject itself, it is also a prescription by which some are told that they are less than human, resisted as the very negation of agency and will. Macherey, "Figures," 17, 18, 19.

29. Macherey, "Figures," 19.

30. Fanon, *Black Skin*, Philcox, 95, 96.

31. Fanon, *Black Skin*, Markmann, 120.

32. Fanon, *Black Skin*, Philcox, 96.

33. Fanon, *Black Skin*, 97–98.

34. Fanon, *Black Skin*, 99, translation modified.

35. On the *il y a*, see Emmanuel Levinas, *Totality and Infinity*, trans. Alphonso Lingis (Pittsburgh: Duquesne University Press, 1969).

36. Fanon, *Black Skin*, 95.

37. See chapter ten, "The Abyssal" in my *Whither Fanon?*

38. Fanon, *Black Skin*, 111.

39. Fanon, *Black Skin*, 114.

40. Fanon, *Black Skin*, 93, translation modified.

41. Fanon, *Black Skin*, 206.

42. Frantz Fanon, *Towards the African Revolution*, trans. Haakon Chevalier (New York: Grove Press, 1967), 27.

43. Fanon, *African Revolution*, 19.

44. Fanon, *African Revolution*, 26, 25.

45. Fanon, *African Revolution*, 24–25.

46. Paul de Man, *The Aesthetic Ideology*, (Minnesota: Minnesota University Press, 1996), 178.

47. Fanon, *African Revolution*, 17.

48. Pierre Macherey, *A Theory of Literary Production*, trans. Geoffrey Wall (London: Routledge & Kegan Paul, 1978), 101.

49. On denegation, see Jacques Lacan, "Response to Jean Hyppolite's Commentary on Freud's 'Verneinung' (1954)," in Écrits, *The First Complete Edition in English*, trans. Bruce Fink (New York: W. W. Norton, 2006), 308–33. For an elaboration of Fanon's relation to Lacan, see my *Lacan Noir* (London: Palgrave Macmillan, 2021); Macherey, *Literary Production*, 85, 86.

50. Macherey, *Literary Production*, 53.

51. Macherey, *Literary Production*, 12.

52. Macherey, *Literary Production*, 13.

53. Fanon, cited in Macherey, "Figures," 14.

54. Fanon, *Black Skin*, 186–7, translation modified.

55. Fanon, *Black Skin*, 187.

56. Fanon, *Black Skin*, 186.

57. Sartre, *Being and Nothingness*, 57. Reading across from *Pour une théorie de la production littéraire* to *Black Skin, White Masks*, it is precisely absence that can be described as a situation of being overdetermined by, and an indeterminate relation to, a desire that reproduces itself as impossibility. As *ruinare*, the n'est pas is not, or not only, a negation: we could also say that it subsists as an ontological impurity that is the trace of the other within us; consequently, there is no defense against it, for it is how blackness absents itself—whitens itself—that overdetermines its own negrophobic appearance. This impurity suggests that anti-blackness must be considered a passion that is violently envious and morally unjust.

Chapter 2

1. Henry Louis Gates, Jr., *The Signifying Monkey: A Theory of African American Literary Criticism* (Oxford: Oxford University Press, 2014), 83.

2. The phrase, "a thought without a thinker" is taken from W. R. Bion, *Attention & Interpretation* (London: Tavistock Publications, 1970), 104.

3. Gates, *The Signifying Monkey*, 5.

4. "Esu's role as the perpetually copulating copula serves to reinforce this notion of linkage, or mediation." Gates, *Signifying Monkey*, 31.

5. Gates, 42.

6. Gates, 37, my emphasis.

7. Gates, 8.

8. Gates, 7.

9. See Immanuel Kant, *Der Streit der Fakultäten* [1798], Akademie-Ausgabe 7 (Berlin: Reimer, 1907).

10. See Martin Heidegger, *Einführung in die Metaphysik* [1935], Gesamtausgabe 40 (Frankfurt: Klostermann, 1983), 47.

11. Gates, *Signifying Monkey*, 54.

12. On *symbola*, see P. Gauthier, *Symbola: Les étrangers et la justice dans les cites grecques*, (Nancy: Université de Nancy, 1972).

13. Gates, *Signifying Monkey*, 11.

14. Gates, 13.

15. Gates, 22.

16. Gates, 25.

17. Gates, 25.

18. Gates, 25.

19. Gates, 26.

20. Gates, 27.

21. Gates, 30.

22. Gates, 31.

23. I will return to this point in chapter 3.

24. Karl Marx, *Capital* [1867], vol 1, trans. Ben Fowkes (Harmondsworth, UK: Penguin, 1990), 255.

25. On *Jemeinigkeit*, see Martin Heidegger, *Being and Time*, trans. John Macquarrie (Oxford: Basil Blackwell, 1995), 41–43.

26. Gates, *Signifying Monkey*, 43.

27. Gates, 45.

28. Jacques Derrida, *Margins of Philosophy*, trans. Alan Bass (Brighton: Harvester Press, 1982), 7.

29. Gates, *Signifying Monkey*, 58.

30. Gates, 58.

31. Gates, 58.

32. Gates, 85.

33. Gates, 116.

34. Gates, 132.

35. Gates, 132, my emphasis.

36. Gates, 134, my emphasis.

37. Gates, 135.

38. Gates, *Figures in Black: Words, Signs, and the "Racial" Self* (New York: Oxford University Press, 1987), 167.

39. Houston A. Baker, *Modernism and the Harlem Renaissance* (Chicago: Chicago University Press, 1987), 15.

40. Baker, *Modernism*, 17.

41. Gates, *Figures in Black*, 168.

42. Gates, 172.

43. Gates, 174.

44. G. W. F. Hegel, *Die Phänomenologie des Geistes* (Frankfurt: SuhrKamp Verlag, 1986): 90, 91.

45. On "ab-sense," see Jacques Lacan, "L'étourdit," trans. J. W. Stone (unofficial), 1972.

46. Gates, *Figures in Black*, 176.

47. Baker, *Modernism*, 50.

48. Gates, *Figures in Black*, 183.

49. Gates, 185, 182.

50. Gates, 191.

51. The allusion here is to the famous prologue of Ralph Ellison's *Invisible Man*, where he writes: "'Now black is . . .' the preacher shouted.

'Bloody . . .'

'I said black is . . .'

'Preach it, brother . . .'

'. . . an' black ain't . .'"

Ralph Ellison, *Invisible Man* (New York: Random House, 1952), 8, ellipses in the original.

52. Gates, *Figures in Black*, 178, 176.

53. David Marriott, *Lacan Noir: Lacan and Afro-Pessimism* (London: Macmillan, 2021).

54. Gates, *Figures in Black*, 247.

55. Heidegger, *Being and Time*, 195.

56. For an elaboration of these arguments, see chapter 1, "N'est Pas."

57. Gates, *Figures in Black*, 275.

58. Werner Hamacher, *Minima Philologica*, trans. Catharine Diehl and Jason Groves (New York: Fordham University Press, 2015), 61.

59. Werner Hamacher, "Ou, séance, touche de Nancy, ici," *Paragraph* 17 (1995), 105.

60. Gates's investment in the "science" of genealogy and its various forms of racial "evidence" could be seen as on a par with his concerns with philological "ancestryness." For a commentary on that science, see Alondra Nelson, *The Social Life of DNA: Race, Reparations, and Reconciliation After the Genome* (Boston: Beacon Press, 2016); and Duana Fullwilley, "Can DNA 'Witness' Race? Forensic Uses of an Imperfect Ancestry Testing Technology," in *Race and the Genetic Revolution*, eds. Sheldon Krimsky and Kathleen Sloan (New York: Columbia University Press, 2011), 116–26.

Chapter 3

A version of this chapter was previously published as "*Nègre, Figura*," *Textual Practice* 35, no. 6 (2021): 997–1013.

1. Frantz Fanon, *Black Skin, White Masks*, trans. Charles Lam Markmann (New York: Grove Press, 1968).

2. Fanon, *Black Skin*, 147.

3. For a detailed exposition of this argument, see chapter 6, "Crystallization."

4. Frantz Fanon, *The Wretched of the Earth*, trans. Constance Farrington (Harmondsworth, UK: Penguin Books, 1967), 166–199.

5. Fanon, *Wretched*, 252.

6. Fanon, *Wretched*, 253, 255.

7. Said's readings of Fanon can be found scattered across several major works, including *Orientalism*, *Culture and Imperialism*, and *Reflections on Exile*. That said, Said appears to have spent his entire intellectual life thinking about style. Long before the postcolonial was defined in terms of discourse, the notion of style in *Culture and Imperialism* was already seeking to bring out—to present—a dimension that is not so much opposed to discourse as it is to a certain "style of historical writing." *Culture and Imperialism* (New York: Vintage Books, 1994), xxvi. Style, he suggests, gives expression to a text's "worldliness" on account of the

fact that texts, too, are part of the world in their complex affiliations. As such, Said is wedded to the idea that these affiliations are historically determined, even if those affiliations are not always decidable as to their truth or falsity, and especially when meaning and truth are reduced to "simple diametric opposition[s]" without reference to "real historical circumstances." *The World, the Text, and the Critic* (Cambridge, MA: Harvard University Press, 1983), 32, 34; *Culture and Imperialism* (New York: Vintage Books, 1994), 436. Structuring, to different degrees, the different levels or types of style (of art, politics, rhetoric, criticism and literature), worldliness or "circumstantial reality" constitutes a kind of leitmotiv, a kind of preoccupation that questions the "style of rule," a mode of thinking, of interpretation, that always proceeds from, and is always mediated by, structures of power and orthodoxy. *The World*, 35; *Culture and Imperialism*, 131. In short, style is not only one of the ways in which texts become worldly; it also undoes the opposition between text and circumstance (and, as we've seen, meaning and interpretation). The non-oppositional structuring of rule and style comes into its own in Said's analyses of empire—its metaphysics, discourses, and ideologies—with style providing the hinge, as it were, or the bridgework, between representation and reality. And "style [not only] conceal[s] rivetingly complex contradictions" between text and events; it also always reveals their fissure, or what interrupts them, this interruption being a mark of a new *contrapuntal*-dialectical emergence as "new literary style[s]" enter the world, no less, calling forth an interpretation that bespeaks a new "critical intellectual style" that is not one of rule, but one of exilic, dialectical thinking. *The World*, 185, 328. In Said's oeuvre, running all the way from *Beginnings* to *On Late Style*, style thus takes the form of a contrapuntal principle at work in any discourse, and amounts to a rhetoric (of signification) that conceals-reveals what it also disseminates as truth in both its expression and affect, its signification and its rationality. *The World*, 185, 243, 328). In bringing out the question of style in Said's work, what interests me here is how it seems to be saying and implicitly claiming that each culture has its own dominant style—as mode, genre, period, authorship, etc.—that defines its self-understanding.

8. Edward W. Said, *Freud and the Non-European* (Verso: London, 2003), 21.

9. Fanon, cited by Said, *Freud*, 20, 21.

10. Said, *Freud*, 24.

11. Said, 25.

12. Said, 25.

13. Said, 54.

14. Said, 53.

15. Said, 55.

16. Edward W. Said, *Reflections on Exile, and Other Essays* (Harvard University Press, 2000), 446, 445.

17. Said, *Reflections*, 447.

18. Said, 447, my emphasis.

19. Said, 448.

20. Said, 451.

21. Fanon, *Wretched*, 251.

22. Fanon, 253.

23. Said, *Reflections*, 450.

24. This is obviously not the place to look into the history of interpretation of Said's definition of *figura*, but see: Aamir R. Mufti, "Auerbach in Istanbul: Edward Said, Secular Criticism, and the Question of Minority Culture," *Critical Inquiry* 25, no.1 (Autumn 1998): 95–125; Evgenia Ilieva, "Said, Auerbach, and the Return to Philological Hermeneutics," *The European Legacy* 25, no. 2 (2000): 134–153; Emily Apter, "Saidian Humanism," *boundary* 2 31, no. 2 (Summer 2004): 35–53; Wolfgang Holdheim, "The Hermeneutic Significance of Auerbach's Ansatz," *New Literary History* 16, no.3 (Spring 1985): 627–631; and Avihu Zakai, *Erich Auerbach and the Crisis of German Philology* (Germany: Springer International, 2017).

25. Edward W. Said, "Introduction," in Erich Auerbach, *Mimesis: The Representation of Reality in Western Literature* (Princeton, NJ: Princeton University Press, 2003). See also Konuk Kader, *East West Mimesis: Auerbach in Turkey* (Stanford University Press: Stanford, 2010); Robert Doran, "Erich Auerbach's Humanism and the Criticism of the Future," *Moderna* 11, no. 12 (2009): 1000–1010.

26. Erich Auerbach, "Figura," in *Scenes from the Drama of European Literature*, trans. Ralph Mannheim (New York: Meridian, 1959), 53.

27. Said, *Freud*, 23.

28. Said in Auerbach, *Mimesis*, xiii.

29. Said in Auerbach, xiii.

30. Auerbach, *Mimesis*, xiii.

31. Said in Auerbach, xvi.

32. Said in Auerbach, xvi.

33. Said in Auerbach, xvi.

34. Said in Auerbach, xvi.

35. Said in Auerbach, xxi.

36. Said in Auerbach, xxxi.

37. Auerbach, *Mimesis*, 195.

38. Fanon, *Wretched*, 254.

39. Fanon, 254.

40. Edward W. Said, "I find myself instinctively on the other side of power," *The Guardian*, December 10, 2001, https://www.theguardian.com/books/departments/politicsphilosophy andsociety/story/0,6000,616545,00.html.

41. Edward W. Said, *Culture and Imperialism* (New York: Vintage Books, 1994), 235–236.

42. Said, *Culture*, 270.

43. Said, 270.

44. Said, 270.

45. Said, 271.

46. Said, 261.

47. Said, xxv.

48. Said, *Reflections*, 182.

49. Said, *Freud*, 54.

Chapter 4

1. Jean-Claude Milner, *For the Love of Language*, trans. Ann Banfield (London: Macmillan, 1978), 51.

2. Werner Hamacher, "What Remains to Be Said: On Twelve and More Ways of Looking at Philology," in *Give the Word: Responses to Werner Hamacher's 95 Theses on Philology*, eds. Gerhard Richter and Ann Smock (Nebraska: Nebraska University Press, 2019), 313.

3. For examples of this genealogy, see Frank M. Snowden, *Blacks in Antiquity: Ethiopians in the Greco-Roman Experience* (Cambridge, MA: Harvard University Press, 1970); Martin Bernal, *Black Athena: The Afroasiatic Roots of Classical Civilization* (London: Free Association Books, 1987); and Henning Trüper, *Orientalism, Philology, and the Illegibility of the Modern World* (London: Bloomsbury, 2020).

4. See David Marriott, *Lacan Noir: Lacan and Afro-pessimism* (London: Palgrave Macmillan, 2021).

5. In this chapter, reference will be made to the following works by Lacan: *Écrits*, trans. Bruce Fink (New York: W. W. Norton, 2006); *The Four Fundamental Concepts of Psychoanalysis: The Seminar of Jacques Lacan Book XI*, trans. Alan Sheridan (New York: W. W. Norton, 1998); *The Other Side of Psychoanalysis: The Seminar of Jacques Lacan Book XVII*, trans. Russell Grigg (New York: W. W. Norton, 2007); *Encore: The Seminar of Jacques Lacan Book XX*, trans. Bruce Fink (New York: W. W. Norton, 1999); *RSI: The Seminar of Jacques Lacan Book XXII*, trans. Jack W. Stone (unofficial), PDF. Published online: https://static1.squarespace.com/static/5d52d51fc078720001362276/t/5ee21894c2d74f6080bf56ac/1591875734235/19741119+rsi+0-11-19-74+Stone.pdf. ; "Remarks on Hysteria," trans. Jack W. Stone (unofficial), 1981, PDF. Published online: https://static1.squarespace.com/static/5d52d51fc078720001362276/t/600db082a597784f94c80603/1611509890608/19770226+Remarks+on+Hysteria+Jacques+Lacan+Propos+sur+Hysterie.pdf.

6. Lacan, "Remarks on Hysteria," 1.

7. On ex-sistence see Lacan, *RSI*, January 14 1975.

8. Lacan, "Remarks on Hysteria," 1.

9. Milner, *Love of Language*, 66.

10. Lacan, "January 21, 1975," *Crucial Problems for Psychoanalysis, 1964–5*, trans. Cormac Gallagher (unofficial), PDF. Published online by *Jacques Lacan in Ireland*, http://www.lacaninireland.com/web/wp-content/uploads/2010/06/12-Crucial-problems-for-psychoanalysis.pdf.

11. See Jacques Lacan, "La troisième," *La cause freudienne* 79, 11–33, trans. Russell Grigg (unofficial), personal communication.

12. In SXXIV, March 8, 1977, Lacan writes: "Making a reflexive verb of this *s'embler*, detaches it from this coming to fruition which being is." The word *s'embler* or the phrase *de s'y embler* (never coming to fruition), is a homophone that suggests the difficulty of "stealing away *(embler)*" being from the semblance that resembles *(sembler)*, figures, represents it. The intimation seems to be that any discourse that claims to know (possess, purloin) being unequivocally, or absolutely, is also a kind of pretense or counterfeit. See Jacques Lacan, *L'insu que sait de l'une-bévue s'aile à mourre: The Seminar of Jacques Lacan Book XXIV*, trans. Cormac Gallagher (unofficial), PDF. Published online by *Jacques Lacan in Ireland*, http://www.lacaninireland.com/web/wp-content/uploads/2010/06/insu-Seminar-XXIV-Final-Sessions-1-12-1976-1977.pdf.

13. Jean Laplance and Serge Leclaire, "The Unconscious: A Psychoanalytic Study," trans. Patrick Coleman, *Yale French Studies* 48 (1972): 175.

14. Lacan, *Other Side*, 152.

15. See Sigmund Freud, *The Interpretation of Dreams* (SE, IV), *Beyond the Pleasure Principle* (SE, XVIII), and *The Question of Lay Analysis* (SE, XX). See also Jacques Derrida, *Resistances of Psychoanalysis*, trans. Peggy Kamuf, Pascale-Anne Brault, and Michael Naas (Stanford: Stanford University Press, 1996). For various figures of blackness in Lacan see Marriott, *Lacan Noir*, Part 1.

16. Lacan, *Encore*, 49.

17. Lacan, *Four Fundamental Concepts*, 20.

18. Lacan, *Other Side*, 51.

19. Lacan, *Écrits*, 161–162.

20. Lacan, *Other Side*, 56.

21. John Forrester, *The Seductions of Psychoanalysis: Freud, Lacan, and Derrida* (Cambridge, UK: Cambridge University Press, 1990), 181.

22. Lacan, *Écrits*, 174. Lee Edelman's comment on this "conclusion" is incisive: "What makes this pseudo-logic so striking is that its initial proposition presupposes a knowledge rooted in ontology . . . only to be followed immediately by a de-ontologizing counter-assertion. . . . This generates, in place of a logical conclusion that demonstrates one's manhood, only the fear, the ontological anxiety, of being convinced one is not a man, which prompts a declaration of manhood deprived of any ontological ground." Lee Edelman, "White, Black, Non-Black: Lacan and the Logic of Race" (unpublished manuscript, 2022).

23. Lacan, *Écrits*, 163.

24. Lacan, 165.

25. Marriott, *Lacan Noir*, 22–37.

26. Lacan, *Écrits*, 162.

27. Lacan, 162.

28. Lacan, 164.

29. Lacan, 174.

30. Lacan, *Four Fundamental Concepts*, 138.

31. Lacan, 139.

32. Frantz Fanon, *Peau noire, masque blancs* (Paris: Éditions du Seuil, 1995), 14.

33. Marriott, *Lacan Noir*, 85–87, 91–9.

34. Lacan, *Encore*, 139.

35. Marriott, *Whither Fanon?: Studies in the Blackness of Being* (Stanford: Stanford University Press, 2018), 314–363.

36. See Jared Sexton, "The Social Life of Social Death: On Afro-Pessimism and Black Optimism," *InTensions* 5 (Fall/Winter, 2011): 28.

37. The implications of this reinflection for Lacan's formula of metaphor (see below) could be indicated as follows: the S (signifier) is not only a figure that allows substitution to take place in the production of a new signified (s), but it is also that which remains unreadable as figure (i.e., is more than crossed out), and is thus unable to engender any substitution of itself into a signified.

$$\frac{S'}{S} \quad \frac{S}{s} \quad \frac{I}{s}$$

$$-x \longrightarrow S' x—$$

38. See Hortense Spillers, *Black, White, and in Color: Essays on American Literature and Culture* (Chicago: Chicago University Press, 2003), for an influential example of this pathos.

39. Lacan, *Encore*, 142.

40. See Martin Heidegger, *Ponderings II-VI: Black Notebooks 1931–1938*, trans. Richard Rojcewicz (Bloomington, IN: Indiana University Press, 2016).

41. Frantz Fanon, *Black Skin, White Masks*, trans. Richard Philcox (New York: Grove Press, 2008), 27.

42. As such, it is worth bearing in mind Lyotard's admonishment: "The closer we get to true language, the more vulnerable we become to the true lie." Jean-François Lyotard, "The Dream-Work Does Not Think," *The Lyotard Reader*, trans. Mary Lydon (Cambridge, UK: Blackwell, 1989), 50.

Part II

1. *Conversio* (conversion) is the onto-theological unconcealing of an essence, and its ecstatic revelation in language.

2. Jacques Lacan, "L'étourdit – Second Turn," trans. Cormac Gallagher (unofficial), 20, PDF. Published online by *Jacques Lacan in Ireland*, http://www.lacaninireland.com/web/wp-content/uploads/2010/06/etourdit-Second-turn-Final-Version4.pdf.

Chapter 5

A version of this chapter was previously published as "The X of Representation: Rereading Stuart Hall," *New Formations* 2019, no. 96–97: 177–228.

1. Stuart Hall, "New Ethnicities," in *Black Film, British Cinema* (London: ICA Documents 7, 1988), 28.

2. Stuart Hall, "What is this 'Black' in Black Popular Culture?," In *Black Popular Culture*, ed. Gina Dent (Seattle: Bay Press, 1992), 32.

3. See Walter Benjamin, "Critique of Violence," in *Selected Writings* (1913–1926), vol. 1, eds. Marcus Bullock and Michael W. Jennings (Cambridge, MA: Belknap Press, 1996), 236–253; and Frantz Fanon, "On Violence," in *The Wretched of the Earth*, trans. Richard Philcox (New York: Grove Press, 2004), 1–52.

4. See Geoffrey Bennington, *Scatter 1: The Politics of Politics in Foucault, Heidegger, and Derrida* (New York: Fordham University Press, 2016).

5. Stuart Hall, "Cultural Studies and Its Theoretical Legacies," in *Stuart Hall: Critical Dialogues in Cultural Studies*, eds. David Morley and Kuan-Hsing Chen (London: Routledge, 1996), 269.

6. On "es gibt" see Martin Heidegger, *Unterwegs zur Sprache* (Pfullingen: Neske, 1971), 192–93.

7. See W. E. B. DuBois, *The Souls of Black Folk* (New York: W. W. Norton, 1999); Edward W. Blyden, *Christianity, Islam and the Negro Race* (Baltimore: Black Classic Press, 1994).

8. For an elaboration of this trope see Alexander Crummell, *Destiny and Race: Selected Writings: 1840–1898* (Amherst, MA: University of Massachusetts Press, 1992).

9. Paul de Man, *The Rhetoric of Romanticism* (New York: Columbia University Press, 1984), 72.

10. On prosopopoeia, see de Man, *Rhetoric of Romanticism*, 249, 250.

11. See Jacques Derrida, *"Différance,"* in *Margins of Philosophy*, trans. Alan Bass (Brighton, NJ: Harvester Press, 1982), 1–29; and Louis Althusser, *For Marx*, trans. Ben Brewster (London: Verso, 2005), 87–129.

12. Malcolm X, *The Autobiography of Malcolm X* (London: Penguin Books, 1965); Eldridge Cleaver, *Soul on Ice* (New York: Dell, 1968); Leroi Jones, *Dutchman* (London: Faber, 1965); Fanon, *Wretched*.

13. Stuart Hall, "New Ethnicities," 28.

14. See Stuart Hall, *The Fateful Triangle: Race, Ethnicity, Nation*, ed. Kobena Mercer (Cambridge, MA: Harvard University Press, 2017), 132.

15. Stuart Hall and Les Back, "At Home and Not at Home," in *Stuart Hall and "Race,"* ed. Claire Alexander (London: Routledge, 2011): 494.

16. de Man, *Rhetoric of Romanticism*, 81.

17. See Stuart Hall, *Familiar Stranger: A Life Between Two Islands* (Durham: Duke University Press, 2017).

18. "Articulation contains the danger of a high formalism. But it also has the considerable advantage of enabling us to think of how specific practices (articulated around contradictions which do not all arise in the same way, at the same point, in the same moment), can nevertheless be thought *together*." Stuart Hall, "Cultural Studies: Two Paradigms," *Media, Culture and Society* 2 (1980): 69. See also Lawrence Grossberg, "On Postmodernism and Articulation: An Interview with Stuart Hall," *Journal of Communication Inquiry* 10, no. 2 (1986): 45–60. Articulation is then this awareness of something that gathers itself only in dividing itself, but only as the new phrasing of difference emerges, a difference that begins by always doubling back on that which precedes it, that is to say, that divides it, from the very start, as both an essential possibility and as a representation.

19. Hall and Back, "At Home," 486.

20. Stuart Hall, *The Hard Road to Renewal: Thatcherism and the Crisis of the Left* (London: Verso, 2021).

21. Hall, "What is this 'Black,'" 32.

22. Michel Foucault, *The Hermeneutics of the Subject*, trans. Graham Burchell (New York: Picador, 2005), 210.

23. John L. Williams, *Michael X: A Life in Black and White* (London: Century, 2008), 131.

24. The phrase "linguistic predicament" is borrowed from Paul de Man's iconic sentence: "Death is a displaced name for a linguistic predicament." *Rhetoric of Romanticism*, 81.

25. Williams, *A Life*, 3.

26. Hall and Back, "At Home," 503.

27. From this, it follows that meaning and position may be regarded as conflicting tendencies. Ideological critique is not meant to reconcile the two. For what is meant by ideology but that its sense is not so easily rendered? Only if there is no equivalence between the signifier and its positioning does some ultimate, decisive element remain beyond all communication—inscribed and yet neither concealed nor clearly distinguishable. In all ideological discourse there remains then an addition to what can be conveyed, something that cannot be communicated; depending on the context in which it appears, it is something that neither symbolizes nor is symbolized, but something in whose traces there is always something incommensurable, unsettling. Though concealed and enigmatic, this something

actively penetrates or inhabits representation, which it weights with non-meaning. Meaning ceases to be the arbiter here, because of the way in which sense (or representation) is touched by dissociation. I have said that this excess (this x) is that which, in racist ideology, pertains to an absence that can neither be, nor be conceived without, blackness, and vice versa, a blackness that can neither be, nor be conceived without, that of a void that falls without end. That is to say, to seek to know this x, to embrace it, is to confront the experience of meaninglessness itself.

28. V. S. Naipaul, *The Return of Eva Peron with the Killings in Trinidad* (New York: Alfred A. Knopf, 1980): 23.

29. Naipaul, *Return of Eva Peron*, 25.

30. Naipaul, 63, 88, 73. Strangely enough, the very phrase linking black writing to a public relations exercise as well as a lie also recurs in "New Ethnicities," where the question of innocence is brought up once again in relation to a new "politics of criticism." Hall cites the following sentences from Hanif Kureishi that, whether knowingly or not, curiously echo Naipaul: "The writer as public relations officer, as hired liar. If there is to be a serious attempt to understand Britain today, with its mix of races and colours, its hysteria and despair, then, writing about it has to be complex. It can't apologize or idealize. It can't sentimentalize and it can't represent only one group as having a monopoly on virtue." Kureishi, quoted in Hall, "New Ethnicities," 30. And, after informing us that such criticism is necessary if "black culture is to grow up, to leave the age of critical innocence," Hall seems to be taking Kureishi at his word. Whether the source of these cited expressions is Naipaul, or whether it results from a new form of black criticism, both stand as condemnations of the essential ignorance of black writing. Symptomatically speaking, this unknown or repressed quotation may thus fulfill the end of critical innocence, but it can only do so by innocently repeating the *content* of a political *positioning* that is decidedly anti-black.

31. Malcolm X, "Saved," *Autobiography*, 175.

32. These inversions remind me of Paul de Man's point that "autobiography veils a defacement of the mind of which it is itself the cause." *Rhetoric of Romanticism*, 81.

33. Paul de Man, *Allegories of Reading: Figural Language in Rousseau, Nietzsche, Rilke, and Proust* (New Haven: Yale University Press, 1979), 292.

34. In this regard, Naipaul's review of the case oddly echoes that of the appeal judges who sought to uphold the literal meaning of the law when condemning Michael X to death. No consideration is given of whether the charges, the trial, and the sentence are just, and no attempt to question whether a blameless man has been allowed to hang. "It beggars belief," writes John Williams, that "neither Naipaul nor any of the other observers seems to have seriously considered the fact that much of the evidence against Michael was literally incredible." Williams, *A Life*, 246. It is this discrepancy between Naipaul's and William's use of the word "literal" that also implies a difference between a naïve faith in law and a radical distrust of any legalistic approach. Those who want to save literality as law condemn Michael, but those who want to save him only do so, however, because they want to condemn law as lie, or fantasy. There can be no innocence or justice if there is lie or fantasy. One may therefore ask whether the literal interpretation of the case depends as such on the presumption of an essential guilt, and, if so, on a certain phantasmatic cruelty. For, as Geoffrey Robertson, one of Michael's defense lawyers, reminds us, it is not as a lie or a fantasy that Michael X was

put to death but as a black human being. Interestingly enough, in extolling the view that in law "the plainest statement is best," Robertson also condemns the Privy Council's defense of Michael X's murder as "cruelty masquerading as mercy." Geoffrey Robertson, *The Justice Game: Tales from the Bar* (London: Chatto & Windus, 1998), 98. In this regard, in his retelling of the story of Michael X, the literal thus changes places with cruel masquerade, and fiction becomes truly merciful only when it fails to resort to "a safe, legalistic approach." Robertson, *Justice Game*, 96.

35. Naipaul, *Return of Eva Peron*, 74.

36. For an elaboration of this complex figure, see my *Whither Fanon?: Studies in the Blackness of Being* (Stanford: Stanford University Press, 2018).

37. Conatus, or striving, is a term taken from Spinoza's *Ethics*, trans. Michael Silverthorne and Matthew J. Kisner (Cambridge, UK: Cambridge University Press, 2018).

38. The literature here is vast, but see for example: James Hunt, "On the Negro's Place in Nature," *Journal of the Anthropological Society of London*, vol 2 (1864): xv–lvi; Dorothy Roberts, *Fatal Invention: How Science, Politics, and Big Business Recreate Race in the 21st Century* (New York: The New Press, 2011); and Troy Duster, "A Post-Genomic Surprise: The Molecular Re-inscription of Race in Science, Law, and Medicine," *British Journal of Sociology* 66, no.1: 1–27. For Hall's own discussion of race in science, see *The Fateful Triangle*.

39. As a sign of this irony, I do no more than note here that Michael X was the first man to be charged and imprisoned for violating the 1965 Race Relations Act, which was designed to counter racial discrimination! For an account see Williams, *A Life*.

40. Pierre Hadot, "*Epistrophē* and *metanoia*," *Actes du XI congrès international de philosophie, Bruxelles, 20–26 août 1953*, vol. 12, (Louvain-Amsterdam: Nauwelaerts, 1953), 31–36.

41. Louis Althusser, *Reading Capital*, trans. Ben Brewster and David Fernbach (London: Verso, 2015), 12, 13.

42. Hall, "What is this 'Black,'" 24, 25.

43. Althusser, *For Marx*, 93.

44. Althusser, *For Marx*, 99.

45. Stuart Hall, *Cultural Studies 1983: A Theoretical History*, eds. Jennifer D. Stack and Lawrence Grossberg (Durham: Duke University Press, 2016), 123.

46. Louis Althusser, *Reading Capital*, 16, 17.

47. Althusser, *Reading Capital*, 25.

48. Althusser, *For Marx*, 111.

49. Althusser, *Reading Capital*, 21.

50. Stuart Hall, "Marx's Notes on Method: A 'Reading' of the '1857 Introduction,'" *Cultural Studies* 17, no. 2 (2003): 113

51. Hall, *Cultural Studies 1983*, 113.

52. Hall, 113.

53. Hall, "Marx's Notes," 130.

54. Hall, 115.

55. Zoe Williams, "The Saturday Interview: Stuart Hall," *Guardian*, February 11, 2012, www.theguardian.com/theguardian/2012/feb/11/saturday-interview-stuart-hall.

56. Stuart Hall, "The Problem of Ideology—Marxism without Guarantees," *Journal of Communication Inquiry* 10, no. 2 (1986): 43.

57. Louis Althusser, "Contradiction and Overdetermination," in *For Marx*, trans. Ben Brewster (London: Verso, 2015), 113, translation modified. For a lucid commentary, see Warren Montag, "To Shatter All the Classical Theories of Causality: Immanent and Absent Causes in Althusser and Lacan (1963–1965)," In *The Concept in Crisis: Reading Capital Today*, ed. Nick Nesbitt (Durham: Duke University Press, 2017), 166–189.

58. Hall, "Problem of Ideology," 43. In his reading of this and other sentences, David Scott reduces such indeterminacy to a thinking about time, or, more accurately, about the need to think the "contingency' of the present." But this is a view that seems to elide the question of the relation between political economy and its theoretical representation in Hall's account. There is also the more difficult question of the relation between contingency and representation, or whether the former is ever strictly representable, which I shall be addressing throughout this chapter. See David Scott, "Stuart Hall's Ethics," *Small Axe* 9, no. 1 (March, 2005): 5.

59. Althusser, *Reading Capital*, 32.

60. Althusser, 34, 42.

61. Althusser, 55.

62. Hall, "Marx's Notes," 146.

63. Hall, 122.

64. Hall, 147.

65. Hall, 126.

66. Hall, 127.

67. Hall, 128.

68. Hall, *Cultural Studies 1983*, 123.

69. Hall, "Problem of Ideology," 77.

70. Alex Callinicos, "Stuart Hall in perspective," *International Socialism: A Quarterly Review of Socialist Theory* 142 (April, 2014): 4, http://isj.org.uk/stuart-hall-in-perspective/.

71. Hall, "New Ethnicities," 28.

72. Hall, "Marx's Notes," 133–134.

73. Hall, "What is this 'Black,'" 31.

74. Stuart Hall, *Policing the Crisis: Mugging, the State, and Law and Order* (London: Macmillan Press, 1978).

75. Hall, *Cultural Studies 1983*, 150, 151.

76. Hall, 153.

77. Hall, 153.

78. Hall, 154.

79. Man, *Allegories of Reading*, 293.

80. Hall and Back, "At Home," 494.

81. Hall and Back, 497.

82. Hall and Back, 497.

83. Hall, *Cultural Studies 1983*, 149.

84. "Afterwardsness" is Jean Laplanche's translation of Freud's *Nachträglichkeit*. See Jean Laplanche, *Life and Death in Psychoanalysis*, trans. J. Mehlman (Baltimore: John Hopkins University Press, 1976).

85. Hall, *Cultural Studies 1983*, 149.

86. Hall and Back, "At Home," 496.

87. Hall, "New Ethnicities," 29.

88. Hall, 29.

89. Hall, *Fateful Triangle*, 134.

90. Derrida cited in Hall, *Fateful Triangle*, 133.

91. Hall, *Fateful Triangle*, 172.

92. Stuart Hall, "Cultural Identity and Diaspora," in *Identity: Community, Culture, Difference*, ed. Jonathan Rutherford (London: Lawrence and Wishart, 1990), 222–237.

93. Hall, "Cultural Identity," 222.

94. Hall, "New Ethnicities," 27.

95. Hall, 27.

96. Hall, 27.

97. Hall, 27.

98. Homi K. Bhabha makes a related point that "there is, however, a recognizable difference between *position* in *war of position* and *positionality* as deployed in the vocabulary of the politics of representation." "'The Beginning of Their Real Enunciation': Stuart Hall and the Work of Culture," *Critical Inquiry* 42 (Autumn 2015): 25.

99. Robertson, *Justice Game*, 78.

100. Robertson, 76.

Chapter 6

An earlier version of this paper was published in *Critical Times* 4, no. 2 (2021): 187–232.

1. Stendhal, *On Love*, trans. H. B. V (Liveright: New York, 1947), 365.

2. Stendhal, *On Love*, 363.

3. "The figure in question is one of showing and hiding: If you throw a hornbeam bough, stripped of its leaves by winter, into the depths of a salt-mine; two or three months later you will find it covered in glistening diamonds, as the crystallization of the salt has covered its blackened surface with diamonds so brilliant and so numerous that it is only here and there that you can catch a glimpse of the real twig." Stendhal, *On Love*, 362. For a commentary, see Julia Kristeva, *Tales of Love*, trans. Leon S. Roudiez (New York: Columbia University Press, 1987), 341–365.

4. "C'est elle enfin qui, en faisant naitre en moi la phénomène que Stendhal appellee *cristallisation*, m'a enseigné à jouir délicieusement de toutes les délices que je découvre en celle que j'aime sans espoir." ["It is she, finally, who bringing to birth in me the phenomenon that Stendhal called *crystallization*, taught me to enjoy deliciously all the delights/pleasures that I discover in one that I love without hope"]. René Maran, *Un homme pareil aux autres* (Éditions A Michel: Paris, 1962), 80, my translation. Note the inversion here: instead of the lover concocting an ideal image of the beloved, it is the ideal image (of whiteness) that allows blackness to be seen, that *creates* it, allowing the black lover to enjoy the imaginary image of its refracted *perfectibility*. I leave to one side the accuracy of this inversion in order to discuss its effects—the delight, the hopelessness; and, therefore, the delight in hopelessness—that will be my focus throughout.

5. Frantz Fanon, *The Wretched of the Earth*, trans. Constance Farringdon (Harmondsworth, UK: Penguin Books, 1967), 239.

6. Frantz Fanon, *The Wretched of the Earth*, trans. Richard Philcox (New York: Grove Press, 2004), 167. See also Keïta Fodéba, "Aube Africaine," *Présence Africain* 12 (1951): 175–178. This version of the poem differs slightly from the one collected in *Poèmes africains*; and these textual differences will also, in fact, play a role in the history of its interpretation. As we shall see, when Christopher Miller is criticizing Fanon for supposedly misquoting the poem, it is to this later version he is referring. Accordingly, Miller's analysis of Fanon can only pose the question of misquotation by misquoting (with seeming sincerity) the literal object of his analysis! See Christopher L. Miller, *Theories of Africans: Francophone Literature and Anthropology in Africa* (Chicago: University of Chicago Press, 1990). Miller's repetition of the very gestures he is criticizing does not in itself invalidate his criticism of Fanon's interpretation, but it does problematize his larger statements about the ethics of a reading that totalizes, while suppressing, the *unique* contents of cultural difference. On the other hand, Miller's own reading of Fanon's text does not question, even for a moment, whether the latter's reading can be characterized as an example of hermeneutics. The consequences of this blind spot are explored in section five of the present chapter. On Fodéba's work more generally, see: Andrew W. M. Smith, "African Dawn: Keïta Fodéba and the Imagining of National Culture in Guinea," *Historical Reflections* 43, no. 3 (Winter, 2017): 102–121; Mairi S. MacDonald, "Guinea's Political Prisoners: Colonial Models, Postcolonial Innovation," *Comparative Studies in Society and History* 54, no. 4 (2012): 898–899; and Sabrina Parent, *Cultural Representations of Massacre: Reinterpretations of the Mutiny of Senegal* (New York: Palgrave Macmillan, 2014).

7. Fanon, *Wretched* (2004), 167.

8. Fanon (2004), 167, my emphasis.

9. It will one day be necessary to define the fundamental form and category of this term. For now, let us simply say that it emerges out of Fanon's discussion of the relation between revolutionary form and colonial disidentification: "Gradually, an attitude, a way of thinking and seeing that is basically white, forms and crystallizes in the young Antillean." Frantz Fanon, *Black Skin, White Masks*, trans. Richard Philcox (New York: Grove Press, 2008), 126. Elsewhere, Fanon refers to "the moment of symbolic crystallization." Fanon, *Black Skin*, 164. In both of these examples, what begins as a fairly routine metaphor of concretization tends, in the course of its elaboration, to move from something that is gradual to what individualizes itself as the sudden coalescence of a misrecognition that is also, simultaneously, the recognition of one's actual mirror image in the cultural imago it mirrors. Now, insofar as Fanon does not oppose politics to self-love, but views narcissism as politics most intimate staging, his central concern (in *Black Skin, White Masks*) is with the racial politics of love: its subterfuges, schemas, and passions. Therefore, by saying that whiteness crystallizes a negrophobic misrecognition, Fanon does not mean that whiteness simply functions as an *identity*, but that it makes difference identifiable *only* as misrecognition. That is to say, while Fanon sees a direct relation between crystallization and political struggle, that relation also establishes a non-relation to the political: what gets crystallized is a complex relation where thought—and consciousness—far from being a controlling center of being, is at odds with, and inseparable from, those misrecognized or rejected parts of the subject that it refuses to admit form part of its (black) individuation. Those rejected parts are connected to the systematic denigration of blackness as knowledge and being.

10. Fanon, *Wretched* (1967), 167.

11. Fanon, *Wretched* (2004), 171.

12. On the relation between charisma and authority, see Max Weber, *Theory of Social and Economic Organization*, trans. A. M. Henderson, Talcott Parsons, ed. Talcott Parsons (New York: Oxford University Press, 1947).

13. For an elaboration of this figure see David Marriott, *Whither Fanon?: Studies in the Blackness of Being* (Stanford: Stanford University Press, 2018).

14. Keïta Fodéba, "Preface," in *Les hommes de la danse* (Éditions Clairfontaine, Lausanne: 1954), 7. Translation by Ella Lebeau (unpublished).

15. Fodéba, *Hommes*, 8.

16. Fodéba, 14.

17. Keïta Fodéba, "La danse africaine et la scène," *Présence Africain* 14–15 (1957): 205. Translation by Ella Lebeau (unpublished).

18. Fodéba, "La danse," 206.

19. Fodéba, *Hommes*, 14.

20. Fodéba, 13.

21. Fodéba, *Hommes*, 8.

22. Miller, *Theories of Africans*, 50. For a contrasting, less tendentious account of Fanon's relationship to Fodéba, and literature more generally, see: Alexander Fyfe, "The Specificity of the Literary and its Universalizing Function in Frantz Fanon's 'On National Culture,' *Interventions* 19, no. 6 (July 2017): 764–780; and Jane Hiddleston, "Fanon and the Uses of Literature," *Nottingham French Studies* 54, no. 1 (2015): 38–51

23. Miller, *Theories of Africans*, 62, 50.

24. "Infinitely-finite": albeit obscure, what I am trying to indicate with this phrase is Fanon's writing of the event, which is written in three different ways: psychoanalytical, philosophical, and political. In *The Wretched of the Earth*, for example, he refers to a "will to particularize [*se fait volunté particularisante*]," whose speculative form is neither opposition nor mediation, neither perficient nor absolute, but occurs *through* and *by* aporia and suspension—an aporia that is also, so to speak, rigorous, corrective, and supremely vigilant. *Wretched* (2004), 173. The relation between this vigilance and what I call a black parabasis will be taken up and further explored in sections four and five of the present chapter. On the meaning of the word "speculative," see Gillian Rose, *Hegel Contra Sociology* (London: The Athlone Press, 1995), 48–49.

25. Fanon, *Wretched* (2004), 173.

26. Frantz Fanon, "Letter to Ali Shariati," in *Alienation and Freedom: Frantz Fanon*, eds. Jean Khalfa and Robert J. C. Young (London: Bloomsbury, 2018), 669, my emphasis.

27. ʿAli Shariʿati, cited in Arash Davari, "A Return to Which Self? Ali Shariʾati and Frantz Fanon on the Political Ethics of Insurrectionary Violence," *Comparative Studies of South Asia, Africa and the Middle East* 34, no. 1 (2014): 95, my emphasis. For a more incisive reading of Shariʿati's relation to Islam, see Mojtaba Mahdavi, "One Bed and Two Dreams? Contentious Public Religion in the Discourses of Ayatollah Khomeini and Ali Shariati," *Studies in Religion* 43, no. 1 (2014): 25–52; and Siavash Saffari, "Rethinking the Islam/Modernity Binary: Ali Shariati and Religiously Mediated Discourse of Sociopolitical Development," *Middle East Critique* 24, no. 3 (2015): 231–250.

28. Fanon, *Wretched* (2004), 180.

29. For example, when Shari'ati writes, "I speak of a religion which is not realized yet," one does indeed hear echoes of Fanon's nation to come; but that realization is immediately proposed as a "continuation of history." See Ali Shari'ati, *Collected Works 22* (Tehran: Chapakhsh, 1998), 18.

30. See G. W. F. Hegel, *Phenomenology of Spirit,* trans. A. V. Miller (Oxford, UK: Oxford University Press, 1977), 27–8.

31. See: Edward Said, *Humanism and Democratic Criticism* (New York: Columbia University Press, 2004); Homi K. Bhabha, *The Location of Culture* (New York: Fordham University Press, 2015); Partha Chatterjee, *The nation and Its Fragments* (Princeton, NJ: Princeton University Press, 1993); Achille Mbembe, *Necropolitics (Theory in Forms)* (Durham: Duke University Press, 2019); Gayatri Spivak, *An Aesthetic Education in the Era of Globalization* (Cambridge, MA: Harvard University Press, 2013); Jasbir K. Puar, *Terrorist Assemblages: Homonationalism in Queer Times* (Durham: Duke University Press, 2017).

32. Fanon, *Wretched* (1967), 122.

33. Fanon (1967), 123, 120, 125.

34. Fanon (1967), 165.

35. Fanon (1967), 148.

36. Fanon (1967), 132.

37. Fanon (1967), 135.

38. Fanon (1967), 134, 208.

39. Fanon (1967), 136.

40. Fanon (1967), 137.

41. Fanon, *Wretched* (2004), 137.

42. Fanon, (2004), 127.

43. Fanon, *Wretched* (1967), 163.

44. Fanon (1967), 165.

45. Fanon (1967), 144.

46. Fanon, *Wretched* (2004), 159–61, my italics.

47. Fanon (2004), 158.

48. Paul de Man, "Aesthetic Formalization: Kleist's *Über das Marionettentheater,*" in *The Rhetoric of Romanticism* (New York: Columbia University Press, 1984), 290. De Man's famous reading of the aestheticization of politics is worth considering again here. On at least two occasions in his lecture on "Kant and Schiller," included in *Aesthetic Ideology,* de Man makes a link between the "aesthetic state" and what he calls a certain "popularization of philosophy" that, in writers such as Schiller, or Goebbels, reproduces a concept of art as a fundamental metaphor of politics. Paul de Man, *Aesthetic Ideology* (Minnesota: University of Minnesota Press, 1986), 154. Even though he is careful to describe this use as itself an aesthetic "misreading" (of philosophy), de Man also says that it is a fundamental consequence of Schiller's seductive vision of "the ideal of a beautiful society" as a "well-executed English dance." In his essay on Kleist, de Man shows how such notions always conceal a violence that is mutilating, a mutilation that reveals how the aesthetic harmony of the state can only appear by settling scores with—that is to say mutilating, disfiguring, murdering—those forces that oppose it. (This situation, including the language used, is strikingly similar to Fanon's account

of the colonized intellectual and the bourgeoisie.) Thus, hidden within the aesthetic appeal of state harmony (what Schiller calls the drive to form or the *Formtrieb*) is another drive— that of *Erkenntnistrieb*—which enjoys violating the very possibility of such individuation. This is also perhaps why de Man was keen to dispute Schiller's formulations of chiasmic reversibility, because in formulating them Schiller could only disarm the disfiguring enjoyment he bore in writing them. And yet even as he settles scores with this aesthetic ideology, by revealing the limits of these various chiasmas, was de Man not still compelled (or even "seduced") by these very same forms at the level of reading and rhetoric? It could be objected that the true limit of the aesthetic for de Man was not the popular misreading of the philosophical, but his own unwillingness to depart from "the canonical principles of literary history" (in his own words). I have no further comment to make on this point, but I do note that Gayatri Spivak, in her reading of de Man and Schiller on aesthetic education, does not fundamentally challenge this aestheticization, but rather encourages a shift in reading it to that of "subalternity." See Gayatri Spivak, *An Aesthetic Education in the Era of Globalization* (Cambridge, MA: Harvard University Press, 2013). Neither truly independent of de Man—"her teacher"—nor immutable to these forms of seduction, since they are also a political question for her generation, Spivak can only repeat them as the double-bind of what she refers to as subalternity. But, for reasons that will become obvious, what she means by this word bears no relation to what Fanon refers to as "les damnés," whose wretchedness has nothing at all to do with education, aesthetic aspiration, or the critical task of pursuing a reading that can only display—but not unmask—its own ideological complicity with what now passes for globalization (which is where, supposedly, any enquiry of the aesthetic must now be negotiated). I am reminded of Barbara Johnson's chiding, but powerfully resonant sentence: "His [de Man's] unmasking of aberrant ideologies maintains a metaphorical, rather than a metonymical, relationship to history." Barbara Johnson, "Poison or Remedy? Paul de Man as Pharmakon," in *The Barbara Johnson Reader*, eds. Melissa Feuerstein, Bill Johnson González, Lili Porten, and Keja L. Valens (Durham: Duke University Press, 201), 360. If unmasking here stands as the *formal* task of avoiding the "too easy leap from the linguistic to the aesthetic, [from the] ethical to political structures," while at the same time remaining vigilant against such seduction, let us also recall that such a task also necessarily remains blind to the transcendental whiff of its own formalism (whether couched in generational terms, or presented as a globalized *ressentiment* that, despite all its critical effort, remains devoted to the world of its own theory). Johnson, 360. To name this double-bind "subalternity" does not so much escape it as confirm its transcendental delusion-dereliction.

49. Fanon, *Wretched* (2004), 163.

50. Fanon, 163.

51. Fanon, 163.

52. The allusion here is to the final lines of Aimé Césaire's *Cahier d'un retour au pays natal*: "and the great black hole where I wanted to drown a moon ago/ this is where I now want to fish the night's malevolent tongue in/ its immobile revolution!" Aimé Césaire, *Notebook of a Return to My Native Land*, trans. Mireille Rosello and Annie Pritchard (Newcastle: Bloodaxe Books, 1995), 135.

53. Frantz Fanon, *Doozakhian-e rooy-e zamin* (*Les damnés de la terre*), trans. Abolhasan Banisadr (publisher unknown, 1971); Abolhassan Benisadr, "Preface: About Fanon and His

Thoughts," trans. Khashayar Beigi and Naveed Monsoori (unpublished manuscript). For background on the Benisadr translation, see Eskandar Sadeghi-Boroujerdi, *Jadaliyya*, August 13, 2020, "Who Translated Fanon's *The Wretched of the Earth* into Persian?," https://www.jadaliyya.com/Details/41564.

54. Banisadr, *Doozakhian-e*, n.p.

55. Banisadr, *Doozakhian-e*, n.p.

56. For a nuanced reading of Shari'ati's philosophy, see Ali Rahnema, *An Islamic Utopian: A Political Biography of Ali Shariati* (London: I. B. Tauris, 2013); and Naghi Yousefi, *Religion and Revolution in the Modern World: Ali Shariati's Islam and Persian Revolution* (Lanham, MD: University Press of America, 1995).

57. Ali Shari'ati, "*Shahadat*," in *Jihad and Shahadat: Struggle and Martyrdom in Islam*, eds. Mehdi Abedi and Gary Legenhausen (Baltimore, MD: Islamic Publications International, 1986), 194, 200, 206, 214.

58. Shari'ati cited in Davari, "Which Self?," 96.

59. Shari'ati cited in Davari, "Which Self?," 93, ff 31.

60. The question of exemplarity also relates to that of a model to be followed. The Greek word *habitus* may be of some use here, as it specifically relates to repetition and performance. In *The Politics of Piety: The Islamic Revival and the Feminist Subject* (Princeton, NJ: Princeton University Press, 2011), Saba Mahmood evokes Islamic reformulations of the term to mean a specific pedagogical process by which "external performative acts (like prayer) are understood to create corresponding inward dispositions," or how piety is formed through repeated practice. Mahmood, *Politics of Piety*, 135. In other words, we are not pious because we have faith—we have faith because we are pious. At first glance, *habitus* might seem to bring mimesis into play, but it is quite significant, in this regard, that this process is pre-reflexive, or nonreflexive, and is based on repetition rather than on representation. First, and crucially, the act must be repeatedly performed en masse "until that practice leaves a permanent mark on the character of the person"; or, for methexis to work, and work well, it has to take place without egoic or mimetic identification. Mahmood, 136. Secondly, *habitus* makes explicit what it enacts by the exact repetition of it: both Mahmood and, more importantly, Shari'ati, tell us that *habitus* is the process through which cultural praxis acquires an authoritative worldliness and one that at the same time closely relates cultural practices to that of pedagogy. In this sense, *bazgasht* is also *habitus*. This suggests, as a corollary, that an ability to articulate a new world and a new set of meanings, is, collectively, oriented around practices of iteration and participation that require an almost pre-reflexive form of realization, allied to a constant need to maintain *vigilance* (a key word for Fanon) if these new practices of iteration are not, by that very token, to be betrayed—that is to say, ossified or reified as knowledge-relations. Indeed, Fanon conceives of this vigilance as a kind of *enraged precision* (and no doubt something quite different, and not at all identical with, pedagogy), because it has to first *move* the (lytic, mortified) body with exactitude. We must in fact imagine a community of bodies, a "corps à corps," suddenly finding itself moving in unison: at first tenuous, then sumptuously massive, this massification is brought into being by its own unprecedented movement; but what precipitates this movement also problematizes the very concept of iteration as a performative mode.

61. Fanon, *Wretched* (2004), 179.

62. Shariʿati cited Davari, "Which Self?," 99.

63. Fanon, *Wretched* (2004), 167.

64. Fanon (2004), 160.

65. Fanon, *Wretched* (1967), 163; Fanon (2004), 174.

66. Fodéba, "Aube Africaine," cited in *Wretched* (2004), 166.

67. Fodéba, "La danse," 209.

68. On the reading of *pas* as aporia, see Jacques Derrida, *Aporias*, trans. Thomas Dutoit (Stanford: Stanford University Press, 1994); and for a reading of repose as a speculative, rather than a dialectical, form, see Gillian Rose, "From Speculative to Dialectical Thinking—Hegel and Adorno," in *Judaism and Modernity: Philosophical Essays* (Oxford, UK: Blackwell, 1993): 53–65.

69. Fanon, *Wretched* (2004), 168.

70. Fanon (2004), 160, 161.

71. These two terms—*déchirure, détraquer*—if followed back to their sources (Bataille and Fanon), reveal two different orientations to avant-garde writing: In *L'Impossible*, Bataille, for example, writes: "Poetry which does not raise itself up to the level of the non-sense of poetry is only empty poetry." Georges Bataille, *L'impossible*, in *Oeuvres complètes*, vol. 3, ed. Thadée Klossowski (Paris: Gallimard, 1974), 20. Poetry (if we no longer identify it with style or literature) rejects all attempts to make this *non-sens* representable, graspable, or reproducible, as knowledge; for poetry is not only contrary to meaning, law, discourse, politics, and philosophy, but it is not even poetry until it becomes an experience of the impossible. And yet its absolute audacity does seem to invoke a plenitude of another order. If poetry is to overcome the inert, empty structures of metaphysics, it must sacrifice itself to the *there is*, the void, or base matter that is its own organizing principle. However, if the essence of such sacrifice does not correspond to the inertia of bourgeois culture, it nonetheless remains coextensive with the singularity of its own sacrificial principle. Thus, poetry is not truly sovereign until it sacrifices itself to the nonsensical mastery of its own impossible truth, and only then does it open up to a being beyond all order and movement. Everything depends on the lifting up—the *relevé*—of base matter into an irreversible becoming. But then Fanon's conception of the crystalline as a moment of precarious decision that is always on the road to *ruination (détraquer)*, introduces a blackness that cannot be imitated or identified with because it is distant to all idioms, including that of the sacred and of sovereignty, doubtless because it is incommensurable, or in any event impossible. Bataille, by contrast, continues to talk about *déchirure* as a moment of sacrifice (of poetry to that of heterology): it should be borne in mind that even if the sovereign moment occurs as a cut or interruption that is discontinuous, unassimilable, inimitable, or disintegrative, any attempt to link it to what sacrifice is—as tribute or donation, say, *sacrificium* or *sacer*—fails to ask why, in the idiom of sovereignty, sacrifice remains unsacrificeable, or why the concept of sacrifice is linked to that of poesis; a logic that some would say leads back to an economy, a desire, that is still too theological.

72. Fodéba, "La danse," 205.

73. Fanon, *Wretched* (1967), 13.

74. Fanon (1967), 13.

75. Miller, *Theories of Africans*, 63.

76. Miller, *Theories of Africans*, 48.

77. It is worth pondering why the word *"politics,"* for Miller, represents the dialectic between ethnicity and ethics (Miller, *Theories of Africans*, 65, author's emphasis); or why politics is the *"means* by which these seemingly exclusive terms can (and must) be worked out
and brought into dialogue" (Miller, 65, my emphasis). Miller himself reproaches mere the-
oreticist approaches to politics, in that they constitute a fundamentally abstract, or exclu-
sionary oppressive approach to difference, and one that situates the other outside of history. If theory always might be unethical, it is clearly as a moralist that Miller condemns it,
to the extent that theory "overlooks" or "liquidates" that which "deviates" from its absolut-
ist truth (and all theory supposedly risks doing this), then theory is a form of political terror, even, as ethics, the demand that theory *relativize* itself is seen as a less naïve or oppressive politics (Miller, 64). In other words, only politics can reveal, dialectically, the violent
limit of politics, as—in the case of political ethics—only theory can reflect on this politics of
politics. At this point, I would have to say that Miller, who declares this position to be more
ethical, more dialectical, than, say, Fanon's, displays what has been repressed by this "relativism," which is no more than a theoretical dogmatism that can only compromise with relativism insofar as it is possible to theorize it. Thus, the importance for Miller of the notion
of dialectics, and thus, also his use of the thought of relativism to disguise his own decidedly
(white) ethnocentric intolerance—a word that he lovingly, repeatedly invokes—of a decidedly black philosophical text such as *The Wretched of the Earth*. In any event, the demand
that *"there is no real ethics without ethnicity"* (Miller, 63), not only theoretically hides its own
intolerance of theory, but refuses a black theory of blackness that refuses the traps of either "ethics or ethnicity," and their ambiguous relation to an account of the political (whose
transcendental configurations are always suspiciously white) that remains masked as such.

78. Miller, 63.

79. Fanon, *Wretched* (2004), 168.

80. Fanon (2004), 166.

81. Fanon (2004), 168.

82. If colonial culture thereby disguises and covers up native culture, the point here is
not to conceive of an essence placed out of sight, or hidden by deception and illusion, but to
know why, in each scene of crystallization, there is nothing beyond reality and so, by implication, nothing to be engaged or disengaged with at the core. But it is the impossibility of
ever knowing the point where the lines of history and truth meet that, in Fanon's work, betrays an ironic attitude to any language of authenticity/inauthenticity, and which generates
a decidedly more complex set of questions than the notion that true culture produces authentic being (and it is no coincidence that Shari'ati's thought here reveals the influence of a
certain Heideggerianism, which sees in *shahadat* something to be revived or retrieved as the
alethic task of political ideology). If, as I am suggesting, these distinctions are themselves
consequences of a different understanding of truth and martyrdom, and thereby of liberation and politics in their differing accounts of revelation and redemption, this is not because
Fanon lacks a proper account of universality (which is itself a reductive opposition), but because of the more subtle point wherein what is distorted is inherent to political decision as
such, and because what is hidden may itself lead to a deceptive, or misleading sense of concealment, thereby usurping any possibility of any authentic or genuine decision; whether

that conviction is one based on historical truth or that of faith, Fanon's argument is to say that the very possibility of crystallization is no more originary than delusion, nor does it reveal a more authentic essence, for what it discloses is an anessential essence of being.

83. G. W. F. Hegel, "'Introduction' and the 'Concept of Religion,'" vol 1 of *Lectures on the Philosophy of Religion*, ed. Peter Hodgson, trans. R. F. Brown, P. C. Hodgson, and J. M. Stewart (Oxford, UK: Oxford University Press, 2008), 354.

84. Fanon, *Wretched* (2004), 169.

Chapter 7

1. Huey Newton. *Revolutionary Suicide* (London: Penguin Books, 2009).

2. With the word "afformation," which here means an ellipsis that checks and interrupts any ipse, I intend to show how resistance, in taking leave of itself also resists itself, but not because it strives to *be* resistant. In this study, *suicidium* thus resists rule and law; but not because of the violence of what it afforms. Rather, in revolutionary suicide, there is a bold and confident attempt to challenge the violence of the anti-black world; and in the nonviolence of its deposing, there is nothing but an attempt to rouse the socially dead to justice. See Werner Hamacher, "Afformative, Strike," *Cardozo Law Review* 13, no. 4 (1991): 1139.

3. "Killing oneself is a crime (a murder). It can also be regarded as a violation of one's duty to other people." Immanuel Kant, *The Metaphysics of Morals*, trans. Mary Gregor (Cambridge, UK: Cambridge University Press, 1996), 176.

4. In John Singleton's *Boyz n the Hood* (1991), these two principles are shown to be intermingled.

5. See David Marriott, "The Perfect Beauty of Black Death," *Los Angeles Review of Books*, June 5, 2017, https://thephilosophicalsalon.com/the-perfect-beauty-of-black-death/; and the final chapter of *Haunted Life* (New York: Columbia University Press, 2007).

6. Compare, in this regard, Michel Foucault, *The Will to Knowledge*, vol. 1 of *The History of Sexuality* (London: Penguin Books, 2008); Gilles Deleuze, *Foucault*, trans. Sean Hand (Minneapolis: University of Minneapolis Press, 1988); and Jacques Derrida, *Resistances of Psychoanalysis*, trans. Pascale-Anne Brault (Stanford: Stanford University Press, 1998).

7. On "afformation," see Hamacher, "Aforrmative," 1133–1158.

8. Newton. *Revolutionary Suicide*, 202.

9. Howard Caygill, *On Resistance: A Philosophy of Defiance* (London: Bloomsbury, 2013), 163–4. See also "Philosophy and the Black Panthers," *Radical Philosophy* 179 (May-June, 2013): 10. For a brilliant reading of the limits of Caygill's analysis, see Peter Hallward, "Defiance or Emancipation?," *Radical Philosophy* 183 (Jan-Feb, 2014): 21–32.

10. Friedrich Nietzsche, *The Anti-Christ, Ecce Homo, Twilight of the Idols, and Other Writings*, eds. Aaron Ridley and Judith Norman (Cambridge, UK: Cambridge University Press, 2005), 210.

11. Gillian Rose, *Mourning Becomes the Law: Philosophy and Representation* (Cambridge, UK: Cambridge University Press, 1996), 139–140. But, she adds, "to reduce the notion of 'voluntary death' to suicide, self-destruction, is to fail to hear the affirmation of the will in the idea of the voluntary, which may prevail in any 'natural' death." Rose, *Mourning*, 140. But this goes against what Nietzsche himself says: the reason why will to power is irreducibly opposed to voluntarism is because it has either gone astray, or is anxiously sought for, *as an*

egoic desire, whereas it is nothing but the affect of unknowable, non-egoic drives. Suicide is the resistance of those drives in those alive enough to want to renounce them.

12. Nietzsche, *Anti-Christ*, 210.

13. Caygill, "Philosophy," 21. See also *On Resistance*, 164.

14. This question should not be confused with Jean Genet's distinction between resistance and spectacle in his writings on the BPP. See Jean Genet, *Prisoner of Love*, trans. Barbara Bray (New York: New York Review of Books, 2003). On the relation between resistance and illegalism, Foucault and the Black Panthers, see Delio Vasquez, "Illegalist Foucault," *Theory & Event* 23, no. 4 (Oct, 2020): 935–972; and Brady Heiner, "Foucault and the Black Panthers," *City* 11, no. 3 (2007): 313–356.

15. The phrase means death at point blank range or suicide by firearm. See Frantz Fanon, "Medicine and Colonialism," in *Studies in a Dying Colonialism*, trans. Haakon Chevalier (London: Earthscan Books, 1989), 121–147.

16. Whenever the phrase appears in *Revolutionary Suicide*, it is negated; this maybe because the phrase was used by Eldridge Cleaver, who is the great antagonist of the book. With reference to Fanon, Cleaver writes of a "racial death-wish." *Soul on Ice* (New York: McGraw Hill, 1968), 102–103.

17. ʿAli Shariʿati, *Husayn, vâres-i adam*, vol. 19 of *Majmuʿah asar* (*Collected Works*) (Tehran: Qualam, AH 1361/AD1982), 207–8.

18. I will be referring mainly to: *Erotism: Death and Sensuality*, trans. Mary Dalwood (San Francisco: City Lights, 1986); *The Accursed Share*, vols. 2 and 3, trans. Robert Hurley (New York: Zone Books, 1991); *Inner Experience*, trans. Stuart Kendall (New York: SUNY Press, 2014); and *On Nietzsche*, trans. Stuart Kendall (New York: SUNY Press, 2015).

19. The phrase "will to chance" is the subtitle of *On Nietzsche*.

20. See Georges Bataille, *The Sacred Conspiracy: The Internal Papers of the Secret Society of Acéphale and Lectures to the College of Sociology*, eds. Marina Galleti and Alastair Brotchie (London: Atlas Press, 2018).

21. "To sacrifice is not to kill, but to abandon and to give." Georges Bataille, *Theory of Religion*, trans. Robert Hurley (New York: Zone Books, 1992), 48–9.

22. Georges Bataille, "Hegel, Death, and Sacrifice," in *The Bataille Reader*, eds. Fred Botting and Scott Wilson (Oxford, UK: Blackwell Publishing, 1997), 293.

23. Georges Bataille, *The Accursed Share*, vols. 2 and 3, trans. Robert Hurley (New York: Zone Books, 1991), 256.

24. See Georges Bataille, "Sacrifices," in *Visions of Excess: Selected Writings, 1927–1939*, trans. Allan Stoekl (Minnesota: University of Minnesota Press, 1985), 130–137.

25. Jean-Luc Nancy, "The Unsacrificeable," trans. Richard Livingston, *Yale French Studies*, no. 79 (1991): 20–38.

26. Bataille, *Accursed Share*, 198.

27. Bataille, *Accursed Share*, 222.

28. This problem is also writ large in Jean-Luc Nancy's 1991 essay, "The Unsacrificeable." Nancy's attempt to shift the terms of debate from that of mimesis to that of singularity, from sacrifice to that of community, is part of a much larger debate on metaphysical fascism. However, my problem with his reading is as follows: in it the concept of the *West* remains metaphysical (as both end and origin) and the relation of sacrifice to modern biopolitics remains wholly ignorant of blackness. Nancy, "Unsacrificeable."

29. Friedrich Nietzsche, *On the Genealogy of Morality*, ed. Keith Ansell-Pearson, trans. Carol Diethe (Cambridge, UK: Cambridge University Press, 2013), 86.

30. Achille Mbembe, "Necropolitics," *Public Culture* 15, no. 1 (2003): 11–40. Due to constraints of space, my focus here will be solely on this 2003 essay and not on the later book, *Necropolitics*.

31. Mbembe, "Necropolitics," 38.

32. Mbembe, 38.

33. Mbembe, 38.

34. Mbembe, 37.

35. Mbembe, 19.

36. Mbembe, 35.

37. Mbembe, 38.

38. Mbembe, 16.

39. Jasbir Puar, *Terrorist Assemblages: Homonationalism in Queer Times* (Durham: Duke University Press, 2017), 216.

40. Puar, *Terrorist Assemblages*, 216.

41. Spivak, cited in Puar, *Terrorist Assemblages*, 218.

42. Charles V. Charles, "Optimism and Frustration in the American Negro," *The Psychoanalytic Review* 29, no. 3 (July 1942), 270.

43. Mbembe's decidedly odd arguments about race and technology can be found in *Critique of Black Reason*, trans. Laurent Dubois (Durham, Duke University Press: 2017). For a critique of this "critique," see David Marriott, "The Becoming Black of the World," *Radical Philosophy* 2, no. 2 (June 2018): 61–71.

44. Nancy, "Unsacrificeable," 24.

45. Nancy, 21, 25.

46. Mbembe, "Necropolitics," 17, 27.

47. Arendt, cited in Mbembe, "Necropolitics," 24, my italics. What is the relation between the outside and the beyond? Or, as Hannah Arendt puts it in *The Origins of Totalitarianism* (1951), a key text for Mbembe, in the colony, savage life was, in the eyes of the colonist, "a horrifying experience, something alien *beyond* imagination or comprehension." Mbembe, 24, my emphases. This, then, is the paradox, which Arendt presents in similar terms when she suggests that the "horror [of the camps] can never be fully embraced by the imagination for the very reason that it stands *outside* of life and death." Cited in Mbembe, 12, my emphases. What's the difference between being outside and being beyond? Are they the same? Do they signify the same forms of exclusion? And is the being beyond, evoked here as the unimagined and unaware, simply to be understood as the *racial* limit of sovereignty? Although Mbembe doesn't seem to notice it, I do happen to think that the two words represent different possibilities that are at once racial—and hence political—in nature. It is just this Arendtian notion of a *beyond*, of a life that can never be fully embraced, that rhetorically performs what the theory of exception of the camps is meant to explain (a theory in which black life, unlike Jewish life, exists so far beyond the limits of imaginative sympathy, it becomes the *outside* that makes the outside of life and death both imaginable and comprehensible), and whose meaning is beyond relation as such.

48. Mbembe, "Necropolitics," 21.

49. Mbembe, 24.

50. At the same time, I would suggest that the pursuit of freedom remains an ambiguous theme on which to understand the being of the slave—at least it risks falsification and wishful thinking. To argue for freedom as agency (that is to say, the belief that every human life ardently desires its freedom, or that freedom is immanent to human existence), is to confuse the appropriation of death, of death as theologized, with a people's struggle for justice in the face of earthly dishonor. Why? Because if suicide is the act through which freedom and being become transcendent then their difference is already sacrificial. The act that separates me from myself (from myself as slave, thing, object) may be an escape from actual siege but there is no path here to transcendence *or* immanence; indeed, it might simply be the letting go of the unbearable, the impossible, a passive acceptance rather than an active contestation. But it is precisely because a sacrificial meaning is required here that there is no longer a basis for thinking freedom as an end. And this is precisely why Newton's analysis of black revolutionary suicide calls this rhetoric out, as both a nihilism and a writing of consolation.

51. Bataille, *On Nietzsche*, 40.

52. Mbembe, "Necropolitics," 37, 35.

53. Friedrich Nietzsche, *The Will to Power*, trans. Walter Kaufmann and R. J. Collingdale (New York: Random House, 1968), 55.

54. Newton, *Revolutionary Suicide*, 613–614.

55. Newton, 613.

56. Huey P. Newton, "Intercommunalism: February 1971," in *The Huey P. Newton Reader*, ed. Donald Weise (New York: Seven Stories Press, 2002), 181–200.

57. Mbembe, "Necropolitics," 39.

58. See Huey P. Newton. "The Will to Power: A Talk before the Southern California Counseling Center, May 20, 1972 (Draft)," series 1, subseries 5, box 48, folder 17, Dr. Huey P. Newton Foundation Collection, Stanford University, Green Library Special Collections. Also see: "Thoughts on the Will to Power," 1977–1978, series 1, subseries 4, box 40, folder 2–3, Dr. Huey P. Newton Foundation Collection, Stanford University, Green Library Special Collections.

59. Or, as Nietzsche writes in the third essay of the *Genealogy of Morals*, "We stand before a discord that wants to be be discordant, that enjoys itself in this suffering." Friedrich Nietzsche, *On the Genealogy of Morality*, trans. Carol Diethe (Cambridge: Cambridge University Press), 86.

60. Compare Caygill on Clausewitz's *On War*, in *On Resistance*, 15–23.

61. On the figure of the *ot-one*, see my *Lacan Noir: Lacan and Afro-Pessimism* (London: Palgrave Macmillan, 2021), 19.

62. On the (Fanonian) relation between *devoit* and *on doit* see Hallward, "Defiance," 31.

Chapter 8

1. See Malcolm X, *The Autobiography of Malcolm X* (London: Penguin, 1965).

2. For a similar position on revolution as law-annihilating violence, see Walter Benjamin, "Critique of Violence," in *Selected Writings*, vol 1, *1913–1926*, eds. Marcus Bullock and Michael W. Jennings (Cambridge, MA: Harvard University Press, 1996), 236–253. See also Frantz Fanon, *The Wretched of the Earth*, trans. Richard Philcox (New York: Grove Press, 2004).

3. The "all but" is borrowed from John Henry Newman, *Waiting for Christ* (Greenwood Village, CO: Augustine Institute, 2018). See also Gillian Rose. *Mourning Becomes the Law: Philosophy and Representation* (Cambridge, UK: Cambridge University Press, 1996), 107–8.

4. Martin Luther King Jr.'s "Letter from Birmingham City Jail (1963)" and "Black Power Defined" are of critical relevance here. See Martin Luther King Jr., *A Testament of Hope*, ed. J. M. Washington (San Francisco: Harper Collins, 1991), 289–313.

5. According to Walter Benjamin, "the expressionless [*das Ausdruckslose*] is the critical violence which, while unable to separate semblance from essence in art, prevents them from mingling. It possesses this violence as a moral dictum. In the expressionless, the sublime violence of the true appears as that which determines the language of the real world according to the laws of the moral world." "Goethe's Elective Affinities," in *Selected Writings*, 340.

6. Malcolm X, *Malcolm X Speaks: Selected Speeches and Statements*, ed. George Brietman (New York: Grove Weidenfeld, 1965), 9.

7. Malcolm X, *Malcolm X Speaks*, 22.

8. Malcolm X, 24.

9. Malcolm X, 29.

10. Malcolm X, 40.

11. Malcolm X, 50.

12. Malcolm X, 69.

13. Malcolm X, 68.

14. Malcolm X, 68–69.

15. Malcolm X, 69.

Part III

1. Fanon, *Black Skin, White Masks*, trans. Charles Lam Markmann (New York: Grove Press, 1967), 8. See also my *Whither Fanon?: Studies in the Blackness of Being* (Stanford: Stanford University Press, 2018), 245–246.

2. The honorable exception remains Gillo Pontecorvo's *The Battle of Algiers* (1966).

3. *Invisable*: see Jean-Luc Marion, *Being Given: Toward a Phenomenology of Givenness*, trans. Jean-Luc Kosky (Stanford: Stanford University Press, 2002).

Chapter 9

1. Donald Rodney, interview with Ruth Kelly, Iniva (Institute of International Visual Arts), March 11, 1994, accessed in 2011, https://www.iniva.org/autoicon/DR/Interv2.htm.

2. "Boy, 4, died alone in Hackney flat two weeks after his mother's death," *Guardian*, June 8, 2017, accessed April 17, 2023, https://www.theguardian.com/uk-news/2017/jun/08/boy-4-died-alone-in-hackney-flat-two-weeks-after-his-mothers-death.

3. Martin Heidegger, *Unterwegs zur Sprache, Gesamtausgabe* 12: 24. Translation by Andrew Mitchell (unpublished).

4. In the film, *Three Songs on Pain Light and Time* (1995), Rodney recounts how green went from being his favorite color to being associated inevitably with visits to hospitals and being operated on due to the pervasive use of green as a contrast color to red, i.e., blood. Here again a passage about losing is itself related to a passage about what can no longer be painfully looked upon.

5. That said, the work *Psalms* (1997) provides an interesting point of comparison. In this work, a solitary wheelchair fitted with sensors sits motionless in a gallery. When it does move, it is in response to the proximity and presence of the viewer. To that extent, the viewer observes how seeing is bound to the machinic, by giving them to understand how Rodney's art—Rodney, who, at this time, was confined to a hospital bed—is bound to his malady. If one is disturbed by the contemplation, perhaps it is because, as viewers, we see how the machine is enabled by our presence but in ways that makes us admit that, since we do not know the pain that led to its creation, or what causes it to move, we can learn of it only by watching the odd, arbitrary movements of this body-in-effigy, which is the lot of the corpus exanime. What the machine's motion discloses to us, in brief, is the recognition of a certain homophony: of a vision split between the experience of a maze and the miseries by which black being is amazed by a pain that no thought or image can stifle. At least, that will be my argument in what follows.

6. I borrow this neologism from Emmanuel Levinas, *On Escape*, trans. Bettina Bergo (Stanford: Stanford University Press, 2003), 54. However my usage of this word is markedly different.

7. On the notion of "monstration" see Jacques Lacan, *RSI: The Seminar of Jacques Lacan Book XXII*, trans. Jack W. Stone (unofficial), PDF. Published online: https://static1.square space.com/static/5d52d51fc078720001362276/t/5ee21894c2d74f6080bf56ac/1591875734235 /19741119+rsi+0-11-19-74+Stone.pdf. See also chapter 4.

8. The term is taken from Book XXI of Saint Augustine's *De Civitate Dei*, where he writes: "We cannot say that 'the body without its soul' feels pain, or, still less, that 'the body outside of the soul,' *corpus exanime*, feels pain." Augustine, *City of God*, trans. Henry Bettenson (London: Penguin Books, 2004), 341. My use of the term, however, will be focused on the "black" meaning of this "outside."

9. Immanuel Kant, *Anthropology from a Pragmatic Point of View*, trans. Robert B. Louden (Cambridge, UK: Cambridge University Press, 2006), 126. Compare Nietzsche's comment in *On the Genealogy of Morality*, when, to illustrate the point that "[pain] did not hurt as much then as it does now," he suggests that Negroes, being more primeval, have a higher capacity for pain. *On the Genealogy of Morality*, ed. Keith Ansell-Pearson, trans. Carol Diethe (Cambridge: Cambridge University Press, 1997), 44. What is one to make of this *racial* nostalgia for pain, for a purer experience of pain, for a being-rent that is indifferent to pain's confirmations? And why is blackness so important for the technique and for the hypothetical imperative of a *cruelty*, whose practice does not concern law or the categorical imperative, but precedes from a racialized indebtedness situated above being and prior to moral knowledge and ignorance? This black capacity for pain that has no equal, and which seems to involve a more radical distinction between thought and being—why is it the measure here of pain's endurability and/or intelligibility? And why does it also appear to involve modalities that are no longer known to us ("us" humans)? Is the black disinterestedness of pain necessary for Nietzsche's original genealogy in which drive and conscience are always in a relation of reciprocity and compensation? If so, why does it conserve (*aufhebt*) what being denies it? We shall come back to these questions in another work.

10. For Heidegger on pain, see Andrew J. Mitchell, "Entering the World of Pain: Heidegger," *Telos* 150 (2010): 83–96; and Ian Alexander Moore, "Pain is Being Itself: Heidegger's Algontology," *Gatherings: The Heidegger Circle Annual* 12 (2022): 1–38.

11. On "flesh" see Hortense Spillers, *Black, White, and in Color: Essays on American Literature and Culture* (Chicago: Chicago Univeristy Press, 2003).

12. For an elaboration of these figures see David Marriott, *Whither Fanon?: Studies in the Blackness of Being* (Stanford: Stanford University Press, 2018); Frank Wilderson, *Red, White, & Black: Cinema and the Structure of US Antagonisms* (Durham: Duke University Press, 2010); and Calvin Warren, "The Karen Call," *Critical Philosophy of Race* 10, no. 2 (2022): 141–157.

13. On the transitional object, see D. W. Winnicott, *Playing and Reality* (London: Tavistock, 1971).

14. See Virginia Nimarkah, "Image of Pain: Physicality in the Art of Donald Rodney," in *Donald Rodney: Doublethink*, ed. Richard Hylton (London: Autograph, 2003), 85.

15. Martin Heidegger, *Über den Schmerz*, in *Jahresgabe der Martin-Heidegger-Gesellschaft 2017–2018*, 35.

16. See Kader Attia, *Repair* (Paris: Black Jack Editions, 2014).

17. Martin Heidegger, *The Question Concerning Technology, and Other Essays*, trans. William Lovitt (San Francisco: Harper Row, 1977). See in particular division 1, chapter 6.

18. G. W. F. Hegel, *Phenomenology of Spirit*, trans. A. V. Miller (Oxford: Oxford University Press, 1977), 125. Translation modified.

19. Jean-Paul Sartre, "Orphée Noir," *Situations, III* (Paris: Gallimard, 1976), 229–289.

20. See Martin Heidegger, *Being and Time*, trans. J. Macquarrie and E. Robinson (Oxford, UK: Blackwell, 1962).

21. Frantz Fanon, *Black Skin, White Masks* (1968), trans. Charles Lam Markmann (New York: Grove Press, 1967), 8, 9.

22. "The worm-eaten roots of the structure." Fanon, *Black Skin*, 11.

23. Fanon, *Black Skin*, 13.

24. René Descartes, *Meditations on First Philosophy* (Cambridge, UK: Cambridge University Press, 2017).

Page numbers in *italics* refer to figures.

Inventions: Black Philosophy, Politics, Aesthetics
Edited by David Marriott

Le véritable saut consiste à introduire l'invention dans l'existence—the real leap consists in introducing invention into existence. Among this and other demands for a thought, a blackness of thought that is itself an act of liberation, for Frantz Fanon, the critical task of any aspirational black philosophy is its ability to tell apart blackness from its mirages and impossibilities in science, art, and European history and philosophy. Is it still possible to pursue this goal today, within the ongoing reaches of anti-blackness? And what could this "leap" be given the undecidability of blackness as a concept, feeling, or figure? The premise of the series is that blackness cannot be subsumed under the prevailing forms of philosophy, politics, or aesthetics without putting into question what this leap could be, or mistaking invention for their presuppositions, and so losing sight of what this invention could be *in its very difference*. To that end, *Inventions* seeks to publish works that set the agenda for what this leap would look like or be.

Anteaesthetics: Black Aesthesis and the Critique of Form
Rizvana Bradley

Printed in the USA
CPSIA information can be obtained
at www.ICGtesting.com
JSHW020924280923
49162JS00001B/1